M000303072

THE CASTLE AT WAR
IN MEDIEVAL
ENGLAND AND WALES

THE CASTLE AT WAR
IN MEDIEVAL
ENGLAND AND WALES

Dan Spencer

AMBERLEY

To Hannah

First published 2018

Amberley Publishing
The Hill, Stroud
Gloucestershire, GL5 4EP

www.amberley-books.com

Copyright © Dan Spencer, 2018

The right of Dan Spencer to be identified as the Author of this work has been asserted in accordance with the Copyrights, Designs and Patents Act 1988.

All rights reserved. No part of this book may be reprinted or reproduced or utilised in any form or by any electronic, mechanical or other means, now known or hereafter invented, including photocopying and recording, or in any information storage or retrieval system, without the permission in writing from the Publishers.

British Library Cataloguing in Publication Data.
A catalogue record for this book is available from the British Library.

ISBN 978 1 4456 6268 8 (hardback)
ISBN 978 1 4456 6269 5 (ebook)

Typesetting and Origination by Amberley Publishing.
Printed in the UK.

Contents

List of Maps and Illustrations

The inner ward of Harlech Castle, Gwynedd. © Crown copyright (2017) Cadw, Welsh Government.

Raglan Castle, Monmouthshire. © Crown copyright (2017) Cadw, Welsh Government.

Corfe Castle, Dorset. Photograph taken by Helen Hotson. © Shutterstock.

Rochester Castle, Kent. Photograph taken by Paulina Grunwald. © Shutterstock.

Launceston Castle, Cornwall. Photograph taken by Elena Barsottelli. © Shutterstock.

Dover Castle, Kent. Photograph taken by Alexander Gold. © Shutterstock.

Pendennis Castle, Cornwall. Photograph taken by Jamie William. © Shutterstock.

The capture of Wark Castle by a Franco-Scottish army in 1385. Jehan Froissart, *Chroniques*, late fifteenth century. British Library, Royal 18 E 1, f. 345. Creative Commons CC0 1.0 Universal Public Domain Dedication.

A stone throwing siege engine known as a trebuchet in action. *Les Grandes Chroniques de France*, early fourteenth century. British Library, Royal 16 G VI, f. 345v. Creative Commons CC0 1.0 Universal Public Domain Dedication.

Besiegers undermining a tower. *Les Grandes Chroniques de France*, early fourteenth century. British Library, Royal 16 G VI, f. 74. Creative Commons CC0 1.0 Universal Public Domain Dedication.

Battle fought outside a castle. *Les Grandes Chroniques de France*, early fourteenth century British Library, Royal 16 G VI, f. 427. Creative Commons CC0 1.0 Universal Public Domain Dedication.

The Tower of London in the fifteenth century. Charles, duke of Orléans, *Pseudo-Heloise*, late fifteenth century. British Library, Royal 16 F II, f. 73. Creative Commons CC0 1.0 Universal Public Domain Dedication.

Carisbrooke Castle, courtesy of Peter Burka.

Scarborough Castle, courtesy of Tim Green.

Sherborne Castle courtesy of Glen Bowman.

Skipton Castle, courtesy of Afshin Darian.

Bodiam Castle, courtesy of Paul Stephenson.

Bodiam Castle, interior courtesy of Dan Davison.

Preface and Acknowledgements

Ever since I was a small child I have had a fascination with history, particularly the Middle Ages. This interest was fostered by my parents, who frequently purchased books for me and took me to visit museums and castles. Since then I have made numerous castle hunting trips across the British Isles and am always on the lookout to see more with my dogs Daisy and Archie. My academic interest in castles stems from my Master's dissertation on Sir Edward Dallingridge, the builder of Bodiam Castle in East Sussex. This was an area that I explored further as part of my PhD thesis on medieval English gunpowder weapons, which was awarded in 2016. I was inspired to write this book by my experience of teaching modules on castles to students at the universities of Southampton and Canterbury Christ Church. This obliged me to expand my understanding of the topic to incorporate the whole period of the Middle Ages. During the process of reading books and articles on castles in preparation for my teaching work, I realised there was a gap in the literature that I could address on the subject of medieval warfare. There are many excellent books on castles, but few in my opinion that seek to place them within the context of military history in general.

This book focuses on the role that castles played in conflicts in England and Wales from their introduction by the Normans in the eleventh century to the death of Henry VIII in 1547. The latter has been chosen as an end-date as his break from Rome can be identified as marking the end of the Middle Ages in England

and Wales. (Not all historians will agree with that date of course.) Chapter 1 includes a discussion of the origins of the castle in northern France, but otherwise the emphasis is on castles in England and Wales. An exception to this rule is chapter 8 where English-held Scottish castles are included in the narrative. But this is a narrative account of the military history of castles in England and Wales. Where appropriate I have incorporated analysis of these buildings and the sources used into the discussion, but the framework is chronological. I have utilised primary sources as much as possible, including unpublished manuscripts from The National Archives in Kew; though this book in its wide range is perforce a work of synthesis.

The focus of castle studies in recent years has been to explore the non-military aspects of these buildings. This includes the examination of their role as residences, status symbols and centres of administration, as well as studying them in relation to their wider landscapes and in literature. Much valuable research has been produced by historians, archaeologists and other scholars, which has gone a great way towards overturning the traditional view of these structures as merely being fortresses. This has resulted in a more nuanced understanding of these buildings and how they were used in the Middle Ages. Nonetheless, it is undeniable that castles did play an important part in medieval warfare. This book is not intended to challenge or downplay the work of these scholars, but to explore the story of the castle specifically in relation to military history.

I would like to thank Amberley for publishing this book, Scott Hall for drawing the maps and my mother, Elizabeth, for reading and commenting on drafts of the book. I am especially grateful to my partner, Hannah, for all the time and effort she has spent in providing feedback and encouragement, without which this book would not have been finished. I dedicate this book to her.

The Origins of the Castle

The foreigners then had built a castle in Herefordshire, in Earl Swein's province, and inflicted every injury and insult they could upon the king's men thereabouts.

Anglo-Saxon Chronicle, manuscript E[1]

The foreigners who had inflicted such insults and injuries were the French followers of the half-Norman English king, Edward the Confessor (1042–1066), who had been invited to settle in England. Their activities provoked a strong reaction from the author of the *Anglo-Saxon Chronicle* and the native population. One reason for this was their decision to construct a new type of fortification that was previously unknown in England, the castle. These new structures were very different from the fortified settlements called burhs that had previously been used by the English in warfare. Burhs were intended to provide protection to local communities in times of strife; by contrast, the castle was the private fortified dwelling of a lord. The English and Normans clearly had very different traditions concerning fortifications. This reflected profound military and social differences between these two peoples. At least two castles were constructed in England during the reign of Edward the Confessor. The first was Ewyas Harold in Herefordshire, built by the Norman knight Osbern Pentecost to help secure the border against the Welsh, whereas the second was known as 'Robert's Castle' and may have been located in Essex. Yet at the time these structures would have seemed insignificant compared to the network of fortified towns that were distributed across the country. Their military value was also called into question when the Norman colony in Herefordshire, centred upon Ewyas Harold Castle, was unable to stop Welsh raiders from harrying the county. By comparison, the burghs had repeatedly proved their worth in the wars of the previous two centuries.[2]

Anglo-Saxon Fortifications

The creation of the Anglo-Saxon system of fortified towns or burhs was a response to the specific circumstances of the ninth century. A devastating raid on the isolated Northumbrian monastery of Lindisfarne, in 793, was followed by many years of Viking attacks throughout the British Isles. In 865, a large force known as the Great Heathen army landed in East Anglia. Unlike previous attackers, however, this was to be an army of conquest. Over the following nine years, the Great Heathen army succeeded in conquering the kingdoms of Northumberland, Mercia and East Anglia. This left Wessex as the last remaining English kingdom by 874. Danish successes meant that by this point English resistance must have seemed hopeless. Yet King Alfred the Great of Wessex (871–899) was able to defeat the Danish ruler King Guthrum at the Battle of Edington in 878 and afterwards negotiated a peace treaty that secured the safety of the kingdom. Key to Alfred's success were his military reforms, which included re-organising the local militia, known as the fyrd, 'so that always half were at home and half on service' and building larger ships. Yet the most crucial initiative was devising a new system of fortifications to improve the defences of the kingdom. Fortified settlements were constructed at intervals throughout Wessex to provide protection against Danish attacks. This can be seen at Worcester where the church was granted a charter to found a borough to be 'built for the protection of all the people, and also to exalt the praise of God'. Carrying out a programme of works on such a large scale was clearly a major challenge. This is borne out by the testimony of Alfred's biographer, the Welsh monk Asser, who chastised the supposed negligence of the king's servants: 'I am speaking here of fortifications commanded by the king which have not yet been begun, or else, having been begun late in the day, have not been brought to completion.' Asser was being unduly pessimistic, however, as the scheme was clearly a success. This can be seen from a manuscript dating from the reign of Alfred's son and successor, Edward the Elder, known as the *Burghal Hidage*, which shows the extent of the programme of works carried out at this time. The document lists thirty-three fortified settlement or burhs ranging from Lydford in Devon, Worcester in the West Midlands and Hastings in East Sussex. Each fortification was allocated a specified number of units of taxation known as 'hides' to provide for their maintenance and defence. This was calculated at a fixed rate with every five-and-a-half yards of wall guarded by four men. Some of these burhs were founded on the sites of old Roman settlements, such as the former 'Saxon Shore' fort at Portchester in Hampshire. This was no doubt intended to take advantage of the substantial masonry defences that still existed in these places. Elsewhere it was necessary to construct new fortifications, as can be seen at Wareham in Dorset, which was enclosed with a substantial rampart and ditch, with a length of just over 2,000 metres.[3]

These fortifications played a crucial part in protecting Wessex from Danish attacks and in securing conquered territory in other parts of England. Edward the Elder (899–924) continued his father's work by constructing new fortresses throughout the Midlands and surrounding regions: Chester in 907, Hertford in 911, Stafford in 913, Warwick and Buckingham in 914, Maldon in 916 and Towcester in 917. The newly constructed forts created a barrier that blunted the advances of Danish armies from the north and East Anglia. This can be seen in 917, when multiple Danish armies launched attacks on the frontier settlements. At Towcester they succeeded in storming the defences but were driven away soon afterwards, whereas attacks on Bedford and 'Wingamere' were defeated. An English counter-attack under Edward succeeded in capturing Derby and the fortress at Tempsford, with the latter attack resulting in the death of the last Danish king of East Anglia. By the end of the campaign, the kingdom of Wessex was in the ascendant – due in large part to the military value of the fortified settlements. Campaigns of conquest were continued by his son and successor, Athelstan (924–939), who succeeded in acquiring the northern kingdom of Northumberland in 927. Later Athelstan won a great victory against an allied force of Vikings from Dublin, Britons from Strathclyde and Scots at the

Battle of Brunanburh in 937. As a result of this victory, he succeeded in unifying all the kingdoms of England under his rule and became the most powerful monarch in the British Isles.[4]

However, the Viking threat was to re-emerge at the end of the century, during the reign of Athelstan's descendant, Ethelred II, the Unready (978–1016). The first raids took place in 980, with the coastal regions of Cornwall, Hampshire and Kent harried by Viking raiders. In the following decade, the scale of attacks intensified with an English army defeated at the Battle of Maldon in 991. The failure of English military counter-measures prompted Ethelred to attempt to buy off Viking fleets through cash payments, which were financed by taxes known as 'Danegeld'. This policy was only able to bring temporary relief, at a great financial cost, and did nothing to dispel the image of England as a tempting target. In 1013, years of devastating Viking raids culminated in an invasion of England by the Danish king, Swein Forkbeard. English resistance, weakened by previous attacks, quickly collapsed and Ethelred and the royal family were forced to flee to Normandy. Swein died during the next year and was succeeded by his son Canute. The English nobility took advantage of the change in Danish leadership and invited Ethelred to return to the kingdom, which he was able to regain. His restoration was to be brief, however, as Canute invaded England in 1015. Canute was able to take advantage of divisions among the Anglo-Saxon ruling elite to rapidly overrun most of the kingdom. Ethelred's son and successor, Edmund 'Ironside', put up a determined resistance to the Danes but was later defeated at the Battle of Assandun on 18 October 1016. A treaty was agreed soon afterwards, whereby England was divided between the two men. However, Edmund died later that year, with King Canute (1016–1035) taking possession of the whole kingdom.[5]

Canute died in 1035 and was succeeded by his son, Harold Harefoot, and then by another son, Harthacnut, in 1040. The death of the latter gave an opportunity for the last surviving member of the house of Wessex, Edward, later known as the 'Confessor', a chance to return from exile and become king of England. Edward was the seventh son of Ethelred II and his second wife, Emma, sister of Richard II, Duke of Normandy. After the accession of Canute to the throne in 1016, Edward was forced to flee to his relatives in Normandy, where he was to remain for many years. In 1036, the turmoil caused by the death of Canute prompted Edward and his brother, Alfred, to mount separate expeditions to England to attempt to regain the throne. However, the venture was to prove disastrous. Edward was forced to withdraw after fighting a battle near Southampton, whereas Alfred was captured by the powerful nobleman Earl Godwine, near Guildford. Alfred was then handed over to Harold Harefoot who had him blinded and soon afterwards he died of his injuries. Edward was invited by his half-brother Harthacnut to return to England in 1041; he succeeded him as king after his death in the following year. One of the challenges that the new monarch faced was how to deal with his most powerful subject, Earl Godwine, who, with his sons, virtually controlled most of southern England. Godwine had been a loyal supporter of Canute and had been richly rewarded for his services. His influence continued to grow in the early years of Edward's reign. Godwine's eldest son, Swein, was appointed Earl of Hereford in 1043 and his second son, Harold, Earl of East Anglia in 1044; this was further strengthened by the marriage of his daughter, Edith, to Edward in the following year. The king appears to have resented the power wielded by his over-mighty subject but he was unable to make a move against him until 1051. In that year, a fight took place between the retinue of his brother-in-law, Eustace of Boulogne, who was on a visit to England, and the inhabitants of Dover. In response, Edward ordered Godwine to lead an army to Kent with orders to punish the townspeople. The latter's refusal led to a confrontation, with armies raised by the supporters of both men. Efforts were made to resolve the dispute through diplomacy, but Edward had not forgotten the part Godwinson had played in the death of his brother fifteen years earlier. This was made apparent during negotiations when the king was said to have joked that he would forgive Godwinson if he could restore his brother Alfred back to life. At this point, the earl's supporters lost heart and he was forced to flee abroad. Godwine's exile proved to be temporary, however, as he returned to England with a fleet the next year, with the prospect of bloodshed prompting negotiations. This time Godwine was forgiven by the king and was restored to his lands.[6]

This reconciliation marked a turning point in the relationship between Edward and the Godwine family, thereafter they remained on good terms. Godwine died in 1053 with his position as head of the family taken by his son, Harold Godwinson. Edward appears to have felt no personal animosity towards Harold and even gave him the important task of defeating the powerful Welsh ruler Gruffudd ap Llywelyn in 1062. A surprise attack was launched on Llywelyn's court at Rhuddlan. As with other Welsh settlements, the palace was not fortified and the prince was forced to flee by sea. During the next year, Harold and his brother Tostig launched an invasion into northern Wales. Llywelyn fled inland, hoping to use the mountainous terrain of Snowdonia to defeat the invaders rather than confront them in battle, but he was killed by his domestic enemies. The safety of the English realm was to be threatened, however, by the issue of the succession. Edward's marriage to Edith was a childless one, with the king's closest male relatives being his great-nephew Edgar, who was a grandson of Edward Ironside, and his nephew, William, Duke of Normandy. Yet Edgar's youth and William's absence in Normandy meant that Edward's brother-in-law, Harold, was in a strong position to assert his own (far more dubious) claim to be his heir. Norman chroniclers were later to argue that Harold had recognised the legitimacy of William's claim. According to this account, Harold was sent by the king to Normandy as an envoy to acknowledge William as Edward's heir. During Harold's time in Normandy he was said to have sworn allegiance to William on the sacraments, a scene that is vividly portrayed in the Bayeaux Tapestry. Whether this episode took place or not is highly debatable, but it reflects the views of Norman writers that their duke was Edward's rightful heir. Yet Normandy was a very different place to England. This was most apparent in the distinctive military traditions of both peoples, with Norman warfare dominated by a reliance on heavily armoured knights and castles, in stark contrast to the Anglo-Saxons, who only made use of infantry and fortified towns. The very different methods of war employed by the Normans derived from their unique French and Scandinavian heritage.[7]

The Normans and Early Castles

The Duchy of Normandy was founded by Viking settlers who had carried out raids on northern France since the early ninth century. In attempt to stop these raids, the Carolingian king, Charles III

(879–929), made an agreement with the Viking leader Rollo in 911 at the Treaty of Saint-Clair-sur-Epte. By the terms of this treaty, Rollo was appointed as Count of Rouen (911–927) and was granted lands in Upper Normandy in return for providing military assistance and converting to Christianity. In the following years, Rollo and his successors expanded the territory under their control, with Bayeux acquired in 924, followed by the Avranchin and Contentin in 933. This was a period marked by intense violence, with the Normans, often supported by war-bands from other parts of the Viking world, carrying out devastating raids into the lands of their neighbours. Yet the pressures of war meant that the survival of the new state was not guaranteed. The periodic arrival of new contingents of Viking warriors threatened the authority of the Counts of Rouen, whereas neighbouring states were eager to reclaim territory from the Normans. In 942, the territory was threatened by a powerful coalition of enemies, with Louis IV, king of West Francia, launching an attack on Rouen, and his ally, Hugh the Great, Duke of the Franks making a simultaneous assault on Bayeux. Both these offenses were defeated, however, and over time Normandy became one of the most powerful states in northern Europe. The Normans had started out as Viking warriors reliant upon hit and run attacks using longboats and lightly armed infantry to carry out devastating raids on their enemies. Yet their ability to successfully maintain their new state was due to their willingness to adapt to Continental methods of waging war, notably the use of mounted cavalry and castles.[8]

Castles first emerged in northern France at some point between the late-ninth and late-tenth century as a result of the breakdown of authority in the Carolingian Empire. The Carolingian dynasty had ruled over an empire that at its peak, under the Emperor Charlemagne, stretched from northern-eastern Spain to western Germany. However, after the death of Louis the Pious in 840, the empire was divided among his three sons, with Charles the Bald receiving the western part, which later became the kingdom of France. Rivalry among Charles's successors and external threats on the frontiers contributed to the fragmentation of power, which became increasingly localised. New aristocratic elites emerged in Western Europe, who were keen to assert their authority through the construction of buildings to demonstrate their wealth and power. This included ecclesiastical buildings, such as monasteries and churches, as well as fortified residences that came to be called castles. It is unclear when these new types of fortifications began to be built, but it may have been as early as 864. In that year, Charles the Bald, king of West Francia (which later became the Kingdom of France) issued an edict ordering that 'whoever at this time has made castles (*castella*) and fortifications (*firmitates*) and enclosures (*haias*) without our permissions shall have them demolished by the 1st of August'. However, there is no further evidence for the presence of castles until the following century, when they begin to be regularly recorded by chroniclers. One of the main difficulties involved with tracing the origins of the castle is caused by language. The word castle derives from the Latin word for fortress *castrum* and its diminutive form *castellum*. In the time of the Roman Empire, these words were often used to refer to legionary forts or other types of fortifications – but during the Early Middle Ages its meaning gradually changed so that it came to be used to describe fortified residences.[9]

Early castles took two main forms. The first consisted of masonry towers called *donjons*, often with walled circuits, whose name derived from the Latin word *dominium* for lordship. The design of these structures was influenced by Late Roman villas and Carolingian palaces. In the late third century the increasing instability of the Roman Empire led to the construction of villas with defensive features such as turrets and enclosing walls, particularly in south-eastern Europe. Carolingian palaces in the eastern border regions of their empire also incorporated defences, including fortified enclosures and towers. The architecture of these buildings, as well as ecclesiastical structures, inspired the design of the early *donjons*. One of the oldest surviving castles of this type is at Langeais in Indre-et-Loire in northern France. This was constructed by the renowned castle builder Fulk Nerra, Count of Anjou, in 994 (although the *donjon* itself may have been built slightly later). Langeais was rebuilt in the fifteenth century, but enough of the original structure survives to indicate its original form. The tower was part of a complex of residential buildings surrounded by a walled enclosure and consisted of a two-storied structure, which was entered at first floor level. As their name suggests, *donjons* were intended to demonstrate the wealth and power of their lordly owners. Their strong defensive features also meant that they could be used as fortresses. This can be seen at Langeais, which was unsuccessfully besieged by Odo, Count of Blois, on two occasions, in 994 and 996. The second and most common type of castle consisted of timber structures that were surrounded by earthwork defences. These included structures known as motte and baileys, as well as ringwork. Mottes were artificial mounds that were formed by labourers digging substantial quantities of earth that was then piled up to create a hill. The motte was linked to one or more outer enclosures known as baileys. Both parts of the castle were surrounded by ditches and wooden walls, with the higher status structures, such as a great tower, being located in the motte. These were clearly large and imposing edifices, which made a striking impression on the landscape. This can be seen from the account of the author of the *Annals of the Angevins and Vendômoises*, who mentions the construction of 'a timber tower of marvellous height upon the motte' at La-Motte-Montboyau near Tours in 1026. In some cases, a natural feature was used for the motte, as can be seen at Tchesté de la Rotche in Belgium. A castle was constructed upon the site of a large rocky outcrop, with post-holes cut into the rock to form the foundations of a wooden tower, with an outer bailey created by carving a ditch across the hilltop and plateau. Ringworks were similar to baileys in that they consisted of an enclosure of wooden buildings surrounded by a ditch. Timber castles were less visually impressive and more prone to being damaged by fire than their stone counterparts, yet these buildings came to play an equally important part in the wars of the tenth and eleventh centuries.[10]

The first castles in Normandy are recorded during the reign of Richard I (942–966), with one of the earliest examples being the construction of a *donjon* at the ducal palace at Rouen. In the following century, their numbers increased under his successors Richard II (996–1026) and Richard III (1026–7), with castles built at Falaise, Tillières, Le Homme, Brix and Cherbourg. Most castles in Normandy at this time belonged to the dukes (a title they used in addition to that of count) and were often in the custody of aristocratic officials called *vicomtes*. These fortifications were crucial for the defence of the duchy, as Normandy was often at war with its neighbours. On its western frontier the duchy was threatened by the ambitions of the Dukes of Brittany, to the east by the wealthy rulers of Flanders and in the south by the powerful Counts of Anjou. This can be seen during the reign of Robert I (1027–35) who was obliged to go to war with his southern neighbour William de Bellême in 1027, intervened in the civil war in Flanders in 1030, and supported Henry I, king of France, in his war against Alan III, Duke of Brittany, in the early 1030s. During the latter conflict, Robert secured his western border by constructing a castle at Cherrueix in the Cotentin. This proved to be useful, as the garrison of the castle, commanded by the *vicomtes* Nigel and Alfred, confronted and defeated in battle a Breton army, led by Alan, that was carrying out a raid into Normandy. The success of these campaigns helped to secure the safety of Normandy and the prestige of its ruler. However, the death of Robert in 1035 and the minority of his illegitimate son and heir, William II (1035–1087) plunged the duchy into anarchy.[11]

William the Conqueror

William was perhaps as young as seven years old upon his accession as duke, with power vested in the hands of a group of guardians. They included his uncle, Robert, the Archbishop of Rouen; Alan, Count of Brittany (who was now on good terms with Normandy), and Osbern, the steward of the court. Yet these men were unable to maintain order in the duchy, which soon descended into a state of disorder and violence. When the duke's uncle, Robert, died in 1039, the situation deteriorated even further, with the Norman magnates vying with each other for power and territory. Private castle building proliferated in this period, with even the ducal castles of Alençon, Ivry and Tillières passing out of the control of the duke's government and into the hands of the aristocracy. In 1046 a major rebellion broke out, led by a powerful coalition of Norman nobles; they intended to depose William and replace him with his cousin, Guy of Burgundy. According to the account of the twelfth-century chronicler Wace, an attempt was made to assassinate the duke while he was in Valognes. He was able to escape from his assailants, however, by fleeing on horseback to the safety of Falaise during the night. William responded by raising an army and calling upon his overlord, Henry I, king of France, to come to his assistance. The support of the latter was to be crucial at the Battle of Val-és-Dunes in 1047, with the rebels decisively defeated. This became a turning point in William's reign as duke; he would demonstrate his formidable skills as a military leader in the campaigns of the following years.[12]

Despite being victorious in battle, the young duke was obliged to lead expeditions against those of his subjects who still challenged his authority. His first task was to capture the castle of Brionne. This was in the possession of Guy of Burgundy who had managed to escape from the battlefield and had taken refuge there. The duke surrounded the castle with his forces and ordered the construction of temporary siege fortifications, including wooden towers, to provide protection for his soldiers. The defenders of the castle were able to hold out for three years before eventually being compelled to surrender. The lengthy duration of the siege and resistance by other rebel lords meant that William continued to experience difficulties in asserting his control over the duchy during this period. Another threat was posed by the activities of Geoffrey Martel, Count of Anjou, who was expanding northwards into Norman territory. In 1051, William led an army into Maine and besieged the town and castle of Domfront. Geoffrey attempted to mount a rescue, but his forces were driven off in some disorder. Yet the Normans were still unable to capture the town and faced the prospect of having to slowly starve the defenders into surrender. This deadlock was soon to be broken by a brilliant tactical move. From his camp before the walls of Domfront, William launched a surprise attack on the nearby town of Alençon and succeeded in capturing the settlement by assault. Then the unfortunate inhabitants of Alençon were subjected to a horrendous massacre. Fearing a similar fate, the garrison of Domfront soon yielded. Any respite was to be short-lived, however, as news of William's victories and growing power prompted Henry of France to change sides and to ally with Geoffrey. William was also forced to contend with a rebellion led by his uncle, William, Count of Arques, who was a leading landowner in Upper Normandy and whose estates were centred upon his strongly fortified stone castle at Arques. The count sought to depose his nephew and become duke in his own right. This rebellion was particularly dangerous due to the prospect of outside intervention. However, Duke William was able to quickly isolate the rebels by leading a force to besiege his uncle's castle at Arques. This was a sensible move, as the duchy was soon afterwards invaded by a French army, commanded in person by Henry of France in 1053, in an attempt to relieve the castle. William chose not to confront the invaders in battle but was able to inflict heavy casualties on them by ambushing part of their army near Saint-Aubin. These losses prompted the French army to withdraw from Normandy, with the abandoned garrison of Arques surrendering in return for having their lives spared in late 1053. The French king was undaunted by this setback and in the next year he assembled a powerful coalition of allies from across northern France to attack the duchy. A two-pronged offensive was planned, with one army to invade from the south and another from the east. To counter this invasion William divided his forces in half. One part, which he led himself, was to oppose the invaders in the south, while another force, under the command of Robert, Count of Eu, confronted the attackers from the east. Robert was able to launch a surprise attack on the French army at Mortemer, which was routed with heavy losses. News of this defeat prompted the main French army to withdraw and the alliance against William dissolved soon afterwards. These against-the-odds victories not only secured William's control over Normandy but also cemented his reputation as a great warrior.[13]

In the following years William extended his influence southwards in the county of Maine, in direct opposition to Geoffrey of Anjou. This prompted Geoffrey to again enter into an alliance with the king of France, with the allies launching a joint invasion of Normandy in 1057. However, their army was ambushed by the Normans while in the process of crossing the River Dives, near Varaville, and their rearguard was routed. The war was eventually ended by the deaths of Geoffrey Martel and Henry I in 1060. Two years later, the death of Herbert II, Count of Maine, gave William the opportunity to annexe the territory. He was able to do so due to an agreement struck nine years earlier, whereby Herbert had agreed to recognise William as his heir, should he die without children, in return for Norman military support. Yet William's attempt to take over the county faced intense opposition from the local nobility, who instead supported the cause of Walter, Count of Mantes. William responded by invading the county in force and systematically reduced the ability of the rebels to resist by burning their lands and besieging their castles. His success at siege warfare in this campaign is evident from the account of the chronicler, William of Poitiers, who describes the capture of Mayenne Castle in detail. This was a strong castle situated on a rocky outcrop, protected on the one side by a river and on the other by stone fortifications. Yet the attackers were able to throw the defenders into confusion by shooting burning arrows into the castle, setting the buildings inside it on fire. The besiegers were then able to storm the castle, with the garrison retreating into the citadel, which was surrendered the next day. By the end of 1063, the city of Le Mans had surrendered and all resistance had ended.[14]

During the next year, William was able to secure the western frontier of his duchy by taking advantage of a rebellion in Brittany against its duke, Conan II. The details of this campaign are relatively obscure, but it is known that he invaded Brittany at the head of an army, which forced Conan to lift the siege of the rebel-held town of Dol. The Normans then besieged and captured the town of Dinan, before withdrawing to Normandy. The war was inconclusive, but it deterred Conan from interfering in Norman affairs for the remaining two years of his life. By 1066, William had successfully defeated all opposition to his rule. The rebellious nobility of Normandy had been subdued and he was in firm control of the duchy and its castles. He had substantially expanded the borders of his territory, through the conquest of Maine, and had led victorious campaigns against all his neighbours. The fortuitous deaths of his main rivals in quick succession also meant he was unlikely to face any external threats to his duchy in the immediate future. As a result, he was well placed to expand his horizons and to assert his claim to the English throne. This was fortunate, as his cousin, Edward the Confessor, died that year on 5 January. Harold Godwinson was crowned by an assembly of the English nobility on the next day, but his right to rule was disputed by both William and the Norwegian king, Harald Hardrada, the latter making the claim that he was the lawful heir of Harthacnut. Both men were prepared to use violence to enforce their claim to the English throne. England faced the dangerous prospect of being simultaneously invaded by the armies of two foreign rulers. William's first move was to seek the counsel of his nobles, who agreed to support his English expedition. Perhaps mindful of the limited resources of his duchy, versus the wealth and manpower available to Harold as the de facto king of England, he embarked upon a successful diplomatic campaign. Papal recognition of his claim was duly granted, with support also offered by the young king of France, Philip I, and the Holy Roman Emperor, Henry IV. This allowed him to attract large numbers of recruits to his army from all over northern France. Efforts were also made to construct a large fleet to transport the expeditionary force to England. Harold was aware of the pending invasion and undertook countermeasures to guard against it. This included calling out the fyrd to guard the south coast and gathering a fleet to protect the Channel. However contrary winds delayed the departure of the invasion in August. This proved to be a blessing in disguise for the Normans, as the delay meant that the fyrd were forced to disband due to a lack of supplies and the English ships were dispersed by a storm. Therefore, William and his army faced little immediate opposition when they finally made landfall at Pevensey in East Sussex on 28 September.[15]

The Normans: 1066–1135

To meet the danger the king rode to all the remote parts of his kingdom and fortified strategic sites against enemy attacks. For the fortifications called castles by the Normans were scarcely known in the English provinces, and so the English – in spite of their courage and love of fighting – could put up only a weak resistance to their enemies.

Orderic Vitalis, *The Ecclesiastical History*[1]

This account was written by the chronicler Orderic Vitalis in the early twelfth century, who sought to explain how the Normans succeeded in conquering England some years earlier. He identified the introduction of the castle as being crucial to the success of the Norman Conquest and the reason why English rebellions after the Battle of Hastings in 1066 were unsuccessful. Vitalis provides a unique perspective on these events due to his Anglo-French heritage. He was born near Shrewsbury on 16 February 1075, the product of an illicit relationship between an unknown English woman and the French chaplain, Odelerius of Orléans. At the age of ten Vitalis was sent by his father to become a monk at the famous Abbey of Saint-Evroul in Normandy and never saw England again. Yet many years later, when he came to write his chronicle of the abbey, he identified himself as 'Vitalis the Englishman', and gave ample attention to English affairs in his writings. However, his account of the Norman Conquest does need to be treated with some caution. Chronicle writers rarely left the confines of their monasteries and abbeys so they usually relied on information that was, at best, second-hand. Yet Saint-Evroul was a rich abbey that received the patronage of prominent members of the Anglo-Norman nobility. Monks, such as Vitalis, were often visited in their cloisters by knights and other visitors, who conversed with them on practical as well as spiritual matters. He was therefore able to draw upon the testimony of well-informed knights and nobles, as well as on older chronicle accounts, in writing his history. The prominence given to castles in his narrative is testament to the role that these buildings played in securing the Norman Conquest.[2]

The Norman Invasion of England

Soon after making landfall in England, William ordered the construction of a castle at Pevensey and another at nearby Hastings. These castles were intended to provide places of safety for the invaders in a hostile land. The Bayeux Tapestry depicts the construction of what appears to be a motte and bailey castle at Hastings in 1066, with labourers shown as being hard at work in creating a mound of earth. However, the construction of a motte was a time-consuming task requiring a large workforce of labourers. Instead these castles were likely to have been far simpler structures, consisting of ditches and wooden palisades, constructed in great haste. These castles were also deliberately sited so as take advantage of the existing Iron Age fortifications at Hastings and the ruins of the Roman fort at Pevensey. From these secure bases, the Normans scouted and raided inland while waiting for the English response. This was not immediately forthcoming due to events, which had taken place in the north. Earlier in the same month that the Normans arrived, the Norwegian king, Harald Hardrada, had landed in Yorkshire and defeated a northern army led by the earls Edwin and Morcar. Harold responded by quickly marching his army northwards to confront the invaders. At Stamford Bridge, on 25 September, he launched a surprise attack on the Norwegian army, who were utterly defeated. Yet Harold did not have long to savour his victory, as news of William's invasion of England reached him soon afterwards at York. His response was to move rapidly southwards to confront the invaders, perhaps in the hope of repeating his success at Stamford Bridge by using the element of surprise. This gambit was to prove to be mistaken one, as reports of Harold's movements reached William who advanced his army to confront the weary English army near Hastings on 14 October.[3]

The different fighting traditions of the English and Normans were exhibited at the Battle of Hastings. The English fought entirely on foot, adopting a defensive formation of locked shields known as a shield wall. By contrast, the Norman-French army consisted of infantry and missile troops, as well as mounted knights. At first the defending English army, deployed on a hill, had the advantage, with several attacks beaten off. Yet the Normans were ultimately able to prevail. According to the chronicler William of Poitiers, the turning point in the battle occurred when part of the Norman army turned to flee, and were pursued by some of the English defenders. William was able to rally his soldiers and launch a counter-attack that defeated the pursuers, with the depleted English ranks further thinned by feigned flights and missile fire. Harold and his two brothers, Gyrth and Leofwine, were killed in the fighting – with the English in full flight by nightfall. Hastings was to prove to be a decisive victory for William, but did not mark the end of English resistance. After the battle, William moved eastward to secure the ports in Kent, with Romney and Dover occupied by his forces. At Dover he was said to have spent eight days improving its existing Anglo-Saxon fortifications through the construction of a castle at the site. Meanwhile, in London, the Archbishop of Canterbury, Stigand, with other members of the English nobility, had chosen Edgar the Atheling as their new king. However, their ability to oppose William was fatally undermined by the lacklustre support of the northern earls, Edwin and Morcar, as well as the submission of the important cities of Winchester and Canterbury. In December, William received the surrender of Archbishop Stigand and other leading nobles at Berkhamsted and was later crowned as king in Westminster Abbey, on Christmas Day 1066.[4]

Soon afterwards William left London and travelled to nearby Barking, where he received the submission of the other English nobles, such as Edwin and Morcar. Nevertheless, he felt the need to strengthen his control over the city and ordered the construction of a castle in its south-eastern corner, later to be known as the Tower of London. Vitalis explains that this fortification was built 'as a defence against the numerous and hostile inhabitants', although the early castle most probably took the form of a simple ringwork, consisting of a palisade surrounded by a ditch. Work was also begun on building a motte and bailey castle in Winchester, on its western edge. At the time, this was one of the largest cities in England and the location of an important royal palace. By March, William felt his position in England was secure enough to return to Normandy to settle the affairs of the duchy, accompanied by a substantial number of English captives of high rank. In his absence he left behind lieutenants to rule over his newly conquered kingdom. These included his half-brother Odo, Bishop of Bayeux, who was entrusted with the custody of Dover Castle and the county of Kent, while another relative, William fitz Osbern, was tasked with overseeing southern England. They sought to bolster Norman control over the southern and south-eastern parts of England through a programme of castle-building. Their activities, however, quickly sparked resentment, with the *Anglo-Saxon Chronicle* claiming that the people were much oppressed during this time. In the west, an English magnate Eadric the Wild allied himself with the Welsh prince Bleddyn ap Cynfyn of Gwynedd and launched a raid into Herefordshire. A more serious rebellion occurred in Kent, in response to an appeal for help sent by the rebels across the Channel to Eustace, Count of Boulogne. In the autumn, Eustace landed with an army at Dover and laid siege to the castle there. The garrison, although being understrength at the time, responded by sallying forth from the gates and they routed the attackers.[5]

News of these events reached William in Normandy and prompted him to return to England in December. This was timely as the new king was soon to face serious threats to his rule. The first challenge was posed by the citizens of Exeter, who rose in rebellion in early 1068 in response to an attempt to increase their tax liability to the Crown. William led an army to the south-west to quell this uprising which, for the first time, included English soldiers. After reaching Exeter he called upon the inhabitants to surrender and after receiving word of their refusal, he laid siege to the city. This was a major undertaking. Exeter was a large and wealthy city, protected by a circuit of masonry walls and, on one side, by the course of the River Exe. The inhabitants were prepared to put up a determined resistance, with reinforcements called in from the neighbouring regions. Vitalis records that William carefully observed the defences of the city before ordering his forces to surround it, with attempts made to capture Exeter by storm. After eighteen days the citizens, fearful of the consequences should Exeter be sacked, surrendered on the condition that their traditional privileges should be reaffirmed. To ensure their future compliance, William ordered that a castle should be built against the northern edge of the city walls. The castle initially consisted of a timber palisade surrounded by a ditch, but soon afterwards a stone gatehouse, originally entered at first floor level, was added to the site, which still exists today. Unusually for a castle, it incorporates Anglo-Saxon architectural features – reflecting William's early efforts to pander to English cultural sensitivities. This enlightened policy was later to change, however, after sustained resistance to his rule.[6]

Having subdued the south-west, William proceeded eastwards to Winchester, where he spent Easter. Yet his hold on power was far less secure than it appeared to be. Rumours had already been circulating of an impending Danish invasion, with the northerners said to be ready to rise in rebellion to assist the invaders. Edgar the Atheling had fled across the border to Scotland, where he was welcomed by Malcolm III of Scotland, while Edwin and Morcar had withdrawn from the court to their northern lands. To pre-empt his enemies from uniting against him, William led his army northwards to impose his authority on the more restive parts of the kingdom. A key part of this campaign was the construction of castles in strategic locations across the Midlands, East Anglia and the north, which were garrisoned and entrusted to lieutenants. Advancing northwards, he briefly stopped at Warwick and Nottingham, where he gave orders for the building of castles in these locations. This show of force persuaded the rebels to submit to royal authority, with his army admitted into York and a truce agreed with King Malcolm. To assert his authority over the inhabitants, William constructed a castle in the middle of the city then he proceeded southwards, with further castles built at Lincoln, Cambridge and Huntingdon. Yet the success of this campaign was more apparent than real. In the next year, major rebellions broke out in the north, which posed a threat to William's control over his newly won kingdom.[7]

The Norman presence in large parts of England, particularly in the far north, was still minimal at this point. In an attempt to rectify this, the king granted the earldom of Northumbria to one of his followers, Robert de Comines, who was sent to take control of the region. However, Robert and his men were set upon by rebels soon after their arrival in Durham in late January and were slain. The news of this massacre spread across the north and prompted the outbreak of another rebellion in York. The garrison of the Norman castle in the city were soon hard pressed by the insurgents, with their commander, William Malet, sending a desperate plea for assistance to the king. William responded decisively by leading his army northwards with great speed. The rebels were caught by surprise and were defeated in battle, with York sacked by the vengeful Normans. Afterwards work was begun on constructing a second castle at the city, on the western side of the walls, and the king returned to Winchester for Easter. However, the kingdom remained in a state of turmoil and unrest due to rumours of an impending invasion by the Danish ruler Swein II in support of Edgar the Atheling. Swein had his own claim to the English throne, as he was a nephew of King Canute, and could therefore expect to receive support from the inhabitants of the Danelaw regions of eastern and northern England. In the summer of 1069 he despatched a large fleet, said to have numbered as many as 300 ships, in support of his English ally. The invaders first appeared off the coast of Kent at Dover, where they attempted to make landfall but they faced determined resistance from the Norman garrison of the castle and were soon forced to return to their ships. Another attempt to make landfall further east, at Sandwich, was also repulsed by the defenders, which prompted the fleet to sail northwards, up the east coast of England, to find an easier landing site. Support for the new regime in East Anglia was strong, so their attempts to capture Ipswich and Norwich were defeated. It was only when the Danish fleet appeared at the River Humber that they could safely disembark from their vessels. The invaders were soon able to join forces with Edgar the Atheling and his supporters, who included among their number the prominent English earls Waltheof and Gospatric. News of this invasion sparked a new uprising in the north, with their ranks swelled by men from across the region.[8]

The allied army at once moved against the Norman garrisons in the area. A small contingent under the command of Edgar the Atheling launched a raid into Lincolnshire but it was repulsed by the garrison of Lincoln Castle. Meanwhile, the main Anglo-Danish force marched on York. The garrisons of the castles in the city, whether due to overconfidence or desperation, chose to confront them in the field by sallying forth from their fortifications. The Norman forces were annihilated, with the now undefended castles falling into the hands of their enemies, who attempted to render them unusable. News of this defeat encouraged the spread of new rebellions across the kingdom, with the settlements of Exeter and Shrewsbury attacked by the rebels. The Scottish king, Malcolm III, emboldened by this turn of events, broke the truce with the Normans to ally with Edgar the Atheling, whose sister, Margaret, he married. By the autumn of 1069, there was the very real possibility that William would lose control of his new kingdom. Yet he ultimately prevailed against this powerful alliance of enemies due to the strength of his resolve and his skills as a military commander. Having gathered his army, William marched swiftly to confront the rebels. The Danes had meanwhile withdrawn the bulk of their forces north of the River Humber to take up a defensive position for the winter, while awaiting the arrival of their king with reinforcements. At first the Anglo-Danish strategy appeared to be a success, with the Norman army initially unable to cross the River Aire, due to enemy resistance. Yet a crossing point was eventually discovered after three weeks, with King William then able to advance on York. It was at this point that the vengeful Normans embarked on a campaign of retribution against the northerners that was later to be known as the 'Harrying of the North'. This was a deliberate policy to inflict widespread suffering on the population of northern England through the destruction of crops and houses. News of William's coming prompted his enemies to flee before him, with the king celebrating Christmas in the ruins of the devastated city. He left York soon afterwards to pacify the region north of the River Humber, with a small contingent of men remaining behind to garrison and repair the damaged castles. The army travelled northwards as far as the River Tees, in the depths of winter, inflicting death and destruction on the unfortunate inhabitants of the areas they passed on the way.

Vitalis claimed that as result of these actions a terrible famine afflicted the country with as many as 100,000 people starving to death. William's enemies, not for the first time, had been utterly confounded by the brutality and decisive nature of his actions. The leading English rebels either made their peace with William, a course of action taken by the earls Waltheof and Gospatric, or alternatively, like Edgar the Atheling, fled to Scotland. Meanwhile, the Danish fleet was increasing isolated and vulnerable on the River Humber, with their leader later accepting a bribe to return home to Denmark. Having subdued the north, William then led his army across the Pennines to punish the men of Chester. Work began on constructing royal castles at Chester and Stafford before the king returned to the south, where the army disbanded at Old Sarum.[9]

King Swein belatedly arrived in England in the spring of 1070. He joined forces with the remnants of his fleet from the previous year's expedition and received some support from the inhabitants of the Humber estuary and Fenlands. Soon afterwards a contingent of local men under the command of a Lincolnshire thegn, Hereward the Wake, attacked and looted the treasures of Peterborough Abbey. The willingness of the northerners to resist the Normans had been dealt a fatal blow, however, by the Harrying of the North. Swein was soon forced to come to terms with William and left England, never to return. The last English diehards, led by Hereward and Earl Morcar, retreated to the Isle of Ely in the Cambridgeshire Fens, where they held out for some time in a futile act of defiance. Initially, the marshy terrain presented a problem to the Normans, who according to chronicle accounts from the early twelfth century, were said to have resorted to employing a witch against the defenders. She was described as cursing and insulting the rebels from a wooden tower, before being incinerated when the rebels set the structure alight. Yet the huge disparity in numbers and the isolation of the rebels meant that they were ultimately forced to surrender to the Normans. The capture of the Isle of Ely effectively marked the end of English resistance to the Norman Conquest. In the following year, a major expedition was launched against Scotland, where Edgar the Atheling and other English exiles had taken refuge. This soon forced Malcolm to come to terms with William, with Edgar expelled and the Scots acknowledging English overlordship.[10]

These victories meant that the king was able to increasingly spend much of his time in Normandy in defence of his Continental possessions, from the early 1070s onwards. Responsibility for safeguarding his kingdom of England was therefore entrusted to lieutenants, notably Archbishop Lanfranc, who governed the land on William's behalf. This arrangement proved to be a successful one, despite challenges. In 1075, a revolt was planned during a feast celebrating a marriage alliance made between two of the king's leading noblemen, Ralph, Earl of East Anglia, who married Emma, the sister of Roger, Earl of Hereford. At some point during the proceedings these two men, in conjunction with Waltheof, Earl of Northumbria, formed a scheme to overthrow William. These noblemen controlled significant territories in western, northern and eastern England and could expect to rally large numbers of men to their banners. Vitalis records that they prepared for the rising by improving the defences of their castles, buying weapons, summoning their knights to them and sending messengers far and wide to encourage support. They also sought help from abroad, with appeals for help sent to King Swein and to the Welsh princes. Yet, in the event, the rebellion proved to be an abject failure. In the west, Earl Roger struggled to raise much of an army, and was trapped by the forces under the command of Bishop Wulfstan of Worcester and Walter de Lacy. At the same time, Earl Ralph's army was defeated in battle near Cambridge and he was forced to retreat to Norwich. Leaving his wife Emma behind to hold the castle there, he fled to his lands in Brittany – promising to return with reinforcements. Meanwhile Earl Waltheof, whose commitment to the uprising appears to have been half-hearted at best, soon gave up and threw himself on the king's mercy. The garrison of Norwich Castle was hard pressed by a besieging army that used siege weapons to launch frequent attacks on the defences. The pressure eventually took its toll, with dwindling food supplies prompting Emma to surrender after a three-month siege.[11]

The Welsh Marches

The conquest of England did not mark the end of Norman territorial ambitions. From an early date attempts were made to expand Norman control into the lands of the Welsh rulers. This was not just an act of territorial aggrandisement. The Welsh had a long history of raiding into the lands of their English neighbours, with the border settlements of Hereford, Shrewsbury and Chester under constant threat of attack. In the years leading up to the conquest, these attacks had intensified under the leadership of the Welsh king, Gruffudd ap Llywelyn, who had temporarily succeeded in uniting all of Wales under his rule. However, his death at the hands of Harold Godwinson in 1063 led to a vicious struggle for power. In the absence of a strong centralising figure able to impose his will on a politically divided nation, the many minor kings and lords of the land were able to reassert themselves. In many ways, this marked a return to the normal state of affairs in the country. The Welsh had a strong sense of identity as a people but the physical geography of Wales, characterised as it was by mountains and rivers, mitigated against the emergence of any strong centralised state. This was exacerbated by Welsh inheritance laws, which recognised the rights of illegitimate children and junior family members. The martial nature of Welsh society also meant that the minor rulers of the land were often at war with one another and despite the presence of powerful kingdoms, such Gwynedd in the north-east, Powys in the east and Deheubarth in the south, it was rare for one prince to achieve hegemony across the country. The divisions within Wales presented the Normans with an opportunity for territorial expansion, yet it also meant that the process of conquest was often tedious and tenuous in nature. It was for this reason that responsibility for dealing with the Welsh was delegated to powerful noblemen.[12]

The need for these measures was demonstrated in 1067 when a Welsh prince, Bleddyn ap Cynfyn of Gwynedd, launched a raid into Herefordshire. The pre-conquest castle of Hereford had been reoccupied and garrisoned by the Normans a short time before, but the defenders were unprepared to resist the Welsh. The *Anglo-Saxon Chronicle* records that the raiders 'attacked the castle-men in Hereford, and did them many injuries'. This prompted the king to appoint William fitz Osbern as Earl of Hereford with responsibility for guarding the border against the Welsh. Fitz Osbern soon extended the territory under his control by mounting an invasion of the kingdom of Gwent and defeated the Welsh kings Rhys,

Cadwgan and Maredudd. He and his followers then cemented their control over the area by building a series of castles. Many of these were constructed on the western edge of his earldom, with castles built at Wigmore, Clifford, Monmouth and Chepstow. Use was also made of pre-existing structures with the pre-conquest castles of Harold Ewias and Richard's Castle being refortified. These fortifications served as the territorial basis for landholding in the area, with estates allocated to provide men and resources for their defence and upkeep. After Fitz Osbern's death in battle in Flanders in 1071 he was succeeded by his son Roger.

In the early 1070s earldoms were also created further north on the Welsh border at Shrewsbury and at Chester. The former was granted to Roger de Montgomery, whose power in the earldom was based around his newly built castles at Montgomery, now known as Hen Domen, and another at Shrewsbury. The construction of the latter was responsible for widespread damage and disruption being caused to the town, with fifty-one houses destroyed for the site of the castle and another forty-three houses occupied by French settlers. Roger was described by Vitalis as 'a wise and prudent man', who benefitted from the advice of learned councillors, including the chronicler's father, Odelerius. The defence of the territory was delegated to the earl's tenants, who included his nephew-in-law, Warin the Bald, who was appointed as sheriff of Shrewsbury. These men were said to have enabled him to 'crush the Welsh and other opponents and pacify the whole province placed under his rule'.[13]

Further to the north the earldom of Chester was created for Hugh d'Avranches in 1071. He was the most active of the earls of the march at the time and was said to have been accompanied by 'an army instead of a household'. This force was used to invade north-east Wales where he 'wrought great slaughter among the Welsh'. One of his leading supporters, Robert of Rhuddlan, built a motte and bailey castle in the newly conquered territory in 1073. Two years later, a counterattack was mounted by the ruler of Gwynedd, Gruffudd ap Cynan. His forces succeeded in capturing and setting fire to the bailey but were unable to capture the tower on the motte. By 1078 Robert had been able to penetrate as far west as Degannwy where he constructed another castle. The creation of the three border earldoms did much to increase the security of western England and began the slow process of conquering Wales. Yet royal interest in subduing the Welsh was limited. In 1081 the king did travel as far west as St Davids in Wales, but this was to compel the Welsh to recognise traditional English claims of overlordship. Of far greater concern to William was ensuring that the Duchy of Normandy was adequately protected from attack. Therefore it was not to be until after his death that a serious and sustained attempt was to be made to conquer Wales.[14]

Domesday: The Great Survey

The threat of a Danish invasion in the autumn of 1085 prompted William to travel from Normandy to England. A great army accompanied him from the Continent to defend his lands from the expected onslaught. Yet as the winter closed in, the prospect of an invasion became ever more unlikely and the king retired to Gloucester to celebrate Christmas. It was there, as the *Anglo-Saxon Chronicle* records, that he 'had great thought and very deep conversation with his Council about this land, how it was occupied, or with which men'. Soon afterwards men were despatched throughout England to carry out a great survey of landholding across the kingdom. The commissioners were given specific instructions to determine how many units of land, known as hundreds, were present in each county. Furthermore, they were tasked with discovering who held land before 1066, during the reign of Edward the Confessor, and in the present day, as well as information on the inhabitants and economic resources of each area. The author of the *Anglo-Saxon Chronicle* went so far to claim that so thorough was the survey that not even 'one ox, one cow, one pig that was omitted, that was not set down in his record'. This information was later recorded in manuscript form, known as the Domesday Book, which provides an unparalleled insight into the economy and society of late eleventh century England. It also demonstrates that a profound change had occurred in landholding with the almost wholescale dispossession of the old English nobility, who had been replaced with Norman and French newcomers. One of the ways in which the new elite displayed their wealth and power was through the construction of castles, which proliferated across the realm after the Norman

Conquest. The commissioners of the great survey were primarily interested in recording land tenure, as opposed to the locations of fortifications – yet at least forty-eight castles are recorded in Domesday Book. Many of these castles were built to form the centre of manorial estates and to assert a lord's control over the region. This can be seen with William Malet, a Norman lord who was granted the wealthy honour of Eye in Suffolk by the king, as a reward for his loyal service. The grant from the king made him the wealthiest landowner in East Anglia, but his dominance of the local economy was contested by another major landholder, the Bishop of Norwich. Malet successfully challenged his rival by holding a weekly market on Saturdays inside his newly constructed castle in the town of Eye, in direct competition with the bishop's market at his nearby manor of Hoxne, which was held on the same day. Malet was able to use his influence over his tenants to compel them to favour the market at Eye, which meant that the market at Hoxne lost out as a result and was thereafter described as being 'of little worth'. The entries from Domesday also reveal that the process of castle-building could be a destructive process, particularly in the case of castles built in urban settlements. This ranged in scale from Wallingford, where eight houses where demolished to make way for a castle, to as many as ninety-eight houses in Norwich.[15]

Yet the castles recorded in Domesday represent only a tiny fraction of the total number of castles constructed in the years following the Norman Conquest. Approximately 1,000 castle sites dating to the period 1066–1200 have been identified in England and Wales, most of which date from the late eleventh century. Comparatively little is known about many of these structures and their occupants, particularly as only a small number of castles are mentioned in documentary sources. Yet their very existence provides evidence of a boom in private castle building in the reign of William the Conqueror. These early castle builders included both major landholding barons and men of knightly rank. The former group included nobles who had been richly rewarded with lands in the aftermath of the Conquest, with their manors and estates organised into lordships. These estates or fiefs were held directly from the king and the nobles that held them were known as tenants in chief. In return for holding their land by feudal tenure (the term feudal being derived from the Latin word *feodum* for fief), they were expected to provide a specified number of knights at their own expense for forty days, when the king required it. This type of castle builder included William de Warenne, 1st Earl of Surrey, who built a large castle with two mottes at Lewes, on a prominent position overlooking the River Ouse. In other areas, particularly in the Welsh Marches, comparatively modest ringworks were constructed by minor landowners, including sub-tenants who held land from another lord, as opposed to directly from the king. One of the methods used to garrison these castles involved another form of land tenure known as castle-guard. This was a system whereby land was granted to tenants in return for providing military service at the castle, for an agreed length of time. At least forty-two castles in England are known to have made use of this type of arrangement. At Richmond Castle in the mid-twelfth century, 186 knights were organised into six groups, which each served for two months at a time, with a larger contingent serving during the summer. The later part of William's reign also saw the rebuilding and improvement of existing royal castles, which had been constructed during the early years of the Norman Conquest. The most notable example of this is the Tower of London, whose names derives from the great keep, known as the White Tower, which was constructed from 1079 to 1093. The White Tower was built using Caen stone and was inspired by earlier Norman keeps such as Ivry-la-Bataille in Normandy. Undoubtedly it was intended to overawe the inhabitants of London and to serve as a striking visual symbol of the new order.[16]

The Anglo-Norman Realm Divided

William's last campaign took place in July 1087 when he invaded the French Vexin at the head of his army. During the sack of Mantes he fell ill and was taken to Rouen, where he died on 9 September and was buried at Caen in the church of St Étienne. Reflecting on his reign, the author of the *Anglo-Saxon Chronicle* praised the firmness of his rule but also bitterly noted that: 'He had castles built and wretched men oppressed'. Yet as brutal as William's methods had sometimes been, they also ensured that the Norman Conquest was a success. His victorious campaigns throughout his lifetime meant that he became one of the most powerful rulers in Western Europe. However, on his death the Anglo-Norman realm was divided. His eldest son, Robert Curthose, succeeded to the Duchy of Normandy, while his second son, William Rufus, inherited the kingdom of England. This division stemmed from a family dispute, which had taken place some years earlier. According to an account provided by Vitalis, this conflict was sparked by a fracas between Robert and his younger brothers, while they were staying in L'Aigle in Normandy, most likely in 1078, which involved the latter pouring urine onto their eldest brother. William was said to have tried to reconcile his sons, but Robert and his followers, infuriated by the insult he had suffered, slipped away and tried to seize Rouen Castle by force. After the failure of this desperate enterprise, they fled into exile. Robert soon joined forces with his father's enemies and was granted a castle at Rémalard, from which he launched raids into southern Normandy. The following year father and son reconciled but the relationship between the two men remained tense and never recovered. It is, therefore, not surprising that William chose to leave his most valuable dominion, the kingdom of England to his second son, William Rufus. However, having previously designated Robert as his heir in Normandy some years earlier, he felt obliged to grant him the Duchy of Normandy. This division of lands was to lead to future conflict. Robert felt cheated by this outcome and was determined to wrest control of England from his brother. Meanwhile, the Norman nobility, who held land both sides of the Channel, owed allegiance to two different lords and so were divided in their loyalties.[17]

Soon after the death of his father, on 9 September 1087, William Rufus crossed over to England. He was crowned as king in Winchester by Lanfranc the Archbishop of Canterbury on 26 September. Thereafter he took control of royal government and strengthened his position among the ruling elite through a liberal distribution of wealth from the treasury. However, William was soon to be challenged by his brother's supporters in England. In the spring of 1088, he was forced to contend with a rebellion led by his uncle, Odo, Bishop of Bayeux and Earl of Kent, as well as other leading nobles, such as Roger de Montgomery, Earl of Shrewsbury. The plan appears to have been for the rebels to seize key towns and castles in England, particularly on the south-east coast, in advance of Robert landing with his army a short time afterwards. They therefore improved the fortifications of their castles, increased the size of their garrisons and supplied them with provisions. The rebellion broke out with raids being launched from their castles in the south-east, Welsh Marches and the north into the surrounding areas. However, most of the nobility remained loyal to William together with the English population. The rebel assaults were beaten back and they were soon cut off and isolated in their castles. William raised a large army with which he systematically captured Odo's main castles in Kent and Sussex. The first target was Tonbridge Castle, held by Gilbert fitz Richard, whose garrison was forced to surrender after a short siege. William then proceeded southwards to Pevensey Castle, which he blockaded by land and sea. After a six week siege, the defenders' supplies ran out and they too were forced to surrender. The royal army then marched on Rochester, which had served as Odo's headquarters and was well defended. The attackers closely blockaded the city and built two siege towers or counter-castles to put the garrison under pressure. This pressure eventually told, with the will and ability of the defenders to resist gradually reduced by the outbreak of disease and the absence of a relieving army from Normandy. Robert's failure to lead an army to England to assist the rebels resulted in the garrison being forced to surrender under terms, with the lives of their leaders spared, in return for being exiled from England. Therefore by the summer of 1088, the rebellion had been completely crushed.[18]

In the following years, William went on the counteroffensive against Robert by undermining the latter's position in Normandy. He initially used his superior financial resources to tempt the Norman nobility to desert his brother and to join his allegiance. This led to the outbreak of a rebellion in Rouen in October 1090, which was followed by an invasion of Normandy by William the next year, in February. Robert struggled to maintain his control over the duchy, but the support of his younger brother, Henry, proved to be critical, and the two sides eventually came to terms. At the Treaty of Rouen, Robert granted territory in Normandy to William, including the county of Eu and the town of Cherboug. In return for which,

William agreed to help his brother regain control of the duchy and to give him some lands in England. However, William's stay on the Continent was cut short by news of a Scottish invasion of the north, which prompted him to return in May. William quickly raised an army and a fleet, which invaded Scotland and soon forced Malcolm III to come to terms. Yet the need to assert Norman authority in the far north of England, prompted the launching of another expedition in May of 1092. An attack was launched on Cumberland, which had been ceded to Scotland by Edmund the Elder in the tenth century. Its ruler, Dolfin, was soon forced to flee and the region was incorporated into the kingdom of England. A royal castle was constructed in the city of Carlisle and English settlers were encouraged to move into the region. This action had long-time consequences as it firmly established the western border between England and Scotland, which remains little changed to this day. The situation was very different in Wales, where the ongoing conflict between the Normans and the Welsh meant that territory frequently changed hands. Warfare was conducted by the king's lieutenants, with limited royal involvement. This changed in 1095 when a remarkable upturn in Welsh fortunes forced the king into a direct intervention.[19]

The Welsh Revival

The 1070s had seen significant Norman penetration into Wales, particularly in the north, but the rate of expansion slowed in the following decade. In southern Wales, they faced fierce opposition from the powerful king of Deheubarth, Rhys ap Tewdwr. His position as effective ruler of the south was recognised by William the Conqueror in 1081, in return for an annuity of £40. By contrast in the north, despite the capture of the most powerful ruler in northern Wales, Gruffudd ap Cynan, king of Gwynedd, the Normans initially chose to consolidate their gains. The situation was transformed in 1093, when Rhys was defeated and killed by a Norman force at Brecon. His death in battle led to a power vacuum that plunged the whole of Wales into chaos, which was rapidly exploited by the Normans. A Welsh chronicler describes the onslaught in stark terms: 'and then the French seized all the lands of the Britons'. The first region to be attacked was the south-east, where Robert Fitzhamon launched an invasion of the kingdom of Morgannwg, later known as Glamorganshire, from his base in Bristol. He then secured his conquests through the construction of castles, including one at Cardiff, which was built on the site of a Roman fort. An even more successful offensive was undertaken by Roger de Montgomery, Earl of Shrewsbury, who invaded Deheubarth by land and sea. Ceredigion (Cardiganshire) and Dyfed (Pembrokeshire) were soon overrun, with the conquered territory secured through the construction of castles at Pembroke, Cardigan and Rhydygors. In the north, the Normans experienced some setbacks during 1093. Robert of Rhuddlan was killed in a skirmish with the Welsh, and Grufffudd ap Cynan was rescued from his prison in Chester, and thereafter fled to Ireland. Yet the Normans had strengthened their hold over the coastal region of Gwynedd through the construction of castles at Caernarfon, Anglesey and Bangor. Thus within a short space of time almost the entire area of Wales had been brought under Norman rule. However, the cruelty and oppression of the Normans provoked a strong Welsh reaction.[20]

The first uprising broke out in north Wales in 1094 and quickly led to a collapse of Norman authority in Gwynedd. All the castles west of the River Conwy were overrun; a force sent to confront the Welsh was defeated in battle by an army led by Cadwgan ap Bleddyn, a prince of the kingdom of Powys. Gruffudd ap Cynan was also able to recover Anglesey at this time, according to a biography of his life written in the early thirteenth century. He was said to have landed at the island, with the support of men and ships provided by Godred Crovan, king of Man, and defeated the Normans in battle. Thereafter his forces laid siege to Castell Aberlleiniog and succeeded in burning part of the castle, as well as killing its commander and 124 men of the garrison. The Norman response to these assaults was hampered by a lack of effective leadership, due to the recent death of Robert of Rhuddlan and the absence of Hugh d'Avranches, Earl of Chester, who was in Normandy. Rebellions rapidly broke out elsewhere in Wales, with almost the whole of the south-west liberated by the Welsh. Only the garrisons of the castles of Pembroke and Rhyd y Gors managed to resist the onslaught. The scale of the disaster prompted

William to return to England in December. Any plans for a royal expedition to Wales were soon thwarted by a dispute with Anselm, the Archbishop of Canterbury, and the discovery of a baronial conspiracy to overthrow him, led by Robert de Mowbray, Earl of Northumberland. In response, the king led an army to the north in the summer to neutralise this threat. First he attacked Newcastle, which surrendered after a two-month siege, before proceeding to Robert de Mowbray's stronghold at Bamburgh Castle. The strong natural defences of the castle, which is situated on a volcanic rock adjacent to the sea, made it a difficult fortress to capture. In recognition of this, he decided to construct a counter-castle called *Malveisin* (Bad Neighbour) next to Bamburgh, to exert pressure on the defenders. The decisiveness of William's northern campaign meant that most of the conspirators lost heart and came to terms, leaving Robert de Mowbray cut off and isolated. It was at this point that the king received the news that Hen Domen Castle had been captured and destroyed by the Welsh. The situation was now so serious that without royal intervention, the Normans faced the very real prospect of losing most of their territory in Wales. William therefore left part of his army to continue the siege and marched southwards to raise a new army for an expedition into Wales.[21]

This new army was divided into separate contingents that invaded Gwynedd from different directions in September. The fear of being ambushed and the rough terrain meant that woodcutters were used to cut down the trees and thickets that lay in the army's path. Nevertheless, numerous casualties were suffered before it reassembled in Snowdonia at the beginning of November. This sacrifice proved to be in vain because the Welsh wisely refused to give battle and William was forced to return to Chester, having achieved very little. The chronicler William of Malmesbury noted that many knights and baggage animals were lost during this campaign, the failure of which he attributed to the 'roughness of the country and the inclement climate' which 'were as much a handicap to his prowess as they were a positive aid to the rebels'. Despite this setback in Wales, the king was more successful in the north of England, where the capture of Roger de Mowbray, after an unsuccessful escape attempt, led to the surrender of Bamburgh. William's attention was soon afterwards diverted to Continental affairs as a result of the preaching of the First Crusade by Pope Urban at the Council of Clermont in November 1095. Robert Curthose decided to join the crusade in the following February and agreed to mortgage his duchy to William for three years, in return for 10,000 silver marks. During the king's absence in Normandy, the Welsh inflicted further defeats on the Normans in 1096. The death of William fitz Baldwin led to the abandonment of Rhyd y Gors Castle by its garrison, which left Pembroke Castle as the sole remaining Norman possession in the south-west. Further to the east, Welsh insurgents in Gwent managed to defeat Norman armies from Glamorganshire. Crucially, however, the Welsh were unable to fully capitalise on these victories due to their failure to capture the castles of the region. Furthermore, the garrison of Pembroke Castle, despite being completely isolated from their compatriots, managed to hold out, thereby providing a base from which a counter-offensive could later be mounted. William returned to England in 1097 to lead another expedition to Wales, but again was unable to bring his enemies to battle, although he did order the construction of further castles in the Welsh Marches.[22]

Despite these setbacks, the Normans were still determined to recover the territories they had lost in Wales. A major offensive was planned to capture Gwynedd, led by Hugh d'Avranches, Earl of Chester, and Hugh de Montgomery, Earl of Shrewsbury. News of this attack prompted the Welsh and their leaders, Gruffudd ap Cynan and Cadwgan ap Bleddyn, to withdraw to Anglesey with their forces. To counter the naval superiority of their enemies, they hired a fleet of ships from the Vikings of Ireland. Yet the latter were bribed by the Normans to change sides, prompting Gruffudd and Cadwgan to flee to Ireland. The Normans then attacked Anglesey, whose now leaderless defenders were quickly overcome. The island was then put to the sword over the course of a week, with many atrocities committed by the victors. This situation was transformed, however, by the unexpected arrival of a fleet led by Magnus Barefoot, king of Norway. The Norwegians at once attacked the Normans who were routed and suffered many losses, including Hugh de Montgomery, who was said to have been struck in the eye by an arrow shot by Magnus. The severity of this defeat prompted the Normans to abandon their attempts to conquer north

Wales. Instead, a policy of securing treaties with native Welsh rulers was adopted. During the next year, Gruffudd ap Cynan returned to Gwynedd with the support of Hugh d'Avranches, and Cadwgan ap Bleddyn was installed as ruler of Powys, with the backing of the new Earl of Shrewsbury, Robert de Bellême.[23]

England and Normandy Reunited

William Rufus was hunting in the New Forest, accompanied by his younger brother Henry, on 2 August 1100 when he was accidentally struck by an arrow and killed. Henry quickly rushed to Winchester to secure the royal treasury and was crowned there three days later. This action went unchallenged at the time, as Robert did not return to Normandy from the Holy Land until the following month. Confronted with this fait accompli, Robert at first professed to be content only with his duchy as opposed to asserting his claim to the English kingdom. However, he had changed his mind by the next year, in part due to the influence of Ranulf Flambard, Bishop of Durham. Ranulf had played a leading role in William's government, but after the accession of Henry was imprisoned in the Tower of London, before later escaping to Normandy. By the summer, an invasion force had been prepared, with Robert hoping that he would receive baronial support after landing in England. Henry was aware of these preparations and led his army to Pevensey Castle on 24 June to await his brother and assembled a fleet to oppose the crossing. Yet Robert, supposedly on the advice of Ranulf, bribed at least some of the crews of these ships to defect to his side. His crossing was therefore unopposed when his fleet sailed from Le Tréport in Normandy and disembarked at Portsmouth on 20 July. The ranks of his army were soon swelled by contingents provided by some of the leading barons in England, including Robert de Bellême and William of Warenne. He then marched his forces inland towards Winchester and camped near the city, to await the arrival of Henry's army, who swiftly moved westwards from Sussex. The two armies eventually confronted each other near Alton, but fighting was averted by negotiations. By the terms of the agreement, Robert agreed to give up his claim to the English throne in return for territorial concessions in the Cotentin in Normandy, which he had sold to his brother some years earlier, and an annuity of 3,000 marks.[24]

This outcome was highly advantageous to Henry, who for a time appeared to have been in very real danger of losing his throne. Yet he was aware of how precarious his rule remained while Robert still had powerful supporters in England. Therefore in the following years he gradually strengthened his hold on power and moved against some of his overmighty vassals. In 1102, he summoned Robert de Bellême to come to his court and to answer for forty-five 'offences in deed or word committed against him'. Robert was undoubtedly aware of the king's hostility towards him and refused to go. Instead he decided to strengthen the fortifications of his castles and appealed for assistance from his allies. Henry responded by raising an army and laying siege to Arundel Castle. However, the strong defences of the castle meant that it could not be captured quickly. Consequently, he decided to construct siege castles outside Arundel and left a small force of men behind to continue the siege. Meanwhile, Robert de Bellême and his men launched raids from his castles in Shropshire into the surrounding areas to ravage the lands of the king's men. Yet the rebellion against Henry was fatally compromised due to the reluctance of Duke Robert and the other barons to join it. What is more, they actively assisted the king in repressing the uprising, with Duke Robert even laying siege to some of Robert de Bellême's castles in Normandy. Henry was therefore able to isolate and capture each of the rebellious castles, one by one. The garrison of Arundel Castle surrendered after a three-month siege, whereas Tickhill Castle was soon reduced by an army led by Robert, Bishop of Lincoln. Finally, Henry laid siege to Robert's newly constructed castle at Bridgnorth in Shropshire, which was described by Vitalis as being 'very strong'. Yet the lack of relief meant that the garrison were soon persuaded to surrender. Thereafter Robert de Bellême was banished from the kingdom and suffered the forfeiture of his English estates. The suppression of this rebellion greatly increased Henry's authority in England and made it possible for him to challenge his brother's hold over Normandy. Over the following few years he did this by suborning the Norman nobility and pressuring Robert into granting him territorial concessions. Eventually in 1106, he invaded Normandy and defeated his brother at the Battle of Tinchebrai, with Robert thereafter spending the remainder of his life in prison.

The Anglo-Norman realm was therefore reunited under one ruler once again.[25]

The frequent outbreak of rebellions in Normandy and conflict with the king of France meant that Henry spent most of the rest of his reign overseas attending to the defence of his continental lands. Nevertheless, he was concerned with enhancing his prestige and authority in England through the construction and rebuilding of castles. The early twelfth century saw the construction of many new castles, which were now increasingly made of stone, as opposed to wood. This period was also characterised by the building of large masonry towers, which since the late Middle Ages have been referred to as keeps, entered at first floor level through a forebuilding. These massive structures were primarily intended to visually symbolise the great wealth and power of their owners, and served as palaces, with their internal layouts designed to accommodate public ceremonies, which took place in their great halls and great chambers. However, they could also be used in a military capacity as a refuge in desperate circumstances during sieges. At Canterbury, an earlier motte and bailey castle, now known as Dane John mound, had been built on the southern edge of the city by William the Conqueror. This older castle was later superseded by a new structure made of stone that was constructed further to the west of the city during the reign of Henry I. The main feature of the new castle is the keep, which currently has two storeys (a third was demolished in the nineteenth century), whose dimensions from its plinth, where the walls are forty metres thick, are thirty metres by twenty-six metres. Henry also built or rebuilt other castles that incorporated keeps, such as at Gloucester (in existence by 1112), Norwich and Corfe. This type of architecture was also adopted by aristocratic and ecclesiastical castle builders. In 1127, the king granted Rochester Castle to the Archbishop of Canterbury, William de Corbeil. The chronicler Gervase of Canterbury records that Corbeil subsequently ordered the construction of a large tower of coursed rubble within the existing walls of the castle. This building is one of the largest Norman keeps in England and consists of four storeys, which originally had four square corner towers (one was later rebuilt as a round tower after it was destroyed during the siege of 1215).[26]

The Settlement of South Wales

The reign of Henry I saw the firm establishment of Norman control over southern Wales. Such was his reputation that a native Welsh chronicler described him as having 'subdued all the sovereigns of the isle of Britain by his power and authority'. Crucially this was attributed not just due to his prowess in warfare but also by his adroit use of 'innumerable gifts of gold and silver' to his followers and vassal rulers to maintain his authority. Henry effectively exercised overlordship over both the native princes of Wales, such as Gruffudd ap Cynan of Gwynedd and Cadwgan ap Bleddyn of Powys, as well as the Norman barons of the marches of Wales. In the south-west in Pembrokeshire, Flemish migrants were encouraged to settle in the area to bring the area firmly under Norman control. This policy was such a success that the area was organised and administered as an English county, despite its physical isolation from England. Further north in Ceredigion, the territory was taken from its ruler, Cadwgan ap Bleddyn, by Henry I on the pretext he was unable to control the area due to the depredations of his son, Owain, and instead granted to Gilbert fitz Richard of Clare. Territory was also granted in south-east Wales as a form of patronage, with land given to Robert, Earl of Gloucester, in Glamorgan and Henry de Beaumont, Earl of Warwick, in Gower. Essential to this process of colonisation was the construction of castles, which served as military bases in times of war and as centres of local administration. This can be seen in Ceredigion, where Gilbert fitz Richard built two castles, one at Cardigan and another near to Aberystwyth. New castles were also constructed in Pembrokeshire, including Haverford, Carew and Manorbier. Royal influence was maintained in the region due to the retention of major fortresses, such as Carmarthen, which were held by constables appointed directly by the king. This policy was greatly assisted by the forfeiture of Roger de Bellême's possessions in 1102, as his territories in Shropshire and Pembrokeshire came into royal hands, including the castles of Pembroke and Shrewsbury.[27]

Henry's priorities for much of his reign were focused elsewhere, particularly in Normandy, yet he was obliged to directly intervene in Welsh affairs in both 1114 and 1121, when he led military expeditions into the country. On the former occasion, this display of force so terrified the Welsh that it was said that he intended to 'exterminate all the Britons entirely, so that they should never more bear the British name'. Despite these efforts, the activities of the Normans did provoke sporadic reactions from the Welsh. In the spring of 1116, Gruffudd ap Rhys, the son of the last Welsh ruler of Deheubarth, Rhys ap Tewdwr, sought to reclaim his patrimony in south Wales. He and his followers first attacked and burnt Narberth Castle in Pembrokeshire, after which they moved eastwards to Carmarthenshire where they attempted to capture Llandovery Castle. They succeeded in setting fire to its outer defences but were unable to capture the castle itself, due to the determined resistance of its garrison. Soon afterwards they attempted to capture Henry Beaumont's castle at Swansea, but after causing some damage they were forced to withdraw. Despite these setbacks, Gruffudd succeeded in attracting enough support to mount an attack on Carmarthen Castle, which was the centre of royal government in south Wales. Gruffudd and his men launched a surprise night attack on the castle and managed to burn its outer ward as well as killing the commander of the garrison, Owain ap Caradog. Yet they were unable to capture the main part of the castle, which consisted of a great tower, to which the garrison had withdrawn for safety. Gruffudd's exploits and the failure of the Normans and their Welsh allies to quickly defeat the rebellion meant that his ranks were swelled by men from the area. Ultimately, however, his failure to take any of the major castles of the region prevented him from fully exploiting his victories. Later that year he was defeated in battle after laying siege to Aberystwyth and his rebellion came to an end.[28]

3

The Anarchy: 1135–1154

Then when the traitors realised that Stephen was a mild men,
gentle and good, and imposed no penalty, they committed every
enormity ... every powerful man made his castles and held them
against him, and filled the land full of castles. They greatly
oppressed the wretched men of the land with castle-work; then
when the castles were made, they filled them with devils and evil
men ... I do not know nor can I tell all the enormities nor all the
tortures that they did to wretched men in this land. And it lasted
the 19 years while Stephen was king, and it always grew worse
and worse ... and they said openly that Christ and His saints
slept.

Anglo-Saxon Chronicle, manuscript E[1]

The vivid account of the *Anglo-Saxon Chronicle* refers to the events
that followed the death of Henry I in 1135. His nephew, Stephen
of Blois, quickly seized the throne and was crowned king, but he
faced opposition to his rule, particularly from the supporters of
Henry's daughter, Matilda. This led to the outbreak of a prolonged
period of civil war and unrest that has been commonly referred to
as the 'Anarchy' since the late nineteenth century. The description
of this conflict as the Anarchy is largely derived from contemporary
narrative accounts. These clerical chroniclers were adamant in their
condemnation of the outrages committed by the aristocracy and their
soldiers in despoiling the possessions of the church and oppressing
the common people. They also emphasised the breakdown in law

and order, as well as a collapse in the authority of royal government during the civil war. This impression is supported by coin hoards dating from Stephen's reign. They reveal that his government lost control of minting coins over a significant part of the kingdom, particularly in the west and north of England. Castles were clearly identified as playing a major role in this conflict, as well as serving as instruments of oppression and tyranny. The monastic chronicler, William of Malmesbury, claimed that there 'were many castles all over England, each defending its own district or, to be more truthful, plundering it. The knights from the castles carried off both herds and flocks, sparing neither churches nor graveyards'. The castles were constructed partly through the imposition of forced labour services on the local communities, who were also extorted for protection money by their garrisons. The author of the *Stephani Gesta* (Acts of Stephen), though he praised Robert, Earl of Gloucester, for bringing a semblance of peace to the territory under his control, nevertheless condemned him for his use of forced labour in building castles. Only two major set-piece battles were fought during this period, the Battle of the Standard in 1138 and the Battle of Lincoln in 1141, yet there were numerous sieges of castles. Some fortifications were subjected to multiple sieges, such as Wallingford Castle, which was unsuccessfully besieged by Stephen's forces on three separate occasions.[2]

The White Ship Disaster and the Problem of the Succession

On 25 November 1120, Henry I and his court set sail from Barfleur in Normandy on a voyage to England. The fleet of ships included a large vessel called the *White Ship*, which was said to have 300 passengers onboard, many of illustrious rank, including William, the son and heir of the king. During the crossing the ship struck rocks and sank, resulting in the death of almost all the crew and passengers. Blame for the disaster was attributed by chroniclers to the reckless actions of the young aristocrats onboard and the sailors who had been drinking heavily. The death of the young prince was to have profound consequences. Henry had fathered numerous children through his mistresses, but only had two legitimate children from his wife Matilda, who had died two years previously, namely his son William and a daughter called Matilda. The issue of the succession therefore became a pressing concern for the king in his later years. Although he married Adeliza, daughter of Godfrey I, Count of Louvain, soon after he became a widower, the marriage proved to be childless. This meant that his closest male relatives were his nephews, who were decended from his brother Robert Curthose and from his sister Adela. William Clito was the only child of Robert Curthose and thereby posed a threat to his uncle's rule throughout his lifetime. William spent most of his life in exile at the courts of Flanders and France where he sought military assistance to support his claim to the Duchy of Normandy and kingdom of England. His death in 1128 removed a serious threat to Henry's plans for the succession. By contrast, Henry was on much better terms with his sister's sons, especially with Stephen and Henry of Blois, who substantially benefitted from their uncle's patronage. Stephen was appointed as Count of Mortain in Normandy in 1113, and received the honours of Eye and Lancaster in England. He later married Matilda, the daughter and heir of Eustace III, Count of Boulogne, in 1125, with his uncle's blessing. Through this accumulation of lands and titles in England and France, Stephen became one of the leading Anglo-Norman magnates. His younger brother, Henry, meanwhile was marked out for a career in the church, being selected as Abbot of Glastonbury in 1126 and three years later as bishop for the wealthy bishopric of Winchester. Nevertheless, despite the favour shown to his nephews, Henry wished to be succeeded by his daughter Matilda, commonly referred to as 'the empress' by historians. She had been married to Henry V, the Holy Roman Emperor, in 1114, but after her husband's death in 1125, continued to style herself as empress for the rest of her life. Her father the king compelled the magnates and ecclesiastics at his court, which included his nephews Stephen and Henry, to swear an oath of fealty to her, on 1 January 1127, thereby recognising her as his heir. In the following year she married Geoffrey Plantagenet, Count of Anjou, one of the most powerful rulers in northern France. The marriage was a turbulent one, in part due to the significant age difference between the couple with Matilda being eleven years older than her husband, however, the union resulted in the birth of three sons.[3]

King Stephen

Henry I died on 1 December 1135 in Normandy. Upon receiving news of his uncle's death, Stephen quickly left the county of Boulogne and set sail for England, where he made landfall at Dover. He travelled to London where his arrival was greeted with enthusiasm by the inhabitants, who pledged their support to his claim to be king. Stephen then went to Winchester, the administrative capital of the realm, where he was given the royal treasury by its custodian, William de Pont-de-l'Arche. He also received the backing of the church, with assistance provided by his brother, Henry, Bishop of Winchester, and Roger, Bishop of Salisbury, as well as from officers of the dead king's royal household. This support proved to be crucial in his bid for power, with Stephen's coronation taking place on 22 December in Westminster Abbey. The speed with which Stephen had taken possession of the crown, a mere three weeks after the death of Henry I, confounded his rivals. His older brother, Theobald, Count of Blois, was said by Orderic Vitalis to have been the choice of the Norman magnates, and to have been at Rouen when he received news of his brother's fait accompli. Yet faced with the prospect of a division of the Anglo-Norman realm, the Normans soon recognised Stephen as Duke of Normandy. Matilda's absence in Anjou also meant that she was slow to react, although her husband, Geoffrey, used the opportunity to launch raids into Normandy. Stephen's position at the beginning of 1136 therefore appeared to be strong, but he was immediately faced with challenges to his rule. The death of Henry I had led to the outbreak of unrest and disorder across the kingdom, with the Scottish king, David I, using the opportunity to launch an invasion of northern England. His forces quickly took possession of the chief castles of the region, namely Carlisle, Wark, Alnwick, Norham and Newcastle-upon-Tyne. Stephen responded by raising a large army to confront the invaders, with his army reaching Durham on 5 February. An agreement was soon reached with the Scots, with David paying homage to Stephen, in return for territorial concessions, notably the counties of Cumberland and Northumberland.[4]

Stephen held court at York during Easter and thereafter planned to visit Normandy to settle the affairs of the duchy, which was in a state of disorder. His departure was postponed, however, due to news of a dispute between the citizens of Exeter and Baldwin de Redvers, who had seized the royal castle. The king responded by marching to Exeter at the head of an army, where he was admitted into the city by its inhabitants, and laying siege to Rougemont Castle. The pro-Stephen author of the *Gesta Stephani* chronicle emphasised the strong defences of the castle, which he described as being 'raised on a very high mound surrounded by an impregnable wall and fortified with towers of hewn limestone'. The strength of the fortifications and the determination of the garrison to resist the king meant that this would prove to be a difficult siege. Stephen's measures to cut off the garrison from outside aid included the construction of a fortification, known as a siege or counter-castle, on the edge of a ridge overlooking the castle. Archaeological excavations of the site of this counter-castle, known as Danes Castle, shows it was a circular ringwork surrounded by a ditch and rampart. The construction of this fortification was a testament to the king's determination to capture the castle and allowed the besiegers to put pressure on the garrison. The author of the *Gesta Stephani* states that the king took an active role in prosecuting the siege, by employing slingers and archers to rain missile fire on the defenders, as well as using miners to undermine the walls, and stone-throwing siege weapons to launch projectiles into the castle. Frequent attacks were made against the garrison, with one assault succeeding in taking an outwork on a mound outside the castle. Further pressure was exerted by means of throwing flaming torches over the battlements, which set fire to the buildings inside. Eventually a lack of food and drink compelled the defenders to surrender; who were given generous terms by the king, and allowed to depart. Baldwin de Redvers at once proceeded to the Isle of Wight, where he had a castle at Carisbrooke which was said to be 'very finely built of stone and very strongly fortified'. Yet his scheme for harassing England with a pirate fleet was undone due to a lack of provisions. He therefore threw himself on the king's mercy at Southampton and was exiled to the Continent. Stephen's failure to punish Baldwin was condemned by many of the chroniclers, who believed that the king's leniency was a major reason for a decline in the power of royal government and the cause of future outbreaks of unrest.[5]

In the spring of 1137 the king travelled to Normandy to confront the growing Angevin threat from Matilda and her husband Geoffrey. During his absence the situation in Wales significantly deteriorated due to a major revival in Welsh power. The death of Henry I had prompted the outbreak of a series of rebellions that severely curtailed Norman power in the region. The Normans were defeated in battle in Gower in January 1136 and three months later, Richard de Clare, Lord of Ceredigion, was killed in an ambush by the Welsh in Gwent. The collapse in Norman power prompted the joint rulers of Gwynedd, Owain and Cadwaladr, the sons and successors of Gruffudd ap Cynan, to launch an invasion of Ceredigion. They soon overran the region and took the castles of Walter de Bec and Rickert de la Mere, which they burnt after capturing them. Later that year they launched another invasion of Ceredigion, when they were confronted by a Norman army outside Cardigan. After a hard-fought battle the Normans were routed and the town was sacked, with the survivors retreating to the castle. Owain and Cadwaladr launched another raid into southern Wales in the following year, capturing the castles of Ystrad Meurig, Llansteffan and Humphrey's Castle, as well as the town and castle of Carmarthen. The loss of the latter was a devastating blow to Norman prestige, as it was the centre of royal power and administration in the region. In other circumstances this disaster would have prompted a royal response. Yet Stephen's need to devote his time and resources to maintaining control over England and Normandy meant that the prospect of a royal expedition to subdue the Welsh was unfeasible. Instead, piece-meal efforts were made by the Marcher lords to confront the Welsh, occasionally with royal backing. An expedition led by Miles of Gloucester, Earl of Hereford, succeeded in rescuing Richard de Clare's widow, Alice, from Cardigan Castle, but other expeditions did not fare so well. Baldwin de Clare, brother of the slain Richard, was tasked with reconquering Ceredigion and was provided with a large sum of money to raise an army. Yet Baldwin appears to have balked at the prospect of facing the triumphant Welsh in battle and withdrew after having achieved very little.

The Normans were still able to retain control of their territory in the far south-west, in Pembrokeshire, and in the south-east, but were put under severe pressure by the Welsh.[6]

Stephen returned to England in December 1137. He was soon involved in a dispute over the custody of Bedford Castle, which had been seized by Miles de Beauchamp. The king was said to have been 'violently incensed against Miles' when he received news of this and resolved to deal with the matter in person. Yet when confronted by Stephen and his army, Miles refused to hand over the castle to the king, who responded by laying siege to it on Christmas Eve. This decision was criticised by the chronicler Henry of Huntingdon, as waging war over Christmas was an action that was said to have displeased God. Bedford Castle was a potentially difficult place to capture due to its strong defences and as it was well supplied with provisions. The *Gesta Stephani* described the castle as being 'surrounded by a very lofty mound, encircled by a strong and high wall, fortified with a strong and unshakeable keep'. After a five week siege, the castle was surrendered under terms – with the garrison permitted to leave. Meanwhile war had broken out with the Scots, who had invaded Northumberland. Stephen responded by leading a counter-invasion of Scotland, with his men laying waste to the land by 'fire and sword', before retiring to Northampton for Lent. The king subsequently travelled to Gloucester, where he was well received by the inhabitants and celebrated the Feast of the Ascension. Afterwards he was informed that Hereford Castle was being held against him by Geoffrey Talbot. Stephen therefore besieged the castle and captured it after a two-week siege, then garrisoned it with his soldiers. This was only the beginning of the king's problems, however, as soon afterwards 'the treason of the English nobles burst forth with great fury'.[7]

The Outbreak of Civil War

Soon after Whitsun (15 May) in 1138 Stephen received a message from Robert, Earl of Gloucester, in Normandy, that he had renounced his homage to him. Robert justified this act of defiance because the king had unlawfully acquired the throne, due to his earlier oath to support the Empress Matilda, and as he had failed to keep promises made to him. This defection was a serious challenge to Stephen as he was one of the most powerful magnates in the realm and a half-brother of the Empress. Robert was an illegitimate son of Henry I, who had been granted substantial lands and titles by his father, including the earldom of Gloucester. According to William of Malmesbury, he had originally intended to support his sister's claim to the throne in 1135, but was deterred by Stephen's rapid success in gaining the throne so offered him homage. However, relations between the two men continued to be fraught and marked by a lack of trust. It was therefore only a matter of time before hostilities broke out. Robert acted first by taking advantage of Stephen's difficulties in suppressing rebellions to plan an uprising against him by persuading his fellow magnates in the west of England and the Welsh Marches to support him in this venture. The castles held by his supporters included Castle Cary and Dunster in Somerset, Ludlow and Shrewsbury in Shropshire, Wareham in Dorset and Dover in Kent. Yet the centre of Robert's powerbase was the town and castle of Bristol. From this stronghold, his supporters carried out raids into the surrounding areas and attempted to capture the city of Bath. Stephen responded by raising an army to confront the rebels, first stopping at Bath, whose defences were repaired by his soldiers, before proceeding to attack Bristol. Yet the formidable defences of the city meant that it was an especially difficult fortress to capture. It was one of the largest ports in England and was surrounded on three sides by the Rivers Frome and Avon. The one side directly approachable by land was protected by a castle which, according to the *Gesta Stephani,* was situated 'on a vast mound, strengthened by wall and battlements, towers and divers engines'. Stephen and his advisors debated various proposals for blockading the town, through the construction of counter-castles and by filling in the channel leading to the harbour with rocks, but ultimately decided to attack more vulnerable nearby targets. His forces first attacked Castle Cary, whose defenders were put under severe pressure by the projectiles thrown by his siege weapons, and who capitulated after running low on food. Stephen next captured the castle of Harptree by taking advantage of a foray by the garrison, which had left it undermanned, before proceeding on to Shrewsbury Castle. The besiegers succeeded in filling in the ditch and setting fire to the castle, after which they stormed the main gate, with many of the surviving defenders hanged on the king's instructions. Elsewhere, the rebels were besieged in Dover Castle by an army led by Stephen's wife, Queen Matilda. The castle was blockaded by both land and sea, with assistance provided by a fleet from Boulogne, which soon forced the defenders to surrender. Despite these successes, Stephen was rapidly losing control over large parts of the kingdom. The author of the *Gesta Stephani* compared the king's situation to that of Hercules when tasked with killing the hydra 'when one head was cut off two or more grew in its place'.[8]

In April, the Scots renewed their attacks on the north of England and caused considerable damage in the counties of Northumberland and Cumberland. They succeeded in capturing Norham Castle after a short siege and then took possession of Alnwick Castle, which was handed over by its owner, Eustace Fitz John. The absence of the king in the south meant that Thurstan, the Archbishop of York, took charge of the situation and mobilised the northern nobility to confront the invaders. They made their stand outside Northallerton in the north of Yorkshire, where they fixed their standard that consisted of a ship's prow from which was hung a pyx containing the consecrated host and the standards of St Wilfred of Ripon, St John of Beverley and St Peter the Apostle. The name of the battle that took place on 22 August, the Battle of the Standard, derived its name from this altar. Despite having superior numbers, the Scottish army was decisively defeated, with King David barely escaping with his life. Due to the turmoil of the civil war, the English were unable to capitalise on this victory, other than besieging the castle of Malton, which was held by Eustace Fitz John. The Scots were also able to continue their siege of Wark Castle throughout the autumn, with the garrison finally surrendering later that year. This meant that the Scots were in a strong position in the subsequent negotiations, with Stephen forced to acquiesce in the transferral of Northumberland to Scottish control in April 1139.[9]

Later that year, the royal court assembled at Oxford to celebrate the feast day of St John the Baptist on 24 June. Tensions were running high due to rumours of further defections from Stephen's cause and the atmosphere was one of mutual suspicion. A dispute over accommodation in the town led to a skirmish between the men of Roger, Bishop of Salisbury, and Alan, Earl of Richmond, with the latter forced to flee for their lives. The king's response was to order that the castles held by Roger, as well as those of his nephews, Alexander, Bishop of Lincoln; and Nigel, Bishop of Ely; should be handed over into his custody. After the bishops refused to comply, they were placed under arrest and were threatened with being stripped of their bishoprics, before later being released. This action shocked contemporaries, particularly as these bishops had hitherto been staunch supporters of Stephen. The clerical chroniclers of the time, such as Orderic Vitalis, blamed the influence of nobles close to the king who were jealous of the wealth and power of the bishops. They were also envious of their castles, which in size and splendour were said to rival those of the greatest magnates of the land. According to William of Malmesbury, Roger had 'wished to be thought of as a great builder' and at Malmesbury had even 'begun a castle in the churchyard itself, hardly a stone's throw from the abbey'. He also made castles at Sherborne and Devizes by constructing 'ranges of buildings surrounded by great towers'. The latter was described by Henry of Huntingdon as 'one of the most stately in Europe'. His nephews were also noted castle builders, with Alexander's castle at Newark said to have built 'in a florid style of architecture, on a charming site, among the meadows washed by the river Trent'. The legality of the king's contentious actions was debated at a church council held in Winchester on 29 August 1139. Despite being the king's brother, Henry of Blois, Bishop of Winchester, took the side of his fellow bishops. He complained that they had been mistreated and that their castles should be returned to them. The king's case was made by Hugh, Archbishop of Rouen, who argued that the possession of castles by the clergy was not supported by canon law. What was more, according to William of Malmesbury, he argued that 'as it is a time of uncertainty, all the chief men, in accordance with the custom of other peoples, ought to hand over the keys of their fortifications to the disposal of the king'. This argument was compelling and ensured that these castles remained in the king's hands. Yet Stephen's reputation was undoubtedly damaged by his move against his erstwhile supporters.[10]

In the meantime, hostilities between the supporters of Stephen and the Empress continued throughout the year, particularly in the south-west of England. The king led an army into Somerset to counter the depredations of William de Bohun, whose chief stronghold was Dunster Castle. The *Gesta Stephani* states, however, that Stephen refrained from leading a direct assault on the fortress due to its 'unconquerable fortifications'. On the one side the castle was inaccessible as it was 'washed by the waves' and on the other was 'rendered very strong by towers and walls, a rampart and stockade'. He therefore decided to construct a counter-castle near Dunster to restrict the activities of the castle's garrison, and he left the counter-castle under the command of Henry de Tracy. Henry's exploits included an incursion into Devon where he caught the defenders of Torrington Castle off guard, as most of the garrison were absent on a raiding mission. He led a surprise night attack on the castle and he and his men managed to enter it by stealth. His soldiers then threw flaming torches inside the windows of the keep, which set the building on fire. After this, they succeeded in capturing the owner of the castle, 'singed as he was', and the contents of his treasury. Elsewhere, Baldwin de Redvers returned from exile in Normandy and landed in Dorset, where he was admitted into Wareham and Corfe Castle. Stephen responded by leading his army against Baldwin and laid siege to Corfe Castle. He spent a considerable length of time besieging the place and constructed a counter-castle on the high ground overlooking the castle, now known as the 'The Rings'. This counter-castle takes the form of a ringwork and bailey fortification, with both features surrounded by a ditch and which originally contained wooden structures within them. However, Stephen was forced to abandoned this enterprise after receiving news that Robert, Earl of Gloucester, and the Empress, were soon due to make landfall in England with their forces.[11]

The Arrival of the Empress

Stephen had given firm instructions that the ports and coasts of England should be carefully watched. Nevertheless, the Empress and Robert succeeded in landing at Arundel in West Sussex. Robert left soon afterwards and travelled overland to his stronghold at Bristol, leaving his sister at the castle. The king prepared to lay siege to Arundel Castle but was persuaded by his advisors, including his brother, Henry, to allow the Empress and her followers to leave for Bristol under a safe conduct. This noble but strategically unwise decision was motivated partly by the desire to avoid the embarrassing situation of attacking a castle which belonged to Adeliza, widow of Henry I. Stephen's poor judgement was condemned by Orderic Vitalis who stated that the episode demonstrated that the king was 'either very guileless or very foolish, and prudent men must deplore his lack of regard for both his own safety and the security of the kingdom'. This assessment was shared by the leading laymen of the realm, some of whom shortly afterwards defected to the Empress. These individuals included notables such as Miles of Gloucester, Earl of Hereford, and Brian Fitz Count, Lord of Wallingford. Stephen responded by laying siege to the town and castle of Wallingford. This settlement was of strategic importance due to its location between Oxford and Reading on the River Thames and as it was the most easterly place held by the Empress's supporters. It therefore was a key objective for Stephen's forces, as the garrison posed a threat to his control over territory in Oxfordshire and Berkshire. Yet the strong fortifications of the settlement meant that it was a challenging place to capture. Wallingford had formerly served as an Anglo-Saxon burh in the ninth century and its defences included a substantial ditch and rampart, which was protected on its eastern flank by the river. The castle adjoined the northern side of the town and consisted of a motte and two baileys. According to the *Gesta Stephani*, the castle was 'securely fortified by impregnable walls', and its garrison consisted of 'a very strong force of invincible warriors, that were well supplied with provisions'. Therefore, as on previous occasions, Stephen decided to build two counter-castles near the settlement rather than being personally embroiled in a lengthy siege. He then led his army into Wiltshire, taking South Cerney Castle by storm and Malmesbury Castle after it was surrendered by its garrison. Yet in the meanwhile, Miles of Gloucester launched a surprise night assault on the soldiers left behind at the counter-castles outside Wallingford and succeeded in breaking the siege. Stephen suffered further setbacks at the end of the year, with both Worcester and

Hereford taken by storm, although at the latter a small force of knights succeeded in taking refuge in the castle.[12]

In January 1140, Stephen led an army into East Anglia to confront Nigel, Bishop of Ely. Nigel's loyalty had been suspect since his arrest in the previous summer and he was said to have wished to avenge the wrongs that he and his family had suffered at the king's hands. The bishop had prepared for his rebellion by hiring a force of knights, which 'molested all his neighbours, and especially those who supported the king'. He had also fortified Ely by constructing a new castle of timber and by rebuilding an earlier one at the causeway leading to the island at Aldreth. The presence of these fortifications, as well as the difficult natural terrain of the Isle of Ely, surrounded as it was by fenland, posed a formidable obstacle to any attackers. Realising that a direct assault would be too risky, Stephen instead instructed his men to construct a bridge made from boats and hurdles to outflank the defenders. His forces were then able to overrun the island, in the process collecting 'booty of great value and treasures in extraordinary quantity'. They also succeeded in capturing Aldreth Castle into which the king installed a garrison. Later that year, Stephen was active in the south-west of England and led an expedition into Cornwall, which had fallen under the control of Reginald, an illegitimate son of Henry I. In the meanwhile, a Flemish adventurer called Robert Fitz Hubert succeeded in taking control of Devizes Castle by a surprise attack. The *Gesta Stephani* states that the attackers used scaling ladders to gain entry to the 'impregnably walled' castle, thereby throwing the royalist garrison into confusion. The defenders retreated into a 'very high tower' but were forced to surrender soon afterwards due to a lack of provisions. Robert then used this castle as a fortified base from which he plundered and terrorised the surrounding communities. His reign of terror was finally ended by a follower of the Empress, John Fitz Gilbert the Marshal, constable of Marlborough Castle, who took him prisoner. Afterwards he was tortured in an attempt to compel his men to surrender the castle and upon their refusal to do so, was hanged outside of the walls. The Empress's supporters also continued to be active in campaigning against the adherents of the king. At Hereford, Geoffrey Talbot and his men laid siege to the castle, which was still held by Stephen's men. According to the *Gesta Stephani*, the besiegers desecrated the cathedral's graveyard by digging it up to form a rampart. Siege weapons were also mounted on the top of the cathedral tower, from which they bombarded the castle, until its garrison surrendered. At the end of the year, negotiations to end the conflict took place between representatives of both factions but they were unable to resolve their differences.[13]

The Battle of Lincoln and its Aftermath

Prior to 1141 the war had primarily consisted of numerous raids, skirmishes and sieges, with neither side able to achieve a decisive advantage in the struggle. This was changed by a major battle that took place outside the walls of Lincoln. The clash was sparked by the seizure of the castle in the city by Ranulf, Earl of Chester, in a dispute over its custody. Control of this fortification was important as Lincoln was the largest city in the east of England and therefore of strategic value. The most vivid account of this event is provided by Orderic Vitalis, who claimed that the castle was captured by Ranulf and his half-brother, William de Roumare, through a trick.

> They cunningly found a time when the household troops of the garrison were widely dispersed, and then sent their wives ahead to the castle under the pretext of a friendly visit. While the two countesses were passing the time there, laughing and talking with the wife of the knight who ought to have been defending the castle, the earl of Chester arrived, unarmed and without his cloak, as though to escort his wife home, and three knights followed him without arousing any suspicion. Once inside the castle they suddenly snatched crowbars and weapons which lay to hand and violently expelled the king's guards. Then William burst in with a force of armed knights, according to a pre-arranged plan, and in this way the two brothers took control of the castle and the whole city.

Stephen responded by rapidly leading his forces northwards and laid siege to the castle in late December 1140. Ranulf succeeded in escaping from the city and went westwards to seek support from Robert, Earl of Gloucester. The latter agreed to aid him and a large army was raised to lift the siege of the castle, which included a sizeable contingent of Welsh soldiers. Stephen received news of the approach of his enemies, but was determined to continue the siege of the hard-pressed garrison. The two sides met in battle on 2 February 1141 and after a brief engagement, the king's forces were routed and he was taken prisoner, with the city being sacked by the victors. Stephen was initially taken by his captors to Gloucester and afterwards to Bristol, where he was initially treated well but subsequently was kept in chains.[14]

The Empress was said to have been delighted by the unexpected victory and the capture of her rival. However, she was unsure how to proceed further, as Stephen, despite being her captive, was an anointed king. She was therefore advised to court the assistance of Henry, Bishop of Winchester, whose positon as papal legate gave him considerable authority. Henry's position was a delicate one, as he was the king's brother, nevertheless after negotiations he agreed to admit her into the city of Winchester and to support her right to the throne. The Empress and her entourage subsequently entered Winchester on 3 March and took possession of the royal castle and palace. She therefore appeared to be in a strong position to secure the deposition of Stephen and to assume the throne in her own right. Yet she immediately ran into problems due to a reluctance by many magnates and churchmen to abandon the king's cause, as well as the unwavering efforts made by Queen Matilda to secure her husband's release. The queen raised an army, partly made up of Flemish mercenaries, which raided the area outside London. Meanwhile, relations between the Londoners, who had been firm supporters of the king, and the Empress broke down, with the latter forced to flee the city on 24 June. She joined forces with her supporters in Oxford but at the end of July decided to travel to Winchester. This move prompted Henry, who had clearly had second thoughts about his earlier decision to abandon his brother, to flee the city and take refuge in his castle at Farnham. Yet he left behind sizeable forces in Winchester to garrison both the royal palace in the centre of the city and his own palace at Wolvesey on its south-eastern corner. Henry had fortified the latter by building a curtain wall around its perimeter and a strong keep. The Empress and her forces in the royal castle at once laid siege to the bishop's men in Wolvesey and the royal palace. The defenders responded by throwing flaming torches from their battlements, which set fire to the city and caused considerable damage on 2 August. In the meanwhile, Henry raised an army of hired knights who were recruited at 'very great expense' and from contingents provided by barons loyal to the king's cause and the Londoners. This force then besieged the Empress and her supporters in the city, thereby beginning a double siege of the city. The Empress's supporters attempted to keep their supply lines open by garrisoning and fortifying the nunnery at Wherwell, some ten miles to the north-west but they were attacked and driven off by a force of the king's men. Eventually the pressure became too much for the Empress and her supporters and they fled the city on 14 August. They were closely pursued by their opponents and the rear-guard was intercepted and defeated at Stockbridge, with Robert, Earl of Gloucester, taken prisoner. The Empress herself managed to escape, but this setback was a serious blow, particularly as half-brother was her leading supporter and advisor. Negotiations between the two sides began soon afterwards to arrange a prisoner exchange, with both Stephen and Robert released in early November.[15]

The Struggle for the West Country

The first few months of 1142 were uneventful in England, with William of Malmesbury noting that both factions 'behaved with calm restraint from Christmas to Lent'. Both sides had experienced reversals in the previous year and needed time to assess the situation. The Empress sought to break the deadlock by sending a message to her husband Geoffrey, requesting his support. He had succeeded in making major inroads into the territory of the Duchy of Normandy, since having received news of the Battle of Lincoln, and had considerable military resources available. Yet he refused to come to her assistance, as the war was still being fought on the Continent and instead requested aid from her supporters in England. The prospect of achieving a decisive victory in Normandy proved to be compelling and a sizeable contingent, including Robert, Earl of Gloucester, left to join Geoffrey's army in the summer. Stephen sought to take advantage of the situation by leading his army westwards deep into the territory of the Empress's supporters. His forces first captured Wareham, which had been left undefended, and a garrison was installed in the castle. Cirencester Castle was also left unprotected as its garrison 'had stolen away' and Stephen ordered its destruction. He then moved towards Oxford, where the Empress was based, and overran the two nearby castles of Bampton and Radcot. Her forces attempted to prevent the passage of the king's army across the river to the town, but they were defeated and driven back to the castle, which was then besieged. The castle would prove to be difficult to capture, however, as its defences were formidable, which the *Gesta Stephani* described as being 'an impregnable castle and tower of great height'. Nevertheless, Stephen was determined to achieve a decisive advantage through the capture of his rival and remained at the siege for the next three months. News of the Empress's plight prompted Robert to return to England. His fleet landed at Wareham and after taking the town, laid siege to the royal garrison in the castle. The defenders were eventually forced to surrender, with his forces also succeeding in capturing the Isle of Portland. He then assembled an army with which to break the siege and rescue his sister. Yet before this could take place, she succeeded in escaping from the castle and evading Stephen's sentries, by fleeing through the snow one night in early December. The garrison of the castle surrendered a short time afterwards, but Stephen had again failed to capture his rival.[16]

In the following year, further campaigning took place in the south-west of England. The king moved against Wareham, but finding that its defences were too strong to capture easily, he decided instead to lay waste to the surrounding area 'with fire and sword'. Afterwards he went to Winton in Wiltshire and attempted to fortify the abbey there, but was attacked by an army led by Robert, Earl of Gloucester, on 1 July. The royal army appears to have been taken by surprise and was routed after a short engagement, with the victors capturing important prisoners such as William Martel, the royal steward. William was only released after the king paid a ransom of £200 and surrendered Sherborne Castle, which was described by the *Gesta Stephani* as 'the master-key of the whole kingdom'. Robert exploited his victory further by gaining control over more territory in Wiltshire and Devon. Stephen's reputation was particularly damaged by this defeat as he was said to have fled the field in a shameful manner. The king also became more insecure and mistrustful of some of his closest followers, as can be seen by his decision to arrest one of his leading supporters, Geoffrey de Mandeville, Earl of Essex, at the royal court held at St Albans in the autumn of 1143. Despite his years of loyal service to Stephen, Geoffrey appears to have been the victim of a whispering campaign by courtiers who had the king's ear and were jealous of his wealth. In return for his freedom he was forced to hand over control of his castles, including Pleshey, Walden and the Tower of London. Outraged by his treatment, he began a rebellion in East Anglia soon after his release. His men first burnt the town of Cambridge before proceeding onto the Isle of Ely, where he received the support of the local inhabitants. From this secure base, raids were carried out into the surrounding area with the *Gesta Stephani* reporting that he 'raged everywhere with fire and sword'. To guard the approach to the island, Geoffrey built castles at Wood Walton and Benwick, with the monks at the nearby abbey of Ramsey evicted so that their residence could be fortified. He also laid siege to the castle of Aldreth, which was held by the king's men, just outside of the Isle of Ely. Stephen arrived in the area with his army in early 1144, but was deterred from launching a direct attack on the island, due to the strength of the newly erected fortifications. Instead he constructed counter-castles in the nearby area and left behind a strong force of men to contain the ravages of Geoffrey's supporters, while he campaigned elsewhere. One of these fortifications was erected at Burwell to the south-east of Ely, on the site of a former Anglo-Saxon aristocratic residence. Archaeological excavations reveal that this was not a temporary campaign castle but was intended as a major fortification. The castle is rectangular in form and consists of a raised platform some thirty metres by sixty metres, which was surrounded by a ditch, together with masonry walls and a great tower. Work on the structure was never fully finished, as can be seen from the presence of nearby spoil heaps overlooking the site. Burwell played a crucial part in the rebellion, as Geoffrey was fatally wounded by an arrow shot by a royalist archer while besieging the castle in the autumn of 1144.[17]

Meanwhile, the king had attempted to capture Lincoln, but abandoned the venture after eighty of his labourers were suffocated to death by the collapse of earthworks they were building outside the city. Afterwards he returned to the south-west to counter the activities of his enemies in the region. Robert, Earl of Gloucester, and his supporters, had constructed new castles in Wiltshire, which threatened the safety of Oxford and royalist castles in the area. These fortifications included three counter-castles built near the royalist-held castle of Malmesbury, whose garrison was soon put under pressure and ran low on provisions. Another castle was erected by William Peverel of Dover at Cricklade, which according to the *Gesta Stephani* was 'inaccessible because of the barrier of water and marsh on every side'. From this stronghold, William carried out 'forays in every direction' targeting the adherents of the king in the region, through frequent ambushes and raids. Stephen succeeded in resupplying the garrison of Malmesbury Castle and laid siege to the nearby castle of Tetbury, but was forced to withdraw after being confronted by a force led by Earl Robert. In the following year (1145), Earl Robert sought to put pressure on the garrison of Oxford by building a counter-castle at Faringdon, twenty miles to the south-west. This was described by the *Gesta Stephani* as being 'strongly fortified by a rampart and stockade' and as being garrisoned by 'the flower of his whole army'. Stephen responded by raising a large army, including a force of Londoners, and laid siege to the castle. The besiegers constructed a palisade to protect themselves from counter-attacks and used stone-throwing artillery and missile weapons to rain projectiles down on the besieged. Earl Robert failed to come to the aid of the beleaguered garrison, which was eventually forced to surrender. This victory was identified by Henry of Huntingdon as a decisive point in the conflict as thereafter 'the king's fortune began to change for the better'. The king attempted to build upon this success by renewing the siege of Wallingford town and castle in 1146. A counter-castle, now known as 'Stephen's Mount' in Crowmarsh, was constructed on the east side of the River Thames and according to the *Gesta Stephani* was 'a work of wondrous toil and skill' and as being situated on 'a very high mound'. Nevertheless, little effort was made to capture the settlement, although the besiegers were able to 'check for a time their accustomed raids'. Stephen had greater success in the north-east, where he succeeded in capturing Lincoln Castle after arresting Ranulf, Earl of Chester, at court in

August. Ranulf had rejoined Stephen's service earlier in the year and taken part in the siege of Wallingford. Yet this reconciliation ended abruptly after Ranulf suggested that the king should lead an expedition to Wales to check the advances of the Welsh. This suggestion was interpreted by Stephen's advisors as part of a plot to capture the king and led to the earl's imprisonment. Ranulf was forced to hand over custody of his castles, which included Lincoln and Coventry, in return for his freedom, with his nephew, Gilbert Fitz Richard, Earl of Hereford, agreeing to hand himself over as a hostage as surety for Ranulf's good behaviour. However, the latter at once defected to the Empress's side and Gilbert was therefore imprisoned.[18]

Henry Plantagenet

The imprisonment of Gilbert Fitz Richard prompted another one of his uncles, Gilbert de Clare, Earl of Pembroke, to request that the king hand over his nephew's castles into his custody. This demand was rebuffed by the king, which prompted the Earl of Pembroke to fortify his castles in the south-east of England, an action that was interpreted as an act of rebellion. Stephen led his army to Kent, where he quickly captured three castles belonging to the earl, before proceeding to Pevensey Castle. Pevensey was described by the *Gesta Stephani* as 'a castle rising on a very lofty mound, fortified on every side by a most beautiful wall, fenced impregnably by the washing waves of the sea, almost inaccessible owing to the difficulty of the ground'. These strong defences meant that the king decided to leave a force of soldiers behind to continue the siege by land, with a fleet of ships to blockade the castle by sea. This eventually prompted the garrison to surrender after their provisions ran short. Meanwhile in Hampshire, the Bishop of Winchester's castle at Merdon was seized by one of the followers of Brian Fitz Count. Bishop Henry responded by laying siege to Merdon and constructed two counter-castles nearby, which he strongly garrisoned with knights and infantry. Robert, Earl of Gloucester, marched eastwards from Bristol to relieve the defenders, who had run low on food, but fled after being confronted by the king's army. The garrison of the castle surrendered soon afterwards. In the spring of 1147, Henry Plantagenet, son and heir of Geoffrey, count of Anjou, and the Empress made landfall in England. The fourteen-year-old Henry with only a small force of mercenaries under his command, attempted to capture the castles of Cricklade and Purton. However, he was quickly repelled by the defenders of the castles, so returned a short time later to Normandy, having successfully sought the payment of the wages of his soldiers from his relative King Stephen. This astonishing act of generosity by Stephen was entirely in keeping with his past acts of benevolence. Yet the course of events was to demonstrate the folly of this action. Towards the end of the year, Earl Robert died of a fever on 31 October at Bristol and five months later, in March 1148, the Empress departed for the Continent and never returned to England. Thereafter Henry Plantagenet assumed the position of leader of the Empress's supporters in England. As a grandson of Henry I he had a strong claim to the throne, which meant that he was to pose a grave threat to Stephen's authority when he reached manhood. However, this danger was less apparent at the time, as the king had recently crowned his eldest son and heir, Eustace.[19]

The focus of the struggle between the two sides in 1148 continued to be in the south-west of England. Henry de Tracy was in the process of besieging Castle Cary in Somerset and had begun work on constructing a counter-castle, when he and his men were attacked by a force led by William, 2nd Earl of Gloucester. Taken by surprise, Henry and his followers were forced to flee and the counter-castle was destroyed. At around the same time, Christchurch Castle was seized in a surprise attack by Walter de Pinkney, a supporter of Stephen, from its Angevin owner Baldwin de Redvers. According to the *Gesta Stephani*, the cruelties Walter had inflicted on the local community encouraged them to plot against him, with assistance provided by knights sent by Baldwin. After encouraging Walter and his men to leave the castle to a meeting in the town's church they ambushed and slew him. The Angevins also succeeded in capturing the Bishop of Winchester's castle at Downton by stealth. Bishop Henry raised a force to besiege the castle and built a counter-castle to pressure the defenders, which eventually resulted in their surrender. In the spring of the next year, Henry Plantagenet returned to England and landed in the south-west. After meeting with the principal magnates of the region at Devizes, he went north to Carlisle where he was knighted by his uncle, David I, king of Scots, on 22 May. The king moved northwards to York to counter this threat, but after a standoff both Henry and Stephen returned to southern England. The king then led his army on a devastating raid into Wiltshire, with his soldiers said to have ravaged the region with 'bestial cruelty', particularly around Salisbury, Marlborough and Devizes. He was soon forced to leave the region, however, in response to news of an incursion into Lincolnshire, led by Ranulf, Earl of Chester. Henry took advantage of his absence from the area and with a strong army, attacked the lands of Henry de Tracy. His forces succeeded in capturing Bridport and ravaged the lands of the king's supporters. Eustace responded by laying siege to Devizes Castle, but was driven off by the defenders and forced to retreat. Yet neither side could break the stalemate to gain a decisive advantage in the war. Therefore, Henry acted on the advice of his leading supporters and returned to Normandy to seek reinforcements from his father, leaving England on 1 January 1150.[20]

The Resurgence of the Welsh

The long years of civil war in England gave the Welsh the opportunity to reassert themselves and drive back the Normans. In the north-east of Wales, Owain Gwynedd, king of Gwynedd, succeeded in regaining the cantref of Tegeingl between the River Clwyd and the Dee estuary by the 1150s; whereas Madog ap Maredudd, ruler of Powys, had expanded his power and influence in central Wales sufficiently to acquire Oswestry in Shropshire, where he built a castle in 1149. In southern Wales, the sons of Gruffudd ap Rhys reformed the kingdom of Deheubarth by successfully driving the Normans from Dyfed and Hywel ab Owain Gwynedd from Ceredigion by the early 1150s. These successes were partly due to the preoccupations of the Norman lords of the Welsh Marches in the civil war in England, many of whom supported the cause of the Empress. They even employed the services of Welsh soldiers in this conflict, with large numbers of men taking part in the Battle of Lincoln in 1141, led by Cadwaladr ap Gruffudd, co-ruler of Gwynedd. The Welsh had also adapted to Norman warfare by making use of castles. In the late eleventh century, the practice of the Welsh had been to destroy any castles that they succeeded in capturing, such as during the rebellion of 1096 in Gwynedd. Yet in the first half of the following century, they began to build castles of their own on a regular basis, which they called 'castells'. Cadwgan ap Bleddyn, ruler of Powys, was recorded as being killed while constructing a castle at Trallwyng Llwelyn, near Welshpool in Montgomeryshire in 1111. Further to the north in Denbighshire, Owain Gwynedd constructed the castle of Tomen y Rhodwydd at Llandegla in 1149 to protect the eastern edge of his territory. The Welsh also rebuilt Norman castles that had previously been destroyed. Humphrey's Castle in Ceredigion was demolished after being captured by the Welsh in 1137, but a new castle was constructed on its site by Hywel ab Owain Gwynedd, eldest son of Owain Gwynedd, in 1151, which was called Ystrad Meurig.[21]

The End of the War

Stephen attempted to exploit the absence of Henry from England by attacking Worcester in the summer of 1150. His forces succeeded in storming the city, which was burnt by the attackers, but was unable to capture the castle. Frustrated by this failure, the royalists took out their fury on the local area, which was savagely plundered, before returning to the south. In the following year, Stephen returned and laid siege to the castle, with two counter-castles constructed nearby to pressure the garrison. Yet after he had left the area, the royalist soldiers left behind were defeated due to the treachery of Robert de Beaumont, Earl of Leicester, and the counter-castles were demolished. This setback reflected the difficulties that the king faced in enforcing his control over large parts of the kingdom. Sensing that his authority was weakening, earlier in the year Stephen had sent an ambassador to the Papacy to request that his son, Eustace, be recognised as the heir to the throne. Yet Eugenius III refused to agree to this request as the succession was disputed. The leading figures of the English church in turn refused to assent to the king's wishes as it was not customary in England to crown a son while his father was still alive. Stephen also suffered the misfortune of losing his wife, Queen Matilda, who died on 3 May 1152. She had been his foremost supporter and had stayed unshakeably loyal to him, particularly during the crisis year of 1141, and her death was a serious blow. By contrast, Henry Plantagenet's cause was in the ascendant. He had been invested as Duke of Normandy by his father in 1150, and after the death of the latter during the next year, had defeated a coalition of enemies, including Louis VII of France and Eustace, on the Continent. Henry's position was also strengthened through his marriage to Eleanor, Duchess of Aquitaine, ruler of most of south-western France. Meanwhile in England, Stephen had captured Newbury Castle and renewed the siege of Wallingford Castle. His forces succeeded in capturing the bridge leading to the town, which they secured by building a counter-castle, with the site of another earlier counter-castle, Crowmarsh, refortified and used by the attackers. The hard-pressed defenders began to run low on supplies and sent an appeal for help to Henry Plantagenet.[22]

Henry responded to this request for assistance by raising an army of mercenaries and landed in south-west England on 6 January 1153. After gathering his forces, he attacked the royalist garrison at Malmesbury. The attackers succeeded in storming the town by using a rain of missile fire to cover their approach and scaling ladders to climb the walls. They then besieged the remaining defenders in the keep of the castle, who were closely blockaded. Stephen responded by leading his army to Malmesbury, with both armies arraying for battle either side of the River Avon. Yet neither side wished to risk the danger of a full-scale engagement, particularly due to the terrible winter conditions, with the soldiers afflicted by snow, wind and rain. Stephen was forced to withdraw his army from the area after which the garrison of the castle surrendered. Unsurprisingly, the king was despondent at this outcome, especially, as the *Gesta Stephani* reports, because 'he noticed that some of his leading barons were slack and very casual in their service' and were secretly negotiating with the enemy. In the spring, Henry moved northwards to the Midlands with his army, where he received the support of notable magnates, such as Robert de Beaumont, Earl of Leicester. His forces then proceeded to overrun many of the royalist towns and castles in the region. Tutbury Castle, described as being of 'wondrous art' and 'impregnably fortified' by the *Gesta Stephani*, was nevertheless besieged and starved into surrender. The towns of Stamford and Bedford were stormed and burnt and Warwick Castle was surrendered by its owner, Gundreda,

Dowager Countess of Warwick. Having secured the Midlands, Henry marched southwards to break the siege of Wallingford in July. He laid siege to the two royalist-held counter-castles, with his men digging a ditch around the walls of his camp. Stephen responded by gathering his forces and confronted Henry's army. Negotiations were soon afterwards initiated, due to the desire of the notables on both sides for peace. A truce was agreed, with Roger de Torigni reporting that the king was permitted to remove eighty of his soldiers from Crowmarsh. A further eighty royalist soldiers had been captured from the castle, of whom sixty archers had been beheaded, but the remaining twenty men were alive in captivity. One of the major obstacles to a permanent settlement was removed by the death of Eustace; he died on 17 August, during a plundering expedition to Cambridgeshire. After months of negotiations, Stephen and Henry met at Winchester on 6 November, where the former recognised the latter as his heir. Relations between the two men continued to be strained, however, due to disputes over their respective rights, particularly regarding the custody of castles. The tense situation between the king and duke was ultimately resolved by the death of the former. Stephen died on 25 October 1154.[23]

The Angevins: 1154–1199

In the eleven hundred and fifty-fourth year from the delivery of the Virgin, Henry, grandson of Henry the elder ... received his hereditary kingdom; and, being greeted by all, and consecrated king with the holy unction, was hailed throughout England by crowds exclaiming, 'Long live the king!' The people, having experienced the misery of the late reign whence so many evils had originated, now anticipated better things of their new sovereign, more especially as prudence and resolution, and a strict regard to justice were apparent in him; and at his very outset he bore the appearance of a great prince ... He next commanded the newly-erected castles, which were not in being in the days of his grandfather, to be demolished, with the exception of a few advantageously situated, which he wished to retain for himself, or his partisans, for the defence of the kingdom.

The History of English Affairs by William of Newburgh[1]

Henry II inherited a realm that had been impoverished and ravaged by years of warfare. The finances of the Crown were in a precarious state and considerable parts of the kingdom were blighted by disorder and violence. The new king was determined to restore royal authority by targeting the most visual symbols of oppression in England. Foreign soldiers, notably the despised Flemings, were expelled from the kingdom, to popular exclaim. He also gave instructions for the destruction of new castles that had been built during the conflict. These unauthorised or 'adulterine' castles were the subject of much hostility from the monastic chroniclers, in part as some were built on ecclesiastical land, notably at Malmesbury Abbey. No formal system of planning permission for fortifications existed in the Middle Ages, but all castles were constructed with the consent of the king. The widespread construction of adulterine castles during the Anarchy was due to a marked collapse in royal power and prestige. Stephen had been helpless to stop the proliferation of these fortifications as he was unable to exert control over large parts of the kingdom. Henry was determined to avoid the mistakes of his predecessor by bringing the nobility to heel, with the castles of recalcitrant magnates destroyed or taken into royal hands. He also did much to restore royal authority in the British Isles during his reign, by recovering the northern countries from the Scots and compelling the Welsh rulers to acknowledge his overlordship. This was despite spending most of his time and resources on Continental affairs, as the ruler of extensive lands in France. Henry also developed a reputation as a great builder of castles throughout his dominions, which included magnificent castles in England, such as at Dover. It is possible to trace his programme of building works due to the survival of financial records of the Exchequer known as the Pipe Rolls. One isolated example of a pipe roll survives from the reign of Henry I for 1129 to 1130, but they only consistently survive from 1155 onwards. These documents list the income and expenditure of sheriffs in each of the counties, including money spent on the construction, maintenance and garrisoning of castles.[2]

Securing the kingdom

Henry was crowned king at Westminster Abbey on 19 December 1154 and at once set out to curb the power of the nobility. He began by heading north to compel the submission of William le Gros, Earl of Aumale. Yorkshire had been under the effective control of William during the years of civil war, where he was said to have 'been more truly a king there than his master'. His principle fortress was at Scarborough, which William of Newburgh described as being a 'costly work', incorporating a wall and a tower. The site of the castle had been carefully chosen, being located on: 'A rock of stupendous height and size, nearly inaccessible on all sides from precipices, repels the ocean by which it is surrounded, except on a narrow ascent which stretches to the west; on its summit is a beautiful grassy plain'. Despite the strength of these defences, William wisely decided to capitulate to the king rather than risk the loss of his lands and surrendered the castle without a fight. Henry also sought to restore royal authority in the Welsh Marches by regaining control of the main fortresses in the region. Despite his long years of service in the Angevin cause during the civil war, Roger, Earl of Hereford, was forced to hand over custody of the castles of Gloucester and Hereford. His fellow magnate, Hugh Mortimer, proved to be more obstinate and refused to hand over his castles of Bridgnorth, Cleobury and Wigmore. These castles were besieged by royal forces and after a few days their garrisons surrendered, with Hugh being pardoned by the king on 7 July 1155. Other notables fled abroad rather than risk a confrontation, with the castles of Henry, Bishop of Winchester, destroyed after he left the realm without royal permission to retire to the Abbey of Cluny in France. Henry spent most of 1156 on the Continent, confronting the rebellion of his younger brother Geoffrey, who had sought to take control of the county of Anjou. He returned to England in April 1157 to deal with a crisis in East Anglia, where a dispute over land ownership between the two leading nobles of the region, Hugh Bigod, Earl of Norfolk, and William of Blois, Earl of Surrey, threatened to escalate into warfare. At a great council held at Bury St Edmunds on 19 May, both men were forced to hand over their castles to the king. Henry's prestige and authority was so great that this action was carried out without resistance, in stark contrast to the circumstances that had prevailed during the reign of Stephen. Royal garrisons of knights and serjeants were installed in the castles of Norwich and Framlingham and castles that had been erected in the time of the civil war were destroyed by the king's command. Henry also compelled the Scottish king, Malcolm IV, to surrender control of the northern counties of Westmorland, Cumberland and Northumberland.[3]

Henry II and Wales

Having secured his control over the kingdom of England, the king decided to reassert royal authority over the Welsh rulers. At a great council meeting held on 17 July 1157 in Northampton, he received support for an expedition to attack Owain, king of Gwynedd. The justification for the campaign was to restore Cadwaladr, in exile at Henry's court, to the lands he had been deprived of by his brother Owain, but it was also intended to recover territory lost in north-east Wales. A combined operation by land and sea was planned to bring overwhelming force against the Welsh. The main army, consisting of a powerful force of cavalry supported by archers from Shropshire, was to march westwards along the northern coast, to be supplied by sea from a fleet, while Henry II with a smaller force moved through the interior. This ambitious venture almost resulted in catastrophe, with the Welsh taking advantage of the difficult terrain to launch an ambush, during which the king was almost killed. Meanwhile, the prospect of plunder had prompted the commanders of the fleet to raid Anglesey, where they were routed by the inhabitants. Undaunted by these setbacks, Henry continued to proceed westwards with his forces and reached Rhuddlan, which had been left undefended. This show of force prompted Owain to seek terms, with peace granted in return for the cessation of territory in north-east Wales, between the River Clwyd and the Dee estuary, and the restoration of Cadwaladr to his lands. In the following year, Rhys ap Gruffudd, ruler of Deheubarth, was compelled to offer homage to Henry II and to surrender extensive territories in southern Wales, including Ceredigion, to avoid an invasion of his lands. Yet a raid by one of the Marcher lords, Walter de Clifford, soon led to a renewed outbreak of fighting. Rhys responded by seizing Llandovery Castle, while his nephew, Einion ab Anarawd, captured and burnt Castell Hywel in Ceredigion. Henry reacted by leading an expedition to south Wales, which prompted Rhys to again seek terms. However, the latter was still keen to recover his lost lands and in 1158 led an expedition into Dyved and besieged Carmarthen. He was confronted in the field by an army led by Reginald, Earl of Cornwall, but after a stand-off, a truce was agreed and both sides disbanded their forces.[4]

Later in 1162, Rhys yet again seized control of Llandovery Castle, prompting Henry to lead another expedition to south Wales in the next year. Rhys was unwilling to confront the might of the royal army unaided and quickly surrendered. He was thereafter taken as a prisoner to England where he gave homage to the king for his lands, before being released. During his captivity, Roger de Clare, Earl of Hertford, incited the murder of Rhys' nephew, Einion ab Anarawd, by one of Einion's own men. Rhy decided to seek revenge by allying with many of the other major Welsh rulers, including Owain Gwynedd, against Henry. The king responded by preparing a massive expedition to subjugate the Welsh once and for all. A substantial army was raised, which included soldiers from his Continental lands and mercenaries from Flanders. Henry made use of the border town of Oswestry as his base for the forthcoming campaign against Owain Gruffudd, with the castle's peace time garrison of one knight, two porters and two watchmen augmented by a force of 100 serjeants for forty days. Yet the expedition was a fiasco, with the army defeated by the weather and the difficult overland terrain of central Wales. The remnants of his starving forces were forced to withdraw in ignominy to England, having achieved nothing. This setback gave the Welsh the opportunity to recover some of the territory they had lost in recent years. In the north-east, Owain Gwynedd succeeded in recovering Rhuddlan and Basingwerk, whereas in the south, Rhys ap Gruffudd regained Cardigan and Cilgerran. The debacle also prompted a major rethink in Henry's policy for Wales. Rather than seeking to impose his supremacy on the Welsh rulers through force, instead he worked in partnership with them. In 1171 he confirmed Rhys as ruler of Ceredigion and other disputed territories and in the following year went so far as to appoint him as 'justice in all south Wales'. This was a marked change from the earlier years of conflict and allowed Rhys to become the pre-eminent native ruler in Wales. The policy of rapprochement with the Welsh also had the result of encouraging the Marcher lords to shift their energies away from the subjugation of Wales to the conquest of Ireland.[5]

The Great Rebellion

Henry's desire to seek good relations with the native rulers of Wales had also been motivated by the growing problems he was facing elsewhere in his dominions. His quarrel with Thomas Becket, Archbishop of Canterbury, had caused a crisis that damaged his relationship with the papacy. Thomas had previously been a royal favourite who had served as chancellor for the king, but after his election as archbishop the two men fell out over the liberties of the English Church. After years of dispute, Thomas was eventually murdered in Canterbury Cathedral on 29 December 1170 by four knights in the king's service. Henry also had difficulties in contending with the ambitions of his sons. The coronation of his eldest son, Henry the Young King, as his successor, rather than securing the succession prompted the younger man to present his demands for a greater share of power in his father's lands. The family problems of Henry II were exploited by his rival, Louis VII, who was determined to break-up his great territorial holdings in France, which were far more substantial than those held by the king of France himself. A grand conspiracy was hatched to build a powerful coalition of enemies against Henry in both France and the British Isles. The Anglo-Norman poet Jordan Fantosme states that the strategy used by the allies in the campaign was to lay waste the lands of the king's supporters and to isolate them in their castles. This approach was said to have been outlined by Count Philip of Flanders, who stated that to obtain victory you needed 'First to destroy the land and then one's enemy'. In England, the rebels were mainly concentrated in the Midlands, led by Hugh Bigod, Earl of Norfolk; Robert Blanchemains, Earl of Leicester; Hugh, Earl of Chester, and William de Ferrers, Earl of Derby. The defence of the realm was led by the justiciar of England, Richard de Lucy, during the absence of the king in Normandy, with many castles prepared for warfare. At the king's newly constructed castle at Orford in Suffolk, these measures included digging a ditch around its perimeter and fixing wooden hoardings onto its battlements, to make it easier for the defenders to shoot missile weapons from its walls. The garrison of twenty knights, two mounted serjeants and twenty foot serjeants was also supplied with 200 cartloads of grain, 200 sides of bacon and 500 cheeses. Garrisons were also provided for other castles, such as at Wark in Northumberland, which was defended by a force of ten knights and forty serjeants. These forces were reinforced during periods of crisis, with the regular garrison of ten knights at Northampton Castle temporarily augmented by 118 hired knights for twenty days led by the constable of the castle, Humphrey de Bohun. Yet the royalists were not content to remain on the defensive. Richard de Lucy succeeded in capturing the town of Leicester but was forced to temporarily lift the siege of the castle when he received news of a Scottish incursion led by William the Lion, King of Scots. The Scottish army laid siege to Carlisle, but the arrival of an English army soon afterwards prompted the Scots to break the siege and a truce was agreed until January of the following year.[6]

In the meantime, Robert, Earl of Leicester, had landed with a force of Flemish mercenaries in East Anglia and succeeded in taking control of Haughley Castle. He then marched his army westwards to relieve the garrison of Leicester Castle but they were intercepted and defeated by the royalists at the Battle of Fornham on 17 October, with Earl Robert captured. During the next year, William the Lion again invaded the north of England. His forces overran the badly defended castles of Appleby, Burgh, Harbottle and Warkworth, and laid siege to Carlisle and Prudhoe Castle. Further south, the royalists besieged Huntingdon and Tutbury but lost control of Nottingham. They had more success in the north-east, where Geoffrey Plantagenet, a bastard son of the king, took Roger de Mowbray's castles at Axholme and Malzeard. Despite these successes, the royalists were rapidly losing ground in East Anglia, where a force of Flemings had landed and assisted Hugh Bigod, Earl of Norfolk, in taking control of Norwich. This setback prompted Henry to leave Normandy and to return to England on 8 July. He soon received good news from the north. William the Lion had been taken by surprise and captured by a force of cavalry from Yorkshire, while besieging Alnwick Castle in Northumberland. This defeat led to a collapse of morale in the rebel camp, whose leaders soon afterwards surrendered to the king's mercy. The king subsequently returned to Normandy and in September he agreed a peace treaty with Louis VII. Henry was magnanimous in victory and refused to punish his English vassals through executions or forfeiture of their lands. Yet he sought to reduce their ability to rebel again in future by ordering the confiscation and destruction of their castles.[7]

Royal Castle-building
The Pipe Rolls of the Exchequer reveal that castle building comprised a significant part of royal expenditure in the reign of Henry II. Between the years 1155 and 1189 as much as £21,000 was spent on the maintenance or construction of castles, for an

average of £650 per annum. This was a substantial outlay as the ordinary revenues of the English Exchequer were less than £10,000 a year in the period. Work was carried out on ninety royal castles across the realm, but the bulk of the expenditure was lavished on a small number of high profile sites. For the castles of Windsor, Nottingham, Newcastle upon Tyne, Winchester and Orford more than £1,000 was spent, with the massive sum of almost £6,500 expended on Dover. These works were carried out under the personal direction of the king, whose court was highly itinerant and moved frequently across England and his other dominions. Responsibility for carrying out his instructions were delegated to the sheriffs in each of the counties who, as the main royal officials in their localities, were charged with carrying out the building projects. In most cases, these works consisted of the rebuilding or maintenance of existing sites, as opposed to the construction of entirely new castles. These projects often took the form of the rebuilding of older timber castles, replacing them with new stone buildings. The growing popularity of stone resulted in a gradual decline in the total number of castles in the late twelfth century, due to its greater expense as a building material. The work itself was carried out by teams of carpenters, masons, sawyers, labourers and other workers, under the supervision of professional craftsmen called engineers. Some of these engineers were specialists in castle building, for example Richard of Wolviston. Richard was employed by Puiset, Bishop of Durham, in extending the keep of Norham Castle, and by the sheriff of Yorkshire, Robert de Stuteville, in the construction of the keep of Bowes Castle in the early 1170s.[8]

The defence of the realm was an important consideration in the king's programme of castle-building. Improvements were carried out to significant castles on the frontiers, in the far north of England, the Welsh Marches and on the coast, particularly during times of warfare. Yet much of the major construction work was motivated by ideological reasons, to enhance the prestige of the king, through the construction of grand imposing structures, notably keeps, to dominate their surrounding landscapes. At Scarborough Castle, a new mighty keep was built between 1158 and 1169 to replace an earlier tower erected by its previous owner William le Gros, Earl of Aumale, which had since collapsed. This imposing square structure originally had four storeys and stood at some thirty metres in height, with a turret on each corner, and walls three-and-a-half metres thick. Other keeps were constructed at Newcastle-upon-Tyne, Nottingham and Bridgnorth castles. Works were also carried out to ensure that royal castles could serve as suitable residences for the king. Sizeable sums were spent on improving the castle at Winchester, with its walls rebuilt and work carried out on the domestic apartments inside, including the queen's chamber and the royal chapel. The castle was clearly a comfortable residence for Henry II, as can be seen from Gerald of Wales description of the king's chamber as having been beautifully decorated with 'various painted figures and colours'. This included a painting of an eagle that was being set upon by four of its offspring, which was said to represent Henry II's turbulent relationship with his rebellious sons. The one exception to the programme of rebuilding older castles was the construction of an entirely new castle at the coastal town of Orford in Suffolk between 1165 and 1173. This castle was built in an area dominated by Hugh Bigod, Earl of Norfolk, and was intended to assert royal authority in the region. The keep has an unusual polygonal shape with three rectangular towers and a forebuilding that was surrounded by a curtain wall with mural towers. Yet as important as these building projects were, they paled in significance when compared with the scale of the works carried out at Dover Castle from 1180 to 1189. The decision to rebuild the castle on a massive scale was influenced by the establishment of a new pilgrimage route to the shrine of Thomas Becket in Canterbury, who had been made a saint in 1173, with overseas visitors landing at Dover. Henry felt the need to erect an imposing structure on the cliffs overlooking the town to impress foreign travellers. At the centre of the castle, a huge keep was erected, which was surrounded by a curtain wall with fourteen rectangular towers.[9]

The Struggle for Power

Henry II died on 6 July 1189 and was succeeded by his eldest surviving son, Richard I. Richard was determined to go on crusade to the Holy Land, where the Christians had suffered numerous setbacks including the loss of Jerusalem after being defeated at the Battle of Hattin in 1187. England was taxed heavily to fund the enterprise, with the king being said to have been willing to have sold London if he could find a buyer. Richard was aware of the problems that might occur during his absence on crusade, so he arranged for England to be governed by loyal officials, which included William Longchamp, Bishop of Ely, who was appointed as chief justiciar. He attempted to bribe his troublesome younger brother John through granting him extensive lands and titles in England and France. John was also tasked with meeting with Lord Rhys, the principal Welsh ruler in southern Wales, to ensure his co-operation. Yet Richard sought to exclude his younger brother from any active involvement in government, by extracting a promise that he would leave England and not return for three years, due to the danger he posed to his rule. However, he was soon persuaded by his mother, Eleanor of Aquitaine, to release John from this promise. This would prove to be a serious mistake as John worked tirelessly to take control of the government of England during his absence. William Longchamp, as a Norman of humble birth, found it difficult to assert his authority over the barons of England, and alienated them further through his high-handed actions in promoting his followers to positions of power. Richard of Devizes remarked that this was a time of tension: 'As the earth grows dark when the sun departs, so the face of the kingdom was changed by the absence of the king'. The barons were said to have been unsettled and had prepared for war, which meant that 'castles were strengthened, towns fortified, ditches dug'. Custody of the royal castles was disputed by both parties, with William laying siege to Lincoln Castle, after the sheriff of Lincolnshire, Gerard de Camville, refused to hand it over to the justiciar's men. John responded by taking control of the castles of Tickhill and Nottingham and demanded that the siege of Lincoln Castle be lifted. The outbreak of civil war was averted, however, by the arrival of Walter de Coutances, Archbishop of Rouen, in September 1191. Walter had been sent by Richard to take charge of the situation in England, in response to troubling reports the king had received while in Sicily en route to the Holy Land. William was deposed as justiciar at a council held in London in the following month, after his men attacked Geoffrey, Archbishop of York, and was replaced in office by Walter.[10]

In early 1193, the peace of the realm was again disturbed by the news that Richard had been captured while returning from the Holy Land and was held by Henry VI, the Holy Roman Emperor. John attempted to exploit this situation by allying with the French king, Philip Augustus, and led a rebellion against his brother's government in England. His forces succeeded in taking control of the castles of Windsor and Wallingford, but elsewhere faced firm resistance from the royalists who went on the counter-offensive and besieged Windsor. The failure of John's rebellion to gain any traction led to a truce being agreed between both sides that was to last until November, with the important castles of Windsor, Wallingford and the Peak handed over into the custody of his mother Eleanor. John and his ally Philip now pinned their hopes on persuading Henry VI to hand custody of Richard over to them in return for paying his massive ransom. Yet the emperor was unwilling to do this, as he feared that it would lead to a breakup of the Angevin empire, which would strengthen the power of the king of France. According to the chronicler Roger of Howden, Philip received news that an agreement had been reached between Richard and the emperor in early autumn. He immediately sent a message to his ally with the warning: 'Look to yourself for the devil is loosed', which panicked John into fleeing to France. News of the imminent release of Richard from captivity in early 1194 prompted the royalists to attack castles held by John's supporters in England. Hugh du Puiset, Bishop of Durham, laid siege to Tickhill Castle in Yorkshire, while Ranulf de Blundeville, Earl of Chester, and David, King of Scots, besieged Nottingham. Elsewhere, Hubert Walter, Archbishop of Canterbury, captured Marlborough Castle after a short siege, and his brother, Theobald, seized control of Lancaster Castle. The return of Richard to England in March prompted the garrison of Tickhill to surrender immediately, but the defenders of Nottingham were more resolute. It was only after the king arrived at the siege in person later that month, and siege weapons were drawn up in front of the castle, that they eventually capitulated. The capture of Nottingham effectively ended the rebellion, with John reconciling with Richard later that year.[11]

King John and the First Barons' War: 1199–1217

John, as soon as he heard that William d'Albiney and his followers had entered the city of Rochester, marched thither ... and on the third day after they had entered the castle, he blocked up all their ways of egress and besieged them... The siege was prolonged many days owing to the great bravery and boldness of the besieged, who hurled stone for stone, weapons for weapons, from the walls and ramparts on the enemy: at last, after great numbers of the royal troops had been slain, the king, seeing that all his warlike engines took but little effect, at length employed miners, who soon threw down a great part of the walls. The provisions of the besieged too failed them, and they were obliged to eat horses and even their own costly chargers. The soldiers of the king now rushed to the breaches in the walls, and by constant fierce assaults they forced the besieged to abandon the castle, although not without great loss on their own side... The king then applied his miners to the tower, and having after much difficulty broken through the walls, an opening was made for the assailants... At length, not a morsel of provisions remaining among them ... all the garrison almost unhurt left the castle.

Roger of Wendower's Flowers of History[1]

This account by the chronicler Roger of Wendower vividly portrays one of the most dramatic events of the First Barons' War, the siege of Rochester Castle in 1215. The siege was exceptional both due to the strenuous efforts made by the attackers in besieging the castle and the fierce determination of the defenders to resist these attacks. This reflected the depth of hostility between King John and his baronial opponents and their eagerness to achieve victory in the war. The conflict had been sparked by baronial unrest, due in part to the loss of most of the Angevin empire in France, culminating in the outbreak of civil war. Wendower, though a fierce critic and opponent of King John, was forced to admit that the capture of Rochester Castle was a serious setback for the baronial cause. Other chroniclers were similarly impressed. The Barnwell chronicler remarked that: 'Our age has not known a siege so hard pressed nor so strongly resisted… Afterwards few cared to put their trust in castles'. Yet this assessment was an exaggerated one, as only a year later, the royalist garrison of Dover Castle successfully resisted a full-scale siege. On the contrary, castles continued to play a crucial role in warfare, both to deny control of territory and as bases from which to conduct offensive operations. The eventual royalist victory was to owe much of its success to the retention of key castles. King John clearly appreciated the importance of castles, as military fortresses as well as symbols of power. Royal investment in castle building was undertaken in his reign on a far greater scale than that of his Angevin predecessors, with very substantial sums spent on a small number of favoured castles. The outbreak of civil war in England also provided an opportunity for Llywelyn ap Iorwerth, ruler of Gwynedd, to assert his dominance over most of Wales.[2]

The Loss of the Angevin Empire

King Richard was besieging the castle of Châlus-Chabrol in Limousin in 1199, when he was struck and wounded by a crossbow bolt. The wound became infected and he died soon afterwards. His death led to a disputed succession – with the throne claimed by both his brother John and his nephew Arthur of Brittany. John succeeded in gaining the upper hand in the war in France with Arthur and his French allies, notably the king of France, Philip II, and by the treaty of Le Goulet in 1200, was recognised as Richard's successor. However, relations between John and Philip remained tense and fighting resumed two years later. John achieved an early success through the capture of Arthur at the Battle of Mirebeau but was soon forced onto the defensive. The superior financial resources of the French king and the outbreak of rebellions across the Angevin lands eventually led to the loss of most of his Continental lands. By 1204, John had lost all of his ancestral lands in northern France, including Normandy and Anjou. In the following years, he attempted to recover these territories by sending military expeditions to the Continent. Yet he was repeatedly thwarted by baronial resistance to his financial extortions and methods of government. The barons refused to provide the customary service of providing knights for forty days at their own expense for overseas expeditions. Instead they were only willing to offer military service for campaigns in the Britain Isles. In the face of this resistance, the king was forced to abandon his plans to recover the lost lands of the Angevin empire. John had greater success in asserting his authority in the British Isles and in Ireland. At the beginning of the reign, William the Lion, King of Scots, attempted to assert his own claim to the northern English counties of Northumberland and Cumberland by refusing to visit and give homage to John when summoned. The threat of military action soon prompted William to change his mind and the two kings met in November 1200. Yet Anglo-Scottish relations remained tense over the following years, prompting John to lead an expedition to Scotland in 1209. His army reached Norham Castle in August, at which point he threatened to invade Scotland unless William came to terms. War was narrowly averted by William surrendering three castles and two of his daughters as hostages. During the next year, John asserted his authority over his barons in Ireland by leading an army to the island.[3]

The situation in Wales was to prove more challenging. The good relations that had existed between Henry II and the Lord Rhys of Deheubarth were ended by Henry's death in 1189. War broke out soon afterwards with the Lord Rhys leading his forces against the lands of the Anglo-Norman lords in south Wales. He succeeded in capturing the castles of Llanstephan and Laughharne and besieged the royal castle of Carmarthen. King Richard sent John with an army to cower the Welsh, who quickly came to terms, but the submission of Rhys and his allies proved to be temporary. The struggle resumed when Richard left England to go on crusade to the Holy Land with Rhys making further gains, including Castell Nanhyfer in Pembrokeshire. The height of his success occurred in 1196, when his forces successfully captured and burnt the town of Carmarthen – but not the castle. A short time later he defeated an army led by Roger Mortimer and Hugh de Say at the Battle of Radnor in Powys. The victorious Welsh then laid siege to nearby Painscastle and assailed the defenders with siege weapons and other types of missiles, forcing its owner, William de Briouze, to come to terms. Yet the death of Lord Rhys in 1197 resulted in a power struggle between his sons, which swiftly led to the breakup of the kingdom of Deheubarth. Further north in central Wales, the ruler of south Powys, Gwenwynwyn, attempted to restore the power of his kingdom by inflicting a major blow against the Anglo-Normans. He led a large army to besiege Painscastle but was decisively defeated in battle by an army led by Geoffrey fitz Peter, justiciar of England, on 13 August 1198. This defeat was to prove to be a major setback for Gwenwynwyn's ambitions. The fragmentation of power in Deheubarth and Powys provided an opportunity for Gwynedd to emerge as the most powerful native Welsh kingdom in Wales under the leadership of Llywelyn ab Iorwerth.[4]

Llywelyn had become the sole ruler of Gwynedd by the end of the twelfth century and thereafter sought to expand his territory into other parts of Wales. In 1202, he led an army into south Powys, although a clash with Gwenwynwyn was averted by ecclesiastical mediation. His next opportunity to intervene in central Wales occurred in 1208, when Gwenwynwyn was arrested and stripped of his lands by John. Llywelyn invaded Powys and quickly overran the whole territory. He then advanced into Ceredigion as far southwards as Aberystwyth, whose castle he rebuilt. Crucial to Llywelyn's success was the favour shown to him by King John, who was prepared to overlook his territorial expansion in return for his allegiance. Yet this relationship deteriorated in 1210, perhaps due to the aid offered by Llywelyn to William de Briouze, who had incurred the king's anger. A punitive expedition was sent into north Wales under the command of Ranulf de Blundeville, Earl of Chester, with three castles constructed during the campaign. In the following year, John decided to lead an army into Wales to harry Llywelyn's lands in person. His forces penetrated into Wales as far as westwards as Degannwy Castle in May, but were forced to withdraw back to Chester due to a lack of provisions. John led another army into Gwynedd from Oswestry in July and ordered the construction of castles in the region, which forced Llywelyn to flee into Snowdonia. This prompted the latter to capitulate to the king soon afterwards in return for major territorial concessions in north-eastern Wales and the handing over of thirty hostages. However, the expansion of royal power into Wales encouraged the rivals of Llywelyn to ally with him in a rebellion against John. Taking advantage of the king's absence in Scotland in the summer of 1212, they launched an assault on the newly constructed royal castles in northern and southern Wales. Llywelyn succeeded in overrunning all the newly constructed castles in Gwynedd, except for Degannwy and Rhuddlan. John responded by issuing orders for the raising of a large army, intended to destroy the power of Llywelyn through the conquest of the whole of Gwynedd. Contingents of soldiers were sought from all parts of his dominions, with William Marshal and the justiciar of Ireland, John de Gray, Bishop of Norwich, ordered to lead 200 knights and as many serjeants as they could raise from the lordship of Ireland. Royal representatives were sent to hire mercenaries from Flanders and Scotland, with the towns of England ordered to raise and send 800 foot serjeants to the muster of the army. An ambitious scheme of castle building was intended for the campaign, with instructions sent out on 10 July to the sheriffs of thirty counties for the hiring of over 2,000 ditch diggers and carpenters and 6,000 labourers. On 14 August, five days before the planned date of the muster, John demonstrated his resolve to crush Llywelyn by ordering the hanging of the thirty hostages that had been handed over to him in the previous summer. Yet the expedition was ultimately aborted by the king due to the rumours of a baronial conspiracy against his life.[5]

Magna Carta

John moved against his enemies by ordering the seizure of castles and the handing over of hostages by barons whose loyalties he suspected. Two prominent noblemen who were suspected of having taken part in the plot, Eustace de Vesci and Robert FitzWalter, fled abroad. The king responded by ordering the seizure of their lands and issued instructions that FitzWalter's castles of Hertford, Bennington and Baynard's Castle should be destroyed. Meanwhile in the north, William de Warenne, Earl of Surrey, and Philip Oldcotes, took possession of Vesci's castle at Alnwick, which was garrisoned with a force of thirty men. Efforts were also made to secure the major royal castles in the north. Significant sums of money were expended on repairing fortifications and the purchase of provisions for the newly installed garrisons. The strategic border castles of Norham and Bamburgh were provided with garrisons of twenty-two and thirty men respectively, whereas further south, at Newcastle-upon-Tyne, a force of ten knights and sixty-one serjeants were established. Reinforcements were also sought from further afield, with a contingent of forty-one mercenary knights from Flanders and Hainault sent to reinforce the garrison at York. These decisive measures ensured that the plot failed to materialise, but tensions continued to remain due to the king's style of rulership. John was aware of his unpopularity and attempted to rein in the financial extortions of some of his officials. He also repaired his relationship with the papacy, which had been ruptured by a dispute over ecclesiastical appointments. This argument between Church and State had eventually led to the placing of an interdict on England and Wales, which banned the clergy from carrying out religious services across the kingdom, and the excommunication of the king. In 1213, John achieved a reconciliation with Pope Innocent III by agreeing to accept the pope's demands and by acknowledging papal overlordship over his realm. This bold move transformed his relationship with the papacy, which thereafter was one of his staunchest supporters.[6]

By 1214, John felt secure enough on his throne to proceed with his long-anticipated scheme to recover his lost lands in France. A powerful coalition of allies was assembled on the Continent, which included the Holy Roman Emperor, Otto IV; Henry I, Duke of Brabant; and Theobald I, Duke of Lorraine. The allies planned to launch a two-pronged attack on Philip II of France, with Otto IV and his forces invading from the north-east, whereas John would invade from the south-west via Poitou. However, John's allies were decisively defeated at the Battle of Bouvines and he was forced to withdraw with his army to England, in ignominy. This setback was a major blow to the king's prestige. Opposition had also developed in his absence due to the stern measures taken by his justiciar, Peter des Roches, Bishop of Winchester, and there was a widespread refusal to pay scrutage for the Poitou campaign. Discontented barons sought to exploit the situation by demanding that the king issue a charter to confirm certain liberties. Both sides prepared for war in early 1215, with John hiring mercenaries from Poitou and Flanders and taking the cross as a crusader, in a successful ploy to obtain papal support for his cause. The rebels renounced their fealty to the king on 5 May and laid siege to Northampton Castle. Their attempts to capture the castle failed but they achieved a major coup later that month, when the Londoners admitted them into the city. This reverse prompted John to negotiate with the rebels, which resulted in the issuing of Magna Carta on 15 June. This is a lengthy document, hence its description as the 'great charter', which specified the granting of extensive rights to the king's subjects. These provisions were primarily designed to protect the aristocratic elite from the worst excesses of arbitrary government. The clauses were to be guaranteed by a group of twenty-five barons who were to receive complaints about the king and were empowered to act against him if necessary. Yet despite the later fame of this document in English and British constitutional history, in 1215 it was soon rendered redundant due to the course of events. John bristled at the curbs placed on his power and tensions remained high between the supporters of both sides over the next few months. Then in September, in response to a request by King John, Pope Innocent III annulled Magna Carta and excommunicated the king's opponents, with fighting breaking out soon afterwards.[7]

Civil War

At the outbreak of the conflict, John's position appeared to be a strong one. He had control of numerous castles across the kingdom, with the most important ones garrisoned by seasoned mercenary soldiers. According to an estimate made by the historian Sidney Painter, of the 209 English castles that were used in the conflict, 149 were held by John and his supporters whereas only sixty were in the possession of the rebels. Furthermore, the king had invested large sums of money on royal castles throughout his reign, spending in excess of £1,000 a year on average. Work was carried out at a total of ninety-five castles, with the bulk of expenditure focused on nine castles. Much of this outlay was related to the construction of new residential buildings, such as the magnificent structure at Corfe Castle called 'la Gloriette', and on the day-to-day maintenance of existing buildings, yet the defences of some castles had been significantly augmented. At Scarborough Castle, more than £2,000 was expended on improving the castle, with the works including the building of an outer wall leading to the edge of the cliffs, thereby greatly expanding the radius of the fortress. In 1215, its garrison consisted of a sizeable force of ten knights, seventy-two serjeants and thirteen crossbowmen. The prospect of civil war had also led to increased measures to improve the defences of royal castles from the autumn of 1214 onwards. A fresh ditch was dug outside Corfe Castle, stone-throwing machines were constructed at Knaresborough and Nottingham castles, and mercenary soldiers from the Continent were sent to augment the garrisons of key castles. Yet despite these efforts, the defences of many castles were in a poor state of repair and they were not prepared for military operations. Furthermore, the retention of castles was dependent upon the loyalties of the men who guarded them. John's reliance on large numbers of mercenary soldiers from Poitou and Flanders was in part due to the problems he had in retaining the allegiance of his barons. Since the summer of 1215, he had sent agents to the Continent to raise an army of mercenaries and was awaiting their arrival in Kent at the end of September, when he received news that the castles of Oxford and Northampton had been besieged by the rebels.[8]

John at once set about assembling an army to relieve these castles, with orders issued to the constables of ten castles to detach as many soldiers as they could spare from their garrisons for the campaign. The expedition was led by one of his trusted commanders, Falkes de Bréauté, and succeeded in lifting the siege of both castles. Meanwhile, a rebel force from London commanded by William d'Aubigny took control of Rochester Castle. Rochester was a royal castle in the possession of the Archbishop of Canterbury, Stephen Langton, and held for him by Reginald of Cornhill. Reginald had previously been in the king's service as sheriff of Kent, but he admitted the rebels into the castle without offering any resistance. John was at Canterbury when he received this news, where he had been joined by a contingent of mercenaries from Flanders. He at once marched with his forces to recover the castle. The rebels sought to block his advance at the bridge over the Medway, but they were defeated in a skirmish and his men took possession of the city of Rochester. The defences of the castle were to pose a more formidable obstacle to the royal army, with its stone fortifications defended by a strong force of rebels. According to Roger of Wendower, the garrison comprised 140 knights with an unspecified number of serjeants and crossbowmen. Yet it appears that the defenders had been caught unawares by the speed of John's counter-attack and were not ready to resist a formal siege. Roger of Wendower states that upon taking possession of the castle, the rebels were horrified to discover that it lacked any supplies of provisions, or arms and armour. Nevertheless, the inspired leadership of William d'Aubigny was said to have persuaded them to remain to defend the fortress. The royalists began the siege by surrounding the castle and deploying their stone-throwing siege weapons outside the walls. These machines were said to have been used to hurl projectiles at the defenders by day and night, with frequent assaults made by the attackers. The defenders put up a fierce resistance, despite soon running low on provisions, in the expectation that they would be relieved by the main rebel force at London. However, rather than risking a confrontation with John in the field, the baronial army turned back after only reaching as far as Deptford. In the meantime, the ranks of the royalist army were swelled by reinforcements, with the king sending instructions to the city of Canterbury to forge as many pickaxes as possible. The attackers were eventually able to breach the outer defences of the castle by deploying miners to undermine the curtain wall. This forced the defenders to withdraw to the keep. Miners were then used to undermine one of the four corner towers of the building. A royal writ dated 25 November records that the justiciar, Hubert de Burgh, was commanded to send in all haste 'forty bacon pigs of the fattest and least good for eating'. The fat from these pigs was used to set fire to the mine and to bring the corner tower crashing down. In desperation, the defenders took refuge behind the cross-wall that divided the keep in half, but a lack of provisions forced them to surrender soon afterwards, on 30 November. The lives of most of the defenders were spared, except for some of the crossbowmen who were hanged. William d'Aubigny and other aristocrats were subsequently imprisoned in Corfe Castle.[9]

The capture of Rochester Castle was a great triumph for John and disheartened his baronial opponents, who increasingly looked overseas for military assistance from France. However, this victory came at a great financial cost, with the chronicler Ralph of Coggeshall estimating that the wages for the king's mercenaries had come to the incredible sum of 60,000 marks (£40,000). This figure is undoubtedly an exaggerated one, yet the cost of paying expensive mercenaries was certainly eating into the king's cash reserves, which were already diminished due to the disruption that the civil war had caused to the system of royal revenue collecting. Financial pressures appear to have been partly responsible for John's decision to divide his army in half. One contingent was left to contain the rebels in London under the command of his half-brother William Longespée, Earl of Salisbury; Falkes de Bréauté, and Savaric de Mauléon, while he took the other half to plunder the lands of his opponents in the north. The king left Rochester on 7 December and gradually made his way northwards to the Midlands, spending Christmas Day at Nottingham. The next day he sent messengers to the garrison of Belvoir Castle in Leicestershire, demanding their surrender, which they agreed to do rather than face the wrath of the king. John then proceeded northwards to Yorkshire, while a detachment of his army attacked and burnt Castle Donnington. King Alexander of Scotland had marched as far south as Newcastle-upon-Tyne to support the rebels, but on hearing news of the approach of the royal army fled northwards. John responded by advancing into Northumberland, where he took the castles of Morpeth, Mitford, Alnwick and Wark. He then proceeded to invade Scotland, with his army capturing Berwick-upon-Tweed on 15 January, with raids then launched into the Scottish Lowlands. Meanwhile in southern England, the constables of Hertford, Windsor and Berkhamsted castle had been tasked with harrying the Londoners, while the royalist commanders, the Earl of Salisbury, Falkes de Bréauté, and Savaric de Mauléon, took their forces to harry East Anglia. At the same time, the newly installed royalist garrison at Rochester Castle sallied forth and captured Tonbridge Castle, which belonged to Gilbert de Clare, Earl of Hereford.[10]

Following the capture of Berwick, John marched his army southwards and reached Bedford on 29 February. He then proceeded to attack the lands of the rebels in East Anglia. The first target of the expedition was Framlingham Castle, held by Robert de Vere, Earl of Oxford, which was besieged on 12 March. Framlingham was defended by a sizeable garrison numbering at least twenty-six knights, twenty serjeants and seven crossbowmen. Nevertheless, the constable of the castle, William le Enveise, surrendered after only thirty-six hours. The royal army then captured Colchester after a short siege, before moving onto besiege Hedingham Castle, whose garrison surrendered after three days. Thus within four months, John had plundered and ravaged the heartlands of his enemies, with impunity, facing only limited and half-hearted resistance. The royalist campaign of December 1215–March 1216 appeared to be highly successful with the king's forces sweeping all before them. Roger of Wendower claimed that the king had subdued the northern parts of England, with only the castles of Mountsorrel in Leicestershire and Helmsley in Yorkshire remaining under the control of the barons. Yet the king had failed to deliver a decisive blow against his enemies. The size and location of London meant that it was a difficult city to besiege and the ranks of its defenders had been swelled by a steady influx of French reinforcements. In northern and eastern England, his opponents had withdrawn rather than confront his forces but they remained defiant. Furthermore, the rebels had offered the English throne to the son and heir of Philip II of France, Prince Louis, which was accepted in April. The imminent threat of a French intervention forced John onto the defensive, with the king travelling with his forces to Kent to await the invasion.[11]

The French Invasion

Louis and his army set sail from Calais in mid-May, with Roger of Wendower claiming that his fleet numbered 600 ships and eighty cogs. John had assembled his army at Dover to confront the invaders, but the first line of defence was to be provided by his fleet. The king had invested large sums of money on constructing royal warships, with twenty galleys and thirty-four other ships built between 1209–12, and a dockyard had been established at Portsmouth. Instructions had been issued for these royal warships and merchant vessels to gather at the Dover roads or the mouth of the Thames to confront the invaders. However, on the night of 18 May, the English fleet was caught in a storm which sank many of the ships and scattered the others. Three days later, the French army made landfall at the coast of Kent. The next day, John advanced towards Sandwich to confront the invaders, but soon afterwards changed his mind and withdrew westwards. This decision appears to have been motivated by the fear that his French mercenaries would defect to Louis's army. In such circumstances, it would certainly have been foolhardy to risk his life and throne on the outcome of an uncertain battle. Nevertheless, this decision damaged John's prestige and was to have serious consequences for his cause. Louis and his army rapidly took control of much of south-east England, with the castles of Rochester and Canterbury falling into his hands. He then travelled to London where he was warmly received by the inhabitants, before moving into Surrey, where he captured Farnham and Guildford. Afterwards Louis marched his army southwards to attack Winchester. His forces were admitted into the city without any resistance by the citizens, but the two castles were held against him. The royal castle was located on the western side of Winchester, whereas the bishop's castle of Wolvesey was sited at its south-eastern corner, with the defence of the latter led by Oliver, an illegitimate son of King John. Both castles were eventually captured after being bombarded with stone-throwing siege weapons. Louis then advanced northwards to besiege Odiham Castle. According to Roger of Wendower, the small royalist garrison of three knights and ten serjeants heroically resisted the French attacks for eight days before being forced to surrender. This valiant act of defiance was said to have won the admiration of the besiegers. These victories prompted many barons to defect from John's allegiance and to come to term with Louis. Among their number were some of the king's closest supporters, including his half-brother, William Longespée, Earl of Salisbury.[12]

By the summer of 1216 only two castles remained in the possession of the king's supporters in south-east England, Windsor and Dover. Yet despite being cut off and isolated from other royalist forces, they were well fortified and garrisoned, thus posing a threat to Louis's control of the region. Louis therefore took the decision to focus most of his resources on reducing these castles. A force was sent to besiege Windsor under the command of Hervé IV of Donzy, Count of Nevers, in June, while Louis took the bulk of his army and fleet to attack Dover in July. The location and strength of Dover's defences meant it was of key strategic importance, described by the chronicler Matthew Paris as the 'key of England'. Since the reign of Henry II, large sums of money had been lavished on improving the fortifications of the castle. By 1216 these defences included a keep, as well as an inner and outer bailey, with the walls of the latter extending down to the edge of the cliffs overlooking the port. The defence of the castle was in the hands of one of the king's most trusted lieutenants, the justiciar, Hubert de Burgh, who commanded a large and well-supplied garrison, which according to Roger of Wendower numbered 140 knights and an unspecified number of other soldiers. These defences therefore posed a formidable challenge to the Anglo-French besiegers. The siege began on 22 July, with the attackers deploying stone-throwing siege weapons and a portable wooden tower to target the main gateway of the castle. This consisted of a twin-towered gatehouse that overlooked a deep ditch, which was connected to an outer wooden barbican by a bridge. Miners were used to form a breach in the walls of the barbican, with the miners protected from the missile weapons of the defenders by means of a wooden structure known as a cat. Afterwards the besiegers mounted an assault and succeeded in capturing the barbican. Louis then deployed his miners to undermine the walls of the gatehouse, causing one of its towers to collapse. The attackers stormed into the castle but were beaten back after fierce fighting, with the gap in the wall filled in with timber. The failure of this assault prompted Louis to agree a truce with the Hubert on 14 October.[13]

In the meantime, John had been residing in south-west England where he co-ordinated the delivery of provisions for royalist-held castles in the area, such as at Corfe and Wareham, but was otherwise inactive. Elsewhere, Louis's supporters overran East Anglia, and his ally, King Alexander, again invaded the north, capturing most of Northumberland. Yet his partisans were unable to capture Barnard Castle and Lincoln Castle, which were resolutely defended by their royalist garrisons. Furthermore, tensions had been growing between Louis's English and French supporters, which led some of the barons to return to John's allegiance, including William Longespée, Earl of Salisbury. John sought to exploit this situation by going on the counter-attack with an army raised from the garrisons of his western castles. His objective may have been to break the siege of Windsor Castle, which was held by its constable Engelard de Cigogné, with a force of sixty knights. He advanced as far eastwards as Reading, which prompted Hervé IV of Donzy, Count of Nevers, the commander of the force besieging Windsor Castle, to lift the siege and to move towards John. However, the king evaded the baronial forces that were pursuing him and marched into East Anglia on a pillaging raid. Afterwards he moved westwards to lift the siege of Lincoln Castle, which had been held for him by its hereditary constable, Nicola de la Hay. The king was at King's Lynn in Norfolk, in October, where he contracted dysentery, which according to Coggeshall was caused by overeating. Despite his illness, he then headed westwards, losing part of his baggage train in crossing the Wash, before dying at Newark Castle on 19 October.[14]

The Battle of Lincoln

John was succeeded by his nine-year-old son, who was crowned as Henry III in Gloucester Cathedral on 28 October 1216. John's will specified that thirteen named executors were to assist his heir in recovering his kingdom, with the boy king entrusted to the guardianship of William Marshal, Earl of Pembroke. William Marshal was a highly regarded figure who as a young man had developed a reputation as a celebrated tournament knight, his biographer describing him as 'the greatest knight in the world', and had served all the Angevin kings from Henry II to John. The new regent, although elderly, was therefore highly capable of prosecuting the war against Louis and his supporters. The accession of a child king also gave the new government the opportunity to distance itself from the unpopularity of John's reign. One of Henry III's first acts was to reissue a revised version of Magna Carta on 12 November, to encourage the rebel barons to change sides. Furthermore, the new king placed himself under papal protection by giving homage to the papacy at his coronation, thereby securing the support of Pope Honorius III. Nevertheless, the survival of the Angevin dynasty was dependent upon winning the war by force of arms. At the end of 1216 large parts of England were held by Louis and his supporters. Placed in this unenviable situation, William Marshal knew that the retention of royalist held castles would be a key asset in winning the conflict. Louis was at the siege of Dover when he received news of the death of John. At once he called upon the constable of the castle, Hubert de Burgh, to surrender, but upon the latter's refusal he lifted the siege, after which the defenders sallied forth to destroy the besiegers camp. According to Roger of Wendower, this course of action was motivated by the decision to focus on reducing smaller castles, as opposed to large and well-defended ones such as Dover. The siege had been costly in both time and resources; therefore, it was considered sensible to target weaker castles. However, this decision was undoubtedly a setback for Louis and damaged his prestige. He moved northwards to besiege Hertford Castle, held by Walter de Godarville, on 12 November. The defenders were said to have put up a fierce resistance, despite being bombarded by stone-throwing engines, but were eventually forced to surrender on 6 December. His next target was Berkhamsted Castle, whose defence was led by 'Waleran the German'. The garrison achieved an early success when they succeeded in capturing a banner belonging to William de Mandeville, during a sortie from the castle. Yet a subsequent sally was driven back the same day, and they were subjected to heavy fire from the French artillery deployed outside the walls. This pressure eventually led to the decision to surrender the castle on 20 December, as part of a general truce agreed between William Marshal and Louis. The ceasefire was subsequently extended to last until 23 April, in return for the handing over of further royalist-held castles: Hedingham, Orford, Norwich and Colchester. The terms of this agreement reflected the military balance of power. Louis had a slight advantage in terms of manpower, but the war was effectively a stalemate, with the kingdom divided in half. William Marshal lacked the funds to muster a field army to go on the offensive, whereas Louis was confronted with numerous well-fortified enemy castles that had to be systematically besieged and reduced in turn, as well as tensions between his English and French followers. Therefore, the truce provided an opportunity for Louis to leave for France to gather reinforcements to break the deadlock, and for the royalists to gain some respite.[15]

Yet the truce was only ever a tenuous one, with numerous violations carried out by both sides. As early as 20 January, a raid by the garrison of Mountsorrel was intercepted and defeated by a royalist force from Nottingham Castle. Two days later, Falkes de Bréauté took advantage of the chaotic situation to launch a plundering raid on the town and abbey of St Albans, with the loot taken back to his stronghold at Bedford Castle. Soon afterwards an attempt was made to blockade Louis in Winchelsea on his way to France, by a land and naval force led by Philip de Albini, who had taken possession of Rye. However, this plan was foiled by the intervention of a French fleet led by a pirate called Eustace the Monk, allowing Louis to sail for the Continent. During his time overseas, some of his English supporters defected to the cause of Henry III. These defectors included high-ranking figures such as William Marshal junior, son of the regent. These men had been dissatisfied with their treatment by Louis and were concerned that lands and offices in England were being granted to his French supporters instead of to them. Emboldened by this upturn in fortune, the royalists went on the offensive in March in southern England. They first captured Farnham Castle after a short siege before moving southwards to Winchester, where they were granted entry into the city. Wolvesey Castle was surrendered after an eight-day siege on 12 March, but the garrison of the royal castle held out until late April. The royalists also succeeded in capturing Cirencester, Marlborough, Portchester and Southampton. However, the military situation was transformed by the return of Louis on 23 April, with Winchester recovered by the end of the month. It was at this point that Louis took the ultimately fatal decision to divide his army into two. He resumed the siege of Dover Castle on 12 May with half of his army, deploying for quite possibly the first time in England a powerful stone-throwing siege engine known as a trebuchet, which had been named *Malvoisin* (bad neighbour). Meanwhile, the rest of his forces – under the command of Saer de Quincy, Earl of Winchester, and Thomas, Count of Perche – were sent to relieve Mountsorrel Castle, whose garrison was hard-pressed by a royalist army led by Ranulf de Blundeville, Earl of Chester. News of their imminent arrival prompted the besiegers to lift the siege, so instead they proceeded northwards to join the siege of the royalist-held castle of Lincoln. William Marshal was at Northampton on 13 May, when news reached him that Louis had divided his army into two. At once he sought to exploit this opportunity to achieve a decisive victory by bringing all his forces to bear against Louis's northern army. The royalist army assembled at Newark on 18 May, with the Battle of Lincoln taking place two days later. Outnumbered by their opponents, the Anglo-French army elected to remain within the walls rather than confronting their enemies outside the city. Unfortunately for the defenders, the royalists discovered a weakness in the defences and managed to open the blocked west gate of the city, while a diversion was made to the north. A force led by Falkes de Bréauté entered the castle from its external west gate, with crossbowmen deployed on its battlements to provide covering fire, while he and his cavalry made a sortie from the east gate of the castle. Meanwhile the main part of the army entered the west gate of the city and launched a fierce assault on their opponents. Assailed from multiple sides, the Anglo-French forces were utterly defeated with many taken prisoner. News of this defeat reached Louis at Dover on 25 May. Soon afterwards he lifted the siege and went to London where he sent envoys to negotiate with the royalists and a peace agreement was reached on 13 June. Yet a dispute over the treatment of Louis's English supporters led to the resumption of hostilities a short time later. The conflict was finally ended by the victory of the royalists at the naval Battle of Sandwich on 24 August, with peace concluded with the Treaty of Lambeth on 20 September.[16]

The Rise of Gwynedd

The outbreak of civil war in England provided Llywelyn ap Iorwerth with a golden opportunity to assert his dominance over Wales. In 1213, following the abandonment of the royal expedition in the previous year, Llywelyn succeeded in capturing the last two castles held by the Crown in Gwynedd, at Degannwy and Rhuddlan. Two years later, he allied with the rebellious barons in England and attacked Shrewsbury, with the town and castle surrendered without any resistance being offered. Llywelyn then invaded Gwent in south-east Wales in support of his ally, Giles de Briouze, Bishop of Hereford, and the latter's brother, Reginald, whose nephews had been dispossessed of their lands after the forfeiture of their father, William. Llywelyn and his English allies rapidly captured Abergavenny, White and Skenfrith castles, before moving westwards, where they took Builth and Brecon castles. These castles were handed over to Reginald de Briouze, who cemented his alliance with Llywelyn by marrying his daughter, Gwladus. Meanwhile in south Wales, the grandsons of Rhys ap Gruffudd, Rhys and Owain, allied with their uncle, Maelgwyn, led a rebellion, with their forces ravaging the area between Swansea and Carmarthen. They faced little challenge, as the principal magnate in the region, William Marshal, Earl of Pembroke, who held the royal castles of Cardigan and Carmarthen, as well as his own castles at Pembroke and Cilgerran, was engaged in negotiations with the rebel barons in England. Afterwards they negotiated an alliance with Llywelyn, recognising him as their overlord, in return for military assistance. In early December 1215 Llywelyn, at the head of a grand alliance of native Welsh rulers, invaded south Wales with his forces, taking advantage of an unusually mild winter. First he attacked Carmarthen, the centre of royal power in the region, whose garrison surrendered after a five-day siege. His forces soon afterwards overran many of the other castles in the region, including Narberth, Kidwelly, Newport, Llanstephan and Laugharne. Before the end of the year they had also succeeded in capturing the castles of Cardigan and Cilgerran. He then disbanded his army, with the author of the *Chronicle of the Princes* stating that his men 'returned again to their lands, happily rejoicing with victory'. Llywelyn then wisely decided to hand over the conquered territories to his allies, with the lands divided between the sons and grandson of Rhys ap Gruffudd. By the beginning of 1216, Llywelyn had become the most powerful native ruler in Wales for many years, and effectively cemented the supremacy of Gwynedd over all the other princely states. The death of King John and the succession of Henry III to the throne later prompted some of Llywelyn's English allies to defect from Louis's cause. This included his son-in-law, Reginald de Briouze, who came to terms with the royalists on 23 June 1217. In response, his lands were attacked and ravaged by his Welsh relatives, with Llywelyn leading his forces in an invasion of Breconshire, with Reginald forced to surrender Swansea to avoid any further destruction being inflicted on his territories. Llywelyn's dominant position in Wales and the weakness of the regency government of Henry III, meant that he received generous terms. The Treaty of Worcester was concluded on March 1218. Llywelyn gave homage to the king, and in return was confirmed as the custodian of the royal castles of Cardigan and Carmarthen, until the king came of age. This agreement was a triumph for Llywelyn as it left much of southern Wales under the control of himself and his allies.[17]

Henry III and the Second Barons' War: 1217–1267

From Westminster king Henry and his warlike army proceeded onwards and arrived before Kenilworth, where, without delay, they laid siege to the castle, wishing, but not being able, to make themselves masters of it with their forces. Their army prepared for the assault, but they found very vigorous defenders within... Outside the castle, a great number of engines were erected, and without delay the besieged erected others, similar both in size and number to those of the besiegers... But the engines of the besieged garrison were at last broken by those engines which were outside the walls, though even then the defenders would not surrender the castle; for they preferred dying bravely, to giving it up on compulsion... And neither the sentence of the legate, who was present, nor the power of the king, could induce them to abandon their enterprise. Therefore, by the wisdom of the cardinal, with the sanction of the king, an assemblage of the clergy and laity was summoned to meet at Kenilworth. And there twelve persons were elected from the most powerful of the nobles, and the wisest of the prelates, to whom was given a power of making regulation concerning the condition of those who had been deprived of their property... In process of time, the garrison of the besieged castle of Kenilworth, worn out by famine and misery, making a virtue of necessity, surrendered it to the king, saving all their necessaries.

The Flowers of History[1]

The siege of Kenilworth Castle in 1266 was the last major military action of the civil war between the supporters of Henry III and Simon de Montfort. Defeated at the Battle of Evesham the previous year, the remaining Monfortians took refuge in Kenilworth Castle, where they were besieged by the royalists. A formidable army was brought to bear against the defenders, well-equipped with siege weapons, provisions, and other military equipment, intended to demonstrate the might of the king. Yet the strong masonry defences of the castle, which was encircled by a huge artificial lake, meant that it was a difficult fortress to capture. The determined resistance of the garrison encouraged the king to attempt to reconcile with his opponents to end civil discord by setting up a committee of bishops and magnates to discuss peace terms. These discussions led to the issuing of the Dictum of Kenilworth, which granted the rebels the option to avoid the forfeiture of their lands to the Crown by paying substantial fines. Nevertheless, the garrison of Kenilworth only finally surrendered after running out of food supplies more than a month later. The siege thereby demonstrated that well fortified, garrisoned and supplied castles posed a considerable challenge to any besieging army. Though the total number of castles in England and Wales declined throughout the thirteenth century, due to the greater cost of stone as a building material, they continued to play a vital role in warfare during the long and turbulent reign of Henry III. The possession of royal castles was strongly contested both during the minority of the young king and much later during the civil war. In Wales, meanwhile, the struggle between the Crown and the Marcher lords on the one side and the rulers of Gwynedd on the other, led to an intensive investment in masonry castle-building.

The minority of Henry III

Despite being victorious in the civil war, the minority government of Henry III was faced with a multitude of problems. Years of warfare had led to a breakdown in the system of administration in the counties, with power having devolved into the hands of local officials, who appropriated most of the revenues due to the king rather than paying them into the Exchequer, and kept hold of the royal castles. Yet the weakness of royal authority meant that the Crown was dependent for its support on these men. The implementation of the peace treaty also proved to be problematic, as its terms specified that the lands of former rebels should be restored to their owners. Understandably, royalists who had taken possession of forfeited lands and castles were reluctant to hand them over to their erstwhile enemies. Philip of Oldcoates, a long-time supporter of the Angevins, was ordered to transfer custody of Mitford Castle in Northumberland to its former owner, Roger Bertram, at a great council held at Westminster in October 1217. At the same time, William de Fors, Count of Aumale, was instructed to surrender Bytham Castle in Lincolnshire to William de Coleville. These commands were ignored by both Oldcoates and Coleville who stubbornly continued to retain control of these castles. Yet the weakness of the regency government meant it was unable to compel either of these men to obey its orders or to punish them for their defiance. There were also concerns regarding the existence of unauthorised adulterine castles that had been constructed during the civil war. The reissued Magna Carta of 1217 included a clause 'that all adulterine castles, that is to say, those built or rebuilt since the beginning of the war between the lord John our father and his barons of England, shall be destroyed immediately'. Periodic attempts were made to order the destruction of these structures and to prevent new fortresses being constructed. On 19 July 1218, a letter was sent by the king to Philip of Oldcoates commanding him to demolish the new castle he was building at Nafferton, as Richard Umfraville had complained that it threatened his castle at Prudhoe, which was situated less than a mile away. The government was also keen to restore peace to the Welsh Marches by negotiating a treaty with Llywelyn ap Iorwerth. Discussions between the two parties in March 1218 resulted in the Treaty of Worcester. In return for swearing homage and fealty to the king, Llywelyn was entrusted with the custody of the royal castles of Cardigan and Carmarthen, with much of southern Wales remaining in the possession of his allies, the sons and grandsons of Lord Rhys of Deheubarth. This agreement was a triumph for Llywelyn, which recognised his dominant position in Wales.[2]

Later the same year, the decision was taken to use force against Robert de Gaugi to compel him to hand over custody of Newark Castle to the Bishop of Lincoln, Hugh of Wells. At the beginning of the civil war, Hugh had entrusted Newark to the king for safekeeping, but its custodian, Gaugi, had refused to hand it back to the bishop now that the conflict was over. Therefore the regent, William Marshal, summoned the royal army to assemble at Stamford on 15 July, with the siege of the castle starting four days later. The defenders were said to have sallied forth to attack the besiegers, causing some casualties, but after being bombarded with stone-throwing siege weapons for eight days, they surrendered. Despite the armed resistance shown to the royal army, the lives of the garrison were spared, with Gaugi even paid £100 in compensation for the stores kept in the castle. Furthermore, this action was taken in isolation, with no other firm measures taken to prise disputed castles from their castellans. In the following year, the death of William Marshal led to the formation of a triumvirate, with power exercised in the king's name by three individuals: Hubert de Burgh, the justiciar; Peter des Roches, Bishop of Winchester; and Pandulf Verraccio, the papal legate. The new government, with papal backing, was strongly committed to restoring the authority of the Crown and the recovery of royal castles. It soon faced a challenge from William Longespée, Earl of Salisbury, who attempted to seize Lincoln Castle from its custodian, Nicola del la Hay. In response, the court travelled to the castle on 19 August, whose garrison was reinforced by a contingent of soldiers under the command of Falkes de Bréauté. This measure deterred Longespée from launching a direct assault on the castle, but elsewhere he continued to cause problems. In Devonshire, his partisans had forcibly prevented Bréauté's men from provisioning Plympton Castle, while his attempts to improve the fortifications of Marlborough Castle sufficiently alarmed the government for it to issue instructions forbidding any further construction work. The continuing weakness of royal authority prompted the decision to carry out a second coronation on 17 May 1220. On the next day, the barons swore an oath to surrender royal castles in their possession and render in full the money they owed to the Exchequer. They also pledged to provide military support against any rebel who refused to comply with royal instructions.

This measure greatly strengthened the ability of the Crown to bring force to bear against recalcitrant castellans. At a council held at York in June, Philip of Oldcoates was finally forced to relinquish control of Mitford Castle to Roger Bertram. Later that month, as the court began to move southwards, a surprise attack was made against Rockingham Castle, held by William de Fors, Count of Aumale. Taken unawares, the garrison surrendered soon afterwards on 28 June, with Sauvey Castle and other manors also taken into royal hands. This decisive action did much to demonstrate royal power and enhanced the prestige of the Crown.[3]

Yet two months later, the government was forced to contend with another crisis – this time in Wales. In July, Rhys Gryg had been ordered by the king to hand over custody of the lands he had conquered during the war to Llywelyn, who was acting as the Crown's representative. Llywelyn in response launched an invasion of south Wales in late August and soon forced Rhys to hand over Kidwelly, Gower, Carnwyllion and Widigada to his control. He then used the opportunity to attack the lands of William Marshal, 5th Earl of Pembroke. His forces rampaged through Pembrokeshire, overrunning and destroying the two castles at Narberth, with the town of Haverford said to have been 'burnt up to the gate of the castle'. The inhabitants of the area were only able to secure a truce with Llywelyn by paying £100 and by promising not to rebuild the castles that he had destroyed. William Marshal was unable to respond to this outrage other than complaining to Hubert de Burgh at his treatment. In response, royal letters were issued on 5 October condemning the invasion of Pembrokeshire and excusing the men of the district from the terms of the truce, but otherwise no action was taken against Llywelyn. At the end of the year, the king and his court were celebrating Christmas at Oxford, attended by the earls and barons of the kingdom. In the middle of the night, William de Fors, Count of Aumale, secretly left Oxford without the king's consent and hurried to Bytham Castle to raise a rebellion. This desperate action was sparked by the resentment that Aumale felt at his treatment by the government. He had been forcibly dispossessed of the castles of Rockingham and Sauvey, thwarted in his desire to be appointed seneschal of Poitou and Gascony, and had come under intense pressure to hand over Bytham Castle. His forces first raided the nearby villages of Deeping and Edenham before attempting unsuccessfully to capture the castles of Sleaford, Newark and Kimbolton. Rebuffed by their garrisons, he instead attacked the royal castle of Fotheringhay, which was in the custody of Ranulf de Blundeville, Earl of Chester. According to Roger of Wendower, the attackers used scaling ladders to climb the walls and then quickly overwhelmed the undermanned garrison. Upon learning news of this uprising, instructions were sent out for the royal army to be assembled at Northampton to recover the castle. However, Aumale soon took fright and abandoned Fotheringay. Fleeing northwards, he initially went to his castle at Skipton in Craven, before taking refuge in Fountains Abbey. Soon afterwards, the royal army laid siege to Bytham Castle on 6 February 1221. The besiegers caused considerable damage to the walls with their siege weapons and the garrison of thirteen men surrendered only two days later. Meanwhile, Aumale had surrendered himself to the king through the mediation of the Archbishop of York, Walter de Gray. Despite his act of rebellion, he was treated with remarkable leniency, being allowed to retain his lands without any penalties being imposed on him. Nevertheless, this demonstration of royal power enhanced the prestige of the Crown, which soon afterwards secured the transferal of the important castles of Marlborough and Corfe into its custody. The format of the government also changed, with power now concentrated in the hands of the justiciar, Hubert de Burgh, after the resignation of the papal legate, Pandulf, and the termination of the guardianship of the king by Peter des Roches.[4]

At the beginning of 1223, Llywelyn launched an attack into Shropshire and captured the castles of Kinnerly and Whittington. An attempt was made to negotiate a truce with Llywelyn, through the intermediary of his ally, Ranulf de Blundeville, Earl of Chester, in March, but no agreement was reached. However, the resumption of conflict in the Welsh Marches provided an excellent opportunity for William Marshal to seek revenge for the humiliation he had suffered three years earlier. Having raised an army from his extensive estates in Ireland, he landed near St David's on 15 April and at once moved to attack the castles held by Llywelyn and his allies in south Wales.

His forces soon took control of the towns and castles of Cardigan and Carmarthen without facing any resistance. After an inconclusive skirmish with a Welsh force led by Llywelyn's son, Gruffudd, in Kidwelly, he withdrew northwards, where he issued instructions for the repair of Carmarthen Castle and for the construction of a new castle at Cilgerran. A further attempt was made by the government to negotiate a truce between both sides at a meeting held at Ludlow from 8 to 10 July. However, upon Llywelyn's demand that the seized castles be returned to him, military support was provided to William Marshal, including a cavalry force of around 140 knights. Marshall then proceeded to secure his hold over Kidwelly, before moving northwards to expel Maelgwyn ap Rhys from south Ceredigion. In early September, Llywelyn counter-attacked by laying siege to Builth Castle, held by Reginald de Briouze. In response, the royal army was summoned to muster at Gloucester on 12 September, with the garrison relieved by 23 September. The decision was then taken to move northwards to Montgomery where a new castle was constructed. An earlier motte and bailey castle, now known as Hen Domen, had previously existed nearby, close to a crossing of the River Severn, but had been abandoned during the civil war. By contrast, the new fortress was constructed on the high ground less than a mile away, on a crag of rock. Roger of Wendower states that the position of the castle was chosen by the commanders of the army as 'it seemed to be impregnable' and was intended to counter the incursions of the Welsh into the region. Llywelyn came to terms soon afterwards in early October and in return for peace was forced to concede his territorial losses in south Wales.[5]

The government's attempts to secure the full resumption of royal castles bore fruit at the very end of the year. On 30 December, Ranulf de Blundeville, Falkes de Bréauté, Hubert de Burgh and others surrendered control of their castles. However, this action contributed to the growing tension between the supporters of Hubert de Burgh and dissidents, such as Ranulf and Falkes, who were unhappy about the way he ruled the kingdom in the king's name. In practice many royal castles remained in the hands of the justiciar and his partisans and were at best only nominally surrendered. Falkes soon became a prime target of the government, due to his refusal to surrender Bedford Castle and the lands of his stepson Baldwin de Redvers, Earl of Devon. On 29 February, he was commanded to give up the castles of Carisbrooke and Christchurch, and eleven days later was instructed to vacate Plympton Castle. Falkes refused to obey these orders but was pursued through the courts on various charges, including breach of the peace. His brother William, who was constable of Bedford Castle, decided to take revenge on one of his persecutors by seizing the royal justice Henry of Braybrooke on 17 June while he was on his way to the great council being held at Northampton. The government responded by demanding his release, and upon Falkes's refusal to do so, the royal army laid siege to Bedford Castle on 20 June. This would prove to be a lengthy siege due to the strong fortifications of the fortress and the determined resistance of its garrison. The defences of the castle had been significantly improved in the years immediately prior to the siege, with the addition of two moats, a barbican, large outer bailey and a new keep. Its garrison had also been reinforced and was said to have numbered more than eighty knights and serjeants, well supplied with provisions and military equipment. Falkes avoided being besieged in Bedford and instead went on the run, while sending out messengers requesting assistance from the papacy, due to his status as a crusader, and from his baronial allies. The delay in receiving a response from the pope and the fear of incurring the king's displeasure deterred his supporters from offering aid. The Crown's determination to capture Bedford Castle can be seen from the huge quantities of equipment that were procured to equip the besiegers. On the first day of the siege, orders were sent to the sheriffs of London to send ropes and slings for the royal siege engines as well as 200 picks for miners. Three days later, instructions were sent to the constable of Corfe Castle, Ralf Gernum, to despatch 15,000 crossbow quarrels to equip the crossbowmen in the royal army. Further quantities of equipment were ordered throughout the course of the siege, including more than 28,000 quarrels, with 30 miners recruited from Hereford to undermine the walls, and at least 20 crossbowmen from London.[6]

The attackers began the siege by surrounding the castle before deploying stone-throwing siege weapons outside the walls.

According to the author of the *Dunstable Chronicle*, three were placed on the east side of the castle, two to the west opposite the keep, one to the north, and one to the south. They also erected two large wooden towers known as belfries, which were used by crossbowmen to harass the defenders by shooting bolts at them and by lookouts to observe the course of the siege. Roger of Wendower stated that the garrison were so hard-pressed by this missile fire that 'no one in the castle could take off his armour without being mortally wounded'. The Dunstable chronicler then describes how the castle was captured in four stages by the attackers. Firstly, they stormed the barbican, where they lost four or five men, before proceeding to overrun the outer bailey, where they took possession of large stores of equipment including mail hauberks, crossbows and food supplies. Next they attacked the inner bailey, employing miners, protected by a wooden structure called a cat, to undermine its defences but were only able to occupy it after suffering heavy losses. Finally, they used miners to undermine the foundations of the keep, where the surviving members of the garrison had taken refuge, prompting the defenders to surrender unconditionally on 15 August. Yet this had been a costly victory for the attackers. Ralph of Coggeshall claimed that one lord, Richard de Argentan, was badly wounded by a crossbow bolt, with six knights killed, as well as more than 200 serjeants and labourers who were slain while operating the siege weapons. The king was angered by these losses and the length of the eight-week siege, so he was in no mood to show mercy. What is more, the king's previous leniency in sparing the lives of the garrisons of rebel castles in the past was blamed for Falkes's rebellion. Walter of Coventry relates that Jocelin of Wells, Bishop of Bath, commented 'if those captured at Bytham had been hung, those now taken would not have held the castle against the royal will'. The entire garrison was ordered to be hanged and the castle was systematically demolished. Falkes gave himself up soon afterwards, and although his life was spared, all his estates were confiscated and he was exiled from the kingdom. Despite this powerful demonstration of royal power, the capture of Bedford Castle was a pyrrhic victory, as it diverted resources away from the defence of Poitou at a critical juncture, allowing the French to overrun the county.[7]

Henry III and Gwynedd

The minority of Henry III ended in January 1227 when the king announced that in future all charters would be issued under his own seal. Yet power continued to be exercised by the justiciar, Hubert de Burgh, who was richly rewarded by his royal master, such as being created Earl of Kent. Burgh also held substantial lands and estates in the Marches of Wales, including the 'three castles of Gwent' – Grosmont, Skenfrith and White castles. His territory in the region was augmented in 1228 with the grant of the lordship and castle of Montgomery on 27 April 1228. This brought him into conflict with Llywelyn ap Iorwerth who was keen to assert his control over this strategically important area of Mid-Wales. A Welsh force laid siege to Montgomery Castle, but was forced to withdraw due to the arrival of a royal army in August. A truce was agreed with Llywelyn in September but collapsed soon afterwards when Hubert began constructing a castle in Ceri. The Welsh harried the English army camped beside the castle-building site and subjected them to considerable pressure by cutting their supply lines. The prominent Marcher lord, William de Briouze, was captured in a skirmish and was ransomed in return for the surrender of his castle of Builth and a large cash payment. The English soon ran low on food and the king was forced to conclude what Roger of Wendower described as being a 'disgraceful peace'. Despite the 'impregnable nature of the place' where the castle was sited, the treaty specified that the almost completed building was to be demolished, although Llywelyn paid £2,000 in compensation. It was for this reason that the destroyed castle was mockingly referred to as 'Hubert's folly'. Two years later, William de Briouze was hanged by Llywelyn on the charge of having committed adultery with his wife. In the next year, the Welsh raided the lands formerly held by Briouze, with hostilities quickly escalating into the outbreak of full-scale war. Llywelyn invaded south Wales, burning the towns of Montgomery, Radnor, Hay and Brecon. He failed to capture Caerleon Castle, but took out his fury on the town – which was burnt. Then with the assistance of the Welsh princes of Glamorgan, he captured and destroyed Neath Castle at the end of June, before occupying Kidwelly. Next he laid siege to Cardigan Castle, whose garrison was forced to surrender after being subjected to the furious missile fire of his siege weapons for three days. The royal response to these attacks, at first, was slow. A proposal to send an army from Ireland to Wales failed to come to fruition, although instructions were issued to the sheriffs of Hereford and Gloucester to lead the men of their counties to raise the siege of Newport Castle on 2 July. The royal army assembled at Hereford on 22 July and had reached Elfael by 1 August. As in 1228, the decision was taken to construct a castle in a strategic location to contain the ravages of the Welsh. The new building was constructed on the ruins of an earlier castle at Painscastle in Radnorshire, which had been destroyed by Llywelyn some years earlier. It was described by the author of the *Annals of Wales* as being 'magnificently rebuilt in stone and lime', with the workforce numbering more than 300 carpenters and labourers. Work was mostly finished by 22 September, when it was provided with a strong garrison, after which the king returned to England, with a truce concluded with Llywelyn in November. Again this represented a poor return for a royal expedition to Wales. The new fortress did help to improve the security of part of the border region but elsewhere the ravages of the Welsh went unchecked. As observed by the author of the *Dunstable Chronicle*, while the king and his army were busy rebuilding Painscastle, Llywelyn had destroyed ten other castles in Wales. The failure of this campaign contributed to Hubert's fall from grace in the following year, when he was removed from office.[8]

In early 1233, the king's policy of lavishing patronage on his French favourites led to the outbreak of a rebellion. These men were disparaging referred to as 'Poitevins' regardless of their origin, and included notable figures such as Peter des Roches, Bishop of Winchester, and the latter's relative, Peter de Rivallis. Opposition to this faction was led by Richard Marshal, 6th Earl of Pembroke, with growing tensions between the two sides leading to the outbreak of hostilities in the summer in the Welsh Marches. In response, the king ordered the confiscation of Marshal's estates and then laid siege to his castle at Usk on 6 September. Yet finding that the defences of the castle were strong and the army's provisions were low, he soon sent envoys to negotiate with the earl. This resulted in a truce being agreed on 8 September, whereby as part of a general settlement, the castle would be temporarily surrendered into the king's hands. However, mutual distrust meant that the peace was to be short-lived. In early October, Marshal, who was now in alliance with Llywelyn, invaded Glamorgan and forcibly recovered Usk Castle from its royalist garrison. His supporters also succeeded in dramatically rescuing Hubert de Burgh from Devizes Castle on 29 October. The king was infuriated by these developments and launched an invasion of the Marshal lands in south Wales. He faced determined resistance from the rebels and their Welsh allies, with the royal army routed by a surprise night attack on their camp on 11 November. This setback forced Henry to retire to England, with the royalist-held castles in Wales entrusted to his 'Poitevin' supporters. Fourteen days later, Marshal was defeated and almost captured in a skirmish outside Monmouth Castle. He was to have his revenge in the following month, when his army routed a royalist force led by John of Monmouth on 26 December. In the new year, Llywelyn and Marshal embarked on a joint invasion; their forces laid waste to Shropshire and burned Shrewsbury. Around the same time, an attempt was made to capture Carmarthen Castle by Llywelyn's south Welsh allies. Their scheme to blockade the town by land and sea, which included constructing a bridge across the River Towry, ended in disaster when the siege was raised by a fleet from Bristol; the Welsh were routed, with heavy losses. The inability of the royalists to defeat the rebels and their allies allowed intermediaries, such as Edmund Rich, the Archbishop of Canterbury, to facilitate a truce on 6 March 1234.[9]

Llywelyn died at Aberconwy Abbey on 11 April 1240 and was succeeded by his legitimate son Dafydd ap Llywelyn. Dafydd gave homage to the king at Gloucester on 15 May and in return was recognised as his father's heir as ruler of Gwynedd. He then secured his grip on power by moving against his main rival, his half-brother, Gruffudd, who was imprisoned, with the latter's son, Owain. Nevertheless, Dafydd was in a far weaker position than his father had been. At his meeting with the king, he had been browbeaten into conceding the lands conquered by his father, with territorial disputes now to be decided by a commission of arbitrators. In the following year, Henry decided to further humble his vassal by espousing the rights of Gruffudd who, according to Welsh inheritance laws, was due a territorial share of his father's lands. The king invaded Gwynedd in August and within a week had secured the submission of Dafydd, who had been abandoned by his allies. Harsh terms were imposed upon him, including the cession of his territories in north-east Wales, east of the River Conwy, and the surrender into royal custody of Gruffudd and Owain, whose rights were to be decided at a later date at the king's court. Henry refrained from further weakening Dafydd through forcing the partition of Gwynedd by enforcing the claims of Gruffudd and his son Owain. Instead he moved Gruffudd to the Tower of London, where he was kept as an insurance policy to ensure the future good behaviour of the Prince of Gwynedd. To secure his control over the newly acquired territory in north-east Wales, Henry decided to construct a substantial masonry castle at Dyserth. This new building was situated on a steep hill and consisted of an outer and inner bailey, with the walls flanked by square and polygonal towers. The defences of nearby Rhuddlan Castle on the River Clywyd were also improved. Instructions were sent to John le Strange, justice of Chester, on 18 January, to ensure that it was adequately protected by ditches and had a well of water 'so that the water in the castle cannot be taken away'. Provision was to be made for timber for constructing barriers, towers and siege weapons, as well as adequate quantities of food supplies. In addition to this, thirty-one men were installed in the garrison, which numbered ten knights with twenty-one serjeants and crossbowmen. The king also decided to strengthen his control over the major royal castles in south Wales. An opportunity to acquire the royal castles traditionally held by the Marshal family was provided by the succession of Walter Marshal to the earldom of Pembroke in 1241, following the deaths of his older brothers Richard and Gilbert. Walter was eventually appointed as Earl Marshal in the following year, but he was not permitted to hold the castles of Cardiff and Cardigan. According to the chronicler Matthew Paris, the king 'considered it necessary to retain them, in order to strengthen the weaker parts of Wales, which he had lately obtained possession of, and to fortify them with castles and garrisons'.[10]

The king's dominance over Wales was to be challenged, however, as a result of a botched escape from the Tower of London on

1 March 1244. Matthew Paris relates that Gruffudd had become bored with his tedious life in prison and had spent much time devising a means of escape. Making a cord out of his bed sheets, table cloths and tapestries, he lowered himself from the top of the tower. Yet the generous portions of food provided by his jailors meant that Gruffudd had become overweight and the cord soon snapped plunging him to his death. It was not until the following morning that the 'lamentable spectacle' of his mangled remains were discovered. Dafydd professed to be outraged by his death and soon exploited the demise of his half-brother by raising a rebellion against the king. In alliance with most of the other native rulers of Wales, his forces ravaged far and wide across the Welsh Marches. Henry's response was at first muted, with only a small force of 300 knights despatched under the command of Hubert Fitz Matthew to quash the rebellion. He also released Owain from the Tower of London in the hope that he would cause problems for his uncle Dafydd. The king's attentions were instead focused on a dispute with Alexander II of Scotland, which was threatening to escalate into war. Tensions were caused in part by the fortification of Scottish castles near the English border, with conflict only averted by the signing of a peace treaty in August. Yet news of Hubert's death in a Welsh ambush in February 1245 and the loss of Mold Castle in the following month, prompted the king to intervene directly in Wales. The royal army was assembled at Chester on 13 August and had reached the east bank of the mouth of the River Conwy thirteen days later. Work then began on constructing a large castle, spread across two nearby steep hills overlooking the river, on the ruins of an earlier fortress at Degannwy. A vivid account of the hardships suffered by the English army can be seen in a letter from an unnamed noble, included in Matthew Paris's chronicle. The soldiers were said to have resided in tents around the site, where they spent their time keeping watch, due to the fear of Welsh raids, and were afflicted by cold and hunger. Provisions for the army were supplied by ships from Ireland and Chester, which docked at a small harbour on the river a short distance downhill from the castle. The Welsh frequently sought to harass the English supply lines, with the author describing in detail a skirmish with a Welsh force residing on the other side of the Conwy. An Irish vessel was

said to have run aground on the hostile western side and its crew was immediately attacked by the Welsh. The English responded by sending reinforcements across the river in boats, which drove off the attackers. However, the English became dispersed in pursuing the fugitives and were themselves routed by a Welsh counter-attack with heavy losses. Yet the crew of the stricken ship succeeded in holding their own until midnight, when they evacuated themselves and their supplies in small boats to the other side of the shore. Numerous other skirmishes were also said to have taken place, with the English collecting the heads of 100 Welsh men after one engagement. Eventually a shortage of provisions and the guerrilla tactics of the Welsh forced the English to abandon the campaign, with a strong garrison left behind to hold the castle. According to the author of the *Chronicle of the Princes*, the king returned to England in October 'leaving untold numbers of his host unburied corpses, some having been slain and others drowned'. However, the Welsh cause was dealt a heavy blow a short time later by the death of Dafydd on 25 February 1246.[11]

The realm of Gwynedd was soon afterwards partitioned between his two nephews, Owain and Llywelyn. This settlement meant that the Welsh were divided in their opposition to Henry III and were unable to offer a united front. What is more, they had suffered terribly during the recent war, particularly as the island of Anglesey, the main grain-producing area in north Wales, had been ravaged by an Anglo-Irish force in 1245. Matthew Paris states that the king had forbidden English or Irish merchants from importing foodstuffs into Wales, whose inhabitants were much oppressed by starvation. The new castle of Degannwy was also said to be well supplied with men, provisions, engines of wars, and arms, which made it 'a thorn in the eye' of the 'most wretched Welsh'. Owain and Llywelyn were therefore keen to treat for peace, with the Treaty of Worcester agreed on 30 April 1247. In return for acquiescing in the division of Gwynedd, the king received the homage of the two brothers, as well as all the minor rulers of north Wales. The terms of this treaty reflected Henry's dominant position in Wales. The Crown now held most of north-east Wales, through its acquisition of Gwynedd east of the River Conwy, and the earldom of Chester, following the death of its earl, John of Scotland, without any heirs in 1237. Henry later sought to partition Gwynedd even further by advancing the claims of another brother, Dafydd, in early 1253. However, Llywelyn defeated both of his siblings at the Battle of Bryn Derwin in June 1255 and thereafter became sole ruler of Gwynedd. During the next year, he led a major rebellion against English rule. The uprising was sparked by the visit of Edward, the eldest son of the king, to north Wales in the summer. Edward had been granted extensive lands and castles in Wales in the previous year and his officials soon set to work imposing English methods of law and taxation on the Welsh inhabitants. According to the author of the *Chronicle of the Princes*, Llywelyn was approached by a delegation of nobles who bitterly complained about their treatment, stating 'that they preferred to be slain in battle for their liberty than to suffer themselves to be trampled upon in bondage'. He responded by releasing his brother Dafydd from prison to assist him and invaded the 'Middle Country' east of the River Conwy in November. His forces succeeded in conquering the whole territory within a week, except for the castles of Degannwy and Dyserth, whose garrisons were now dangerously isolated. In the following month, he moved southwards into Merionydd, whose Welsh ruler was forced to flee, and then proceeded to invade Ceredigion.[12]

Llywelyn kept up the pressure in the new year by attacking Powys, before penetrating as far south as Carmarthenshire, with his conquests including Gower, Kidwelly and Carnwyllion. The English response to this rebellion was hampered by bad weather conditions and the poor finances of the Crown. Matthew Paris claims that Edward sought assistance from his father but was rebuffed with the reply 'What is it to me? The land is yours by my gift'. It was not until the king received news of a crushing defeat of an English army led by Stephen Bauzan in June that he summoned the royal army to assemble at Chester for 1 August. Llywelyn's victories meant that he succeeded in uniting almost all of the other native rulers of Wales under his banner, which Matthew Paris states was 'a circumstance never before known'. The fear of English reprisals prompted Llywelyn to send envoys requesting peace with Henry. However, as Matthew Paris relates, the king refused these entreaties and 'like a dragon which knows not how to spare any one, he threatened general extermination to the Welsh'. In the meantime, Llywelyn had made inroads into south-west Wales, where his forces succeeded in capturing the castles of Narberth, Laugharne and Llanstephan. Henry eventually left Chester on 19 August and with the assistance of a naval force succeeded in temporarily relieving the castles of Dyserth and Degannwy. Supply problems meant that the campaign had to be abandoned soon afterwards on 3 September, with the English remorselessly harried during the retreat by the victorious Welsh. This was followed by a brief truce that covered the winter months of 1257–8. Early in the new year, Llywelyn summoned an assembly of the nobility of Wales, where he received their homage and began to style himself as 'Prince of Wales'. In the spring, Henry made plans for another expedition to Wales to take place in the summer. However, the campaign had to be abandoned due to the formation of a baronial movement opposed to the king's unpopular methods of ruling the kingdom. Instead a two-year truce was agreed with Llywelyn at Oxford on 17 June.[13]

Simon de Montfort and Civil War

Henry was unable to counter Llywelyn's territorial advances in Wales due to the political crisis that had arisen in England. This was largely due to his mismanagement of the kingdom and the resultant alienation of most of the nobility. The king's reliance on his Lusignan relatives, who were beneficiaries of lavish patronage, was a source of keen resentment. The Crown was also experiencing significant financial problems, due in part to Henry's attempts to acquire the kingdom of Sicily for his second son, Edmund. Attempts by royal officials to raise the huge sums of money required for this venture were deeply unpopular. Baronial discontent came to a head at the April Parliament at Westminster, when an armed delegate of magnates, including Henry's brother-in-law Simon de Montfort, forced themselves into the king's presence with a list of demands. Henry was compelled to accept these terms, which included the appointment of a committee to carry out reforms to the governance of the kingdom. Further restrictions were placed on his power two months later at the Parliament of Oxford. The complaints of the magnates were drawn up in a document known as the 'Petition of the Barons', which became the basis of the Provisions of Oxford.

Control over the government was transferred to a newly formed council, with new constables installed in royal castles, to reduce the ability of royalists to use military force to overthrow the settlement. In desperation, the king's eldest son the Lord Edward and the Lusignans fled to Winchester Castle at the end of June – but were soon forced to surrender. Edward was compelled to swear an oath to agree to the Provisions and the Lusignans were banished from the realm. The baronial regime further strengthened its position through the enacting of the Provisions of Westminster in October 1259, with the king allowed to depart for France in the following month to finalise a treaty with Louis IX. Henry was forced to relinquish his hereditary claims to the lost lands of the Angevin empire and give homage to the French king at the Treaty of Paris on 4 December. However, his prolonged absence in France allowed him to recruit a small force of mercenaries, with which he landed at Dover on 23 April 1260. Yet the king was at first willing to work with the baronial government, headed by Montfort, with good relations maintained until the end of the year. This changed abruptly in early 1261, with envoys sent to request papal assistance to annul the Provisions, and the aid of Louis IX. In the meanwhile, he took refuge in the Tower of London, whose defences he ordered to be improved. Henry left the Tower in May and seized control of Dover Castle and the Cinque Ports. This allowed his representatives to safely land in England with the papal bulls annulling the Provisions of Westminster, which were publicly proclaimed at Winchester in June. Resistance to the royalist counter-coup had collapsed by the end of the year, with the king reasserting his control over the governance of the realm, with Montfort leaving for France.[14]

However, Henry weakened his authority by making a series of blunders over the course of 1262. This included an attempt to revive the Sicilian venture and the recall of his unpopular Lusignan relatives to the realm. Royalist supporters were alienated, with prominent members of Lord Edward's household, such as Roger de Leybourne, accused of financial impropriety. The king travelled to France in July in the hope of securing French support for resolving his differences with Montfort. Yet these discussions were inconclusive and Henry's court was stricken by the outbreak of a deadly epidemic, which delayed his return to England until the end of December. During the king's absence in France, Montfort made a brief visit to England in October, where he presented a papal bull that endorsed the Provisions. This had the effect of gradually further undermining the prestige of the king and his government. Fighting had also broken out in the Marches of Wales, with Llywelyn attacking the lands of Roger de Mortimer, Lord of Wigmore. In late November, Mortimer's new castle of Cefnllys was captured through treachery, which the Welsh then proceeded to dismantle. Mortimer and Humphrey de Bohun led a counter-attack but were soon forced to withdraw in the face of a superior Welsh force. Llywelyn then proceeded to conquer the lordship of Maelienydd, with a further five castles captured by Christmas. Early in the next year, he advanced southwards into Breconshire, which was soon overrun, with his forces raiding Herefordshire as far east as Wigmore. The English response to these advances was slow and hampered by internal divisions. The Lord Edward finally led an expedition into Gwynedd in April, but the difficult terrain, guerrilla tactics of the Welsh and a lack of supplies eventually forced him to retreat to Chester in May. The hard-pressed garrisons of Dyserth and Degannwy were temporarily relieved, but otherwise the campaign achieved very little. Meanwhile, Montfort had returned to England on 25 April 1263 and attended a secret meeting of reformist magnates at Oxford, who resolved to force the king to accept the Provisions. Henry refused to agree to these demands and issued instructions for the royal army to assemble at Worcester on 25 May. Ostensibly this army was raised to fight Llywelyn, but it was also intended to quell any resistance from discontented barons. Instead, the king's opponents struck first by attacking the lands of royalists in the Marches of Wales. On 7 June, the Bishop of Hereford, Peter of Aigueblanche, was seized from his cathedral and imprisoned in Eardisley Castle. Soon afterwards the rebels advanced southwards and besieged Gloucester, which was held by Matthew de Bezil. According to the author of the *Flowers of History*, the besiegers gained access to the city by burning down one of its gates. Afterwards they were admitted into the postern gate of the castle through treachery, forcing Matthew to retreat into the keep. The attackers then broke down the strong iron gates of the keep with hammers and axes and took him prisoner.[15]

Royalist attempts to counter the rebellion were hampered by a lack of support and money, with the king taking refuge in the Tower of London. In desperation, Lord Edward raided the deposits of money kept by the Knights Templar at the New Temple to pay for his foreign soldiers. Then he took his loot to Windsor Castle, which he fortified and garrisoned with his mercenaries. In July, Montfort advanced to the south-east and secured the Cinque Ports, thereby cutting off the royalists from reinforcements from the Continent. An attempt was made by Queen Eleanor to escape from the Tower on 13 July by boat, but confronted with the hostility of the Londoners, she was compelled to take shelter at the Bishop of London's palace. Two days later, the rebels were admitted into the city and Henry was forced to come to terms with Montfort.

The terms of their agreement specified the imposition of major curbs on the king's power, which included the surrender of the custody of royal castles to baronial supporters. Yet the barons still faced opposition from the Lord Edward, who had led a foolhardy attack on Bristol with his forces. This assault was beaten off by the townspeople, who then besieged him in the castle. Edward extricated himself from this situation thanks to the mediation of Walter de Cantilupe, Bishop of Worcester, and retreated to his base at Windsor. However, he was soon forced to surrender due to the arrival of an army led by Montfort, and his foreign soldiers were expelled from the kingdom. Later in September, Montfort crossed to France with Henry in tow and received support from King Louis. Despite this triumph, Montfort's regime proved to be short-lived, due to a breakdown of law and order and continued opposition from royalists, with prominent men such as Roger de Leybourne defecting back to the king's side. Edward led the royalist counter-attack by seizing control of Windsor Castle on 13 October. Montfort lacked the resources to raise an army to besiege Windsor and sought arbitration from France, with a brief truce concluded in November. This was soon broken by Henry, who seized control of the chancery at Winchester before attempting to gain entry to Dover Castle, on 3 December, to secure an entry point for the mercenary forces being raised by Queen Eleanor from France, but he was rebuffed by the garrison. Both sides later agreed to accept French arbitration of their dispute, which was to be decided by King Louis at Amiens in northern France. After carefully considering the claims of the two parties, Louis gave his judgement fully in favour of Henry at the Mise of Amiens on 23 January 1264, and declared that the Provisions were revoked in their entirety. Meanwhile in Wales, Llywelyn had succeeded in recapturing the last two English-held castles in Gwynedd. Dyserth was taken by assault on 4 August after a siege of five weeks, whereas Degannwy was surrendered by its garrison on 28 September, with both castles then demolished by the Welsh. Llywelyn was now in the ascendency in Wales, with the embattled Marcher lords unable to offer any effective opposition to him due to the domestic turmoil in England.[16]

News of the outcome of the Mise of Amiens led to the resumption of fighting in England, with supporters of Montfort refusing to accept the decision. In the Marches of Wales, Montfort's two sons, Simon and Henry, attacked the lands of Roger de Mortimer and took Radnor Castle with the assistance of Llywelyn. They subsequently captured the castles of Roger Clifford and Thomas Corbet before taking Worcester by storm on 28 February. Lord Edward responded by joining forces with Mortimer at Hereford and then proceeded to take Humphrey de Bohun's castles of Hay and Huntingdon. From there he advanced southwards to Gloucester, which had been captured by the rebels through deception, with the royalist garrison besieged in the castle. Edward succeeded in gaining entry to the castle on 5 March, but was placed in jeopardy soon afterwards by the arrival of the main Montfortian force led by Henry de Montfort. Yet Edward succeeded in removing himself from danger again by negotiating a brief truce with his opponents. Edward then joined forces with his father, who was in the process of assembling the royal army at Oxford. On 3 April, the king led his army northwards and reached Northampton on the following evening, which was held by Simon de Montfort the Younger, with a large garrison. The next day the royalists mounted an assault and quickly made a breach in the walls with their siege weapons. This allowed them to storm the town, with the garrison of the castle surrendering on the following day. According to the chronicler William Rishanger, fifteen barons and sixty knights were taken prisoner by the victors. Further royalist successes came in quick succession, with the royal army entering Leicester without resistance on 11 April and Nottingham on the next day. Henry then sent Edward westwards to ravage the lands of Robert de Ferrers, Earl of Derby, in Derbyshire and Staffordshire. The author of the *Flowers of History* states that his forces 'laid waste with fire and sword' the lands of Robert de Ferrers and 'overthrew his castle of Tutbury, and inflicted miserable destruction on it'. These royalist victories in the Midlands were only tempered by the loss of Warwick Castle, which was captured through treachery by a contingent led by John Giffard from the Kenilworth garrison. In the south-east, Simon de Montfort laid siege to Rochester on 17 April, which was held by the royalist commanders, John de Warenne, Earl of Surrey, and Roger de Leybourne. The assaults of the attackers were initially beaten off by the defenders, but they then used a fireship to set alight the city's bridge, which had a wooden tower on it. In the chaos that ensued, the besiegers resumed their attacks on the walls and succeeded in storming the city. The next day, they took the outer bailey of the castle by subjecting the defenders to heavy missile fire from their siege weapons and crossbows, forcing the garrison to withdraw into the keep. Montfort then set about reducing the keep by deploying siege weapons to bombard the defenders and miners to dig tunnels under its foundations. However, news arrived on 25 April that the king's army was rapidly approaching London, prompting him to withdraw from Rochester with most of his forces to the capital.[17]

The royal army lifted the siege on 28 April and after a brief break moved southwards to receive the submission of the garrison of Tonbridge Castle. Henry next moved to the coast to subdue the Cinque Ports, which submitted without resistance, although his soldiers suffered casualties from local archers while crossing the woods of the Weald in Sussex and Kent. The royal army reached Lewes on 11 May and two days later was confronted by Montfort's army. After peace negotiations were rebuffed by the king, the Battle of Lewes took place on 14 May. Despite their superior numbers, the royalists were quickly defeated, with the king and the Lord Edward taken prisoner. Henry was compelled to agree to the Mise of Lewes, thereby surrendering all effective power to Montfort and becoming a puppet ruler. Montfort was then able to use his control over his royal captives to gradually compel royalist constables to relinquish their castles to his supporters. The author of the *Greater Chronicle* states that he took Henry and Edward 'with him wherever he went, until he had got possession of all the strongest castles in the kingdom'. Yet he faced continued opposition from the powerful Marcher lords in the west, and from Queen Eleanor in Flanders, where she raised an army of mercenaries poised to invade England. The hostility of the former prompted Montfort to lead an army to the Marches of Wales in July, where he received military assistance from Llywelyn. His forces quickly overran the castles of Hay, Hereford and Ludlow, with the Marcher lords soon compelled to treat for peace. The terms of this agreement included the surrender of the royal castles in their possession and the release of the remaining Montfortian prisoners taken at the capture of Northampton. Montfort also succeeded in delaying Eleanor's invasion through engaging in protracted negotiations with her patron, King Louis, and the papal legate, Guy Foulquois. This stalling tactic worked, as the queen's funds were exhausted by October, which led to her army disbanding itself. Undeterred by this development, the Marcher lords rose in rebellion in October and seized control of the castles of Bridgnorth, Gloucester and Marlborough. A bold attempt was also made to rescue Edward from captivity in Wallingford by a contingent from the garrison of Bristol Castle. According to the account of Robert of Gloucester, the force of 300 men managed to gain entry to the castle but were forced to withdraw after the defenders threatened to propel Edward over the battlements from one of their siege weapons. Montfort finally moved against the Marcher lords in November and, with the support of Llywelyn, again forced them to seek terms. This time the conditions were stringent, they had to agree to go into exile to Ireland for a year, after which they would be judged by their peers, with their castles and estates in the meanwhile transferred to the custody of Montfort. The success of this campaign prompted the submission of the garrisons of many of the remaining royalist castles over the following months. By the end of March 1265, only three castles remained under the control of royalist castellans: Bamburgh, Richmond and Pevensey. The latter had been besieged by Simon de Montfort the Younger since September with a strong force, which had dug a ditch outside the defences to confine the garrison within the walls. However, despite deploying siege weapons and blockading the defenders by land and sea, they were unable to capture the castle.[18]

Nevertheless, Montfort was confident enough about his control over the kingdom to agree to the conditional release of the Lord Edward from captivity in March 1265. The latter had restraints put on his movements, including the supervision of an armed escort, and was obliged to transfer five castles into the control of Montfort. Two months later, Edward managed to outwit his guards at Hereford and fled to Roger de Mortimer's castle at Wigmore. He soon raised an army with the forces provided by the Marcher lords, who had delayed their departure to Ireland. Further reinforcements were provided by disaffected Montfortian supporters, such as Gilbert de Clare, Earl of Gloucester, who were dissatisfied with Montfort's increasingly autocratic style of rule. The first blow was struck by James de Audley and Urian de Saint Pierre, who seized control of Beeston Castle on 6 June. They then laid siege to Chester Castle but were unable to take it due to the fierce resistance put up by the defenders, but succeeded in keeping the garrison pinned behind the walls. Edward's supporters soon afterwards took control of Worcester, Shrewsbury, Ludlow and Bridgnorth. Gloucester was taken after a siege on 14 June, although the garrison of the castle held out for a further fifteen days. Montfort's reaction to these events was slow, with the speed of the royalist offensive taking him off-guard. The loss of Worcester and Gloucester meant that he was trapped on the wrong side of the River Severn, and cut off from his supporters in England. In desperation, he sought military assistance from Llywelyn, who was happy to exploit his ally's predicament by exacting substantial concessions.

A treaty was concluded on 19 June at Pipton, whereby the latter agreed to pay a large sum of money and provide soldiers in return for being recognised as Prince of Wales. Montfort then moved his reinforced army southwards to Monmouth on 24 June, whose royalist garrison surrendered after a short siege. He then attacked Gilbert de Clare's castle at Usk and had taken the fortress by 2 July. His next move was to travel to Newport, where he intended to rendezvous with a fleet from Bristol. However, this plan was thwarted due to the defeat of the latter at the hands of a royalist flotilla. To avoid Edward's army that was rapidly closing in from the east, he burnt the bridge at Newport and moved northwards to the territory of his ally Llywelyn in Gwent. From there he then marched eastwards and reached Hereford on 16 July. In the meantime, Simon de Montfort the Younger, in response to his father's increasingly desperate appeals for assistance, had finally lifted the siege of Pevensey Castle and marched to his aid, reaching Kenilworth Castle on 31 July. News of his movements soon reached the royalists at Worcester some thirty miles away. Edward responded by marching his mounted forces through the night to Kenilworth, where they caught their opponents completely unawares. Simon de Montfort the Younger had mistakenly believed that the royalists were much further away and so was safe from attack. Therefore, his army was quartered in the town and priory, rather than behind the safety of the castle walls, and it was swiftly routed. At the same time, Montfort's army succeeded in crossing the River Severn using the ford at Kempsey and moved eastwards to Evesham. It was there that they were intercepted by Edward's army, with the Battle of Evesham taking place on 4 August. The outnumbered Montfortians were utterly defeated, with Simon de Montfort and many of his men killed both during and after the battle.[19]

News of the outcome of the battle led to a collapse in the baronial position, with many castles surrendered by their garrisons to the royalists. Wallingford and Berkhamsted were relinquished on 7 August, while the Tower of London was handed over by Alina, widow of Sir Hugh Despenser, in September. In the following month, the royalist prisoners kept in Dover Castle staged an uprising against their guards and took control of the keep. Lord Edward responded to this development by laying siege to Dover with his army and soon forced Montfort's widow, Eleanor, to surrender the castle. However, the victory at Evesham did not immediately end the war. Royalist reprisals and confiscations meant that some of the surviving Montfortians, known as the disinherited, continued to put up a desperate struggle from their stronghold at Kenilworth Castle. Bands of rebels roamed the countryside carrying out attacks and spreading disorder across the kingdom. Simon de Montfort the Younger left Kenilworth in November and went to the fens of Lincolnshire, using the Isle of Axholme as a base from which to launch raids into the surrounding area.

Edward dealt with this threat by attacking the rebels in the following month. His army succeeded in outflanking the defences of the disinherited, by constructing a wooden bridge across the fens, which forced them to surrender under terms around Christmas. Despite this agreement, the garrison of Kenilworth Castle rejected all calls for them to surrender. The king eventually issued orders for the raising of the royal army in the spring of 1266, with the siege of the rebel stronghold taking place in June. The formidable defences of the castle meant that this would prove to be a difficult and lengthy undertaking. Kenilworth was a large castle, encircled by a huge artificial lake, which contained an outer and inner bailey, with a magnificent keep situated within the inner bailey. Its fortifications had been improved in recent years by Simon de Montfort and according to the author of the *Flowers of History* was said to have been 'furnished in an admirable manner with all kinds of engines, which had never been seen or heard of among us before'. The garrison had also prepared for the siege by laying in substantial quantities of provisions and they were determined to put up a fierce resistance, as they expected to be shown no mercy by the vengeful king.

The royalists began the siege by surrounding the castle and erecting siege weapons. They were well supplied with military equipment, including 60,000 crossbow quarrels and 2,000 wooden hurdles to be used as protective screens against the missile fire of the defenders. The besiegers used their stone-throwing siege weapons to bombard the castle. One of these projectiles was discovered by archaeologists in the 1960s in the outer bailey, which had been hurled more than 300 metres over the lake and had destroyed one of the internal buildings. Nevertheless, the missile fire and frequent sallies of the defenders caused heavy casualties among the attackers, who were unable to undermine the walls due to the lake. The garrison also succeeded in destroying the wooden siege towers deployed against the walls by the besiegers, and defeated attempts by the royalists to use barges to attack the castle from the lake. These setbacks encouraged Henry to change tack and to adopt a more conciliatory approach towards resolving the conflict. A committee of magnates and bishops was appointed by the parliament of August 1266 to draw up a peace settlement, which was known as the Dictum of Kenilworth. This was issued on 31 October with reasonable terms for the Montfortian rebels, who were permitted to avoid the confiscation of their estates in return for paying substantial fines. The garrison of Kenilworth at first rejected these terms, but dwindling food supplies eventually prompted them to surrender on 13 December. During the next year, the war with Llywelyn was also ended through negotiations, with the Treaty of Montgomery agreed on 29 September 1267.[20]

The Conquest of Wales: 1267–1295

In the Welshery a ribald is arisen, who believed that the king was gone beyond sea; he has seized Snowdon as his heritage, caused himself to be entitled prince by name of kindred. He has put to death the English, as many as are found, has broken down to the ground the king's castles. The king cannot suffer his iniquities; he has already delayed the war in Gascony, and has entered under Snowdon into Wales. In Aberconway, a castle well strengthened, he held his Christmas with many of his barons. From Christmas forward till after Easter lasted the war in Wales, very troublesome to the king ... and immediately after Easter the king and the barons drive out the Welsh, and seize Snowdon. The king, when he comes there, causes to be proclaimed everywhere his peace to all who will come to pardon.

The Chronicle of Pierre de Langtoft[1]

The suppression of the rebellion of Madog ap Llywelyn in 1295 marked the end of the Welsh struggle against the English. Over the course of two wars, in 1277 and 1282–3, Edward had defeated the Welsh prince, Llywelyn ap Gruffudd, and had conquered his principality. Uprisings by the Welsh in 1287 and 1294–5 were crushed, leaving the whole of Wales under the control of the English king. The ruling house of Gwynedd was all but extinguished, with the Welsh a conquered people, forced to acquiesce to the imposition of English methods of administration and law. Yet the conquest had been a difficult process, which was only possible due to the substantial resources that Edward was able to bring to bear against the Welsh, in both manpower and finance. The unpopularity of Llywelyn's rule as Prince of Wales meant that he was quickly defeated in the short war of 1277, with his power dramatically reduced. However, the second conflict was of a very different nature. Resentment at the harsh nature of English governance led to the outbreak of a full-scale rebellion across Wales in 1282, with Llywelyn leading the national struggle by the Welsh against Edward. The prosecution of this war was costly for the English, with victory only achieved after a year of hard fighting. To secure the conquest, Edward embarked on a major programme of castle-building in Wales, with eight major royal castles constructed at great expense. These structures are some of the finest castles ever built in Europe, four of which are recognised by UNESCO as world heritage sites: Beaumaris, Caernarfon, Conwy and Harlech. Architecturally they are distinct from earlier castles, except for Builth, as the great tower or keep was no longer the most important part of the structure. Instead the most notable features were now elaborate gatehouses, and a change in style meant that towers were now usually round as opposed to square. The survival of building accounts for these castles means that their construction can be traced in detail, including the leading role played by a master mason from Savoy, James of St George, in supervising the programme of works. They were intended to overawe the Welsh with their size and splendour and to symbolise the permanence of the conquest. Yet the building of these castles did not fully pacify the Welsh for some time to come, with two major rebellions taking place later in the century. What is more, Madog's uprising of 1294–5 occurred at a very inopportune moment for Edward, entangled as he was with affairs in France and Scotland, which distracted his attentions at a critical junction from the war in Gascony.

The Apogee of Gwynedd

The Treaty of Montgomery was a great triumph for Llywelyn; he was recognised by Henry III as Prince of Wales and as the feudal overlord of the other native rulers of Wales, who held their lands as fiefs from him. Llywelyn also retained most of the territory he had conquered during the civil war in England. In return, he had to give homage and fealty to the king and pay the large sum of £16,650 in instalments. The financial terms of this agreement did impose a heavy burden on his administration, but he was left in possession of all of Wales, bar the Marcher lordships in the south-west and south-east. Llywelyn was the most powerful native ruler in Wales since the Norman invasion in the eleventh century. He sought to maintain his power by taking hostages from his vassals and imposing fines on suspected malcontents. Llywelyn also imposed his authority through initiating a programme of castle building. These works included improving existing castles, notably those constructed in Gwynedd during the reign of his grandfather, Llywelyn ap Iorwerth. The castle of Cricieth, situated in a dramatic coastal location on a headland, was an enclosure castle that was entered via an impressive twin-towered three-storey gatehouse. Its extent was significantly expanded through the addition of an outer ward and a large rectangular tower on its south-west side. Work was also carried out at Castell y Bere in the south of Gwynedd, which was located on high ground in the shadow of the mountain of Cadair Idris. The defences of the castle were enhanced through adding a new tower, barbican and gate, and digging a deep ditch around its perimeter, thereby creating a formidable entrance for any visitor or attacker. Llywelyn also built new castles on the eastern borders of his newly acquired territory. Ewloe was constructed in the early 1260s; close to Chester on the north-east frontier of Gwynedd. The castle has an inner and outer ward, with the former dominated by a two-storey apsidal keep, whereas the latter had a slightly smaller round tower on its western side. In the 1270s, Dolforwyn was built in central-east Wales, together with an adjoining town, to contest the dominance of nearby Montgomery. The sizeable rectangular enclosure castle is surrounded by a ditch and incorporated two large towers, one round and the other square, with the courtyard bisected by an inner ditch. Llywelyn's substantial investment in castle-building demonstrated his power and prestige, and showed that the Welsh had adapted to English methods of warfare. Yet these fortresses were greatly overshadowed by the castles constructed by the Marcher lords in the same period. Unlike the small castles generally built by the Welsh on remote rocky outcrops, the English erected much larger structures in the centre of their estates and lordships. Earlier in the century, the Marshal family had spent heavily on castle-building in the Marches, notably at Chepstow, Cilgerran, Pembroke and Usk. Following the failure of the male line after the death of Anselm Marshal in 1245, these castles passed into the possession of the Bigod and Valence families, who further improved them. The most spectacular baronial castle of this period was constructed by Gilbert de Clare, Earl of Gloucester, at Caerphilly in Glamorgan from 1267 to 1290. Caerphilly is a concentric castle, with a middle and inner ward encircled by a moat, bank, two large lakes, dams and outer defences. These features meant that the castle was an imposing fortress and was visually stunning. The possession of these castles gave the Marcher lords well-fortified bases from which they could begin the recovery of the lands they had previously lost to the Welsh.[2]

The costs of Llywelyn's castle-building contributed to the financial problems experienced by his government. His principality was forced to pay a substantial annual tribute to the English Crown, as well as meeting other expenses, including giving rewards to his followers, funding embassies to foreign rulers and paying the wages of soldiers. Traditional Welsh methods of fundraising were inadequate to meet these outgoings, so his officials were forced to resort to ever more exploitative techniques to raise money, which fostered resentment of Llywelyn's government, with the prince driven to imposing fines and demanding hostages from reluctant vassals. He also faced the problem of worsening relations with England. Border disputes with the Marcher lords led to the outbreak of fighting in south-east Wales in the early 1270s. Llywelyn's anger at Gilbert de Clare's decision to build a castle at Caerphilly in 1268 resulted in him attacking and temporarily damaging the incomplete fortress two years later. Hostilities also broke out in Breconshire and Maelienydd, after disagreements over the territorial settlement of the Treaty of Montgomery. Llywelyn's worsening relationship with the English Crown only served to further amplify these existing problems. The Welsh prince continued to meet his financial obligations during the last years of the reign of Henry III, but he quickly fell out with the latter's successor, Edward, on his succession to the throne in 1272.

Llywelyn stopped paying the annual instalments to the English Crown and failed to give fealty to the new king when instructed to do so in January 1273. He also refused a command by Edward's government to stop building his new castle at Dolforwyn. The Welsh prince believed that the English had failed to honour the terms of the Treaty of Montgomery and intended to withhold payment until he received satisfaction. Relations continued to deteriorate in the following year. Llywelyn did not attend the coronation of Edward at Westminster on 19 August 1274, where he was due to pay homage, following the latter's return to England after a four-year absence. Later that year, a conspiracy was discovered against Llywelyn's life, led by his brother, Dafydd, and Gruffudd ap Gwenwynwyn. The fugitives succeeded in escaping to England where they were well treated by Edward. Another point of contention was caused by Llywelyn's provocative decision to go ahead with his arranged marriage to Eleanor, daughter of Simon de Montfort. The marriage was carried out by proxy in 1275, but the bride and her brother, Amaury, were captured at sea in the Bristol Channel and were imprisoned by Edward. Further instructions were issued to Llywelyn to travel to England to give homage to the king in October 1275, January 1276 and April 1276, but he failed to obey these summonses. The Welsh prince was unhappy about the intensification of fighting in the border regions and he feared for his safety should he have visited the English court, especially as Edward was harbouring his enemies.[3]

The War of 1277

Edward publicly announced his decision to go to war with Llywelyn at a council held at Westminster on 12 November 1276. Orders were at once issued for the feudal army to assemble at Worcester on 1 July in the following year. In the meantime, provision was made for the defence of the Marches, with soldiers and supplies sent to reinforce English territory. Payn de Chaworth was placed in command of west Wales at Carmarthen, Roger de Mortimer was appointed to hold the central Marches from Montgomery, and William de Beauchamp, earl of Warwick, was sent to defend the north operating from Chester. A strong contingent of knights and serjeants were sent from the royal household to augment their forces, which were steadily strengthened by the arrival of further reinforcements. Before the end of the year these armies had gone on the offensive against the Welsh. In the south, Payn de Chaworth advanced up the Vale of Towy and by 11 April had compelled the prominent southern lord, Rhys ap Maredudd, to submit to the king and to surrender his castle of Dynevor. Meanwhile in the central Marches, Roger de Mortimer's forces penetrated westwards into Montgomeryshire. They were assisted in this venture by support from Gruffudd ap Gwenwynwyn and other Welshmen in English service, who succeeded in winning over many of the locals to Edward's side, a task made easier by the unpopularity of the Welsh prince's rule. Llywelyn's expensive new fortress at Dolforwyn was besieged at the end of March, with the garrison surrendering after only nine days due to a lack of water. Confronted with this, many of Llywelyn's vassals had surrendered to the king by the beginning of July, leaving only Gwynedd under the control of the Welsh prince. The second stage of the campaign saw a combined assault on Gwynedd, with the king's brother, Edmund Crouchback, Earl of Lancaster, advancing northwards from Carmarthen with one army, while Edward moved westwards from Chester with the main force, which was supplied by a fleet provided by the Cinque Ports. The king was keen to avoid the mistakes made by previous English armies that had invaded north Wales, which had frequently been defeated by the difficult terrain, poor weather and Welsh guerrilla tactics. Therefore, this was a carefully planned and executed operation, with particular attention paid to the organisation of logistics.[4]

The royal army of approximately 800 knights and serjeants and 2,500 infantry was accompanied by a large contingent of auxiliary workers, including axemen who were employed in clearing a passage through the thick woods, thereby reducing the risk posed by Welsh ambushes. After leaving Chester on 21 July, the army marched eleven miles north-westwards to Flint, on the coast, and reached there four days later. Edward then issued instructions for a field camp to be established to serve as a base for the next stage of the offensive, with substantial quantities of equipment and provisions transported there from Chester. A large workforce, numbering hundreds of men, was used to fortify the encampment with banks and ditches, while protected by a sizeable garrison of archers and crossbowmen. In the following month, the army moved westwards across the coast and arrived at Rhuddlan on 20 August, where further field fortifications were erected. Edward now commanded a considerable force of 15,000 infantry, of which 9,000 were Welshmen, although the size of his cavalry arm had been significantly reduced after the expiry of the forty days of unpaid feudal service. Rather than risk advancing into the mountains of Gwynedd, instead he detached a force to occupy Anglesey. At a stroke, this cut off the Welsh from the main area of food production in north Wales, a move that the chronicler Bartholomew Cotton characterised as beginning a siege of Snowdonia. Meanwhile, Edmund Crouchback had advanced to the southern border of Gwynedd and had begun work on the construction of a castle at Aberystwyth. Llywelyn was thus surrounded, having been deserted by many of his vassals, and had little realistic prospect of maintaining himself in the mountains through the winter. He was compelled to seek peace with Edward, with the Treaty of Aberconwy agreed on 9 November. The terms of this agreement saw a severe reduction in the power and prestige of the Welsh prince. He was forced to relinquish most of his territories, with his realm now reduced to the western part of Gwynedd, although he was permitted to retain the title Prince of Wales and the homage of five minor lords.[5]

Edward had therefore achieved a decisive victory over his rival Llywelyn, who was now reduced to ruling over a small client state. By exploiting the grievances of Llywelyn's subjects, including his brother Dafydd, Edward had succeeded in undermining much of his rival's power before the first blow was struck, which meant that the war of 1277 was relatively short and inexpensive. Yet he had refrained from attempting the total conquest of Wales. To achieve a complete victory, he would have had to penetrate into the heartlands of Llywelyn's domains in Snowdonia itself. This enterprise would have been a far more risky and expensive undertaking; instead, he was content to have imposed his mastery with his rival now humbled. To secure his conquests he ordered the construction of four new royal castles to encircle Gwynedd. Work to rebuild the castle of Builth on the Upper Wye, destroyed by Llywelyn in 1260, began as early as 3 May, soon after the area had been occupied by the forces of Roger de Mortimer.

Temporary timber buildings were quickly erected to house the workforce and garrison, while construction began on the keep. Work continued throughout the winter, with the wooden buildings replaced by masonry ones that were covered in straw to protect them from the elements. In the following year, further buildings were finished with the average weekly labour force consisting of around 140 workers, including masons, labourers, mortar makers, diggers, barrowmen and watchmen. By October 1280, substantial progress had been made on the construction of the wall of the outer bailey, as well as six towers, the keep, the wall of the inner bailey and a 'turning' bridge flanked by two large towers. The danger of a Welsh attack meant that the workforce was initially protected by a garrison of fifty men, which was reduced to fourteen men in 1278. By the time that work was completed in September 1282, the castle had cost a sizeable sum – in excess of £1,600. By comparison, more than double this amount was spent in this period on the building of Aberystwyth Castle on the west coast of Wales. Construction of Aberystwyth Castle and its adjoining town started on 1 August 1277, with the initial workforce including a team of 120 carpenters and 120 masons recruited from the West Country. The labour force had increased to more than 1,100 workers in October 1279, by which time work had begun on erecting the inner buildings. Despite this substantial outlay, a critical report on the state of the castle was sent to the king and his council by Bogo de Knovill, the newly appointed justiciar of west Wales in early 1280. According to his testimony, when he took possession of the castle it lacked provisions and supplies, as well as a garrison. What was more, the condition of part of the structure was inadequate and needed to be inspected by a master of the works. The progress of work on the main gate was also hampered by its location, as it was sited too close to the outer ditch, which meant that its foundations were unstable and prone to damage from the sea. Little was done to rectify these problems prior to the outbreak of unrest in 1282, although £200 was spent on the construction of the town wall. By comparison, much greater sums of money were spent on the construction of the castles of Flint and Rhuddlan in north-east Wales.[6]

These castles were intended to secure English control over the newly acquired territory east of the River Conwy and were to be adjoined by new towns inhabited by settlers from England. Work on fortifying these sites began during Edward's campaign in northern Wales in the summer of 1277. The author of the *Chronicle of the Princes* notes that the king 'fortified a court in Flint with huge ditches around it. Thence he came to Rhuddlan and fortified it, too, with ditches around it'. By the end of August, almost 2,300 ditch diggers had been assembled at Flint, although many of these workers subsequently moved to Rhuddlan and other building sites, including the baronial castle under construction at Ruthin. Most of the initial work over the first couple of years was focused on the digging of ditches and erecting a timber palisade around the town. Attention had shifted to the construction of masonry buildings within the castle by 1281, with an average of 190 masons employed between April and August. The finished structure eventually consisted of an outer and inner ward, the latter having towers on three of its corners. It was abutted on its south-east corner by a much larger tower that was separated from the rest of the castle by a ditch, which was filled by water at high tide. The coastal location of Flint meant that equipment, supplies and workers could be easily transported to the site by sea.

By contrast, Rhuddlan was situated more than two miles inland, on the banks of the River Clwyd near the site of an older abandoned castle at Twthill. It was therefore necessary to straighten and dredge the river to make it navigable by ships. Over the course of the next three years, a team of, on average, sixty-six diggers, working six days a week, were employed on the task, which was completed by November 1280. This was a major feat of medieval engineering that meant the new castle and town could be supplied by water. It was intended to serve as the administrative centre of north-east Wales, hence its construction was prioritised by the king's officials, with the structure mostly complete by 1280. Rhuddlan has a similar design to Flint, with an inner and outer ward, flanked on three sides by a moat and the other by the river, with the most prominent features being the two inner gatehouses, each flanked by two towers. Large sums of money were expended on these castles, with more than £7,000 spent on the construction of Flint and almost £9,500 on Rhuddlan, from 1277 to 1285. Further sums were expended on repairs and improvements carried out on Welsh castles that were acquired during the war, such as to Carreg Cennen. Instructions were also sent out to royal officials to clear roads and passes, to mitigate the risk of Welsh ambushes, to aid the movement of soldiers.[7]

The Conquest of Wales

Welsh discontent led to the outbreak of the second war in 1282. The initial uprising was led by Llywelyn's brother, Dafydd, who had fought for Edward in the war of 1277, but who was now dissatisfied with the lands granted to him as part of the territorial settlement. Rather than being given a share of his ancestral lands in Gwynedd, he was instead allocated the lordship of Hope, where he began the construction of a castle, as well as a life interest in two of the Four Cantrefs, Dyffryn Clwyd and Rhufuniog. He was also unhappy about his treatment by royal officials, such as Reynold de Grey, justice of Chester, who were said to have interfered in the administration of his lands. This discontent was shared by other Welsh nobles. Gruffudd ap Maredudd, a descendant of the Lord Rhys, had submitted to the king at the beginning of the previous war and had served at his own expense during the conflict, but still suffered the confiscation of half of his estates. Llywelyn himself was unwilling to abide by the Treaty of Aberconwy and soon joined in the hostilities. At first his relationship with Edward had been positive. He had been treated with leniency in the peace settlement and his marriage to Eleanor de Montfort finally took place with royal consent at Worcester in the presence of the king and court in 1278. Yet a territorial dispute over the lordship of Arwystli alienated the Welsh prince, who also faced harassment at the hands of royal officials. He was therefore a willing participant in the conflict against the king. Hostilities began with Dafydd capturing Hawarden Castle through a surprise night attack on 21 March 1282, with the Justice of Wales, Roger de Clifford, taken prisoner. Three days later Aberystwyth was taken through treachery, with the town and castle burnt by the Welsh. Attacks were also launched on English-held settlements in south Wales, with the castles of Llandovery and Carreg Cennen captured. Unlike in 1277, Edward had not anticipated conflict in Wales and so was taken by surprise by these attacks. Nevertheless, he responded quickly on 25 March by appointing lieutenants to hold key commands. Reginald de Grey was placed in command at Chester, Roger de Mortimer at Montgomery and Robert de Tibetot in south Wales, with the latter replaced soon afterwards by Gilbert de Clare, Earl of Gloucester. As in the previous war, the plan for the campaign was for the king to lead the main army along the coast into north Wales, while his commanders conducted independent operations throughout the rest of the country. Large numbers of soldiers were recruited over the next few months – by 15 June approximately 800 cavalry and 7,000 footmen were serving in Wales. Interestingly, a high proportion of the latter were armed with longbows, in contrast to earlier conflicts where the English had preferred to employ melee armed infantry and crossbowmen. This was almost certainly a reaction to Welsh success in the use of the longbow. While the feudal host was assembling at Rhuddlan, Reginald de Grey was sent to attack Dafydd's castle at Hope, in Flintshire. Rather than risk being trapped behind the walls, the Welsh defenders had abandoned and slighted the fortress prior to his arrival on 16 June. It was therefore necessary to rebuild the castle so that it could serve as a base for future operations. Hundreds of carpenters, woodmen and masons were brought to the site to carry out repairs and refurbishments, which included demolishing the damaged keep. A large garrison of 2,600 archers was allocated to protect this workforce, under the command of the castle's newly appointed constable Hugh de Pulford. By the end of the month, Richard de Grey had taken Ewloe Castle, while Hawarden had been vacated by Dafydd's men. However, the English had less success in the south of Wales, with Gilbert's de Clare army falling victim to a Welsh ambush on 17 June, which resulted in heavy casualties. This led to his replacement by William de Valence, Earl of Pembroke, who led an expedition to pacify Cardiganshire in August and September.[8]

The royal army had in the meanwhile assembled at Rhuddlan, which, by the end of August, comprised almost 9,000 men, approximately 750 cavalry and 8,000 infantry. Edward's next move, as had been the case in 1277, was to send a naval force to occupy Anglesey, to cut off the Welsh from the principal food production region in the north of the country. An ambitious project was conceived to build a bridge of boats across the Menai Strait to link the island to the mainland, with work having started by September. Barges were constructed by carpenters at Chester, which were then transported to the site, where they were linked together to form a platform large enough for the passage of soldiers. Despite the difficulties posed by this enterprise, the bridge was completed by the beginning of November when an English force under the command of Luke de Tany crossed over to the island. Yet this venture ended in disaster, when the English were ambushed after attempting to retreat to the mainland and suffered heavy losses. According to the author of the *Chronicle of St Werburgh's Abbey*, sixteen knights, sixteen esquires and 300 footmen were killed. Edward was undeterred by this setback; he issued instructions for the recruitment of more soldiers to participate in an invasion of Snowdonia. Soon afterwards his ranks were further swelled by the arrival of reinforcements from Gascony. Yet the situation was transformed by Llywelyn's decision to leave the mountains of Snowdonia and to advance eastwards to Builth. By this bold move he hoped to benefit from the disruption that had been caused to the defence of the central Marches by the recent death of Roger de Mortimer. However, Llywelyn's army was intercepted by a force led by Roger Lestrange and his army was defeated and he was killed on 11 December. His death dealt a heavy blow to the Welsh cause. Dafydd assumed the title of Prince of Wales but he lacked his brother's prestige and authority. The resulting chaos gave the king the opportunity to strike a decisive blow by moving into Snowdonia. Edward advanced inland from his base at Rhuddlan into mountains and had reached Betws-y-Coed by 18 January. A detachment of his army took possession of Dolwyddelan Castle at the same time, possibly through a pre-arranged agreement with its defenders. In the meantime, Anglesey had been pacified by an English force, which was then sent to occupy Harlech on the west coast of Gwynedd. In March, Edward moved his headquarters westwards from Rhuddlan to Conwy, where temporary buildings were constructed to house the army and court, with a garrison also having been established at Bangor. From the south, the armies of Roger Lestrange and William de Valence joined forces and laid siege to Castell y Bere, which surrendered after a ten-day siege on 25 April. Dafydd was now hemmed in on all sides into an ever-shrinking pocket of territory so went on the run into the wilds of Snowdonia. He was eventually captured by Welshmen, possibly through treachery, and was handed over to the king in June. Edward was no in mood to show mercy to a man who had betrayed him. After being convicted of treason at the parliament held at Shrewsbury, he was subjected to a gruesome death, being hanged, drawn and quartered. His execution effectively ended any remaining resistance.[9]

Edward's conquest was a great achievement – for the first time all of Wales was now under the control of the king of England and his subjects. Yet experience had shown that the Welsh could recover from serious setbacks. It was therefore necessary to ensure that the conquest was secured by the founding of new castles and towns in north Wales. Thousands of workers were employed by the Crown on these projects, with the work supervised by a master mason recruited from Savoy, James of St George. His skill in organising multiple complex building projects meant that he played a leading role in co-ordinating the king's works in Wales. These buildings were built on a lavish, grand scale, surpassing even the edifices constructed following the war of 1277. The new castles had formidable defences that made them difficult to capture, particularly as they were located on the coast and could be supplied by sea. They were also deliberately situated in areas of great symbolic and cultural importance to the Welsh, thereby demonstrating to the inhabitants that the conquest was permanent. This can be seen at Conwy, where work began on building a new castle and town in March 1282. These buildings were constructed on a site previously occupied by Aberconwy Abbey, which had been founded by Llywelyn ap Iorwerth, and a hall that had served as Llywelyn's ap Gruffudd's main residence. The monks of the abbey were forced to relocate seven miles upriver to Maenan; however, the fabric of the manor house was retained within the walls of the new borough. Conwy Castle was constructed on a prominent rocky outcrop that overlooked the estuary and the adjacent town. However, unlike the nearby site of Degannwy Castle, provisions could easily be transported there by water, thereby avoiding the fate of the castles built in the area by Henry III, which had been cut off and isolated by the Welsh. The castle has a rectangular shape that incorporates an outer and inner ward, which are flanked by eight large round towers. Access from the town was via a fortified bridge that led to the west barbican adjacent to the outer ward, whereas entry by boat was via the Watergate, with stairs leading up to the east barbican by the inner ward. Despite the size of the project, most of the town and castle was constructed quickly over the course of five intensive building seasons from 1283–7 at the cost of £15,000. A garrison was installed in 1284 to protect the fortress, which the king specified should consist of at least thirty men, including fifteen crossbowmen. Yet as grand and imposing as Conwy was and still is, an even more impressive castle was constructed at Caernarfon some twenty-one miles along the coast to the south-west. It was situated near the ruins of the Roman fort of Segontium and was built in a style that resembled Roman architecture, with its distinctive polygonal banded towers. Caernarfon has a rectangular shape with an inner and outer ward, with entry to the castle via two grand twin-towered gatehouses. It was designed to operate as the administrative centre of north-west Wales, with more than £20,000 spent on its construction, from 1283 to 1330. Yet despite this vast expenditure the design was never fully completed, with important features, such as the internal gatehouse that was intended to separate the inner and outer wards, remaining unfinished. A more modest but still substantial castle was constructed at Harlech on the west coast of Wales, which is situated on a rocky crag that faces the sea. Building started in June 1282 and was carried on until the beginning of 1290 when it was finished at a cost of approximately £9,500.

Harlech is a square concentric castle with two layers of wall that enclose the inner ward. As with Conwy and Caernarfon, it could be supplied by sea and was defended by a moat, with its most impressive feature being its twin-towered gatehouse. Work was also carried out at other royal castles in Wales. These works included repairs to fortresses that had been damaged during the war, such as Aberystwyth, as well as improvements that were made to native Welsh castles after they were acquired by the Crown, such as to Cricieth and Castell y Bere.[10]

Welsh Rebellions

The conquest of Wales was followed by the territorial disinheritance of many of the native Welsh noble and princely families, who were punished for their adherence to Llywelyn and Dafydd. Even those Welsh lords who had consistently supported the king, such as Rhys ap Maredudd, Lord of Dryslwyn, were only allocated comparatively modest gains. More substantial grants were made to some of the English Marcher lords, with Roger Mortimer junior given the lordship of Chirk and Henry de Lacy, Earl of Lincolnshire, with the lordship of Denbigh. However, most of the conquered lands, including Gwynedd in the north-west, were kept by the Crown. The governance of these newly acquired royal lands was set out in the Statue of Rhuddlan, which was issued by the king on 3 March 1284. In the north-east the county of Flintshire was formed, under the administration of the justice of Chester, in which the lands formerly belonging to Gwynedd were now assigned to the Principality of North Wales, under the control of a newly appointed justiciar. The title of Prince of Wales was later given to the king's eldest son, also called Edward, in 1301, who had been born at Caernarfon Castle on 25 April 1284. All subsequent heirs to the English throne were to be given the same title, an arrangement that continues to this day. Yet Welsh resentment of this settlement and the imposition of English laws and taxation meant that the threat of rebellion remained, despite the king's substantial investment in castle building. On 8 June 1287 Rhys ap Maredudd rebelled against the Crown by seizing control of Llandovery Castle. He had loyally fought for the king in the wars of 1277 and 1282–3 but had become alienated by his treatment over the intervening years. His long-cherished ambition of obtaining custody of Dinefwr Castle, ancestral seat of the kingdom of Deheubarth, had been denied to him, and he had been subjected to judicial harassment from the justiciar of west Wales, Robert Tibetot. Soon after taking control of Llandovery, Rhys moved southwards with his forces and overran the castles of Dinefwr and Carreg Cennen. He then marched eastwards to burn Swansea before proceeding northwards to Aberystwyth, where part of the town was destroyed, but the garrison of the castle held out. The king was absent in Gascony, so responsibility for suppressing the rebellion fell to his cousin, Edmund, Earl of Cornwall, who was serving as regent of the realm. Edmund responded by raising large numbers of soldiers to crush the uprising, with four separate armies ordered to assemble at Carmarthen in early August, which were to converge from Llanbadarn, Monmouth, Brecon and west Wales. By 13 August the siege of Rhys's castle of Dryslwyn had begun, with the attackers deploying a trebuchet and bringing up miners to undermine the walls. The formidable natural defences of the castle, located as it is on the top of a steep hill, meant that it was difficult to capture. Furthermore, the attackers suffered a setback when a group of knights were killed while inspecting a mine that was being dug by the besiegers. However, the superior numbers and resources of the besiegers meant that the defenders were put under intense pressure. The castle eventually fell on 5 September but not before Rhys and most of his men managed to make their escape. Rhys was now on the run but continued to pose a threat. On 2 November, the castle of Newcastle Emlyn was stormed in a surprise attack and soon afterwards the town of Llandovery was sacked. In the following month, Robert Tibetot, justiciar of west Wales, laid siege to the castle, which was taken within ten days. Yet Rhys once again managed to evade capture. Parties of Welsh soldiers were sent to hunt him down, but he remained at large until 2 April 1292, when he was betrayed to the king's men. Rhys was sent to York in chains and after a trial was hanged, drawn and quartered on 2 June.[11]

Rhys had been a menace to the English authorities, but his rebellion was confined to south-west Wales. By contrast, a far more serious uprising took place in 1294, which affected all parts of the country. This was a delayed response to the levying of a heavy tax on Wales in 1292 to pay for the king's outstanding debts, which exacerbated other grievances with English rule. A suitable opportunity for a rebellion came in 1294 when war broke out between England and France over the Duchy of Gascony. Instructions were issued for the royal army to assemble at Portsmouth at the end of September for the expedition. The demands for Welsh soldiers to participate in the campaign caused yet more resentment and gave a cover for the conspirators to raise forces in preparation for the rebellion. Unlike the uprising of 1287, this was a carefully planned insurrection, with simultaneous attacks made on castles throughout Wales at the end of September. A leading role in this uprising was played by Madog ap Llywelyn, whose father had been dispossessed of his lordship of Meirionydd by Llywelyn ap Gruffudd. He had served the king against Llywelyn in the expectation that his ancestral lands would be restored to him, but was disappointed by the post war settlement, being granted only a modest estate in Anglesey. Madog and his followers began their uprising by pillaging the church of Llanfaes before overrunning the whole island. Then they crossed over to the mainland and attacked Caernarfon, which was the administrative centre of English rule in the north-west. The defences of the town and castle were still incomplete and the rebels succeeded in overrunning the entire settlement. Roger de Pulesdon, the sheriff of Anglesey, was brutally killed and the Welsh caused considerable damage to the fortifications. Afterwards they raided throughout the valley of the Conwy, burning mills and laying waste the land. Meanwhile, attacks were made on castles in southern and central Wales, with Cardigan and Builth besieged by insurgents. The unexpected nature of the rebellion meant that the garrisons of many castles were understrength and had absentee constables. This lack of preparedness contributed to the success of the rebels in overrunning inland castles, particularly in the north, with Hawarden, Mold, Denbigh and Ruthin falling into their hands. By contrast, they were unable to capture the coastal castles, as they could be provisioned by sea, although the constable of Flint, Sir Reginald de Grey, was forced to order the burning of the town. Edward was at Portsmouth when he received news of the rebellion in Wales. The concentration of soldiers at the port for the Gascony expedition meant that it was a straightforward task to redeploy them to Wales, but frustrated the king's plans to recover his lands in France. Instructions were sent for the magnates to gather at Worcester on 21 November, with musters of troops ordered to be held at Chester, Brecon and Cardiff. Strenuous efforts were made to procure supplies for the beleaguered garrisons of the castles, with the isolated defenders of Cricieth and Harlech provided with victuals by ships from Ireland. Expeditionary forces were also sent into the interior of the country to relieve the defenders of the inland castles. A force led by John Giffard succeeded in relieving Builth, but a similar effort to relieve Castell y Bere was unsuccessful.

An attempt was also made by Henry de Lacy, Earl of Lincoln, to recover his castle of Denbigh, but he was attacked by his own tenants and forced to flee on 11 November.[12]

By December three large English armies numbering in excess of 35,000 men had mustered to suppress the rebellion. The main force was at Chester, under the command of the king, with another at Montgomery, led by William de Beauchamp, Earl of Warwick, and the third at Carmarthen, under the joint leadership of William de Valence, Earl of Pembroke, and Roger Bigod, Earl of Norfolk. Before the end of the year, these forces had begun offensive operations against the rebels. In the north, Edward moved westwards with his army and had reached Conwy by Christmas. He was met by a delegation of Welshmen who submitted to him and were pardoned in return for promising to serve in his army in France. At the beginning of the new year, he moved westwards on a raid as far west as Nefyn in the Lleyn peninsular, but suffered a setback on his return to Conwy when his baggage train was attacked and captured by the rebels. This disaster was responsible for a severe shortage of provisions in the army, which meant that for a short time the English were effectively besieged in the castle by the Welsh. According to the chronicler Walter of Guisborough, the king nobly shared the last cask of wine left in Conwy with his soldiers, rather than keeping it for his own use. Eventually further supplies were procured and the king resumed the offensive in March, when a sortie by the infantry routed a local force of rebels. Edward then proceeded to occupy Anglesey in April before crossing back to the mainland in the following month. He then marched along the west coast of Wales towards Aberystwyth. In the meanwhile, a decisive victory had been achieved by William de Beauchamp, who defeated Madog's army at the Battle of Maes Moydog on 5 March, although the rebel leader managed to escape from the battlefield. Further defeats were inflicted on the Welsh in quick succession by Humphrey de Bohun, Earl of Hereford, and Reginald de Grey, which effectively ended the rebellion. Madog eventually submitted to John de Havering, justice of north Wales, in July and he was imprisoned in the Tower of London for the rest of his life. However, the danger of further uprisings by the Welsh meant that large sums of money were spent on repairing and improving castles in Wales in the following years. Edward also decided to construct a new castle on the island of Anglesey called Beaumaris. Building work began in early 1295, with large sums of money allocated for the wages of workers, the purchase of materials and a garrison. Over the next five years the considerable sum of almost £11,500 was spent on its construction before a lack of funds forced the work to come to a halt in 1300. Yet the castle was still far from complete. Problems were identified as early as February 1296 in a report sent to the Exchequer by the supervisors of the work, James of St George and Walter of Winchester. The cost of paying for a large workforce, particularly through the winter, was prohibitive and the men were threatening to desert as their wages were in arrears. This was unfortunate as the war with France and deteriorating relations with Scotland meant that the king's resources were soon stretched to breaking point. After a gap of six years, construction work resumed in 1306 and by 1326 almost £3,000 more had been spent on the castle, although the structure was never fully finished. Work on the upper storeys of the inner towers was never started and it is missing most of its planned residential accommodation. However, even in its incomplete form it is still an impressive fortress, which was garrisoned throughout the Middle Ages. Beaumaris is a symmetrical concentric castle, with successive layers of defence, consisting of a moat, an outer curtain wall and a taller inner wall, together with towers and three gatehouses.[13]

War with Scotland: 1295–1337

Meanwhile Robert Bruce ravaged Northumbria, burned vills and towns, killed men, drove off their cattle, and forced many to pay tribute... He utterly destroyed, too, the walls of the castles and towns in Scotland, lest they should later serve to protect the advancing English. He took two of the King of England's strongest fortresses, namely Edinburgh and Roxburgh; one through the treachery of a certain Gascon, who was Piers Gaveston's cousin, to whom our king had given the custody of the castle... The other castle was taken through the efforts of James Douglas, who was on the side of the Scots. For this James came secretly to the fort one night, brought up ladders stealthily and placed them against the wall; and by this means he climbed up the wall, and led his companions upon the sleeping or careless guards; and he attacked those he found and took the castle, and he would have taken Berwick Castle in the same way except a dog aroused the watchmen. Then Robert Bruce turned to the siege of Stirling Castle... When the keeper of the castle saw that the siege had already begun, that their stores were insufficient, that Robert and the Scots lay continually in ambush, he agreed to a truce on this condition, that he would either get the King of England to come to defend the castle, or, if he could not persuade the king to do this, he would give up the castle without delay.

The Life of Edward the Second[1]

The siege of Stirling Castle by the forces of Robert Bruce in 1314 meant that Edward II of England was obliged to lead an army to relieve the beleaguered English garrison. However, his army was intercepted and defeated by the Scots at the Battle of Bannockburn. This was a crushing defeat, which was a humiliation for Edward II and resulted in the loss of English control over Scotland. The conflict had been inherited from the reign of his father, Edward I, who had exploited a crisis in the succession to the Scottish throne to impose his will over Scotland. Over the course of multiple successful military campaigns, he had repeatedly defeated the Scots and occupied their towns and castles. However, he was unable to achieve a final victory, with opposition to his rule led first by William Wallace and then by Robert Bruce, who was crowned as king of Scots in 1306. Civil unrest in England during the turbulent reign of Edward I's son and successor, Edward II, and the inspired leadership of Robert Bruce meant that the Scots succeeded in driving the English out of Scotland. Bruce then took the war to his enemies, with repeated devastating raids bringing misery to the inhabitants of northern England.

The outbreak of civil war in England and the ineptitude of Edward II meant that the English were unable to counter these successes. The excessive reliance and favour shown by Edward II to his unpopular favourites eventually resulted in his overthrow by his queen, Isabella, and her lover, Roger Mortimer, Earl of March, in favour of his son Edward in 1326. Edward III's desire to seek revenge for past English defeats later led to a renewal of hostilities, when he provided military support for the Scottish pretender Edward Balliol. Castles played a key role in this conflict, with the English occupation of Scotland dependent upon the retention of well supplied and garrisoned castles, which were used as strongholds and bases for field armies. Considerable efforts were also made to garrison and supply castles in northern England, in an unsuccessful attempt to counter Scottish raids. Robert Bruce's decision to destroy the defences of castles that he captured to deny their use to the enemy demonstrates that he recognised their crucial role in warfare.

The Great Cause

On the night of 19 March 1286, King Alexander III of Scotland left a meeting of his council at Edinburgh to return to his wife, Yolande, who was staying at Kinghorn in Fife. In the darkness, he became separated from his companions and was killed after being thrown by his horse. Alexander's death caused a crisis in the succession to the Scottish throne, as his children from his first marriage had predeceased him, leaving as his closest relative his three-year-old granddaughter, Margaret, who was the issue of the marriage between his daughter, Margaret, and Eric II of Norway. While negotiations were initiated with King Eric to arrange for Margaret to travel to Scotland, the governance of the kingdom was entrusted by the Scottish nobility and prelates to a group of six men, known as the Guardians. The Guardians sought assistance from England during this fraught period of transition and sent embassies to Edward I to seek his advice and guidance. This was a reasonable course of action to take as Anglo-Scottish relations had been amicable for most of the thirteenth century. All three parties – the Scots, Norwegians and English – eventually agreed that the issue should be resolved by a marriage between Margaret and Edward's son and heir, Edward of Caernarfon. This union, if it had taken place, would have united the two kingdoms of England and Scotland, thereby bringing all the British Isles under the control of one ruler. However, this scheme was undone in the autumn of 1290 by the death of Margaret, in Orkney, where her ship had stopped off on its way to Scotland. Her death left the kingdom on the verge of civil war, with as many as thirteen claimants stepping forward to contest the throne, some of whom were prepared to use violence to enforce their claims. Edward reacted by summoning the Scottish magnates to appear at Norham in May 1291, where he held hearings to determine the issue of the succession. He then exerted pressure on the candidates to force them to accept his claim to have rights of feudal overlordship over Scotland and to agree to the temporary transfer of royal castles to his custody. The hearings began in August at Berwick-upon-Tweed with much of the proceedings devoted to deciding between the claims of the two main contenders for the throne, John Balliol, Lord of Galloway, and Robert Bruce, Lord of Annandale. This proved to be a long and protracted process but Edward finally gave his judgements in favour of John Balliol on 17 November 1292, on the basis that he had the strongest claim by right of primogeniture. John was inaugurated as king of Scots on 30 November 1292 and custody of the kingdom was handed over to him by the king of England. Thus far Edward's behaviour towards the Scots had been opportunistic but not excessive, but he subsequently began to exploit his rights as feudal overlord to undermine John's authority as king. Appeals were made to the English court by his subjects and he was forced to appear in Parliament in England in 1293. The final straw was Edward's decision to summon King John and eighteen Scottish magnates to provide personal military service in his army in the war against Philip IV of France in the following year. Instead, the Scots chose to defy the English king and sought assistance from the French, with a treaty of alliance agreed in October 1295, later known as the 'Auld Alliance'.[2]

The Outbreak of War

Edward regarded the Franco-Scottish treaty as an act of war and at once began to prepare for an invasion of Scotland. On 16 December 1295, he issued instructions for his magnates to muster at Newcastle on 1 March 1296. The Scottish decision to pre-empt this invasion by launching attacks across the border into England handed Edward a propaganda victory, as it allowed him to characterise them as the aggressors in the conflict. An attempt was made to capture Wark Castle and an English force was ambushed before the invaders were driven off by Edward's army. In the meantime, a larger Scottish army led by seven earls invaded the West March of England and laid siege to Carlisle. Their attempts to storm the city were beaten off by the defenders and they retreated back across the border, leaving a trail of devastation in their wake. Edward waited until the end of Easter before leading his forces northwards, arriving outside Berwick on 30 March. The town lacked any walls or earthwork defences and was quickly stormed by the English, who slaughtered many of the inhabitants, with the garrison of the castle surrendering soon afterwards. Edward recognised the strategic and economic importance of Berwick and four days after its capture, he issued instructions for the sheriff of Northumberland to send ditch diggers, carpenters and other workers to construct fortifications at the town. According to the chronicle of Walter of Guisborough, the finished ditch was forty feet deep and eight feet wide, and was topped by a timber palisade. The Scottish lords were unwilling to confront the English in battle, instead they led another raid into Northumberland, burning the towns of Corbridge and Hexham. On their return to Scotland they seized control of Dunbar Castle; its owner, Patrick, Earl of Dunbar, was serving in the English army. Edward responded by sending a force under the command of John de Warenne, Earl of Surrey, to lay siege to the castle. The Scots attempted to relieve the garrison but were defeated in a cavalry engagement at the Battle of Dunbar on 27 April. This success was hailed as a great victory by the English chroniclers, but in reality was little more than a skirmish. Yet it had important consequences, as the defenders of Dunbar Castle surrendered the next day. Many men of high rank were taken prisoner, including three earls and more than 100 knights and esquires, who were imprisoned in twenty-four castles in England and Wales. This setback was a heavy blow to Scottish morale and led to a collapse in their willingness to resist the invaders, as well as highlighting the ineptitude of King John. Edward's triumphant progression through the heartlands of Scotland saw him taking castles and receiving the submission of the inhabitants. He attacked Edinburgh Castle and deployed siege weapons against the defenders, who surrendered after a short siege. According to the chronicler of Lanercost Priory, the castle had never 'been captured before, owing to its height and strength'.

Numerous other castles were surrendered after little or no resistance, including the strategically important castle of Stirling, which was abandoned by its defenders. King John submitted himself to Edward in July and was forced to abdicate in a humiliating ceremony before being sent to the Tower of London. Yet Edward did not intend to replace him as king, instead Scotland was to be demoted from the status of a kingdom to that of a land governed by the officials he appointed. The royal jewels and records of government were transported from Edinburgh Castle to England, as was the coronation stone from Scone Abbey. Edward's conquest of Scotland had seemingly been a far easier task than his subjugation of Wales, and English writers exulted in the victory of their king. The chronicler Pierre de Langtoft went so far as to claim that his victories surpassed even those of King Arthur in uniting the British Isles under one ruler. Yet in the following year Edward was confronted by a major rebellion in Scotland.[3]

The uprising was sparked by the murder of the English sheriff of Lanark, William Heselrig, at the hands of William Wallace, a man of knightly family, in May 1297. Rebellion soon spread throughout the realm due to resentment at foreign rule and the king's demand for soldiers and money for his war with France. At the head of a growing band of men, Wallace went on to lead a daring raid on Scone, forcing the justiciar, William Ormsby, to flee for his life, before later laying siege to Dundee Castle. Meanwhile, in the north, the revolt was led by Andrew Murray, who succeeded in overrunning most of the English-held castles of the region, including Banff, Inverness and Elgin. A small number of Scottish nobles, including James Stewart and Robert Bruce the Younger, raised an army and took up arms against Edward but gave up the struggle after lengthy negotiations with the English at Irvine. Following this capitulation, leadership of the rebellion was assumed by Wallace and Murray. By 24 July the treasurer of Scotland, Hugh Cressingham, was complaining to the king that not a penny could be raised in the country and that most of the counties lacked keepers due to 'death, sieges, or imprisonment'. The English response was further hampered by the lacklustre performance of the absentee custodian of Scotland, John de Warenne, Earl of Surrey, who was residing at his Yorkshire estates. Warenne and Cressingham finally moved against the Scots in late August when they marched northwards and were confronted by the army of Wallace and Murray at the Battle of Stirling Bridge on 11 September. The English commanders were overconfident due to their superior numbers and were in the process of crossing the bridge when they were attacked by the Scots and suffered heavy casualties. Following this victory, the Scots launched a devastating raid across the border into Northumberland, where they burned and plundered at will, before retiring northwards in November due to bad weather. In recognition of his successes, Wallace was later knighted and appointed as Guardian of Scotland. The shock of defeat prompted the English to prepare for a new expedition to subdue Scotland. On 23 October orders were issued for the assembly of 30,000 infantry to take place at Newcastle on 6 December. However, operations did not begin in earnest until the summer of the following year as the king, who had been serving with another army in Flanders, wished to lead the campaign. The army eventually mustered at Roxburgh on 25 June, at which time it consisted of almost 30,000 men, including 3,000 cavalry and over 25,000 English and Welsh infantry. To counter this formidable host, Wallace adopted a Fabian strategy of laying waste the land to deny food supplies to the enemy. At first this plan was successful, as Edward's army soon began to suffer from a lack of provisions after entering Scotland, leading to a clash between the English and Welsh soldiers. The king was forced to withdraw to Edinburgh by mid-July but once there, learnt that the Scottish army was nearby and advanced to meet them. At the Battle of Falkirk, fought on 22 July, the Scottish infantry, armed with spears and arrayed in tight formations known as 'schiltroms', were defeated by a combination of cavalry charges and missile fire from longbows. Wallace succeeded in escaping from the battlefield, but the Scots suffered heavy losses. After the battle, Edward marched northwards into Fife and sacked Perth. However, a lack of supplies meant that he was forced to retreat to Carlisle, which he reached in September, having captured Lochmaben Castle en route.[4]

The Conquest of Scotland

Edward's attempts to organise another expedition to invade Scotland in the following year were thwarted by political discontent. This allowed the Scots to place the English garrisons in the country under further pressure, which led to the surrender of Caerlaverock and Stirling castles before the end of 1299. It was not until early July that the English army of approximately 10,000 men was mustered at Carlisle. Despite the army being smaller than previous expeditions to Scotland, it was well supplied with provisions by a fleet of ships. Edward's first objective was to recover Caerlaverock Castle on the coast of Dumfries. Caerlaverock is an unusual triangular-shaped castle, encircled by a moat, which he besieged on 8 July. A detailed account of the siege is provided by the anonymous author of the poem called the *Song of Caerlaverock*. Caerlaverock was described as having the shape of a shield and being 'so strong, that it did not fear a siege', amply stocked with supplies and weapons. The English army was divided into three battalions that were quartered outside the walls, housed in a rich array of tents and wooden huts, with provisions and siege weapons transported to the site by sea. After the garrison refused a summons to surrender, the English made repeated attempts to storm the castle but their assaults were repulsed. The poet remarks that the defenders used missile weapons to inflict losses on the besiegers, including 'such kind of stones thrown as if they would beat hats and helmets to powder, and break shields and targets in pieces'. However, the attackers had greater success in using their four stone-throwing siege weapons, which were said to be 'of great power and very destructive, which cut down and cleave whatever they strike'. Under the constant bombardment of these missiles the surviving force of sixty men was soon forced to surrender.

After the end of the siege, Edward marched westwards along the coast, a skirmish with a Scottish force taking place near the estuary of the Cree in early August. However, the ranks of his army were rapidly becoming depleted by desertion and Edward was forced to abandon the campaign and return to Carlisle in September. He travelled to Dumfries Castle with a small force to inspect its fortifications in October, at which time a short truce was agreed with the Scots, before he returned to Carlisle in early November. While at Dumfries he issued orders for its defences to be improved by the addition of an outer enclosure known as a 'peel', that was intended to serve as a secure assembly point for soldiers. The fortifications took the form of a wooden palisade and ditch, which were constructed by a team of more than 300 workers. Work was also carried out to enlarge and extend the existing moats around the castle.[5]

The Scots succeeded in securing support from Pope Boniface VIII, in the form of a papal bull, which stated that the issue of English overlordship should be decided by papal arbitration. Edward rejected this decision using the argument that England had historical rights to supremacy over its northern neighbour, deriving from the mythical landing of Brutus in the British Isles, and also cited Balliol's performance of fealty and homage to him, whereby his rights as feudal overlord had been recognised. The king made plans for another expedition to Scotland in 1301. Unlike in previous years, the English forces were to be divided into two armies, which were to invade the country from separate directions. One force, led by Edward, was to invade from Berwick in the east, while the main army, nominally under the command of his eldest son, Prince Edward, but in practice under the command of Henry de Lacy, Earl of Lincoln, was to attack the west from Carlisle. This decision was prompted by the king's desire to give his son 'the chief honour of taming the pride of the Scots', as he explained in a royal writ sent to de Lacy on 1 March.

The two armies, collectively numbering more than 15,000 men, assembled at their mustering points on 24 June. Edward's smaller force moved upstream along the River Tweed to Coldstream, before striking inland towards Glasgow, arriving there by 23 August. The army then laid siege to the nearby castle of Bothwell. This impressive fortress is situated on a steep bank overlooking the River Clyde and is dominated by a large cylindrical keep. A wooden tower called a belfry was employed by the English in besieging the castle, which had fallen into their hands by 24 September. Meanwhile, Prince Edward's army had travelled inland towards the Firth of Clyde and had captured Turnberry Castle by the beginning of September. He then returned to Carlisle before joining his father at Linlithgow where they spent the winter. According to the author of the *Lanercost Chronicle*, the king decided to prolong his stay in the country after 'considering that whatever he gained in Scotland during the summer he would lose in winter', which meant that the 'Scots were brought far nearer subjection by that occupation than they had been before'. Despite the optimism of the chronicler, the English were experiencing problems with paying their soldiers, which had led to widespread desertion. Therefore, the king agreed a truce with the Scots to last from January to November 1302. The king spent some of this time overseeing improvements made to the fortifications of Linlithgow Castle. His experienced master mason from Savoy, Master James of St George, was appointed to supervise the works, which involved extending the perimeter of the castle by constructing a wooden peel. Building work was in full earnest by the end of the summer, with the urgent need for workers resulting in the employment of 140 women as ditch diggers and the impressment of the 100 foot soldiers in the garrison as labourers. Earlier in the year, Robert Bruce, Earl of Carrick, grandson of the elder Bruce who had sought to become king of Scots ten years earlier, changed sides and joined the English cause. This decision was motivated by the expectation that he would be made king by Edward to replace Balliol. It proved to be a vain hope.[6]

Fighting resumed early in 1303 with the Scots launching attacks on English-held castles. These fortresses were well guarded, with more than 1,000 men stationed in garrisons in southern Scotland, nevertheless, some of these castles, including the newly constructed peel at Selkirk, were overrun in January. The defenders of Linlithgow succeeded in resisting a brief Scottish siege, but were forced to resort to converting the royal chapel in the castle into a granary, which involved filling in the windows and digging up the corpses buried there. During the next month, a mounted force led by the king's lieutenant in Scotland, John de Segrave, led a foray into enemy territory but was ambushed and defeated at Roslin, near Edinburgh. Edward responded to this setback by leading another expeditionary force to Scotland in the summer. The army of approximately 7,500 men left Newcastle in early May and marched northwards through eastern Scotland, with Brechin Castle placed under siege in July. Artillery was transported to the siege via Montrose on the coast, with five cartloads of lead stripped from the local cathedral to furnish counterweights for the trebuchets. According to the author of the *Flowers of History*, the garrison was led by Sir Thomas Maule. The defenders were said to have valiantly resisted the attacks of their enemies for forty days, including a fierce bombardment of stones hurled by the English siege weapons, but yielded after Maule was killed by a projectile. After capturing the castle, the army marched to Aberdeen on the coast, where it was resupplied by merchant ships, before heading northwards to Kinloss Abbey in September. Meanwhile, military operations were also taking place on the west coast. As in previous years, the king drew upon the military resources of the lordship of Ireland to furnish soldiers and ships. In 1303 the main contingent was led by Richard de Burgh, Earl of Ulster, which numbered almost 3,500 men and was transported by a fleet of 173 ships. This force reached Scotland in July and within

Above: Caerphilly
Castle, Caerphilly.
© Crown copyright
(2017) Cadw, Welsh
Government.

Right: Cricieth
Castle, Gwynedd.
© Crown copyright
(2017) Cadw, Welsh
Government.

Major Castles in England and Wales

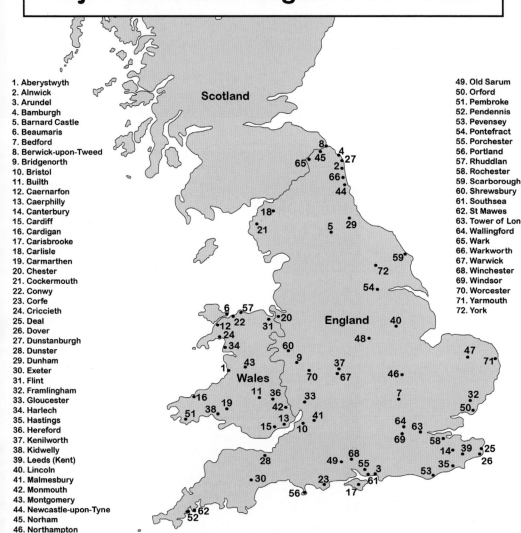

Scotland

England

Wales

1. Aberystwyth
2. Alnwick
3. Arundel
4. Bamburgh
5. Barnard Castle
6. Beaumaris
7. Bedford
8. Berwick-upon-Tweed
9. Bridgenorth
10. Bristol
11. Builth
12. Caernarfon
13. Caerphilly
14. Canterbury
15. Cardiff
16. Cardigan
17. Carisbrooke
18. Carlisle
19. Carmarthen
20. Chester
21. Cockermouth
22. Conwy
23. Corfe
24. Criccieth
25. Deal
26. Dover
27. Dunstanburgh
28. Dunster
29. Dunham
30. Exeter
31. Flint
32. Framlingham
33. Gloucester
34. Harlech
35. Hastings
36. Hereford
37. Kenilworth
38. Kidwelly
39. Leeds (Kent)
40. Lincoln
41. Malmesbury
42. Monmouth
43. Montgomery
44. Newcastle-upon-Tyne
45. Norham
46. Northampton
47. Norwich
48. Nottingham

49. Old Sarum
50. Orford
51. Pembroke
52. Pendennis
53. Pevensey
54. Pontefract
55. Porchester
56. Portland
57. Rhuddlan
58. Rochester
59. Scarborough
60. Shrewsbury
61. Southsea
62. St Mawes
63. Tower of Lon
64. Wallingford
65. Wark
66. Warkworth
67. Warwick
68. Winchester
69. Windsor
70. Worcester
71. Yarmouth
72. York

Major castles in England and Wales. Map drawn by Scott Hall. © Dan Spencer.

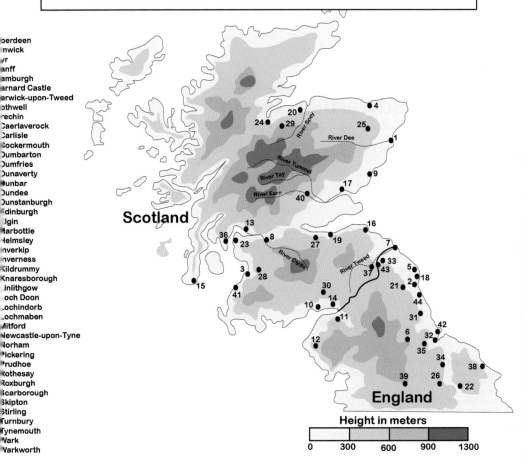

Major Castles of the North of England and Scotland

Scotland

England

Height in meters

0   300   600   900   1300

The North of England and Scotland. Map drawn by Scott Hall. © Dan Spencer.

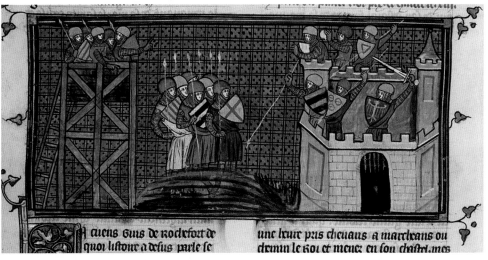

The deployment of a siege tower during a siege. *Les Grandes Chroniques de France*, early fourteenth century. British Library, Royal 16 G VI, f. 280v. Creative Commons CC0 1.0 Universal Public Domain Dedication.

Edwardian Castles of Wales

Edwardian Castles

1. Aberystwyth
2. Beaumaris
3. Builth
4. Caernarfon
5. Conwy
6. Harlech
7. Flint
8. Rhuddlan

Other Royal Castles

9. Cardigan
10. Carmarthen
11. Chester
12. Gloucester
13. Hereford
14. Montgomery
15. Shrewsbury

Major Baronial Castles

16. Abergavenny
17. Brecon
18. Caerphilly
19. Chepstow
20. Chirk
21. Cilgerran
22. Denbigh
23. Grosmont
24. Holt
25. Kidwelly
26. Monmouth
27. Pembroke
28. Usk
29. White Castle

Native Welsh C

30. Carreg Cenn
31. Castell y Ber
32. Criccieth
33. Dinefwr
34. Dolbarden
35. Dolforwyn
36. Dolwyddelan
37. Dynevor

Anglesey

Wales

England

River Dee

River Severn

River Teifi

River Tywi

River Usk

River Wye

Height in meters

0   400   800   1100

Edwardian castles of Wales. Map drawn by Scott Hall. © Dan Spencer.

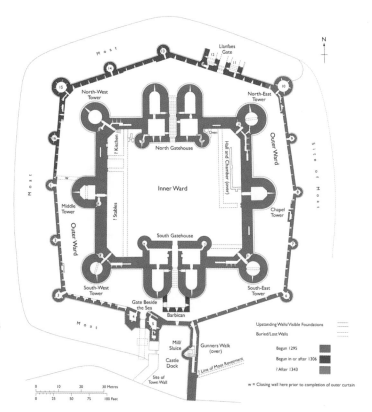

Plan of Beaumaris Castle, Anglesey. © Crown copyright (2017) Cadw, Welsh Government.

Beaumaris Castle, Anglesey. © Crown copyright (2017) Cadw, Welsh Government.

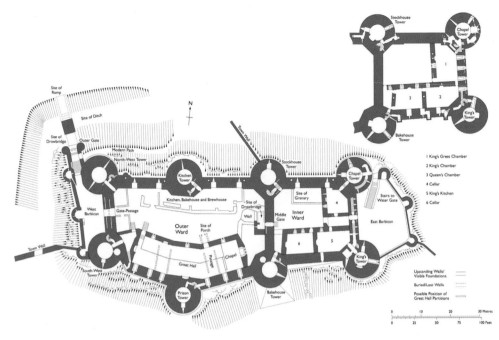

Plan of Conwy Castle, Conwy. © Crown copyright (2017) Cadw, Welsh Government.

Conwy Castle, Conwy. © Crown copyright (2017) Cadw, Welsh Government.

Harlech Castle, Gwynedd. © Crown copyright (2017) Cadw, Welsh Government.

The inner ward of Harlech Castle, Gwynedd. © Crown copyright (2017) Cadw, Welsh Government.

Raglan Castle, Monmouthshire. © Crown copyright (2017) Cadw, Welsh Government.

Corfe Castle, Dorset. Photograph taken by Helen Hotson. © Shutterstock.

Above: Rochester Castle, Kent. Photograph taken by Paulina Grunwald. © Shutterstock.

Below: Launceston Castle, Cornwall. Photograph taken by Elena Barsottelli. © Shutterstock.

Dover Castle, Kent. Photograph taken by Alexander Gold. © Shutterstock.

Pendennis Castle, Cornwall. Photograph taken by Jamie William. © Shutterstock.

Above: The capture of Wark Castle by a Franco-Scottish army in 1385. Jehan Froissart, *Chroniques*, late fifteenth century. British Library, Royal 18 E 1, f. 345. Creative Commons CC0 1.0 Universal Public Domain Dedication.

Right: A stone throwing siege engine known as a trebuchet in action. *Les Grandes Chroniques de France*, early fourteenth century. British Library, Royal 16 G VI, f. 345v. Creative Commons CC0 1.0 Universal Public Domain Dedication.

Besiegers undermining a tower. *Les Grandes Chroniques de France*, early fourteenth century. British Library, Royal 16 G VI, f. 74. Creative Commons CC0 1.0 Universal Public Domain Dedication.

Battle fought outside a castle. *Les Grandes Chroniques de France*, early fourteenth century British Library, Royal 16 G VI, f. 427. Creative Commons CC0 1.0 Universal Public Domain Dedication.

The Tower of London in the fifteenth century. Charles, duke of Orléans, *Pseudo-Heloise*, late fifteenth century. British Library, Royal 16 F II, f. 73. Creative Commons CC0 1.0 Universal Public Domain Dedication.

The gatehouse of Carisbrooke Castle, Isle of Wight, courtesy of Peter Burka.

Scarborough Castle, Yorkshire, courtesy of Tim Green.

Above: The top half of the gatehouse of Old Sherborne Castle, Dorset, courtesy of Glen Bowman.

Below: The gatehouse of Skipton Castle, Yorkshire, courtesy of Afshin Darian.

Above: Bodiam Castle, East Sussex, courtesy of Paul Stephenson.

Below: The courtyard of Bodiam Castle, East Sussex, courtesy of Dan Davison.

two months had succeeded in capturing Rothesay Castle on the Isle of Bute and Inverkip Castle in Lanarkshire. By the end of the year, Edward had travelled southwards to Dunfermline in Fife, where he stayed for the winter. The author of the *Flowers of History* states that this was because 'he had determined that he would not depart from that country till he had either utterly subdued all the Scots, or been himself subdued by them'. The king remained busy throughout the winter, with orders issued to fortify the undefended town of Dunfermline. Plans were also put in place for further campaigning in Scotland in the summer. Edward had failed to land a decisive blow against the Scots, despite years of military operations, but the prospect of contending with yet another English invasion prompted almost all the Scottish leaders to come to terms with him in February 1304. This decision was also motivated by the Anglo-French treaty of the previous year, which eliminated the possibility of French assistance. However, this capitulation did not end the war. Notable figures such as William Wallace and Simon Fraser were still at large, and the strategically important castle of Stirling was held by William Oliphant.[7]

Regaining control of this fortress was Edward's main objective for the campaign of 1304. The strong natural defences of the castle meant that it was difficult to capture, due to its lofty location on a steep crag surrounded on three sides by cliffs. Extensive preparations were made for besieging the castle, with a large siege train assembled by one of the king's engineers, Reginald, with further pieces of artillery supplied from Brechin Castle and Aberdeen. The importance attached to these trebuchets and other stone-throwing engines can be seen from the fact that many of them were given their own individual names. These ranged from unusual ones such as 'the Parson', 'the Vicar' and 'the Veweth Forester', to those named after magnates, including 'Lincoln', 'Gloucester' and 'Segrave'. Stone balls to serve as ammunition for the artillery were carved by masons in nearby quarries, and woodsmen working in Stirling Forest were tasked with making large wooden frames to provide protection from enemy missile fire. A substantial quantity of other equipment was also supplied to the attackers, including bows, crossbows, arrows, quarrels, ropes, pickaxes, mallets and shovels. The siege began in April after the commander of the garrison, William Oliphant, refused a summons to surrender.

According to the author of the *Flowers of History*, the fortress was defended by 'gallant men, whom despair rendered braver', who put up a vigorous defence. The attackers were said to have kept up a continuous bombardment of the castle, with the stones thrown by their artillery causing extensive death and destruction. Yet undaunted by this, the garrison in turn used their own siege weapons and crossbows to great effect and launched frequent sallies into the camp of the besiegers. One particularly vivid episode that took place during the siege is recorded by the chronicler Thomas Gray in his work, the *Scalacronica*. He states that his father, also called Thomas, had just rescued his lord, Henry de Beaumont, who had been caught by a hook thrown from a siege weapon at the barriers outside the walls of the castle. Immediately afterwards Thomas was struck in the face below his eyes by a bolt fired by a large torsion weapon called a springald. He was knocked unconscious by this blow and was presumed to be dead by a group of Englishmen who recovered his body. Yet before he could be buried, he miraculously regained consciousness and subsequently recovered from his injury. Despite the dangers involved, the siege was a grand spectacle that demonstrated the might of the English army. It was for this reason that a viewing gallery was constructed in a house in the town of Stirling, so that Queen Margaret and the ladies of the court could observe the proceedings from a safe distance. Eventually the pressure exerted by the English artillery and dwindling food supplies prompted the garrison to unconditionally surrender on 20 July. However, this offer was at first rebuffed by Edward. A team of five master carpenters, fifty other carpenters and four pages had been hard at work constructing a mighty trebuchet called 'Warwolf'. Such was the king's determination to try out this new weapon that he refused to accept the surrender of the garrison until the castle had been 'struck with the Warwolf'. Once this had been carried out, the defenders were finally permitted to submit on 24 July and were imprisoned in castles in England.

The fall of Stirling Castle marked the end of effective Scottish resistance. In August of the next year, William Wallace was captured near Glasgow by the servants of Sir John Menteith, the constable of Dumbarton Castle, and handed over to the English. Wallace was taken southwards to Westminster where he was brutally executed by being hanged, drawn and quartered.[8]

King Robert I

Yet Edward's triumph proved to be short-lived as six months later, a shocking murder led to a renewal of the conflict. On 10 February 1306, Robert Bruce, Earl of Carrick, met with John Comyn, Lord of Badenoch, son and heir of John Comyn, one of the contenders for the throne in 1292, in Greyfriars Church at Dumfries. The two men were rivals but Bruce wished to gain Comyn's support for his bid to become King of Scots. However, after a short discussion Bruce accused Comyn of treachery and stabbed him with a dagger, with the mortally wounded man then finished off by Bruce's men, armed with swords. According to Scottish accounts this was because Comyn had betrayed Bruce's plans to rebel against Edward, whereas English accounts depict the slaying as part of a plot by Bruce to murder a rival to the throne. Bruce had been in Edward's service since 1302 but had received few rewards from the English king and sensed an opportunity to assume leadership of the nationalist cause. Following the murder, he rose in rebellion against the English administration in Scotland and their Scottish supporters. His partisans soon took control of a swathe of castles in the south-west, including Dumfries, Dunaverty, Ayr and Tibbers. Bruce then received the fealty of numerous men at Glasgow and Rutherglen, before proceeding to Scone where he was crowned king on 25 March 1306 in Scone Abbey. Edward responded by preparing for another expedition to Scotland, with the feudal host summoned to appear at Carlisle on 8 July. The king was now old and increasingly unwell, which meant that the leadership of the campaign was delegated to his commanders. Aymer de Valence, Earl of Pembroke, was appointed as the king's lieutenant in Scotland to direct operations against the rebels, while Prince Edward was tasked with leading the main army from England. The Earl of Pembroke soon achieved successes in eastern Scotland and routed Bruce's army outside Perth in a surprise attack on 19 June at the Battle of Methven. In August, Prince Edward's army left Carlisle and advanced to Lochmaben Castle, which was surrendered by its garrison without any resistance being offered. He then marched across land to the north-east, via Perth, his army savagely laying waste to the land en route, before arriving outside the walls of Kildrummy Castle, which was taken after a short siege.

Bruce had sent his wife, sisters and other ladies of his court to the fortress for safe keeping, but on the approach of the English army they fled northwards. They were intercepted by the forces of William, Earl of Ross, and handed over to the English. In the south-west, John Botetourt and John of Mentieth took Dunaverty Castle in Kintyre in September after employing two siege engines against the defenders. Bruce's own castle of Loch Doon was captured after a waterborne assault using boats later that month. Bruce was forced to flee westwards and eventually reached Ireland, but meanwhile his supporters paid a high price for daring to defy the wrath of King Edward. Prominent adherents such as Simon Fraser and John of Strathbogie, Earl of Atholl, were executed, while Bruce's sister, Christian, and Countess Isabel of Buchan, were imprisoned in cages at the castles of Roxburgh and Berwick respectively. This act of cruelty towards noble-born women was unprecedented and reveals how vindictive Edward had become towards his Scottish opponents. Henceforth they were to be treated as rebels and brigands, with orders issued to hang or behead prisoners. Yet the resentment fostered by this cruelty encouraged resistance to English rule rather than quelling it. During the next year, Bruce returned to Scotland and began to harry the English garrisons in the south-west. He succeeded in outmanoeuvring the English commanders tasked with hunting him down and routed an army led by the Earl of Pembroke at the Battle of Loudon Hill on 10 May. This victory greatly strengthened Bruce's cause, with the author of the *Lanercost Chronicle* noting that henceforth 'the number of those willing to establish him in the realm increased from day to day'. Edward recognised the seriousness of the situation and immediately issued instructions for a new expedition to Scotland. Despite his advanced age and ill health, he decided to lead the campaign in person but died near Carlisle on 7 July.[9]

Piers Gaveston

Upon receiving news of his father's death Prince Edward travelled northwards to Carlisle where he received the homage and fealty of the English magnates on 20 July. Afterwards he went to Dumfries in August to receive the same from his Scottish supporters before returning to England. The royal campaign against Bruce was abandoned, with Amyer de Valence, Earl of Pembroke, and later John of Brittany, Earl of Richmond, appointed as the king's lieutenant in the country. Edward then travelled southwards to Northampton where a parliament was held on 13 October and subsequently to Westminster Abbey on 27 October. He was not to return to Scotland for another three years. The reason for this delay was due to the domestic problems that the new king faced. These were partly owing to the huge debts incurred by the Crown during his father's reign, and resentment at the arbitrary methods employed by the late king's government. Yet another factor was discontent caused by the excessive fondness and favour that Edward showed to his favourite, Piers Gaveston. This would soon cause a serious deterioration in his relationship with prominent members of the nobility. Gaveston was the son of a Gascon lord and had arrived in England in the late 1290s. He came to the attention of Edward I through his service in the royal army in Flanders in 1297 and was made a squire in the royal household in that year. Three years later, he was transferred to the household of Prince Edward and over time the two men developed a close bond. This relationship meant that he became a target of the king's wrath in 1305, following a quarrel between the king and prince over money, which led to his temporary removal from the latter's household. Two years later he was exiled from the realm, which the Lanercost chronicler claims was due to the 'improper familiarity which my lord Edward the younger entertained with him, speaking of him openly as his brother'. One of Edward II's first acts upon succeeding to the throne was to recall Gaveston from exile and to grant him the earldom of Cornwall. Further rewards were lavished on Gaveston including the hand in marriage of Edward's niece, Margaret de Clare, and his appointment as chamberlain of the king's chamber. In January 1308, Gaveston was appointed as regent of England during the king's absence on the Continent. Edward married Isabella, daughter of Philip IV, at Boulogne on 25 January and six days later gave homage for his lands in France to the French king. In the following month, the king returned to England for his coronation, which took place at Westminster Abbey on 25 February. Gaveston's arrogant behaviour and influence over Edward quickly led to a rift with members of the aristocracy. The author of *The Life of Edward II* remarked that 'the great men of the land hated him, because he alone found favour in the king's eyes and lorded it over them like a second king'. Growing tensions in the spring of 1308 prompted Edward to prepare for the outbreak of civil war. Key royal castles were entrusted to loyal supporters and orders were issued for their defences to be improved.

In response, the rebellious magnates under the direction of Henry de Lacy, Earl of Lincoln, gathered their forces at Pontefract Castle. They attended the parliament held at Westminster in April fully armed and demanded that Gaveston be banished from the realm. Under intense pressure from almost all his magnates, the king finally agreed to send him into exile on 18 May, with Gaveston leaving England on 21 June. However, the latter's exile was to last little more than a year. Edward succeeded in reconciling with many of the magnates over the course of 1308 and by the following summer, felt confident enough to recall his favourite.[10]

Yet Gaveston had failed to learn from his previous mistakes and once again managed to anger his fellow earls. This was in part due to his habit of giving them derogatory nicknames, said to be 'Burst-belly' for Henry de Lacy, Earl of Lincoln; 'the Fiddler' for Thomas, Earl of Lancaster, a cousin of the king; and 'the Black Dog of Arden' for Guy de Beauchamp, Earl of Warwick. In February 1310, some of the earls refused to attend parliament as 'their chief enemy, who had set the kingdom and themselves in an uproar, was skulking in the king's chamber'. By the next month, the king was threatened with being deposed and was forced to agree to the appointment of a body of twenty-one men, known as the Ordainers, selected from the ranks of the prelates, earls and barons. The Ordainers were granted full authority to make all necessary changes to reform the governance of the realm and the king's household for one year, from 29 September 1310 to 29 September 1311. Later in the summer, it was brought to the king's attention that his presence was urgently required in Scotland. At a council held at Westminster in mid-June, Edward was informed by those Scottish magnates still loyal to him that unless he soon visited Scotland in person, with an army, he would lose control of the country. Over the past three years, Bruce had succeeded in defeating many of his Scottish opponents and now controlled a swathe of territory in the west and north. The English still controlled many of the major castles in the Lowlands, but their beleaguered garrisons were increasingly isolated behind their walls. Therefore, it was imperative for the king to lead an expedition to Scotland to retrieve the situation, which also had the advantage of keeping Edward and Gaveston as far away as possible from the Ordainers. Instructions were issued soon afterwards for the royal army to assemble at Berwick on 9 September, with the king leaving for the north in July. However, the king was only accompanied by four of the earls, namely Gilbert de Clare, Earl of Gloucester; John of Brittany, Earl of Richmond; John de Warenne, Earl of Surrey; and Gaveston. By contrast, the other earls refused to take part in the campaign – using the excuse that they were too busy working as Ordainers, and only sent the minimal number of knights they were legally obliged to send for the fiefs they held. This decision contributed to the small size of the army, which at its peak numbered some 3,000 infantry and 1,700 cavalry, with further contingents provided by the garrisons of the castles of Roxburgh and Berwick. Edward led his army into Scotland in mid-September and made his way in stages to Edinburgh, via Roxburgh, Selkirk and Glasgow. Yet after arriving in the Scottish capital at the end of October, he returned southwards to Berwick. The Scots refused to offer battle and Edward's limited resources in manpower and finance meant that it would have been risky to pursue them. Instead he remained at Berwick over the winter, from where he oversaw the process of ensuring that his castles were defensible and adequately supplied. Further campaigning took place in the New Year, with Gaveston sent northwards to hold Perth in January. Nevertheless, Edward's failure to raise reinforcements meant that he was eventually forced to return to England in the summer. Fearful of what his opponents would do to Gaveston, he placed him for safe keeping in the royal fortress of Bamburgh.[11]

At the parliament held at Westminster in August 1311, Edward was formally presented with the deliberations of the Ordainers in the form of a lengthy document known as the Ordinances. The Ordinances contained forty-one clauses, which were to place severe restrictions on the king's power to govern the realm. He was forbidden to wage war, to leave the realm, or to make grants of land or offices without the consent of the barons. Specific reference was also made to the baleful influence of 'evil counsellors', who should be dismissed from office. Most distressing of all these clauses to Edward was the one that singled out Gaveston for personal attack. He was characterised as 'the evident enemy of the king and his people', whose bad advice, greed and appropriation of royal authority had threatened 'the ruin of the kingdom'. Edward attempted to resist the publication of the Ordinances, protesting that some of the clauses were detrimental to his rights, but he was soon forced to give in due to the threat of civil war. He was therefore compelled to exile his favourite for a second time, with Gaveston departing for the Continent on 3 November. However, his exile was to last only two months, before he was secretly recalled by the king. Edward travelled to Knaresborough Castle in Yorkshire in January, where he was joined soon afterwards by Gaveston. Both men then travelled to York, where the king ordered the sheriff of York to announce that he had recalled Gaveston as the latter had been 'exiled contrary to law and custom' on 18 January. Thomas, Earl of Lancaster, wrote to Edward to protest at this action and to insist that Gaveston should be surrendered into the custody of the Ordainers or sent back into exile, but was rebuffed by the king. This reckless act meant that a confrontation with the earls was inevitable. Yet Edward's attempts to resist his enemies were lacklustre. On 28 January, he ordered his officials to inspect the defences of ten castles in England, and summoned forty-five northern notables to meet with him at York on 20 February. Meanwhile, the Ordainers had resolved to use force to deal with the situation. The author of the *Life of Edward II*, states that the earls used the pretext of proclaiming tournaments in different places as a cover for gathering their forces. On 4 May, the Earl of Lancaster arrived unexpectedly at Newcastle, forcing Edward, Gaveston and Isabella, who was pregnant, to flee before them. They left in such a hurry that they were forced to abandon many of their belongings, including most of their horses and military equipment. Afterwards they travelled by sea from Tynemouth to Scarborough Castle, where Gaveston was left behind, with Edward and Isabella proceeding first to Knaresborough and then to York.[12]

In the meantime, the other earls had arrived in Yorkshire and at once laid siege to Scarborough Castle. The castle had strong natural defences and under other circumstances could have held out for a long period of time, yet its garrison was undermanned and food supplies were low. Therefore, Gaveston was soon forced to surrender under terms and was taken into the custody of Aymer de Valence, Earl of Pembroke, who escorted himself southwards. During the journey he was temporarily left by Pembroke at a rector's house in Deddington, while the latter went to his manor at Bampton. In his absence, Gaveston was seized by Guy de Beauchamp, Earl of Warwick, and was taken to Warwick Castle, where he was imprisoned. After a short period of captivity, he was executed at nearby Blacklow Hill on 19 June. The king was grief stricken when he heard the news and wished to avenge Gaveston's death. According to the author of the *Life of Edward II*, his counsellors and Gaveston's household knights urged him to 'collect an army from his faithful supporters and boldly attack his enemies'. He also received support from some of his former opponents. The execution of Gaveston had caused a rift to develop between the Ordainers, with Pembroke outraged by his seizure while in his custody. Therefore he now realigned himself with the king and was joined by John de Warenne, Earl of Surrey. Edward moved to strengthen his position in July by extracting a promise from the Londoners that they would hold the city for him against his enemies. In the following month, he issued instructions for the constables of Wallingford and Oxford castles to raise as many footmen as possible and to lead them to London. Having thus strengthened the military resources available to him, he sought to precipitate a showdown with his opponents by summoning a parliament to meet in the city on 20 August. In response, the earls refused to attend parliament but instead gathered their forces at Ware in Hertfordshire. However, a clash between the two sides was averted by negotiations, with a treaty finally agreed in December 1312 whereby the king agreed to pardon the rebellious barons. One of the reasons for this settlement was the threat that the resurgent Scots posed to the realm.[13]

The Battle of Bannockburn and its Aftermath

Following Edward's departure from Scotland in the summer of 1311, the Scots repeatedly raided the northern counties of England. The local system of defence quickly broke down and the lack of military or financial assistance from the Crown meant that the northerners were soon in dire straits. In desperation, the local inhabitants were forced to pay large sums of money to buy local truces with the Scots. By 1313, the northerners were struggling to make these payments, which led to the Scots launching ever deeper raids into England to find more loot and tribute. These forays were designed not only to put pressure on Edward II to come to terms and to recognise the kingship of Robert I, but also to finance the reduction of the remaining English-held castles and towns in Scotland. An attempt to launch a surprise attack on Berwick with scaling ladders on the night of 6 December 1312 was only foiled by the barking of a dog, which alerted the defenders. The Scots had more success at Perth in the following year, where they pretended to lift the siege of the town one day, only to secretly return at night to climb the walls with ladders.

A similar tactic was used at Roxburgh Castle in February 1314. According to the poet John Barbour, a force led by James Douglas scaled the walls on the night of Shrove Tuesday and quickly overpowered the watchmen. The attackers then burst into the great hall where 'at that moment the garrison were in all the hall, dancing, singing, and otherwise at play'. Taken by surprise, the unarmed soldiers were slaughtered, although a small group led by the constable, William de Fiennes, succeeded in briefly holding out in the keep before surrendering the next day. The author of the *Lanercost Chronicle* notes that following the capture of Roxburgh 'they razed to the ground the whole of that beautiful castle, just as they did other castles which they succeeded in taking, lest the English should every hereafter be able to lord it over the land through holding the castles'. This policy of denying strongholds to the English was ruthlessly carried out by Bruce, with few castles spared destruction. The formidable Edinburgh Castle, despite being well garrisoned, was captured by Randolph, Earl of Moray, through a stratagem in March. A small group of men climbed the castle rock and scaled the walls in a surprise night attack, with the defenders quickly overpowered by their assailants. In the same month, the Scots laid siege to the key castle of Stirling, whose commander, Philip Mowbray, agreed to surrender if it was not relieved by 24 June. The loss of these castles caused consternation in England, with the Lanercost chronicler recording that the king 'could hardly restrain his tears' after hearing the news. It was therefore more than ever necessary for Edward to lead an army to Scotland to reverse these setbacks. Even before news of these defeats had reached England, the Crown had been in the process of organising a major royal expedition. Attempts to raise an army in 1313 had floundered due to ongoing negotiations between the king and magnates regarding the settlement of the previous year. These issues were resolved by 1314, with an army of some 15,000 infantry and 2,000 cavalry mustering at Berwick in June. The number of soldiers raised was impressive, with the author of the *Life of Edward II* stating that 'all who were present agreed that never in our time has such an army marched out of England'.[14]

Edward led the army northwards from Berwick on 17 June and six days later reached the vicinity of Stirling Castle. There he was confronted by a smaller Scottish army commanded in person by Bruce, which blocked his path to the castle. Skirmishing between the two sides took place soon afterwards, but the main engagement did not begin until the following morning. Despite their superior numbers, the English were unable to deploy their forces effectively and were routed by the Scots with heavy casualties. The defeat of an army dominated by heavy cavalry at the hands of infantry armed with spears was an important event in military history, which reflected a change in European warfare that took place in the fourteenth century. Infantry gradually began to play a more important role on the battlefield, with knights and men-at-arms often choosing to fight on foot rather than from horseback. The significance of the battle was recognised by contemporaries, with the author of the *Life of Edward II* remarking 'I think it is unheard of in our time for such an army to be scattered so suddenly by infantry, unless when the flower of France fell before the Flemings at Courtrai' (with the latter having taken place in 1302). After escaping from the battlefield, Edward attempted to gain admittance to Stirling Castle. However, he was refused entry by Philip Mowbray, who insisted that as the castle had not been relieved by his army, it would have to be surrendered to the Scots. The king instead rapidly rode eastwards, while hotly pursued by his enemies, until he reached the safety of Dunbar Castle on the coast, from whence he sailed to Berwick. He then travelled to York where he summoned a parliament to meet in September to discuss measures for countering the Scots. Instead his opponents exploited the king's weak position to force him to confirm the Ordinances. Little was done to provide men or resources to protect the north, which was now subjected to intensified raiding from the Scots. In 1315, Bruce opened up a second front by sending his brother, Edward, to invade Ireland. The Scots soon spread havoc throughout the island, thereby cutting off a vital source of manpower and resources for the English war effort. Bruce kept up the pressure in the summer, by laying siege to Carlisle, the gateway to the north-west of England. The defence of the city and castle was led by Andrew Harclay, sheriff of Cumberland, who since the previous year had commanded a force of some 400 men, consisting of men-at-arms, light cavalry called hobelars, and archers. Harclay prepared for the attack by ordering that houses immediately outside the walls should be demolished to deny cover to the Scots and for the three gates to blocked. A detailed account of the siege is provided by the Lanercost chronicler, who records that the Scots first burnt the suburbs before launching their first assault on the city on 22 July. Over the course of ten days they were said to have made repeated assaults on the gates, employing a stone-throwing siege weapon and a belfry against the garrison. Yet their attacks ended in failure due to intensive missile fire from the defenders, who were well stocked with artillery, while the belfry became stuck in the mud and had to be abandoned. Attempts to use a siege weapon, known as a sow, and scaling ladders, were also unsuccessful, with the attackers suffering heavy losses. News of the imminent arrival of an English relief force led by Aymer de Valence, Earl of Pembroke, prompted the Scots to lift the siege on 1 August.[15]

Despite this setback, there was no let-up in Scottish attacks in the following year. The author of the *Lanercost Chronicle* relates that 'one bright moonlit night' in January 1316, Bruce launched a surprise attack on Berwick. It was a combined assault by land and by sea, with the Scots using small boats, which was targeted at a part of the town 'between Brighouse and the castle, where the wall was not yet built'. However, the alarm was sounded by the guards who succeeded in resisting the attackers, which prompted Bruce to abandon the venture. Yet the English were forced to remain on the defensive, as political wrangling between the king and a party of magnates led by Thomas, Earl of Lancaster, frustrated efforts to raise an expedition in 1316.

Resources were also diverted elsewhere due to the outbreak of a rebellion in south Wales. A dispute between a local Welsh lord, Llywelyn Bren, and a royal official, Payn Trubleville of Coety, led to violence in Glamorganshire. Llywelyn led an attack on the constable of Caerphilly Castle, while the latter was holding a court outside the walls on 28 January. The Welsh succeeded in taking the constable prisoner and burnt the outer ward of the castle, but were unable to penetrate its inner defences. The king responded by tasking Humphrey de Bohun, Earl of Hereford, with crushing the rebellion. He led an army of some 150 men-at-arms and 2,000 infantry against the Welsh. Faced with overwhelming force, the rebels soon capitulated with Llywelyn sent to the Tower of London after his surrender on 18 March.

Meanwhile, the Scots continued to launch raids into the north of England. The devastation caused by these forays was exacerbated by the failure of successive harvests from 1315 to 1317, which caused widespread famine and suffering. In these circumstances, the isolated garrisons of northern castles were forced to resort to desperate measures to survive, as can be seen from surviving petitions to the Crown. At Berwick, a shortage of food supplies prompted a large contingent of soldiers to disobey orders from the warden, Sir Maurice Berkley, and to make a raid into enemy territory on 14 February, as 'it was better to die fighting than to starve'. They came to within six miles of Melrose Abbey on their foray and took many prisoners and cattle but on their return, were attacked at a ford, some twenty-one miles from Berwick. Twenty men-at-arms and sixty footmen were killed or taken prisoner in the engagement together with most of their horses and provisions. In the following month, Berkley reported to the king that his soldiers were dying of hunger and of the 300 men-at-arms in the garrison, only fifty could be mounted due to a shortage of horses. Inevitably, the temptation to extort the inhabitants was irresistible for some castle constables. The local people who took refuge in Bamburgh Castle for fear of the Scots complained to the king that they had been charged exorbitant sums of money for bringing their goods within the walls and for taking shelter in the grounds. In response, the constable, Roger de Horsley, was ordered to desist from levying these charges.[16]

The situation in the north was clearly severe yet only limited measures to safeguard the region were undertaken by the Crown. This was due to growing tensions between supporters of the king and those of Thomas, Earl of Lancaster, which threatened to escalate into civil war in 1317. A new element was added to the personal animosity between Edward and his cousin, the Earl of Lancaster, due to the rise of new royal favourites who received rich rewards from the king, including grants of offices, estates and advantageous marriages to wealthy heiresses. These men consisted of Hugh Despenser the Younger, whose father, Hugh Despenser the Elder, was Earl of Winchester and who had been a long-time trusted counsellor of the king, as well as three young knights, Roger Damory, Hugh Audley the Younger and William de Montacute. This new group of royalist supporters was regarded as a threat by the Earl of Lancaster, who sought to counter their influence and power. Tensions were further escalated by an extraordinary attack on Louis Beaumont near to Rushyford, while he was travelling on the road between Darlington and Durham for his consecration as Bishop of Durham on 1 September. He was set upon by Sir Gilbert de Middleton, a Northumbrian knight, and an armed group of men who took him and his brother, Henry, for ransom at Mitford Castle. It was regarded as a particularly heinous act of violence as he was accompanied by two cardinals, Gaucelin de Jean and Luca Fieschi, who were robbed of their possessions but allowed to carry on their way. The king believed the Earl of Lancaster to have been responsible for ordering the attack due to his hostility to the pro-royalist Beaumonts. However, Lancaster sought to disavow himself of any involvement by escorting the cardinals to York and ensuring that their stolen goods were restored to them. At York, the two cardinals and Aymer de Valence, Earl of Pembroke, worked to mediate between the two sides. An agreement was struck whereby the king agreed not to act against the Earl of Lancaster, while the latter promised to attend the next parliament, with one summoned to meet at Lincoln on 27 January 1318. However, this arrangement was swiftly undone by a reckless act of provocation by the king and his supporters. As they travelled from York to London they decided to approach the Earl of Lancaster's castle at Pontefract, where the latter was residing. According to the *Life of Edward II*, the king was goaded on by his favourites to launch an attack on the castle, resulting in an armed standoff. Edward was eventually persuaded by the Earl of Pembroke to desist from violence, but the episode enraged the Earl of Lancaster, who sought revenge. He ordered his followers to launch attacks on castles held by the officials of Roger Damory and John de Warenne, Earl of Surrey, whom he held to be chiefly responsible for the king's behaviour. On 5 October, John de Lilburn seized control of the royal castle of Knaresborough, which had been in the custody of a constable appointed by Damory. Elsewhere in Yorkshire, Warenne's castles of Conisbrough and Sandal were also occupied, despite the protests of the king. Edward prepared for the outbreak of hostilities by issuing instructions for the constables of royal castles to ensure that their fortifications were defensible. Civil war was averted due to negotiations, which began in November and eventually saw a political settlement agreed on 9 August 1318. The Treaty of Leake saw the king agreed to confirm the Ordinances and to appoint a standing royal council. Meanwhile, Sir Gilbert de Middleton had continued his ravages in Northumberland. He succeeded in taking prisoners on his forays and held them in Mitford Castle for ransom, but failed in his attempts to take Tynemouth Castle, which was defended by Sir Robert de la Vale. The constable of Alnwick Castle, Sir John Felton, was captured by Middleton in one raid and was only released on the condition of agreeing to arrange the surrender of the castle. This prompted John's brother, William, and a group of Northumberland gentlemen to band together to deal with the rebels. Mitford Castle was finally taken by a ruse in December 1317, when a group of armed men, on the pretence of visiting the castle to pay ransom money, overpowered the guards and captured Middleton, who was then sent to London for execution.[17]

The English suffered a further setback in April 1318 when Berwick fell to the Scots. It had for a long time been blockaded by land and sea, which caused great hardships for the townspeople and garrison, but was eventually captured through treachery.

One of the English inhabitants of the town, a Peter Spalding, was said to have admitted the Scots into the settlement by allowing them to scale the wall where he was stationed as a sentry, in return for the payment of a large bribe. The garrison of the castle held out for a further eleven weeks but was eventually compelled to surrender due to a lack of supplies. Bruce followed up on this victory by invading Northumberland and capturing the castles of Wark and Harbottle. The loss of Berwick was a major blow to Edward's prestige, which demanded that he make a decisive response. He was in a strong position to do so due to recent events. His reconciliation with Thomas, Earl of Lancaster, meant that he now had the full support of his magnates, and the defeat and death of Edward Bruce at the Battle of Faughart on 14 October 1318 removed the danger of a Scottish conquest of Ireland. Instructions were issued in November for a large army and fleet to assemble on 22 May 1319 for the campaign to recover Berwick. The royal army of some 10,000 men, including 8,000 infantry, supported by a fleet of seventy-seven ships, eventually arrived outside Berwick on 7 September, with the siege beginning the next day. A fierce initial assault was made by the English soldiers, which was said to have almost led to the capture of the town, before the defenders rallied and drove them back. The decision was then taken to pause operations, while stone-throwing artillery and specialist workers, such as ditch diggers, were transported by sea to the besiegers' camp, with operations resuming on 13 September. Further attempts to storm Berwick came close to success, before news arrived on the following day of the defeat of a hastily assembled English force at Myton near Boroughbridge. This reversal led to the abandonment of the siege due to the fear of a Scottish attack on York. Edward attempted to lead the army to intercept the Scots but they succeeded in evading the English and recrossed the border. This fiasco led to the abandonment of the campaign, with mutual recriminations ending the working relationship between the king and the Earl of Lancaster. The failure to recover Berwick also meant that the border castle of Norham remained dangerously isolated. This fortress was held for the Bishop of Durham, Louis de Beaumont, by his constable Thomas Gray, and was frequently subjected to Scottish attacks.

The exploits of the garrison are recorded by the latter's son, the chronicler of the same name, who claimed that it was said to have been 'the most dangerous (and) adventurous place in the country'. Gray states that Norham was besieged on two occasions, once for seven months, then for a whole year, with the sieges broken by the forces of Henry, Lord Percy, and Ralph, Lord Neville. It was not until the agreement of a two-year truce between England and Scotland, which ran from 29 December 1319 to 29 December 1321, that the hardships of the garrison were alleviated.[18]

The Rule of the Despensers

Following the death of Gaveston in 1312, Edward had lavished patronage on a small group of favoured courtiers. Yet over time the influence of Hugh Despenser the Younger gradually increased to the extent that he eventually completely supplanted his rivals in the king's affections. An important stage in this progress took place in 1318, when he was appointed as chamberlain of the king's household, a position once held by Gaveston. This brought him into close proximity with Edward, who soon became completely dependent upon him and his father, Hugh Despenser the Elder, the Earl of Winchester, in governing the kingdom. However, this excessive influence over the king soon earned Despenser the Younger the enmity of many of the magnates. Despenser's unscrupulous attempts to increase his power base in south Wales also brought him into conflict with the Marcher lords. He had acquired extensive lands in the region following the death of his brother-in-law, Gilbert de Clare, Earl of Gloucester, at the Battle of Bannockburn in 1314. Through his marriage to the late earl's sister, Eleanor, he was granted a share in the division of his estates, which took place in 1317. His main acquisition was the valuable lordship of Glamorgan, which was estimated to be worth almost £1,300 per annum, and included the important castles of Caerphilly, Llantrisant and Cardiff. Despenser's avariciousness meant that he ordered his officials not merely to take possession of Glamorgan, but to also take over the neighbouring lordship of Gwynllwg, which had been allocated to Hugh Audley. Despite being ordered by the king to relinquish possession of the lordship, Despenser refused to do so. Audley eventually gave up the struggle in December 1318, by agreeing to transfer ownership of Gwynlleg to Despenser in return for six manors in England that were far less valuable. Later in 1320, his attempt to acquire the lordship of Gower was opposed by many of his fellow Marcher lords, including Humphrey de Bohun, Earl of Hereford, and Roger Mortimer of Wigmore. The king's decision to intervene in the dispute, by ordering that Gower should be confiscated by the Crown on a technicality and then appointing Despenser as keeper, brought matters to a head. The Marcher lords were incensed, as they believed that the special laws and customs of the March had been infringed. In response, they resolved to take direct military action against Despenser and began to muster their forces in January and February of 1321. Aware of their preparations, the king issued instructions forbidding the gathering of unlawful assemblies and ordered his officials to ensure that the royal castles in Wales were defensible. In April, he seized control of Roger Damory's castle of St Briavels and ordered the confiscation of Montgomery Castle, which had been held for the Crown by Audley. Undaunted by these measures, the Marcher lords rebuffed a summons to attend a meeting with the king in May. Instead they began to ravage Despenser's lands in Wales, with the castles of Newport, Cardiff and Swansea taken within two weeks. Their attacks were aided by the unpopularity of Despenser in the region, with the chroniclers claiming that neither the keepers of his castles, nor his tenants, were willing to offer any resistance. It was later estimated that the damage caused to his estates and possessions came to the considerable sum of £14,000. In the following month, an agreement was concluded between Thomas, Earl of Lancaster, and the Marcher lords. Faced with this formidable coalition of opponents, Edward was powerless to retaliate against his enemies. Threatened with deposition by the magnates at the parliament held at Westminster in July, he was soon forced to exile the Despensers, who left the realm before the end of August.[19]

However, Edward was determined to secure the return of the Despensers. He at once began to plot with them through the exchange of letters and quickly formulated a plan to destroy their enemies. On 25 September, Edward sent instructions demanding that Roger Damory, Hugh Audley and Humphrey de Bohun, Earl of Hereford, surrender control of the Despenser estates they had seized. Predictably, these orders were disregarded, but they gave a suitable pretext for the king to move against the Marcher lords. Edward then targeted Sir Bartholomew Badlesmere, who was commanded to give up custody of Tonbridge Castle the next day. Badlesmere had been a trusted royal official, but his decision to dramatically change sides in the summer of 1321, earned him the hatred of the king. He was also detested by some of the barons, including Thomas, Earl of Lancaster, in part due to his recent association with Hugh Despenser the Younger. Soon afterwards Edward and Isabella left Westminster and travelled to Kent, on the pretext of visiting the shrine of Thomas Becket at Canterbury. Instead, Isabella went to Leeds Castle, a royal castle held by Badlesmere, and requested admittance from the latter's wife, Margaret, who had been left in charge. Her refusal to admit the queen led to a violent confrontation in which some members of Isabella's household were killed. Edward responded to this news by gathering his forces to lay siege to the castle. On 16 October, the sheriffs of Essex, Hampshire and Surrey were ordered to raise a force of 3,000 footmen and to send the knights and men-at-arms of their counties to accompany the royal army. These soldiers were to augment the retinues provided by Aymer de Valence, Earl of Pembroke; John of Brittany, Earl of Richmond, and Thomas of Brotherton, Earl of Norfolk, with a further contingent of 400 footmen provided by the city of London. The siege began on 23 October, with the royalists blockading the castle. Leeds had strong defences, surrounded as it was by a large artificial lake; if well provisioned, the castle could be expected to hold out for some time. However, the baronial army was prevented from marching to the aid of the defenders due to the opposition of the Earl of Lancaster. Their failure to break the siege led to the surrender of the castle on 31 October, after which thirteen members of the garrison, including the constable, Walter Culpeper, were executed for treason. The author of the *Life of Edward II* explains that the king took this brutal action 'so that no one in future would dare to hold fortresses against him'. Edward then prepared to move against the Marcher lords in November, by ordering his forces to assemble at Cirencester on 13 December. Instructions were also sent to Sir Gruffudd Llwyd and Rhys ap Gruffudd to raise forces within

Wales to attack the estates of his opponents. Soon afterwards the king succeeded in revoking the sentence of exile imposed on the Despensers following the meeting of a council of loyalist bishops and magnates.[20]

Edward travelled to Cirencester in December and stayed there for Christmas. Meanwhile, his opponents had seized control of Gloucester and had marshalled their forces to resist the royalist offensive. On 27 December, the king led his army northwards to Worcester, which was reached four days later. However, the royalists were unable to cross the River Severn there, as the opposite bank was held by their enemies. Therefore the king despatched a force to take control of Bridgnorth, further upstream. The Marcher lords responded by launching an attack on Bridgnorth Castle on the night of 5 January. Taken by surprise, the royalists were forced to retreat, and the bridge was burnt. Undeterred by this setback, Edward then led his forces northwards to Shrewsbury, which he reached on 14 January. At this point the resolve of the Marcher lords to resist the king began to waver. They were alarmed by the lack of support by Thomas, Earl of Lancaster, and their estates had been ravaged by royalist Welsh forces. Sir Gruffudd Llwyd had achieved notable successes against them, with his exploits including the capture of the Mortimer-held castles of Chirk, Clun and Welshpool. The first defections to the king occurred on 22 January, when Roger Mortimer of Wigmore, and his uncle Roger Mortimer of Chirk, submitted at Shrewsbury. Edward then acted decisively to defeat the remaining Marcher lords, who either surrendered or fled by 6 February. Five days later he issued instructions for his officials to raise a force of 12,000 Welsh and 3,000 English foot soldiers. Edward then marched northwards with the ranks of his army rapidly swelling in number, reaching Lichfield on 3 March. Further to the north, the Earl of Lancaster's forces had initiated hostilities in early January by laying siege to Tickhill Castle, but had failed to take the fortress. News of the king's approach prompted him to withdraw towards his castle of Tutbury, taking up position at the crossing at Burton-on-Trent. After three days of skirmishing between the two armies, the rebels fled when their position was outflanked by a force led by John de Warenne, Earl of Surrey. However, they were intercepted by an army led by Andrew Harclay and were defeated at the Battle of Boroughbridge on 16 March. The Earl of Lancaster was taken as a prisoner to his own castle at Pontefract, where he was executed on 22 March.[21]

Following the royalist victory, the defeated rebels were subjected to savage reprisals, with their leaders punished through executions, imprisonment and confiscation of their estates. The acquisition of these lands led to a marked improvement in the king's finances, even after many of them were distributed to his supporters. Edward used his new-found wealth to finance the raising of a new army for another campaign in Scotland. Soon after the execution of Thomas, Earl of Lancaster, orders were issued for the raising of soldiers and the procurement of provisions. The expedition was conceived on a grand scale, with orders issued for the raising of as many as 38,000 foot soldiers supported by a fleet of ships. A special emphasis was placed on the procurement of well-armed infantry, who were to be equipped with bacinets (helmets), aketons (quilted body armour) and gauntlets. Edward thereby intended to bring the largest possible force to bear against the Scots, in the expectation of achieving a decisive victory on the battlefield. In the event, the size of the army was much smaller, consisting of some 20,000 foot soldiers and more than 3,000 hobelars and men-at-arms, but it was still impressive. Bruce pre-empted the invasion by leading a raid into the north-west of England on 1 July. The Scots swept as far south as Lancaster, which they burnt, before returning to Scotland on 24 July, having inflicted significant damage in Cumberland and Lancashire. From the assembly point at Newcastle, Edward led his army into Scotland on 10 August reaching Musselburgh near Edinburgh nine days later. However, Bruce refused to offer battle and his scorched earth strategy in Lothian meant that the English rapidly exhausted their limited food supplies. Edward was soon forced to retreat to Newcastle, arriving there on 10 September, where he disbanded most of his forces. Nevertheless, he decided to remain in the north of England, issuing instructions for men to be arrayed for the defence of the border counties. The king's frustration at the disappointing end to the Scottish expedition can be seen in a set of letters he addressed to the constables of the principal castles in Northumberland dated 26 September. He wrote that the Scots with only a small force had raided the area near to their castles 'without challenge or damage from the garrisons' to their 'dishonour and shame'. Edward professed astonishment at their lack of scouts and inadequate intelligence, as well as their failure to harass the Scots. They were therefore commanded to 'see and do better' and to carry out 'some exploit on the enemy'. However, they were clearly unable or unwilling to act on his orders, as a short time later Bruce invaded England and defeated an English army outside Byland on 14 October. Edward was taken by surprise and was forced to flee from the nearby abbey of Rievaulx to avoid capture. This debacle prompted Andrew Harclay, Earl of Carlisle, to enter into treasonous correspondence with the Scots. Harclay had hitherto been the king's most loyal supporter in the north and had played a vital role in defeating the rebels at the Battle of Boroughbridge. His loyalty to the Crown was soon afterwards rewarded by his elevation to the title of earl. Yet the king's repeated failure to protect the north led him in desperation to agree a treaty with Bruce, whereby an Anglo-Scottish peace would be imposed on Edward – using force if necessary. Word of his treacherous behaviour eventually reached the king, who despatched Sir Antony de Lucy to arrest him on 1 February. The Lanercost chronicler states that de Lucy visited Carlisle Castle on the pretext of discussing 'household matters' with Harclay, accompanied by a small group of knights and men-at-arms. While some his companions subtly took up position in key locations around the castle, he burst into the great hall with the others, where Harclay was busy composing letters. There he was said to have exclaimed 'My lord earl, thou must either surrender immediately or defend thyself'. The unarmed earl was compelled to surrender to them and was taken into custody. Harclay was condemned to death on 3 March by a panel of royal justices without a trial at Carlisle Castle. He was then systematically stripped of his titles and knighthood in a degrading ceremony before being brutally executed by being hanged, drawn and quartered. In the following month, a lengthy truce was concluded with the Scots, which was to run from May 1323 to May 1336.[22]

Edward's triumph over his domestic opponents appeared to have been complete at the beginning of 1323. Yet a legacy of resentment and apprehension remained in the country due to the brutality of royalist reprisals. This mood of fear can be seen from a statement made by the author of the *Life of Edward II*. 'The king's harshness has indeed increased so much today that no one, however great and wise, dares to cross the king's will'. Hugh Despenser the Younger was the main beneficiary of this situation. He used his influence over the king to significantly increase his wealth, often using unscrupulous methods, becoming even more hated than before. Yet the confidence of the regime was shaken in the summer of 1323 due to the escape of Roger Mortimer of Wigmore from the Tower of London on 1 August. Mortimer afterwards travelled to France where he was well received by Charles IV due to a sudden decline in Anglo-France relations. A border incident in Gascony in October caused a crisis, which eventually led to the outbreak of war in August 1324. The French rapidly overran the badly defended duchy and Edward was forced to sue for peace. During the subsequent negotiations, Queen Isabella was sent to negotiate with her brother Charles IV, with an agreement finally reached in August 1325. As part of the settlement, Edward sent his son, Prince Edward, to perform homage on his behalf to the French king in September. However, both the queen and the prince subsequently refused to return to England. This was due to the breakdown of the relationship between Edward and Isabella. Isabella was angered by the influence that the Despensers had over her husband, and by the seizure of her estates in 1324 due to the government's indiscriminate confiscation of lands belonging to French subjects during the war with France. During her time on the Continent she began a relationship with Mortimer and hatched a plan with him to invade England to overthrow her husband and the Despensers. She gained the support of William I, Count of Hainaut, by betrothing Prince Edward to his daughter, Philippa, and used the latter's dowry to raise a small force of mercenaries. Edward made extensive preparations to resist the invasion, but such was the unpopularity of his regime that resistance rapidly collapsed after Isabella landed at Orwell in Suffolk on 24 September. Edward abandoned the capital on 2 October and fled westwards, with the Tower of London stormed soon afterwards. Hugh Despenser the Elder was handed over to the rebels after the garrison of Bristol surrendered on 26 October and he was executed the next day. Edward and

Despenser the Younger tried to raise an army in south Wales, without success, before attempting to escape to Ireland by ship, but were foiled by contrary winds. They were eventually captured at Llantrisant on 16 November, with Despenser executed eight days later. The only resistance to the invasion took place at Caerphilly Castle, whose defence was led by Sir John de Felton with a garrison of thirty-eight men. From mid-November they were besieged by a force of thirty men-at-arms and 400 foot-men commanded by William la Zouche. The formidable defences of Caerphilly meant a direct assault would be a hazardous undertaking so instead the attackers were forced to blockade the castle. However, this proved to be a very lengthy process as the fortress was amply supplied with provisions and equipment. The defenders were also fearful of reprisals should they surrender without a pardon. Therefore, they only capitulated after receiving guarantees for their safety on 11 March 1327, having held out for almost six months. In the meantime, Edward had been sent to Kenilworth Castle where he was forced to abdicate in favour of his fourteen-year-old son on 20 January. The deposed king was then sent to Berkeley Castle in April, with his death announced at the parliament held at Lincoln on 21 September. Accounts of his demise vary, with the *Lanercost Chronicle* stating that he 'died ... either by a natural death or by the violence of others' and was buried at Gloucester.[23]

Edward Balliol

Edward III was crowned as king on 1 February 1327 at Westminster Abbey. As he was deemed to be of a suitable age to rule the kingdom, a regency was not established. Instead it was decided in parliament that a council of fourteen earls, barons and bishops, presided over by Henry, Earl of Lancaster, should advise him. Nevertheless, royal authority was quickly appropriated by Isabella and Mortimer who marginalised the council and reduced Edward to being little more than a figurehead. The government moved swiftly to finalise a peace treaty with France, but was confronted with a renewed threat from Scotland. On the very same day as the king's coronation, the Scots had broken the truce by launching a surprise night-time attack on Norham Castle. The Lanercost chronicler reports that a small group of sixteen men boldly climbed the walls using ladders, intending to use the element of surprise to overcome the defenders, a tactic they had used with great success against the English in previous years. Unfortunately for them, the constable of the castle, Sir Robert de Manners, had been forewarned of the assault by a Scot in his service. This meant that the attackers were quickly overpowered by the waiting English, with almost all the Scots killed or taken prisoner. The timing of the attack was regarded as a challenge to the new king's honour, which demanded a robust response; therefore instructions were issued for the feudal host to muster at Newcastle in April for an expedition to Scotland. A delayed start to the campaign meant that the assembly point was eventually changed to York, which the army left in early July. By this time, the Scots had launched a pre-emptive strike across the border into Cumberland and it was feared that they intended to besiege Carlisle. Over the course of the next month, the English attempted to bring their opponents to battle. Yet they were repeatedly thwarted by the fast-moving Scots, who were lightly equipped and mounted on small ponies. After a frantic pursuit across Cumberland and County Durham, the English eventually caught up with them at Stanhope in the Wear valley. However, as their opponents had made camp in a strong position on the high ground they were unwilling to mount an immediate assault. On 4 August, a night-time assault led by Sir James Douglas caused havoc in the English camp before the Scots succeeded in slipping away before dawn three days later. This debacle prompted the leaders of the English army to abandon the campaign. According to Thomas Gray, such was the young king's frustration at this development that he burst into tears. The Scots then pressed home their advantage by launching an invasion into Northumberland. Bruce with his main force laid siege to Norham Castle, deploying stone-throwing artillery against the defenders, while another contingent led by Thomas Randolph, Earl of Moray, and Sir James Douglas besieged Alnwick. The risk of losing control of these castles and therefore effective control of Northumberland prompted the English government to sue for peace with the Scots. A treaty was ratified at Northampton on 4 May 1328 whereby Robert I's title as king was recognised in return for the promise of a payment of £20,000 in war reparations.[24]

The grasping nature of the Mortimer and Isabella regime led to the disaffection of prominent members of the nobility. The pair lavished lands and titles on themselves and their supporters, with the vast treasury accumulated by Edward II swiftly dissipated, leaving the Crown in dire financial straits. At the parliament held at Salisbury in October 1328, Mortimer was even granted the novel title of 'Earl of March'. This provoked Henry, Earl of Lancaster, to retire to his estates in the West Midlands and to gather his forces at Kenilworth Castle. He marched on the capital with an armed gathering in January 1329, but the defection of his aristocratic allies forced him to capitulate. Mortimer strengthened his grip on power in the following year when he instigated the arrest, trial and execution of the king's uncle, Edmund, Earl of Kent, on the charge of treason. The latter was said to have been tricked into believing that his brother, Edward II, was still alive and to have agreed to participate in a plot to restore him to the throne. Remarking on this event, the Lanercost chronicler stated that Mortimer 'at that time was more than king in the kingdom, forasmuch as the queen-mother and he ruled the whole realm'. The execution of his uncle persuaded Edward that he had to act decisively against Mortimer. Thomas Gray states that he was encouraged to do so by a member of his household, William Montagu, as 'it is better to eat the dog than to have the dog eat you'. An opportunity was provided by the summoning of a parliament to appear at Nottingham in October, with the royal party lodged in the castle. Edward and a small group of armed companions were said to have secretly entered the inner ward of the castle by means of an underground tunnel. They then gained access to the keep, which had been left purposely unlocked by the constable of the castle, and went into Isabella's chamber. After a short but violent confrontation, that left some of Mortimer's men dead, they arrested the occupants and took control of the castle. Mortimer was subsequently put on trial and executed for treason, but otherwise the coup was bloodless. Edward was keen to restore domestic accord now that he had assumed control of the government. Yet one of the problems he had to contend with concerned the claims of the so-called 'disinherited'. These were English lords whose lands in Scotland had been lost due to the treaty of 1328. Attempts to secure compensation from the government of David II, the son and successor or Robert I, were rebuffed, leading to a deterioration in Anglo-Scottish relations. The disinherited found a useful figurehead in Edward Balliol, son of the deposed king and, in support of his claim to be king of Scots, invaded Scotland with a small force in 1332. On 11 August, they succeeded in winning a remarkable victory against a much larger Scottish army at the Battle of Dupplin Moor. Their defensive deployment of men-at-arms and archers proved to be a highly effective tactic that was used to great effect by the English in future campaigns. This defeat caused consternation in Scotland, due to the heavy death toll, with many Scots of high rank slain. In the confusion that followed, some of the magnates threw their lot in with Balliol, who was proclaimed king of Scots at Scone Abbey on 24 September. However, his reign was to be a brief one. His forces were taken by surprise at Annan in December and he was forced to flee across the border to England. He sought Edward III's assistance by offering to cede the southern counties of Scotland and to recognise him as his feudal overlord. These terms were accepted by Edward who prepared to mount a military expedition to restore Balliol to power.[25]

The advance guard of the invasion was led by Balliol, who laid siege to Berwick in March 1333. Meanwhile orders were issued for the procurement of large quantities of provisions and for the main army to assemble at Newcastle. Artillery was also constructed by carpenters in Yorkshire for the siege, with hundreds of stone projectiles carved by masons. These siege weapons were placed under the supervision of a Flemish mercenary, John Crabbe, who had previously directed the defence of Berwick in 1319, but had been induced to change sides after being captured by the English in the previous year. Edward and the main army arrived at the town in May, which led to an intensification of the prosecution of the siege. The English stone-throwing artillery subjected the defenders to a heavy barrage of missiles, which caused significant damage to the walls and houses of the town. This prompted the garrison to negotiate an agreement with the besiegers, whereby they would surrender if they had not been relieved by a Scottish army by 11 July. The guardian of Scotland, Sir Archibald Douglas, attempted to pressure the English into abandoning the siege, by launching raids into

Cumberland and Northumberland. However, unlike his father in 1319, Edward refused to be deflected from his purpose. Even when the Scots briefly besieged Bamburgh Castle, where his wife Queen Philippa was staying, he refused to let up the pressure on Berwick. This forced the Scots to confront Edward in the field in a desperate attempt to break the siege. On 19 July, the English won a decisive victory at the Battle of Halidon Hill, with Berwick surrendered the next day. Following this triumph, Edward moved swiftly to occupy most of southern Scotland, which was administered by English officials. Balliol established his capital at Perth but quickly faced armed resistance from supporters of David II. By September 1334 he had been forced to flee southwards to Berwick. A new campaign was organised for the following year, with some 13,000 soldiers mustering at Newcastle in July 1335. One army commanded by Edward advanced from Carlisle to Annandale, meanwhile Balliol led the other contingent from Berwick towards Edinburgh.

They joined forces at Glasgow before marching northwards to Perth, which they reached in August, where a short truce was agreed with the Scots. However, Balliol suffered a major blow on 30 November, due to the defeat of one of his principle supporters, David Strathbogie, Earl of Atholl, at the Battle of Culblean. Diplomatic support was also offered by the French king, Philip VI, who made a permanent Anglo-French settlement contingent on the recognition of the rights of the Bruce dynasty. In the following summer, Edward returned to Scotland with a small mounted force of less than 1,000 men. First he made for Perth, where he relieved a hard-pressed English force led by Henry Grosmont, Earl of Lancaster. He then proceeded northwards to break the siege of Lochindorb Castle, held by Katherine, Countess of Atholl, before marching along the north-east coast, with his soldiers burning and ravaging the land and settlements in their path. This destruction was intended to punish his opponents and to deter the French from landing an army on the east coast of Scotland to aid their Scottish allies. Despite these successes, the cause of David II continued to gain strength, with Balliol's pretences to be King of Scots becoming increasingly hollow. However, Edward's attention was now focused on the Continent due to the outbreak of war with France in 1337.[26]

The Hundred Years' War and the Threat of Invasion: 1337–1399

In the same year (1377) on 21 August the French took the virtually impregnable Isle of Wight, though more by guile than valour. If it had been properly defended by the garrison it would not have fallen to anyone. But the careless watch kept by the islanders led to destruction for themselves, an unexpected triumph for the French and disgrace and heavy losses for the English... The French at last reached the castle on the island. They imagined that they could capture it with little trouble, but they found there in Sir Hugh Tyrrell, the castellan, a person able to inspire an unbelievably fierce defence. He boldly met the French near the castle, and inflicted great slaughter upon them. So they stopped attacking the castle, and, thinking it unsafe to live alongside such a dragon in the future, they collected as much booty as they could from the island and forced the inhabitants to beg their friends outside the island for a thousand marks (£666) of silver to save their houses from fire and to secure the rest of their possessions. And they only departed after they had received an oath of good behaviour from the islanders and a promise that for a whole year they would not keep out the French, whenever it pleased them to land on the island.

The Chronica Maiora of Thomas Walsingham[1]

On 24 May 1337, Philip VI ordered the confiscation of the Duchy of Gascony, with a French army invading the territory soon afterwards. This action was taken in response to the failure of

Edward III to perform homage to him as his feudal overlord for Gascony. Anglo-French wars had been fought earlier in the century over the duchy, but this struggle had lasting consequences. It would prove to be the start of a lengthy conflict between England and France that was later described by modern historians as the Hundred Years' War. In 1340, Edward III declared himself king of France, claiming that he was the rightful heir to his uncle, Charles IV, who had died twelve years earlier. Thereafter he attempted to conquer France through force of arms. His claim to the French throne was retained by his successors until the reign of George III. The Hundred Years' War was entwined from the start with the Anglo-Scottish conflict and soon expanded to incorporate the Low Countries and the Iberian Peninsula. Military operations were primarily fought on the Continent, with frequent expeditionary forces sent from England across the Channel. The main strategy used by the English was to employ entirely mounted armies to carry out devastating forays, known as 'chevauchées', to inflict widespread devastation throughout France. However, the French sought to retaliate through raiding the coastal communities of England and the Channel Islands. The impact of these attacks was most keenly felt in the late fourteenth century, with towns such as Rye and Winchelsea burnt by raiders. This pressure peaked in the mid-1380s when there was the very real danger of a French invasion of England. The Crown sought to counter this threat through the garrisoning of strategic castles in southern England, with work carried out to improve their defences. The most notable development of this period was the adoption of gunpowder weapons to provide additional firepower for the defenders of fortifications. These early guns were very small, with their usage limited by the initially high price of gunpowder. Yet over time, gunpowder weapons came to play an increasingly important role in warfare.

King of England and France

By the mid-1330s Anglo-French relations had become severely strained. The main source of this discord was territorial disputes over the border region of Agenais in south-west France but further tension was caused by the war between England and Scotland, due to French support for the latter, which derived from the Treaty of Paris in 1296. The cancellation of a planned crusade to the Holy Land in March 1336 also meant that Philip VI had the opportunity to use a powerful fleet of galleys he had assembled to instead launch an assault on England. In the autumn, attacks were made on English ships anchored at Orford in Suffolk and the Isle of Wight. Existing measures for coastal defence were found wanting, with no effective challenge made to drive off or punish the perpetrators. Therefore orders were issued for the requisitioning of merchant vessels to patrol the sea and for the raising of soldiers to defend the coastal regions. The soldiers were assembled using a system that had been place prior to the Norman Conquest. All men between the ages of sixteen and sixty were obliged to serve in defence of the realm at their own expense. They were to be armed with weapons and armour, according to their means, as was stated in the Statute of Winchester of 1285. In January 1345, it was specified that individuals with an annual income of £5 should serve as mounted archers, those with £10 as hobelars, equipped with a helmet (palet), visor, quilted armour (aketon), iron gauntlets and a lance, whereas men who earnt £25 were to serve as heavily armed and armoured men-at-arms. These men were assembled by specially appointed commissioners of array, who were prominent local landowners appointed by the Crown to supervise the mustering of men in their counties. They were also required to ensure that they were suitably armed and ready for service when required. In addition to this, a series of manned beacons was set up so that fires could be lit to warn the local inhabitants of enemy landings. However, the deficiencies in this system of coastal defence were soon laid bare.[2]

In March 1338, a French force landed at Portsmouth. As it was unwalled and badly defended, the French faced little resistance and they were able to sack and burn the town. Local forces were too slow and reactionary to intervene. In September, a Franco-Genoese fleet attacked Guernsey and succeeded in overrunning the island, with the garrisons of Cornet Castle and Jerburgh Castle overwhelmed. In the following month, an armada sailed into the Solent and landed a force outside Southampton. The French then proceeded to storm the settlement, causing considerable damage to its buildings before they returned to their ships the next day. Their success was largely due to the inadequate state of the fortifications, with only a wooden barbican protecting the seashore, and due to the lack of resistance offered by the townspeople. The king was furious when he received this news and set up a commission headed by Richard, Earl of Arundel, to investigate the debacle. It was reported that the keepers of the coast and commissioners of array in the county had 'not only neglected entirely to provide for the defence of parts threatened but basely fled with the men of the town on sight of the enemy'. Early in the following year, Philip VI decided to strike a decisive blow against his adversary by raising an army for an invasion of England. Upon hearing news of this plan, Edward and his council ordered measures for the defence of the realm. Merchant ships were requisitioned for naval service and men were arrayed to defend the coastal regions. Efforts were also made to improve the fortifications of threatened castles, and to ensure that they were adequately guarded. The garrison of the strategically important castle of Dover was more than doubled from forty-six to 100 men, while a force of thirty men-at-arms and archers was placed in Winchester Castle. Reinforcements were also sent to the Isle of Wight and major repairs were started at Carisbrooke Castle. However, delays in raising the army in Normandy meant that the French offensive was limited to coastal raids. This time the English were better prepared to face them. An attack on Plymouth in May was repelled by the men of Devon, with attempts to make landings in Hampshire, the Isle of Wight and Kent also beaten off. The only French success was the burning of Hastings, as the town was unwalled and its castle was dilapidated. Nevertheless, the threat of invasion was only averted by Edward's expedition to Flanders later that year, which diverted French resources. It was during this campaign that he proclaimed himself king of France, as a means by which to secure military support from the Flemish towns.[3]

Despite Edward's preoccupation with Continental affairs, the war continued unabated in Scotland. Early in 1337, Sir Andrew Murray, the Guardian of Scotland, succeeded in recapturing his ancestral stronghold of Bothwell Castle. He then followed up on this victory by capturing other castles and towns in Fife. In response, Edward entered Scotland in June with a small army to break the siege of Stirling Castle. Yet he was unable to remain in the country for long and after overseeing the provisioning of his fortresses there, returned to southern England. In his absence, a strong force under the command of William Montagu, Earl of Salisbury, laid siege to Dunbar Castle in January 1338. Despite being well supplied with siege weapons they were unable to take the castle due to the determined resistance of the defenders, led by 'Black Agnes' Randolph. Eventually they were forced to lift the siege in June. However, even after this setback, the English still had a strong presence in southern Scotland with sizeable garrisons maintained in the major towns and castles. In 1340, it was recorded that a force of 143 men were stationed at Edinburgh Castle, a further 123 at Stirling Castle, and an additional 135 at Roxburgh Castle. Work was also undertaken to rebuild some of the fortifications that had previously been destroyed by the Scots. In November 1335, it was reported by the incoming constable that the only habitable buildings in Edinburgh Castle were the chapel and a stable block. Over the course of the following year, Master John of Kilburn supervised the reconstruction of the fortress, with teams of masons, carpenters, labourers and carters undertaking work that made the structure defensible. Other projects included the erection of a peel at the ruins of Stirling Castle and the rebuilding of Roxburgh Castle. Nevertheless, most of these fortifications had been recaptured by the Scots by June 1341, with many of their garrisons having been starved into surrender when David II returned from France to take control of his kingdom. These defeats prompted Edward to lead another expedition to Scotland in December, but he soon returned to England having achieved very little. Following his departure, the Scots succeeded in taking Roxburgh Castle in a surprise attack and began to launch raids into northern England. However, the situation was transformed in the autumn of 1346. David II invaded the north of England with a large army but was defeated and captured at the Battle of Neville's Cross on 14 October.[4]

Two months previously, Edward had achieved an even more significant victory at the Battle of Crécy in northern France. The English were significantly outnumbered by their opponents but used a combination of dismounted men-at-arms and archers to devastating effect against the French cavalry. This was to be first in a succession of English victories over the following decade.

Nine years later, his eldest son, Edward of Woodstock, later known as the 'Black Prince', defeated an army led in person by King John II at the Battle of Poitiers in September 1356. The capture of King John during the battle meant that Edward was in a strong position to negotiate a highly advantageous settlement with the French government. His hand was further strengthened by a breakdown in law and order across many regions of France, with a major rebellion known as the Jacquerie occurring in the north in the summer of 1358. This was largely due to the ravages by bands of freebooter soldiers, known as routiers, who professed to be in English service, but mainly operated independently of the Crown's control. Yet it was only following another major expedition to France in 1359–60, led in person by the English king that negotiations led to the Treaty of Brétigny, agreed on 8 May 1360. In return for the release of King John and for renouncing his claim to the French throne, Edward was granted a colossal sum of ransom money, payable in instalments, and the ceding, in full sovereignty, of a huge swathe of territory in south-west France. This settlement was a signal victory for Edward and cemented his reputation as a great warrior king. Peace had already been achieved with Scotland, following the release of David II from captivity in 1357, in return for the payment of a large sum of money. Edward invested part of his windfall from these ransoms in castle-building over the following years. He founded a new town and castle on the Isle of Sheppey in Kent, named Queenborough in honour of his wife, Queen Philippa. Queenborough had an unusual concentric circular design, with an inner ward flanked by six towers, which was encircled in turn by an outer ward and moat. This was one of the biggest building projects of Edward's reign, with more than £20,000 spent on the castle from 1361 to 1377. A later inventory from 1388 reveals that it had substantial stores of arms and armour, including stone-throwing engines. Queenborough is most notable, however, for the presence of gunpowder weapons. In 1365, eleven guns were sent to the castle from the Tower of London by the keeper of the Privy Wardrobe, John Sleaford, a royal official responsible for the supply of the king's arms and armour. It was therefore the first castle in England to be equipped with these new types of weapons. During the same period, substantial works were carried out on the other side of the Thames Estuary at Hadleigh Castle in Essex. More than £2,000 was spent on rebuilding the walls, towers and lodgings in the castle, which became one of the king's favoured residences, along with Queenborough.[5]

The Threat of Invasion

The resumption of war with France in 1369 led to the rapid loss of almost all the territory gained as part of the Treaty of Brétigny. A succession of English expeditions to the Continent failed to reverse these gains with the French now in the ascendant. The situation was made worse by the death of Edward III in 1377. He was succeeded by his ten-year-old grandson Richard II. During his minority, the government of the kingdom was in the hands of his uncles, but they were unable to provide effective leadership to counter French gains. In the summer of 1377, a Franco-Castilian fleet raided the coast of southern England. They first made landfall in East Sussex, with an attack made on Rye on 21 June, which they sacked after overpowering its defenders. Yet they were deterred from assaulting nearby Winchelsea, due to the presence of Haimo of Offington, Abbot of Battle Abbey. The chronicler Thomas Walsingham reports that upon receiving news of their landing at Rye, Haimo had gathered the local men of the area to resist the invaders and led them to the town. An offer was made to spare Winchelsea by the French leader, Jean de Viennes, in return for a large payment, which was rejected by the abbot. In response, the French launched an assault on the town, but after hours of fierce fighting they were forced to withdraw. This prompted the raiders to return to their ships in search of easier prey. They subsequently burnt Hastings and captured the prior of Lewes, John of Charlieu, after defeating him at a skirmish fought at Rottingdean. Later in August they descended on the Isle of Wight. The French quickly overran the island, due to the carelessness of the inhabitants, but faced determined resistance from the constable of Carisbrooke Castle, Sir Hugh Tyrell. He inflicted a sharp reverse on the raiders after leading a sortie from the castle, but was powerless to stop them from burning the adjoining town. Eventually the inhabitants of the island were forced to make a payment of 1,000 marks (approximately £666) to persuade the French to leave. Viennes next sailed his fleet into the Solent and attacked Southampton. However, the town was defended by a large royal garrison of 340 men, led by Sir John Arundel, and their attempts to make landfall were beaten off. Similar attempts to make landings at Poole and Dover were repulsed by the local defence forces, although they did burn Folkstone. Anger at the failure of the government to prevent French raiding later contributed to the outbreak of a major rebellion subsequently known as the 'Peasants' Revolt'. This uprising was motivated primarily by the imposition of a poll tax earlier in the year, with the rebels marching on the capital in the summer of 1381. They were permitted to gain entry to the Tower of London and only dispersed after Richard II agreed to make concessions to them. However, the king went back on his word after gathering his forces and the rebellion was brutally suppressed.[6]

The threat of a French invasion and raiding prompted the Crown to refurbish the defences of strategic coastal castles in southern England in the 1370s and 1380s. More than £300 was spent refurbishing the fortifications at Corfe Castle, with a further £500 spent on Rochester Castle. At Portchester Castle, a new tower called 'Assheton's Tower' was erected in the inner ward. It was named in honour of Sir Robert Assheton, the constable of the castle from 1377 to 1381, and was designed for the use of gunpowder weapons. Five keyhole-shaped gun ports are carved into the walls, from where firearms could be fired; an inventory from 1385 reveals that it was equipped with four guns. The biggest building project took place at Southampton Castle, which was entirely rebuilt between the years 1378 and 1388, at a cost of almost £2,000. A keep was constructed on the site of the old castle, encircled by a curtain wall with four towers, three gates and a bridge. This was intended to improve the defences of the strategic town, which was in the process of being fully enclosed with a stone wall. The stocks of arms and armour in the castle were placed in the keeping of a chaplain called Thomas Tredyngton, who was appointed in July 1386. Despite his clerical background, he was given the responsibility of looking after the castle's arsenal, in addition to his religious duties, because he was said to been 'an expert in guns and the management of artillery'. From the 1370s, royal castles were routinely supplied with firearms from the arsenal at the Tower of

London. For example, in 1380 four guns were sent to Corfe and a further three guns to Dover. The introduction of these weapons led to a gradual decline in traditional forms of defensive artillery, such as springalds, which became increasingly rare. These early guns were mostly small, generally weighing less than 100lbs, and they fired lead bullets for targeting enemy combatants rather than knocking down walls. Yet from these humble beginnings gunpowder weapons gradually transformed the conduct of medieval warfare.[7]

These defensive preparations were crucial as the country faced the very real prospect of an invasion in the mid-1380s. The defeats suffered by the English and her allies on the Continent in the preceding years, notably the French suppression of the rebellion in Flanders, meant that the international situation was bleak. Sir Michael de la Pole, the chancellor of England, outlined the dangers facing the kingdom when he addressed the parliament held at Westminster on 15 November 1384. A powerful coalition, consisting of the French, Castilians, Flemish and Scots, was posed to attack the country, 'entirely surrounded as it was by deadly enemies all in league with one another'. A short time later, Richard II and his council received news that Charles VI of France, intended to invade England via Scotland. It was therefore decided that the king should lead an army in person to launch a pre-emptive strike against the Scots in the summer of 1385. However, a French fleet succeeded in evading English naval patrols and landed a small advance guard, led by Jean de Viennes, on the east coast of Scotland in May. This army then joined forces with the Scots and invaded Northumberland. A vivid account of the campaign is provided by the chronicler Jean Froissart, who states that the invaders first made for Roxburgh Castle. Yet after observing that it was 'large, fair and well provided with artillery' they instead proceeded towards Berwick-upon-Tweed. On their march towards the sea they encountered two peel towers, which they took by storm. Afterwards they came before Wark Castle, which was said to be 'a very strong' fortress held by Sir John Luffebourne, who had furnished the place with soldiers and artillery 'to the utmost of his power, in expectation of the attack'. However, a later inquisition reveals that Froissart's description of the castle was grossly exaggerated. Wark was described as having been in a ruinous state during the reign of Edward III, and it had been badly damaged by the Scots in 1383. Nevertheless, in view of its strategic location close to the border, a royal garrison was installed in the castle in the following year, despite its dilapidated condition. According to Froissart, the French behaved in a far more courageous manner than the Scots by leading an immediate assault on Wark. The attackers first succeeded in making their way past the ditches surrounding the castle, though not without difficulty, before they climbed the walls with ladders. In the hand-to-hand fighting that followed they suffered heavy losses at the hands of the English garrison, who put up a heroic resistance, but the French were finally victorious due to their superior numbers, with upwards of forty prisoners taken. They then slighted the castle, after deciding that it could not be held against the English. Soon afterwards they withdrew back to Scotland, after receiving news that an enemy force was marching to confront them. This army was led by Richard II, which marched northwards from Newcastle on 30 July, crossing the border into Lothian one week later. The English soldiers carried out a savage campaign of destruction, ravaging and pillaging everything in their path, with Edinburgh burnt on 11 August. Yet they soon experienced shortages of provisions due to the huge size of the English army and as the Scots refused to meet them in battle. This quickly led to the decision to abandon the expedition, but not before a heated dispute was said to have broken out between the king and his uncle, John of Gaunt, Duke of Lancaster. According to the chronicler Thomas Walsingham, the latter argued that they should pursue the Scots into the Highlands, but his nephew accused him of traitorously plotting his destruction. This led to the campaign ending in bitter acrimony, with the army returning to Newcastle on 20 August. Following their departure, the Scots and the French retaliated by mounting an incursion into the north-west of England, with the city of Carlisle briefly besieged. However, the relationship between the allies had been increasingly strained and this led to the departure of Viennes and his contingent a short time later. The planned French follow-up expedition to Scotland was also cancelled due to the capture of the town of Dammes in Flanders by a force from the city of

Ghent, an ally of England. The French were forced to direct their resources towards the recovery Dammes, with Charles VI and his ministers instead deciding to organise a direct invasion of England in the following year.[8]

This took the form of a major expedition that was intended to win the war against the English in the summer of 1386. Victory would be achieved either through the conquest of England, or by forcing Richard II to agree to peace terms favourable to the French. A large army and fleet were assembled in Flanders, which Froissart claimed was so great in number 'that the oldest man then living had never seen nor heard of the like'. The expeditionary force was equipped with a sizeable artillery train, consisting of both stone-throwing siege weapons and guns, for siege warfare, as well as a prefabricated castle. According to Thomas Walsingham, this was to be erected after the invaders made landfall in England to provide them with a place of safe refuge. The walls of the fortress were said to be twenty feet in height, with towers placed every twelve feet along its circuit. In response to this news, Richard II issued instructions for commissioners of array to raise a force of 10,000 men from across the country, which was to muster in the area around London. Garrisons were also installed in the main towns and castles of south-eastern England, with 720 men-at-arms and archers stationed at Dover, Portchester, Rye, Sandwich and Southampton. This deployment of forces was partly based on reports of where the enemy intended to land. According to Froissart, the constable of Dover Castle, Sir Simon de Burley, was informed that the French intended to land part of their army at Dover and another at Sandwich. This intelligence came from the fishermen of Kent, who were given this information by their French counterparts from across the Channel, with whom they had a working relationship. Nevertheless, rumours as to the size of the invasion force threw the country into panic. Thomas Walsingham reports that the Londoners were so fearful that they tore down the houses outside the city walls, in anticipation of an enemy siege. Their anxious mood was not helped by the activities of the English soldiers quartered outside of the city. Due to a lack of pay and provisions, they were said to have robbed the local inhabitants and acted 'as though they were in the country of the enemy'. Discontent with the government's handling of the crisis came to a head at the parliament held at Westminster in October, later known as the 'Wonderful Parliament'. The Commons demanded the removal of the chancellor, Michael de la Pole, from office and reforms to the royal household. Richard was initially unwilling to accept these demands, but was forced to capitulate after being threatened with deposition. In the meanwhile, the French government had experienced severe financial difficulties due to the sheer size of the army and fleet they had assembled, which eventually led in November to the abandonment of the expedition. Any further attempts to revive the venture were scotched by an English counter-attack at sea. In early 1387, a fleet commanded by Richard Fitzalan, Earl of Arundel, intercepted and captured many of the French ships in the Channel, even briefly blockading the port of Sluys, where some of them had taken refuge.[9]

The Overthrow of Richard II

Richard's desire to seek revenge against those magnates who had forced him to accept the reforms of the Wonderful Parliament almost led to his downfall in late 1387. The king's favourite, Robert de Vere, Duke of Ireland, raised a royalist army in Cheshire, while Simon de Burley, constable of Dover Castle, attempted to gather support from the Cinque Ports. At the same time, their opponents mustered their forces to resist them by force of arms. They comprised a powerful coalition of magnates, consisting of the king's uncle, Thomas of Woodstock, Duke of Gloucester; Richard Fitzalan, Earl of Arundel; Thomas Beauchamp, Earl of Warwick; his cousin, Henry Bolingbroke, eldest son of John of Gaunt, Earl of Derby, and Thomas Mowbray, Earl of Nottingham. These men were subsequently known as the 'Lords Appellant' as they brought a judicial appeal against five of the king's favourites. There was little support for Richard's cause and de Vere's army was intercepted at Radcot Bridge in Oxfordshire and compelled to surrender. The Lords Appellant then marched on the capital and took control of the government. They considered deposing Richard, but after disagreeing over who should replace him, they left him as king. Nevertheless, they purged the royal household, with the king's favourites condemned to death with confiscation of their lands and goods at the so-called 'Merciless Parliament' of February 1388.

Richard regained power in 1389, but did not immediately seek revenge against his opponents. Instead, he directed his attention to the restoration of royal power in Ireland, by leading an expedition to the island in 1394. Richard also pursued a policy of seeking peace with France, with a twenty-eight-year truce agreed in Paris in 1396. However, in the following year, without any warning, he suddenly ordered the arrest of the Duke of Gloucester and the earls of Arundel and Warwick. Gloucester died in suspicious circumstances while awaiting trial in Calais, whereas Arundel was executed after being convicted of treason at the parliament of 1397. Warwick's life was spared after he admitted his own guilt of the charges put to him, but he was sentenced to life imprisonment on the Isle of Man. In September 1398, the king also ordered the exile of both Mowbray and Derby, following a quarrel between the two men. By 1399, Richard appeared to be firmly in control of his kingdom. Yet his vindictive reprisals against former supporters of the Lords Appellant, which included the levying of heavy fines, fostered popular resentment against his rule.[10]

Richard's decision to confiscate the Duchy of Lancaster, following the death of John of Gaunt in February 1399, incurred the enmity of Henry Bolingbroke, who was denied his patrimony. The latter, with the support of a faction of the French court of Charles VI, began to plot his cousin's overthrow. Henry's opportunity came in May when Richard left England, with many of his most loyal supporters, for an expedition to Ireland. Soon afterwards he sailed from Boulogne with a small band of followers and landed near Ravenspurn in Yorkshire on 4 July. His return was carefully co-ordinated with his network of Lancastrian supporters, who rapidly turned out to join his growing army. Henry then moved quickly to take control of the nearby castles of Pickering, Knaresborough and Pontefract. He enjoyed widespread support from the region, with the author of the *Chronicle of Dieulacres Abbey* stating that 'numerous noble and warlike men from the north and from Lancaster, Derby and Stafford gathered with him'. In the meantime, his followers in other parts of the country had also taken up arms against Richard's government. Sir John Pelham seized control of Pevensey Castle but was then besieged by a royalist force. Elsewhere, Henry's partisans took control of the castles of Kenilworth and Dunstanburgh, which they garrisoned. Responsibility for defending the kingdom had been entrusted by Richard to his uncle, Edmund of Langley, Duke of York, who he appointed as keeper of the realm. Edmund responded to news of Henry's landing in Yorkshire by issuing instructions for a large force of men-at-arms and archers to assemble at Ware in Hertfordshire. Measures were also taken to secure southern England, with garrisons stationed in the castles of Queenborough and Rochester. Yet Edmund's resolve soon wavered. Many of his soldiers were unwilling to fight against Henry and began to desert his army. Therefore, after meeting with his nephew at Berkeley, he switched sides and joined his army. Some of Richard's most ardent and hated supporters, including William Scrope, Earl of Wiltshire, fled in desperation to Bristol Castle. The fortress was said to have had a large garrison and to have ample provisions. Nevertheless, it was surrendered without any resistance being offered on the approach of Henry's army, with the fugitives shown summary justice and executed. By this time, Richard had returned to the realm, having landed at Milford Haven on or about 24 July, yet his cause was already all but lost. Bad weather had led to the dispersal of his fleet, leaving him with only the remnants of the force he had led to Ireland some two months earlier. In a state of panic, he abandoned his army and headed across country with only a small band of followers. Richard intended to rendezvous with John Montagu, Earl of Salisbury, who he had earlier sent on ahead to raise fresh forces from the principality of Wales and Cheshire. Yet upon his arrival at Conwy Castle on 6 August, he was met by the Earl of Salisbury, who informed him of his failure to recruit any soldiers. At about the same time, Henry received the surrender of Chester. He then marched on the nearby castle of Holt, which Jean de Creton, a French esquire who was a companion of Richard's at the time, claims was 'so strong and sound that ... it could not have been taken by force in ten years'. However, despite being well garrisoned and provisioned, the 'faint-hearted and cowardly' defenders surrendered without a fight. The king was then tricked into leaving Conwy by Henry Percy, Earl of Northumberland, and was delivered to Henry's custody at Flint. Richard was subsequently deposed with the assent of parliament on 30 September, with Henry Bolingbroke crowned as Henry IV thirteen days later.[11]

The Lancastrians: 1399–1453

Very powerful and very redoubted liege lord, we recommend us to your very sovereign lordship with all manner of honours and reverences. And may it please your royal majesty to hear that Robert Parys, the deputy constable of Caer-narvon Castle, has informed us through a woman, because there was no man who dared to come, for neither man nor woman dare carry letters on account of the rebels of Wales, whom Owen Glyndŵr, with the French and all his other power, is raising up to assault the town and castle of Caernarvon; and to begin the execution of this operation with engines, 'sows', and ladders of great lengths. And in the town and castle there are not in all more than twenty-eight fighting men, which is too small a force; for eleven of the abler men who were there at the last siege of the place are dead, some of the wounds they received at the time of the assault, and others of the plague. Therefore the castle and town are in great peril, as the bearer of this will be able to inform you by word of mouth, to whom, may it please your highness to give full faith and credence, as he can inform you of the whole matter truly ... Written at Chester the 16th day of January. Your poor lieges. William Venables of Kinderton (Constable of Chester) and Roger Brescy.
A letter to Henry IV dated 16 January 1404[1]

This letter was written at the height of a great rebellion in Wales in January 1404. Some four years earlier, a quarrel between Reginald, Lord Grey of Ruthin, and a Welsh gentleman, Owain Glyn Dŵr, led to the latter launching an uprising. Owain was soon forced to go on the run, but resentment at English rule meant that the rebellion grew in strength to engulf almost all of Wales within a few years. The success of the uprising was due, in large part, to the chaos and unrest caused by the usurpation of Henry IV in 1399. Supporters of the deposed Richard II sought to restore him to the throne by overthrowing the new regime. Henry was also forced to contend with rebellions led by his erstwhile supporters, the powerful Percy family. This meant that the early years of the fifteenth century were characterised by uprisings and conspiracies. The survival of the Lancastrian dynasty was only secured by years of hard fighting and military operations. Crucial to this success was the control of castles, particularly in Wales. Many of these structures dated from the thirteenth century or earlier, were in a poor state of repair and held by tiny, isolated garrisons. Yet they played a vital role in preventing the Welsh from fully driving the English out of the country. Furthermore, they served as bridgeheads for counter-attacks that eventually led to the suppression of the rebellion, which was all but over by the accession of Henry V in 1413. Henry's desire for glory soon led to the resumption of the Hundred Years' War with France. Most of the fighting took place on the Continent, but tensions with Scotland, France's ally, led to occasional border clashes. This period also saw an important technological development with the adoption by the English of a new type of gun, known as a bombard. Bombards were huge guns that weighed thousands of pounds, and could knock down the walls of towns and castles with the large stone projectiles they fired. This later led to significant changes in the design of fortifications to counter the impact of gunpowder artillery.

Plots and Rebellions

Henry's seizure of the throne in 1399 had been remarkably easy, with few men willing to fight for Richard II. Nevertheless, the new king was soon faced with a multitude of dangers that threatened to overwhelm him. Conscious of the need to achieve reconciliation to avoid any further civil strife, he began his reign by pardoning many of the chief supporters of Richard II. Their closeness to the deposed king meant that they were deeply unpopular, and some of them were implicated in the murder of Thomas of Woodstock, Duke of Gloucester. Nevertheless, their lives were spared – although they were demoted in rank, with the titles they had been granted since 1397 removed. Despite this act of clemency, a plot was quickly hatched by John Holland, Earl of Huntingdon; Thomas Holland, Earl of Kent; John Montagu, Earl of Salisbury; Ralph, Lord Lumley, and others, to overthrow Henry and to restore Richard to power. The conspirators gathered their forces under the pretence of participating in a tournament at Windsor Castle, where the king and the royal household were celebrating the Christmas festivities. They planned to strike on 6 January, the day of the Epiphany, and to kill Henry and his sons, with the chronicler Thomas Walsingham claiming that they had a force of 400 men. However, their plot was betrayed to the king who fled to London and sent urgent messages for his forces to assemble. The rebels soon learnt that their scheme had been foiled and after briefly occupying Windsor Castle, most of them fled westwards. At Cirencester they were attacked by the townspeople, with Lord Lumley and the earls of Kent and Salisbury lynched after they surrendered. The other principal conspirators were swiftly hunted down and killed, with a further twenty-seven participants executed at Oxford Castle after being convicted of treason on 12 January. To remove the possibility of any further pro-Ricardian rebellions, Henry issued instructions for Richard II to be killed. According to the testimony of most of the chronicle accounts, he was starved to death by his jailors at Pontefract. Yet the kingdom remained in a state of turmoil, with rumours that Richard was still alive and of plots to murder the new king. It was for this reason that Henry ordered the formulation of a special bodyguard of men-at-arms and archers to protect himself day and night. The Scots sought to exploit the situation by undermining the authority of the English ruler. They had launched a raid across the border into Northumberland and attacked Wark Castle in October. In the following month, Henry was addressed insultingly as 'Duke of Lancaster, Earl of Derby and Steward of England', rather than as king, in a letter sent in the name of Robert III. It was therefore decided in parliament that he should lead an expedition in person to punish the Scots for their transgressions. On 14 August 1404, Henry entered Scotland at the head of a considerable army of

13,000 men. Yet the campaign saw little fighting as a lack of money meant that the English returned across the border less than two weeks later. As the king was travelling southwards he received ominous news from Wales while at Northampton.[2]

The country had been in a state of unrest since the start of Henry Bolingbroke's rebellion against Richard II. Groups of Welshmen were said to have attacked and despoiled English soldiers, with the violence continuing even after the overthrow of Richard. The most notable action took place on 18 September 1400, when a Welsh force of some 300 men led by Owain Glyn Dŵr sacked the town of Ruthin. Owain's men then went on to attack other settlements in north-east Wales, including Denbigh, Flint, Rhuddlan and Holt. This uprising was motivated by a dispute between Owain and his neighbour, Reginald, Lord Grey of Ruthin, over landholding. A short time earlier, a rebellion had also broken out on Anglesey led by the brothers Gwilym ap Tudor and Rhys ap Tudor. Henry responded by issuing instructions to the sheriffs of the Midland and border counties to raise an army to crush the uprising on 19 September. Five days later the rebels were routed near the town of Welshpool by a force led by Sir Hugh Burnell, forcing Owain to go on the run. Henry led an army into north Wales in early October, placing garrisons into the principal castles of the region and presiding over the execution of rebels, before returning to Shrewsbury by the end of the month. The king's decisive actions had seemingly ended the rebellion before it could grow any further, with offers of clemency extended to many of the participants. Yet the decision not to extend pardons to Owain or the Tudor brothers proved to be a costly mistake. On 1 April 1401, Gwilym and Rhys pulled off a spectacular coup by seizing control of Conwy Castle. The pro-English Welsh chronicler Adam of Usk reports that the brothers gained entry to the fortress with a small force of forty men on Good Friday. Taking advantage of the absence of most of the garrison who were attending a church service in the town, a carpenter overpowered and killed the two warders on duty, before admitting his companions into the castle. They were soon afterwards placed under siege by Henry, Prince of Wales, who employed a force of 120 men-at-arms and 300 archers to blockade the castle. Conwy was said to have been well equipped with provisions and equipment prior to its capture, but as they were completely cut off from assistance their food supplies gradually dwindled. According to Usk, the Tudor brothers surrendered the castle to the prince under terms that were 'cowardly for themselves and treacherously for their comrades' at the end of May. In return for sparing their lives, they handed over nine of their comrades, who were said to have been bound in their sleep after attending the night watches. These men were then executed by being hanged, drawn and quartered. Despite the gruesome conclusion of the siege, the success of the Tudor brothers in striking a blow against English rule led to the outbreak of rebellions throughout Wales, with the Welsh gradually uniting under the leadership of Owain. Usk states that by the autumn all of north Wales, Powys and Cardiganshire were in rebellion, with the Welsh having 'sorely harried with fire and sword the English who dwelt in those parts'. Henry led another harrying expedition throughout the country, but this did little to stem the tide of rebellion. By 2 November, Usk reports that Owain had laid siege to Caernarfon Castle. He was accompanied by a great host in the middle of which he 'unfurled his standard, a golden dragon on a white field', but was routed by the garrison, losing 300 in the engagement at Tuthill.[3]

Undaunted by this setback, Owain launched another attack on Ruthin in January 1402. Three months later he had the satisfaction of capturing his adversary Reginald in an ambush, who was only released after the payment of a large ransom. In the summer, Owain led his forces on a raid deep into Powys reaching almost as far as the English border. On 22 June, he was confronted by a sizeable English force, raised from Herefordshire and led by Sir Edmund Mortimer, uncle of Edmund Mortimer, Earl of March, near the village of Knighton and a short distance west of Offa's Dyke. In the engagement that followed, the Welsh were victorious – with many of the English killed and Edmund taken prisoner. The Battle of Bryn Glas was identified as a turning point by the author of *The Life and Reign of Richard the Second*, who stated that 'from that day Owain's cause grew excessively, and our cause began to wane'. Owain followed up on his victory by invading Gwent and Glamorganshire in the south-east. Usk states that he captured the castles of Caerleon, Usk and Newport, and went so far as to compare him to a 'second Assyrian, the rod of God's anger' who carried out 'deeds of unheard-of cruelty with fire and sword'. In response to this news, the king appointed commanders to hold military zones in Wales to combat the further spread of the rebellion. Thomas Fitzalan, Earl of Arundel, was tasked with holding the area from Holt Castle to Wigmore, and Edmund Stafford, Earl of Stafford, the region from Wigmore to Chepstow Castle. The most wide-ranging command was given to Richard, Lord Grey of Codnor, who was responsible for overseeing the defence of a wide swathe of territory from Cardiganshire in the south-west to Breconshire in the east. Prince Henry was also despatched with a force to relieve the hard-pressed garrisons of the north-west, including Harlech and Caernarfon, at the end of August. In the following month, Henry led another expedition to Wales in person, but poor weather conditions soon forced him to abandon the venture. Walsingham claims that Owain attempted to use 'his arts of magic' to destroy the king and his army by summoning 'storms of rain and snow and hail' to afflict the English. Henry was dealt a further blow in November by the defection of the captive Sir Edmund Mortimer, who married Owain's daughter, Catherine. Edmund had been angered by the king's refusal to provide financial assistance towards meeting the cost of his ransom and was therefore receptive to switching sides. Edmund's nephew, the young Earl of March, had a strong claim to the English throne as a great-grandson of Edward III, therefore a Mortimer-Glyn Dŵr alliance posed a serious threat to the Lancastrian dynasty.[4]

By the beginning of 1403, Owain controlled all north-west Wales except for the isolated castles of Aberystwyth, Harlech, Conwy and Caernarfon. The garrisons of these places were hard-pressed and could only now be supplied by sea. Furthermore, the Welsh rebels had penetrated as far eastwards as Flintshire and were carrying out raids across the border into Shropshire. In July, Owain marched through south Wales with a mighty host said to have numbered as many as 8,240 men. His forces overwhelmed many of the castles of the region, with Carmarthen, Newcastle Emlyn and Dryslwyn all falling in quick succession. Yet the king faced an even greater threat from Sir Henry 'Hotspur' Percy, eldest son of Henry, Earl of Northumberland, who had rebelled against him. The Percy family had been richly rewarded for the crucial part that Earl Henry had played in the overthrow of Richard II, being granted offices, lands and castles soon after the accession of Henry IV. Thereafter they assumed a position of dominance in the north of England, with Sir Henry and his father playing a crucial role in defending the Scottish border. It was in recognition of his martial prowess against them that the Scots bestowed upon the former the nickname 'Hotspur'. However, the relationship between the Percys and the king later soured due to claims that the king had failed to meet his obligations towards them for their expenses incurred in resisting Scottish incursions. This rift was partly caused by the Crown's financial difficulties and the perception that the influence of the Percy family was waning. Nevertheless, Sir Henry had until recently served as the king's lieutenant in north Wales, from the summer of 1402. In September, he and his father had also been in command of an English force that defeated a Scottish army at the Battle of Homildon Hill. It was the king's refusal to countenance the ransoming of any prisoners taken at the battle without his leave that was the final straw that led to the Percys rebelling against him. Sir Henry went southwards to Cheshire with his uncle Thomas Percy, Earl of Worcester, where he proclaimed that Richard II was still alive and raised an army. He was expecting reinforcements from his father and had almost certainly been in contact with Owain. Nonetheless, he made the fatal decision to march on Shrewsbury after learning that Prince Henry was there, not realising that the latter had joined forces with the king's army.

The Battle of Shrewsbury took place on 21 July with both sides suffering heavy casualties, which included Prince Henry who was wounded by an arrow in the face. Yet the rebels were finally routed after the death of Sir Henry, with Thomas Percy executed after being captured. Meanwhile, the Earl of Northumberland had been blocked from marching southwards by the forces of Ralph Neville, Earl of Westmorland. After receiving news of the battle, he realised that further resistance was futile and threw himself on the royal mercy soon afterwards. Despite his role in the rebellion the king pardoned him, although he was ordered to hand over control of his castles.[5]

Owain as Prince of Wales

In the meanwhile, Owain continued his ravages in the south, with Usk stating that he 'marched through Wales with a great power as far as the sea of the Severn'. The remaining English-held castles and towns of the region were hard-pressed and in dire straits. This can be clearly seen from surviving letters written by commanders of garrisons and other royal officials. One such individual was John Skidmore, constable of Carreg Cennen, who since the previous November had held the isolated castle in Carmarthenshire, perched on the edge of a lofty limestone precipice, with a force of one man-at-arms, a chaplain and twenty-four archers. In a letter dated 5 July, he wrote to the receiver of Breconshire, John Fairford, with news of the activities of the rebels. The inhabitants of Carmarthenshire, Cydweli, Carnwyllion and Iscennen were all said to have sworn allegiance to Owain and the towns and castles of Kidwelly, Gower and Glamorganshire were under siege. Two days later, Fairford forwarded this correspondence to the king with his own report on the situation in his area. He stated that the rebels in Breconshire had been carrying out 'all the mischief and destruction that they can to its neighbourhood' and implored his majesty to 'ordain a final destruction of all the false nation'. Fairford's pleas were soon answered due to the intervention of the men of Herefordshire. On 13 July, the sheriff, knights, esquires and commons of the county wrote a letter to the king stating that at his command they had raised a force and marched to the rescue of Breconshire. They had defeated the rebels in an engagement, slaying at least 240 rebels in an engagement and had broken the siege of the castle. Yet despite this rare piece of good news, the situation remained grim for the English of the area. This was apparent at the walled town and castle of Kidwelly in Carmarthenshire. Rumours that Owain was planning to attack the region had prompted the inhabitants to hurriedly raise a force of seven archers and seventeen other men to defend the castle a short time earlier. Frantic efforts were also made to improve the fortifications, which included the digging of ditches and the erecting of timber towers. These measures proved to be necessary as the settlement was attacked by the rebels. According to a later indictment submitted in the reign of Henry V, the rebels mounted an assault on Kidwelly on Monday 13 August, with some of the inhabitants killed in repulsing the attackers. Even after this success, the circumstances of the townspeople remained desperate. This can be seen from a letter dated 3 October, sent by the constable of the castle to the king that explained their plight. A rebel force led by Henry Don and including a contingent of Frenchmen and Bretons, had destroyed all the grain in the area, prompting many of the inhabitants to flee to England. Those that were left had taken refuge in the castle and unless they received assistance soon they would be 'destroyed and undone for ever'. Despite this ominous report, Kidwelly remained in English hands, but other places were less fortunate, with Carreg Cennen falling to the rebels at some point in the winter. The victories of Owain in south Wales demonstrated that he was a force to be reckoned with, and prompted many of the Welsh inhabitants of areas hitherto loyal to England to join his cause. By August, the men of Flintshire had joined the uprising and had besieged the castles of Rhuddlan, Flint and Hawarden. Henry led an army to south Wales in September, which recovered Carmarthen and temporarily quelled the rebellion in the region. However, only a month later he had to issue instructions for the raising of an expeditionary force to rescue the besieged castle of Cardiff. By the end of 1403, almost all of Wales had joined Owain's cause.[6]

The new year saw an intensification of the pressure placed on English-held towns and castles. Nowhere was this more so than in the north-west of the country, where isolated garrisons were subjected to frequent attacks. On 10 January, the keeper of Conwy Castle, Reynald Baildon, wrote a letter addressed to William Venables of Kinderton, constable of Chester, and his colleague, Roger Brescy, apprising them of the situation in his area. The rebels, with French assistance, were preparing to assail the town of Caernarfon, which was said to be 'more febil nowe then hit was the last tyme that thae were before hit'. Furthermore, he had just received news that the constable of Harlech Castle, William Hunte, had been captured. Hunte had made the mistake of parleying with the rebels without taking the precaution of asking for hostages beforehand and had been seized along with two sailors who had accompanied him. The ranks of the defenders were also said to have been depleted by deaths from the pestilence, with other men having defected to the enemy or fled into England. Nevertheless, he was confident of the safety of the fortress, as the remaining soldiers were 'kepyn the Castel welynogh yet'. A more pessimistic appraisal of the situation was sent to Venables and Brescy by the receiver of Denbigh, Roger de Bolton, by messenger, whose report they forwarded to the king on 15 February. Following the capture of the constable, the fortress was allegedly in 'great jeopardy', as the garrison now consisted of only five Englishmen and sixteen Welshmen. However, Harlech was not the only castle that was in danger of falling to the rebels. On 16 January they had written another letter to the king with details of an assault that was expected at any moment to be made against Caernarfon Castle. News of the plight of the garrison had been conveyed to them verbally by a woman, as no man dared to make the dangerous journey to Chester. A Franco-Welsh force was preparing to assail the place well-equipped with siege engines, 'sows' and long ladders. To oppose them, the garrison only numbered some twenty-eight men to defend both the walls of the town and castle. This was because eleven soldiers had died since the previous siege, some of them having perished due to injuries they had suffered in repelling the last assault and others from the plague. Five days later, Venables and Brescy passed on further troubling intelligence they had received from Anglesey. The deputy sheriff of the island, Mered ap Ken, had set forth from Beaumaris Castle to collect taxes accompanied by a strong escort of between fifty to sixty soldiers. Yet as they were passing some dense thickets, they were ambushed by a group of 200 rebels, who killed his escorts and sent Mered as a captive to Owain. The loss of these soldiers meant that the safety of Beaumaris was now imperilled with the garrison in urgent need of assistance. During the next month, Venables and Brescy received news that Harlech Castle was on the verge of being captured. Owain was said to have struck an agreement with all bar seven men of the garrison, who had agreed to deliver the castle on a set day in return for payment of gold. This report may well have been accurate as Harlech, along with the castles of Aberystwyth and Criccieth, fell to the rebels at some point in the year, although Caernarfon and Beaumaris remained in English hands. Elsewhere, the Welsh had increased the intensity of their raiding across the border into England. This meant that garrisons had to be installed in English castles to counter these incursions, such as at Bishop's Castle in Shropshire, which was provided with a force of six men-at-arms and thirty archers. Owain's position in Wales was now so strong that he began to act as the ruler of an independent country as opposed to a guerrilla leader. He styled himself as 'Prince of Wales', used a seal with regnal images and adopted other pretentions of rulership in official documents. He was aided in this task by the defection of high-status educated Welshmen to his cause, such as John Trefor, Bishop of St Asaph. These men provided him with invaluable diplomatic and administrative advice. Owain also held a parliament at Machynlleth in Powys and concluded a military alliance with the government of Charles VI of France. Therefore by the close of 1404, the dream of an independent Wales appeared to be a very real possibility.[7]

The extent of Owain's ambitions can be seen from the text of an extraordinary document known as the 'Tripartite Indenture', dating most probably from early 1405. This specified the details of an alliance made between Owain, Henry Percy, Earl of Northumberland, and Sir Edmund Mortimer. According to the document, the kingdom of England was to be divided between the three men, with the Earl of Northumberland receiving the north, East Anglia and part of the Midlands and Mortimer most of the rest. Remarkably, Owain's territorial share was to consist of a principality of Wales with greatly enlarged borders, which would have given him all of Cheshire and much of Shropshire, Herefordshire and Worcestershire. Yet the illusion of attaining these fantastical aspirations was soon to be dispelled by military setbacks. In March, Prince Henry reported to his father the king that he had defeated a Welsh army of 8,000 men outside Grosmont in Monmouthshire, with upwards of 1,000 rebels slain. Two months later, the English had a further success further south at Usk, where the garrison of the castle sallied forth and routed a force led by Owain's son, Gruffudd, who was taken prisoner. This was identified as a turning point for the rebellion in south-east Wales by Usk who noted that 'from that time forth in those parts the fortunes of Owen waned'. A naval force from Ireland also attacked Anglesey and in Flintshire some of the most prominent rebels, including Gwilym ap Gruffudd ap Gwilyn, surrendered. These successes were due in part to a marked improvement in royal finances, which meant that the government of Henry IV could focus more resources on crushing the rebellion. This included the provision of more than 2,000 soldiers for the garrisoning of seven castles alone. Prince Henry was also appointed as the king's lieutenant in north Wales and was allocated a force of some 500 men-at-arms and 3,000 archers to combat the rebels. The arrival of a French expeditionary army at Milford Haven in August did little to change the situation. In conjunction with Owain's forces, they marched through the south-west, burning Haverford and unsuccessfully besieging Tenby. These ravages prompted the men of Pembrokeshire to pay £200 to secure a truce with the rebels. Afterwards the Franco-Welsh force captured the town and castle of Carmarthen following a short siege, although it was soon recovered by the English. Yet these exploits proved to be the only achievements of the campaign. Elsewhere in the country, the rebels continued to be on the offensive, with Rhuddlan besieged and the town of Kidwelly sacked and burnt. Owain also held his second parliament at Harlech in August.[8]

Henry Victorious

Henry was preparing to lead another expedition to Wales in late May 1405 when he received news of an uprising in the north of England led by Henry Percy, Earl of Northumberland, who had been pardoned for his role in the rebellion that took place two years earlier, but had been humbled. He was removed from the royal council and ordered to hand over his castles. The earl was therefore eager for revenge and began to plot against the king. Despite his loss of prestige following the failure of the previous uprising, he still commanded considerable support among his retainers in the north. This can be seen from a letter sent to the king by John Coppyll, constable of Bamburgh Castle, in January 1404. Coppyll informed the king that the castles of Alnwick, Berwick-upon-Tweed and Warkworth were being held against him by supporters of the earl, who had strongly garrisoned them. Furthermore, they had recruited a large force of men to whom they had distributed Percy livery and had sworn to hold these places against him. Coppyll warned that unless the king came in person to the north then the outbreak of a rebellion was inevitable.

His assessment of the situation proved to be prescient. The Earl of Northumberland decided to strike in the early summer of 1405, hoping to take advantage of the king's anticipated absence in Wales. He first moved against Ralph Neville, Earl of Westmorland, his main rival in the north, by attempting to seize him in a surprise attack. However, his quarry was forewarned of the plot and fled from the castle of Witton-le-Wear in County Durham, where he had been staying as a guest of Sir Ralph Euer. The failure of this exploit soon led to the Earl of Northumberland losing his nerve. After arresting a royal envoy that had been sent to negotiate with him on 6 May, he retreated northwards. Subsequently, he gained entry to Berwick by tricking the burgesses into believing that he was still loyal to the king and then took control of the town. Upon receiving news of the earl's treason, Henry travelled to Nottingham where he began to assemble an army. He arrived at York in early June, where an armed protest led by Richard Scrope, Archbishop of York, had recently been suppressed, before proceeding northwards to Northumberland. Henry faced a potentially difficult task in defeating the rebellion, due to the strength of support for the Percys in the region. Furthermore, the rebels held some of the strongest castles in Northumberland and had received Scottish assistance. Yet in the space of a short and decisive campaign he was triumphant. One reason for this was due to his deployment of a formidable artillery train. Henry had a keen interest in gunpowder weapons and had recruited a team of specialist German gunners. These men had been employed in the production of new, large guns called bombards, which fired heavy gunstones that could knock down masonry fortifications. These bombards were soon put to good use against the defenders of Warkworth Castle. After arriving outside the walls of the castle on 1 July, the king called upon the garrison to surrender, which they refused to do. They quickly reconsidered this decision after being subjected to seven shots from the royal guns. Henry then proceeded northwards to besiege Berwick on 6 July, which was held by the rebels and their Scottish allies. According to Walsingham, the king deployed a huge gun against the castle, which with one shot demolished part of one of the towers 'and so frightened the garrison that they preferred voluntarily to expose themselves to the king's swords rather than to wait for a second firing', who then capitulated. News of the fall of Berwick prompted the garrison of Alnwick, the last remaining rebel-held castle, to surrender. The Earl of Northumberland was still at large, having fled a short time earlier to Scotland, but the loss of his lands meant that he no longer posed as much of a threat.[9]

Owain's fortunes continued to decline in 1406. He was still capable of carrying out hit-and-run raids across Wales, but the ranks of his supporters were diminished by defections and military setbacks. Events elsewhere also meant that the prospect of foreign military assistance became increasingly unrealistic. The last remaining French soldiers left Wales in the spring of 1406, with any further expectations of aid from France dashed by the conclusion of an Anglo-French truce in the following year. Meanwhile, the capture of the heir to the Scottish throne by the English at sea, removed the possibility of any relief from that quarter. Furthermore, the English Crown finally dedicated sufficient financial and military resources to suppressing the rebellion. Prince Henry was given the responsibility of carrying out this task and in February was appointed as the king's lieutenant in north and south Wales, with a force of almost 5,000 men. His first objective was the pacification of Anglesey, as a means by which to cut off food supplies for the rebels. A force from Chester was sent to secure the island early in the year, with further reinforcements dispatched in the summer. These measures had the desired effect, with some 2,000 men from Anglesey making their submission to the king at Beaumaris on 9 November. At the same time, English garrisons were also active in other parts of the country in subduing the rebels. By the beginning of 1407, most of Wales had returned to the allegiance of Henry IV. The last remaining challenge was the recovery of the two major castles of Aberystwyth and Harlech, which were still in Welsh hands. To accomplish this objective, considerable efforts were made to assemble a powerful artillery train to batter the defenders of these fortresses into submission. These preparations were completed by the summer, with Prince Henry laying siege to Aberystwyth Castle in July, at the head of a sizeable force of 200 men-at-arms and 600 archers. Yet the besiegers struggled to make much headway against the defenders. The artillery proved to be ineffectual, with some of the guns bursting under the strain of firing, including one large bronze gun called *Messenger*, which weighed as much as 4,480lbs. It was therefore decided to negotiate with the garrison, who agreed to surrender on 1 November, if they were not relieved by Owain. However, the latter succeeded in secretly gaining entry to the castle, leading to the English withdrawing from the siege in disarray. Yet the respite was only to be temporary. In the next year, the siege of Aberystwyth was resumed, with Harlech also besieged at the same time. The defenders of these castles were gradually starved into surrender, with both places having fallen by early 1409. Owain himself remained on the run, but his rebellion was effectively over. Nevertheless, the country was still restless with bands of insurgents periodically carrying out attacks on English soldiers and officials, therefore garrisons were maintained in the principal castles of Wales for years to come.[10]

Border Tensions

Henry IV's reign had been marked by civil strife and rebellions, yet after years of conflict he had emerged victorious. Now that the peace of the realm was secured, he could engage more directly in Continental affairs. The outbreak of civil war in France between the Armagnacs and the Burgundians, provided a golden opportunity for enlarging his overseas possessions. An expeditionary force was sent to the Continent in support of the former in 1412, but achieved little. Henry IV was succeeded by his eldest son and heir, Henry V, in 1413. The new king was eager to achieve glory and two years later invaded France with a large expeditionary force. Concerns over the safety of the realm during his absence meant that soldiers were provided for the defence of vulnerable regions. The defence of north Wales was entrusted to a force of sixty men-at-arms and 120 archers, whereas a smaller contingent of forty men-at-arms and eighty archers was provided for guarding the south of Wales. Greater resources were provided for the defence of the north, with 600 men-at-arms and archers allocated for defending the west and east marches of Scotland. Henry won a great victory over the French at the Battle of Agincourt on 25 October, and followed up on this triumph by conquering Normandy between 1417 and 1419. On 21 May 1420, he was recognised as the successor to Charles VI of France, at the Treaty of Troyes, in a great diplomatic coup for the king. However, this agreement was contested by the Dauphin, the future Charles VII, which meant that the war carried on. Later in 1422, Henry V died of dysentery contracted during the siege of Meaux before he could become king of France. He was succeeded by his nine-month-old son, who became Henry VI. The youth of the new monarch meant that arrangements had to be put in place for the governance of both his English and French realms. His uncle, John, Duke of Bedford, was appointed as regent of France, whereas his other uncle, Humphrey, Duke of Gloucester, was appointed as Lord Protector with responsibility for ruling England. For most of the reign of Henry VI, the resources of the government were focused on the prosecution of the war in France, but provision still had to be made for the defence of the north. On the face of it, Anglo-Scottish relations were relatively peaceful with a series of truces in place, with the goodwill of the Scots guaranteed by the captivity of James I in England. Yet frequent violations of these truces took place. In 1417, the Scots had mounted an incursion across the border known as the 'foul raid' and two years later they briefly occupied Wark Castle.[11]

Later in 1424, the release of James I was secured in return for his marriage to Joan Beaufort, a relative of Henry VI, and for the payment of a large ransom. At first the Scottish king's attentions were focused on establishing his position in Scotland, but tensions with England gradually escalated from the late 1420s onwards. Concerns about the safety of the north prompted the English government to appoint John Skipton, a former Clerk of the King's Works, to oversee improvements to the defences of key border fortifications. Skipton was given nearly £3,100 between 1427 and his death in 1434, which he spent on carrying out repairs to the towns and castles of Berwick, Carlisle and Roxburgh. Efforts were also made to equip them with weaponry, with guns, gunpowder, bows and arrows, sent to augment their arsenals. James's opportunity to strike a decisive blow against the English occurred in 1436. The government of Henry VI was on the defensive and its financial resources were strained due to military defeats in France and a Burgundian siege of Calais. James took advantage of the situation to cross the border and to besiege

Roxburgh Castle with a large army, well equipped with guns, in August. However, news of the imminent arrival of an English army threw the Scots into panic, with the king's expensive artillery abandoned during the chaotic retreat to Scotland. The debacle at Roxburgh dealt a serious blow to James's prestige, but he was eager to renew the struggle in the following year. However, he fell victim to a conspiracy led by his domestic opponents, who had been antagonised by his style of rulership, and he was murdered while staying at Blackfriars, outside Perth, on 21 February. His death led to the restoration of peace with England, as the Scottish government was forced to contend with numerous domestic problems during the minority of James II. Nevertheless, relations between the two countries remained strained, with frequent breaches of the truce taking place, and a brief war breaking out in 1448.[12]

The Wars of the Roses: 1453–1485

The king stayed in the palace of York, and kept his estate solemnly; and there he made Sir John Neville, Lord Montague, Earl of Northumberland. And then my lord of Warwick took upon him the journey, by the king's commandment and authority, to resist the rebellions of the north, accompanied with him my said lord of Northumberland his brother... The 23 day of June, my said lord of Warwick, with the army, came before the castle of Alnwick, and had it delivered by appointment; and also the castle of Dunstanburgh ... my said Lord of Warwick, and his brother earl of Northumberland, the 25 day of June, laid siege unto the castle of Bamburgh, there within being Sir Ralph Grey ... And then my lord lieutenant had ordered all the king's great guns that were charged at once to shoot unto the said castle, Newcastle the king's great gun, and London the second gun of iron; the which afflicted the place, that stones of the walls flew into the sea; Dysyon, a brass gun of the king's, smote through Sir Ralph Grey's chamber oftentimes; Edward and Richard Bombartell, and other of the king's ordnance, so occupied by the ordnance of my said Lord, with men of arms and archers, won the castle of Bamburgh with assault, captured Sir Ralph Grey, and took him, and brought him to the king to Doncaster, and there he was executed.

Manuscript from the College of Arms[1]

The storming of Bamburgh Castle by the forces of Richard Neville, Earl of Warwick, ended the Lancastrian rebellion in Northumberland. Over the course of four years, the Yorkists had been forced to send expeditionary forces to quell resistance in the north of England. They were finally able to prevail in 1464 due to their victory at the Battle of Hexham and the use of their artillery to capture Lancastrian castles. Despite this success, the Yorkist king, Edward IV, continued to face threats to his rule for much of his reign. This was due to the turbulence of the times. The second half of the fifteenth century was marked by a series of conflicts, later known as the Wars of the Roses. These wars were a struggle between the conflicting dynastic claims of the houses of Lancaster and York to the English throne. The shock of defeat in France, economic difficulties, the weak rule of Henry VI, and the ambitions of Richard, Duke of York, led to civil unrest and rebellions in the 1450s. Richard met his end at the Battle of Wakefield in 1460, but his cause was taken up by his son and heir, Edward, Earl of March. The latter triumphed over his enemies at the Battle of Towton in the following year and was crowned Edward IV. He was forced to contend with years of rebellion, including being briefly dethroned between 1470–1, but was ultimately victorious. After Edward's death in 1483, his brother, Richard, Duke of Gloucester, usurped the throne, but was in turn defeated and killed by Henry Tudor at the Battle of Bosworth in 1485. The dynastic nature of these conflicts meant that both the Lancastrians and the Yorkists sought to prevail through victory on the battlefield, as opposed to the conquest of towns and castles. Therefore, castles only played a minor role in many of these campaigns. Yet these fortifications retained their military usefulness, as can be seen with the Lancastrian rebellions in Wales and the north of England in the 1460s. Diehard supporters of the defeated Henry VI seized control of castles, to encourage the outbreak of further uprisings and to provide bridgeheads for the intervention of foreign armies. The Yorkists in turn were forced to maintain garrisons in key fortresses, and to besiege rebel-held castles.

Richard Duke of York

On 17 July 1453, an English army led by John Talbot, Earl of Shrewsbury, was routed by the French at the Battle of Castillon in

Gascony. This defeat led to the loss of England's last remaining lands on the Continent, except for the Pale of Calais. Over the previous three years, the French had rapidly overrun English territory in France. Their success was due in large part to the decision by the French king, Charles VII, to establish a standing army and to reorganise his artillery. The shock of defeat in France destabilised the peace of the realm in England. Returning groups of demoralised and embittered soldiers carried out acts of violence and theft. This disorder aggravated existing problems due to the breakdown of law across the kingdom resulting from aristocratic feuds and economic problems. Dissatisfaction with the government had led to the outbreak of a rebellion in the south-east of England, led by Jack Cade in the summer of 1450. The uprising began in Kent in May, with the rebels gaining support throughout the county. In response to this development, efforts were made to improve the safety of the fortifications of the region. The constable of Dover Castle sent instructions for the Cinque Ports to send men to reinforce the garrison and despatched scouts to keep a careful watch on the rebels. Yet no proactive measures were taken to suppress the rebellion, with the rebels moving westwards to Blackheath just outside London in the second week of June. Meanwhile, the king ordered his magnates to assemble in the city with their retinues. The gatherings of these forces prompted the rebels to withdraw, back to Kent, but a royalist advance guard incautiously pursued them and fell into an ambush. Buoyed by this unexpected success, the insurgents marched back to the capital. This setback and a mutiny among his own soldiers prompted Henry to abandon the city and to flee to the safety of Kenilworth Castle.

Forsaken by the king, the mayor and aldermen of London put up little resistance to the rebels who entered the city on 3 July. Cade tried to prevent his men from carrying out acts of violence by issuing proclamations, but nevertheless widespread looting, killings and disorder took place. The success of the rebels led to a collapse in morale, which meant that no attempt was made to hold the Tower of London against the insurgents, although some efforts had been made by the king to prepare the defence of the castle a short time earlier. Instead, unpopular royalist officials who had taken refuge there, such as James Fiennes, Lord Saye, were taken out and executed, with the armoury looted. Yet soon enough the ravages of the rebels induced the Londoners to take up arms against them to drive them out of the city, which they succeeded in doing after fierce fighting on 5 July. Cade fled eastwards to Rochester before trying to gain admittance to Queenborough Castle. However, the garrison, led by Sir Roger Chamberleyn, repulsed his attacks and captured two of his lieutenants. Cade was finally cornered and mortally wounded in Sussex in late July. Despite the suppression of the revolt, the country remained in turmoil and in a state of unrest. One reason for this discontent was due to the dynastic claims of Richard, Duke of York. His descent from two of the sons of Edward III – Lionel of Antwerp, Duke of Clarence on his mother's side, and Edmund Langley, Duke of York, from his father's line – meant that he arguably had a stronger claim to the throne than the king. The Duke of York's disillusionment with the government of Henry VI, who owed him substantial sums of money for his war service, meant that he became a figurehead for opposition to the Lancastrian dynasty in the early 1450s.[2]

His first move against the government occurred in the autumn of 1450. The Duke of York left his post as Lieutenant of Ireland and landed at Beaumaris in September. His return was not authorised by the king or the court, who were said to have been greatly alarmed by his arrival. Richard sought to benefit from the recent unrest by adopting popular demands, which he presented to Henry in two bills of complaint. He sought to exert further pressure on the king and the government by recruiting a large entourage of men in advance of the parliament that was to be held on 6 November. His intention seems to have been to increase his own influence over the king and to pursue the prosecution of men who he held responsible for English defeats in France, principally, Edmund Beaufort, Duke of Somerset. The latter was briefly imprisoned in the Tower, supposedly for his own safety, but was released soon afterwards. Two years later, in 1452, the Duke of York made a more determined effort to seize control of power. He raised an army and marched on London, while protesting that he was a loyal subject of the king. However, after a standoff with the royal army he was forced to capitulate at Dartford in March, although he received a royal pardon some of his supporters were executed. In August of the following year, Henry was stricken by a serious illness that left him unable to govern the country. This prompted the royal council to appoint York as Protector and Defender of the Realm on 27 March 1454, due to his status as the king's cousin and as the premier duke in the kingdom. Yet Henry soon recovered from his illness and York was dismissed from office in early 1455. A short time later, York and his closest supporters, Richard Neville, Earl of Salisbury, and the latter's eldest son, Richard Neville, Earl of Warwick, later known as the 'Kingmaker', decided to take power by force. They defeated the royal army at the First Battle of St Albans on 22 May, with Somerset and other prominent Lancastrian lords killed. York again became Protector in the aftermath of the battle, but a lack of political support from his peers compelled him to relinquish the office early in 1456. The situation remained tense – with the king, Queen Margaret and the Lancastrian court withdrawing to the safety of Kenilworth Castle in Warwickshire. They spent most of the remaining three years in the West Midlands, with field guns sent from the Tower of London to Kenilworth. An uneasy state of peace remained until 1459, when escalating tensions led to an armed standoff at Ludford Bridge, although the Yorkist lords fled into exile before a battle could take place. However, they returned to England in the next year, and marched on the capital with their army. After engaging in negotiations with the civic authorities, they were admitted into the city, although they faced opposition from the Lancastrian garrison of the Tower of London led by Thomas, Lord Scales. The defenders opened fire on the citizens with their guns, but a lack of provisions meant that they were quickly put under pressure by the besiegers. On 10 July 1460, the Lancastrians were defeated at the Battle of Northampton, with Henry VI taken prisoner by the victorious Yorkists. News of the outcome battle soon prompted the defenders of the Tower to surrender, with Lord Scales lynched after trying to flee to the sanctuary of Westminster Abbey. The Duke of York's attempt to seize the throne was rebuffed by the nobility, but he attempted to use his control over Henry VI to rule in his name. Yet York was killed at the Battle of Wakefield on 30 December 1460, along with the Earl of Salisbury, after having gone northwards to Yorkshire to quell Lancastrian resistance. Queen Margaret and her forces then marched southwards to regain the capital, with a Yorkist army led by the Earl of Warwick defeated at the Second Battle of St Albans on 17 February 1461.[3]

Edward IV

The situation of the Yorkists appeared to be bleak, but the Londoners succeeded in delaying the entry of the Lancastrians into the city through negotiations. Meanwhile, leadership of the Yorkist cause had passed to Edward, Earl of March. The latter succeeded in defeating an army led by Jasper Tudor, Earl of Pembroke, at the Battle of Mortimer's Cross on 2 February 1461, and then advanced towards London. New of his coming prompted Margaret to withdraw with her forces to the Lancastrian heartlands in the north of England. The Yorkists then entered the city on 27 February, with the Earl of March receiving a euphoric welcome from the citizens. He then advanced northwards to confront the Lancastrians and won a great victory against them at the Battle of Towton on 29 March. Following the battle, Edward IV spent three weeks in York before proceeding northwards as far as Newcastle-upon-Tyne. In the meantime, Henry VI and many of his leading followers had fled across the border to Scotland, where they were well received by James III. A treaty was soon agreed on 25 April, whereby the Scots would provide military assistance in return for the surrender of Berwick-upon-Tweed, which duly took place. News of this alliance prompted Edward to install garrison in key castles in the region, including at Newcastle and Tynemouth. Edward soon returned to the south for his coronation, which took place on 28 June, with Richard Neville, Earl of Warwick, and the latter's brother, John Neville, Lord Montague, given the task of subduing the remnants of Lancastrian resistance in the north. In the summer, an attack was made on Carlisle by a Lancastrian and Scottish force, but the siege was lifted by an army led by Lord Montagu, with an attempt to threaten Durham also repulsed a short time earlier. Around the same time, Edward IV entrusted the newly ennobled William, Lord Herbert, with the task of subduing Lancastrian-held castles in Wales. In September of that year, Lord Herbert led an army into South Wales supported by a fleet, which soon resulted in the collapse of Lancastrian resistance, with the castles of Tenby and Pembroke surrendered by their garrisons. The Yorkists subsequently secured their position in the south through the garrisoning of strategic castles, with remaining Lancastrian resistance in South Wales subdued early in the following year.[4]

Meanwhile in the north of England, the Lancastrians succeeded in recapturing the castles of Alnwick and Naworth in the winter of 1461–2. Yet this only proved to be a temporary setback for the Yorkists, who were able to use their superior resources to prevent the Lancastrians or their allies from making any further gains in the early months of 1462. By June, a treaty had been agreed with the Scots, which allowed for the reduction of the remaining Lancastrian castles in Northumberland, which had been recovered by 31 July. Therefore, by the summer of 1462, the Lancastrian cause must have seemed hopeless. Yet the situation was transformed due to an agreement made between Margaret of Anjou and Louis XI, for the latter to provide financial assistance, which was used to hire a fleet of ships and to recruit a small army led by the renowned soldier Pierre de Brézé. On 25 October, Margaret of Anjou and her forces landed on the coast near Bamburgh, which led to the outbreak of a rebellion in Northumberland, with the Lancastrians soon able to capture the three great castles of Alnwick, Dunstanburgh and Bamburgh. In response, Edward IV raised a large army, which was said to have numbered 30,000 men and to have included two dukes, seven earls, thirty-one lords and fifty-nine knights. The king fell ill en route, however, and therefore delegated the conduct of military operations to Richard Neville, Earl of Warwick. News of the arrival of the Yorkist army prompted the Lancastrians to withdraw by sea to Scotland, with most of their forces, although some of their ships were sunk in a storm. The small garrisons left behind in their Northumberland castles were then subsequently besieged by the Yorkists.

Little effort appears to have been made by the attackers to exploit their superiority in manpower or artillery to capture these fortifications by assault, with the defenders instead starved into surrender. Dwindling food supplies and the absence of a relief force soon prompted the garrisons of Bamburgh and Dunstanburgh to capitulate on 26 and 27 December respectively. However, a raid by a Scottish force led by George Douglas, Earl of Angus, forced the besiegers to withdraw from Alnwick Castle on 6 January 1463, which allowed some of the garrison to leave the castle and flee with them, with the others surrendering soon afterwards.[5]

Generous terms were offered to the defeated Lancastrians, many of whom were either allowed to leave the realm, or alternatively were taken into royal service, such as Sir Ralph Percy, who was left in command of Bamburgh Castle. This policy was no doubt intended to induce staunch supporters of Henry VI to transfer their allegiances to Edward IV and thereby end the insurrection in the north. Yet it was to prove to be a mistaken one, due to the treachery of many of these individuals. The castles of Bamburgh and Dunstanburgh were handed over to the Lancastrians by Sir Ralph Percy in March of 1463, whereas Alnwick Castle was betrayed a short time later by its constable, Sir Ralph Grey, who imprisoned its captain, Sir John Ashley. A combined Franco-Scottish-Lancastrian army attacked Norham Castle in July, which was besieged for eighteen days, before it was relieved by a Yorkist army led by Richard Neville, Earl of Warwick, and John Neville, Lord Montagu. This defeat prompted Brézé and the remaining French soldiers to return to France with Margaret of Anjou. The Lancastrians were subsequently abandoned by their allies, with Edward IV making truces with Louis XI in October and James III in December. Yet shortly before Christmas, a conspiracy by Henry Beaufort, Duke of Somerset, to seize control of Newcastle, was discovered and thwarted, with the king despatching reinforcements to the port. Despite the loss of French and Scottish support, the Lancastrians were still capable of conducting offensive operations in early 1464. They succeeded in capturing the tower of Hexham and the castles of Langley and Bywell in Northumberland, thereby threatening communications between Carlisle and Newcastle, as well as taking Norham Castle, and were even able to strike as far south as Yorkshire by seizing Skipton Castle. However, the Yorkists were soon able to recover the initiative with Sir William Stanley able to recapture Skipton by 4 June after it was bombarded by his forces. Yorkist victories at the battles of Hedgeley Moor, on 25 April, and Hexham, on 15 May, followed by the execution of many of the captives of high rank, meant that the Lancastrian position rapidly collapsed in Northumberland, with the garrisons of Alnwick and Dunstanburgh surrendering on 23 June. The only place to offer resistance was Bamburgh, which was besieged two days later. A manuscript in the College of Arms states that Chester and Warwick heralds were sent to offer terms to the garrison, with pardons offered to all of the defenders, except for two of their leaders, Sir Ralph Grey and Sir Humphrey Neville. This account states that the strategic location of the castle meant that Edward IV had 'specially desirethe to have it, hoole, unbroken, with ordennaunce', with the threat that the head of a defender would be taken should 'any greet gunne (be) laide unto the wal, and be shote and prejudice the wal'. These terms were rejected. In response, the besiegers deployed their artillery against the walls of the castle, including the bombards called Newcastle, London and Dijon. These were able to inflict serious damage on the defences of the castle, which was then taken by assault. The capture of Bamburgh effectively marked the end of Lancastrian resistance in the north. Henry VI remained on the run but was eventually captured at Ribblesdale in July 1465.[6]

It was to take a further three years, however, before the Lancastrian-held castle of Harlech in north Wales surrendered. The Yorkists had succeeded in pacifying most of Wales by the beginning of 1462, yet resistance continued in this remote north-western region. Harlech was used as a base for opponents of Edward IV to challenge his rule, with attempts made by dissenters to spark risings in both north and south Wales in the winter of 1463–4. In the south the rebellion was crushed relatively quickly, with the rebels defeated in battle at Dryslwyn in Carmarthenshire. By contrast, the north took longer to pacify. John, Lord Howard was assigned the task of suppressing the rebellion in Denbighshire, serving with a force of 1,200 men, including nine mounted scouts, which operated out of Holt Castle in January of 1464, in a successful attempt to capture a prominent local Lancastrian called John Hamner. The Lancastrians in Harlech continued to pose a threat to the safety of the castles in North Wales over the following years, which necessitated the maintenance of garrisons in the key fortifications of the region. Yet it was not until 1468 that the Yorkists made a serious effort to capture the castle. This was in response to the return of Jasper Tudor, Earl of Pembroke, from Ireland, who had landed with a small force in North Wales in June. He soon raised an army, with which he attacked and burnt the town of Denbigh, and was said to have ridden through the country and held many legal sessions in the name of Henry VI. William, Lord Herbert, was therefore entrusted with the task of capturing Harlech Castle, which included the provision of a large army and artillery train. John Wode, master of the king's ordnance, was paid more than £1,300 for procuring gunpowder weapons, with guns transported to Bristol, and from there by sea to North Wales. On 20 July, an indenture was made between him and Edward IV, for the former to retain an ordnance company of sixty-seven gunners, smiths, carpenters and other professionals, together with 600 sailors and soldiers. A two-pronged attack was planned, with armies to converge on Harlech from both north and south Wales. The Earl of Pembroke tried to pre-empt this by leading his forces eastwards, but was defeated in battle by Lord Herbert. Meanwhile, the latter's brother, Sir Richard Herbert, led another army northwards from Pembroke, and was able to capture Harlech after a short siege, with the garrison surrendering on 14 August.[7]

Therefore, after years of warfare the Yorkists were victorious, with Henry VI a captive in the Tower of London and other Lancastrians, such as Queen Margaret, in exile on the Continent. Yet Edward was soon faced with a new challenge to his rule from his cousin and most powerful supporter, Richard Neville, Earl of Warwick. The two men fell out over Edward's choice of bride, Elizabeth Woodville, and his decision to ally with Charles the Bold, Duke of Burgundy, as opposed to Louis XI, king of France. In 1469, the Earl of Warwick, with the king's brother, George, Duke of Clarence, hatched a conspiracy to seize power. They defeated a royalist army at the Battle of Edgecote and took Edward prisoner, holding him first in Warwick Castle, then afterwards at Middleham Castle. However, they struggled to maintain their control over the kingdom and were soon forced to release him. The failure of a further plot in 1470 prompted Warwick and Clarence to flee to the Continent, where they concluded an alliance with the Lancastrian exiles to restore Henry VI to power. They returned to England a short time later and succeeded in overthrowing Edward. However, the latter managed to flee to the Burgundian-controlled Low Countries, where he received material assistance from his brother-in-law the Duke of Burgundy. Edward used this support to recruit a small army with which he landed in the north of England in March 1471. He then marched southwards to confront the forces of the Earl of Warwick, whom he defeated at the Battle of Barnet on 14 April 1471. Edward had little time to savour his victory as he quickly received news of the landing of Queen Margaret and her son Prince Edward in the south-west of England. He was therefore obliged to raise another army to attack the Lancastrians, whom he defeated at the Battle of Tewkesbury on 4 May 1471. During his absence in the West Country, a force led by Thomas Neville, known as the 'Bastard of Fauconberg', attacked London. Fauconberg was a relative and supporter of the now deceased Earl of Warwick, who commanded a mixed army raised from the men of Kent, various 'shipmen' and members of the Calais garrison. His attempts to gain peaceful admittance to the city in the name of Henry VI were rebuffed by the Londoners. He therefore resorted to attacking London using guns removed from his ships, but the rebel attacks were beaten off by the inhabitants, who were supported by the royalist garrison in the Tower of London. This staunch resistance led to the rebels losing heart and abandoning the siege, with the king returning a short time later to pursue the fugitives into Kent. Edward's victories in 1471 meant that he was now secure on the throne, with the Lancastrian threat effectively eliminated due to the deaths of Henry VI and his son, Prince Edward. The king could now devote his energies to involvement in Continental affairs, leading a large and well-equipped army to invade France in 1475. Nevertheless, the campaign saw little fighting with the French king agreeing to pay Edward an annuity in return for peace. War later broke out between England and Scotland in the summer of 1480, with the Scots raiding the border regions. Edward prepared to lead an expedition to Scotland in 1481, but ill health meant that the campaign was postponed until the following year. Military operations were instead directed by his brother, Richard, Duke of Gloucester, who managed to recapture Berwick after a long siege and to temporarily occupy Edinburgh in 1482.[8]

The Rise of the Tudors

The death of Edward IV on 9 April 1483 set in motion a sequence of events that led to the overthrow of the Yorkist dynasty. Next in line to the throne was the deceased king's eldest son,

Edward, who was twelve years old and residing at Ludlow. Almost immediately afterwards, a royal council under the influence of Edward's maternal Woodville relatives put in place preparations for his coronation on 4 May. Yet as his party moved eastwards from Ludlow towards London, they were intercepted by a force led by his paternal uncle, Richard, Duke of Gloucester, who took Edward into his custody, with the boy's maternal uncle, Anthony Woodville, Earl Rivers, taken prisoner. The coronation of Edward V was postponed and the Duke of Gloucester became Lord Protector of the realm. A short time later, Edward and his younger brother, Richard, Duke of York, were declared to be illegitimate by Gloucester, who then took the throne, being crowned as Richard III on 6 July.

The new king faced an early challenge from his erstwhile supporter Henry Stafford, Duke of Buckingham, but his rebellion was quickly defeated. Rumours soon spread that the sons of Edward IV, who had been imprisoned in the Tower of London, had been murdered by their uncle. Opposition to Richard III therefore coalesced around Henry Tudor, who was in exile on the Continent. His claim to the throne was a tenuous one, being derived from his mother, Margaret Beaufort, who was a granddaughter of John of Gaunt, Duke of Lancaster, one of the sons of Edward III. Henry had only become a viable claimant to the throne due to the near extinction of the Lancastrian line. By 1483, he had spent much of his life in exile in France and Brittany, whose rulers had used his claim to the throne as a means by which to exert pressure on Edward IV. Henry sailed from France in the summer of 1485, with a small force of English exile and French mercenaries. He made landfall in Milford Haven and gradually made his way northwards across Wales, before heading east into England via Shrewsbury. In the meantime, Richard had raised an army and marched to the West Midlands to confront Henry. The two armies met at the Battle of Bosworth on 22 August, which resulted in the defeat of the Yorkist army, with Richard killed during the fighting. Henry then travelled eastwards to London and was crowned king on 30 October 1485.[9]

The Early Tudors: 1485–1547

The king's highness which never ceased to study and take pains
for the advancement for the commonwealth of this his realm
of England, of the which he was the only supreme governor
and head, and also for the defence of all the same, was lately
informed by his trusty and faithful friends that the cankered and
cruel serpent the bishop of Rome, by that arch traitor Reginald
Pole, enemy to God's word and his natural country, had moved
and stirred diverse great princes and potentates of Christendom
to invade the realm of England, and utterly to destroy the whole
nation of the same: wherefore his majesty in person, without
any delay took very laborious and painful journeys towards the
seacoasts. Also he sent diverse of his nobles and counsellors to
view and search all the ports and dangers on the coasts where any
suitable or convenient landing place might be expected, as well
as on the borders of England as also of Wales. And in all such
doubtful places his highness caused diverse and many bulwarks
and fortifications to be made.
  The Union of the Two Noble and Illustre Families of Lancastre
                                    and Yorke by Edward Hall[1]

Henry VIII's decision to annul his marriage to his wife, Katherine of
Aragon, and to marry Anne Boleyn led to the break with Rome in
the early 1530s. This breach meant that England became increasingly
diplomatically isolated from the Catholic powers of Europe. By
the end of the decade, the country faced the threat of an invasion,

with Pope Paul III calling for the overthrow of Henry. The king reacted by sending commissioners to survey the ports and coasts of the kingdom to locate landing sites and weaknesses in existing defences. In response to the findings of these officials, a document known as the 'Device by the King' was formulated in February 1539. This specified a comprehensive scheme of defensive works, with castles, bulwarks and blockhouses to be constructed at key points along the coastline. These fortifications were built at a rapid pace over the following years, at great expense, financed in part by the profits incurred by the Crown from the dissolution of the monasteries some years earlier. In the event, however, the effectiveness of these fortresses was not put to the test as an invasion did not materialise. The larger Henrician forts were called castles, such as Camber Castle in Kent, yet they had a very different form to the older medieval castles. Instead of the tall towers and walls that characterised earlier structures, they were much smaller and thicker in size, designed especially for the use of gunpowder weapons. Furthermore, they were no longer intended to serve as lordly residences or as centres of local administration, but were only inhabited by small garrisons. This reflected an important architectural change that had gradually taken place at the end of the Middle Ages. New aristocratic residences of the late fifteenth and sixteenth centuries were still often called castles and incorporated castle-like features, such as towers and crenellation. Yet increasingly they had limited practical value in warfare, due in part to the growing popularity of large windows, with little provision made for modern artillery. This was in stark contrast to royal and urban fortifications of the period. Therefore, a separation of the traditional residential and military functions of a castle had taken place. This development coincided with the gradual dilapidation of a significant number of medieval castles, many which were in a ruinous condition by the sixteenth century. Yet old castles still had some value in warfare, due to their substantial masonry defences, which meant that the fortifications of some of them were modified for the use of gunpowder weapons, particularly in the border region with Scotland.

Border Conflicts

Despite being victorious at the Battle of Bosworth, Henry VII was forced to contend with years of rebellions and plots against his rule. The most dangerous threat was posed by a Yorkist pretender,

Lambert Simnel, who claimed to be Edward, Earl of Warwick, the son of the deceased Duke of Clarence. He was crowned as Edward VI in Dublin on 24 May 1486. In the following year, Simnel and his supporters invaded England with a mostly Irish and German army, landing at Furness in Lancashire on 4 June. In response, Henry marched northwards to confront the Yorkists and defeated them at the Battle of Stoke on 16 June. Later in the 1490s, he had to deal with the challenge posed by a new Yorkist pretender, Perkin Warbeck. Warbeck claimed to be Richard, Duke of York, the younger brother of Edward V, and sought international assistance to gain the English throne. He proved to be a useful pawn to put pressure on Henry VII, with Warbeck receiving first French and then Burgundian support. In 1495, he attempted to invade England with a small force of English renegades and European mercenaries provided by Maximilian, king of the Romans. Yet the effort was abandoned following a disastrous attempt to make a landing at Deal in Kent, with the advance guard of his army overwhelmed by the local inhabitants. Warbeck went first to Ireland, but after the defeat of his allies there made his way to the court of James IV of Scotland. The Scottish king officially recognised Warbeck as Richard IV and even arranged for him to marry a distant relative of his, Lady Katherine Gordon. James invaded the north of England with a strong force, accompanied by Warbeck, in the autumn of 1496. The Scots destroyed a few peel towers, but the failure to attract any English support for the Yorkist pretender led to the abandonment of the venture. In response to this development, Henry decided to send a punitive expedition to punish the Scots. Preparations were put in place for a large army and fleet, equipped with the latest gunpowder weapons, to invade Scotland. However, the outbreak of a rebellion in Cornwall in May 1497, in response to the imposition of heavy taxes to pay for the Scottish war, led to the postponement of the expedition. James took advantage of the situation by crossing the border in force and laying siege to Norham Castle in early August. A determined effort was made to capture the castle, with the defenders subjected to a heavy bombardment from the Scottish artillery, but a lack of money to pay his soldiers meant that he was forced to break the siege after ten days. The English army, led by Thomas Howard, Earl of Surrey, retaliated a short time later by crossing into Berwickshire and capturing some peel towers. Yet after an abortive standoff between the two armies at Halidon Hill, a truce was concluded at Berwick-upon-Tweed on 20 August. Meanwhile, Warbeck had made his way to Ireland before deciding to travel to the West Country. The Cornish had been defeated at the Battle of Blackheath on 17 June, but his arrival revived the rebellion, with the rebels laying siege to Exeter. However, their failure to capture the city led to the collapse of the uprising, with Warbeck later captured at Taunton on 5 October. He was at first sentenced to life imprisonment in the Tower of London but after becoming involved in a conspiracy with his fellow captive, the Earl of Warwick, was executed in 1499.[2]

Anglo-Scottish relations remained peaceful for the remainder of the reign of Henry VII, with James IV marrying Henry's daughter, Prince Margaret, in August 1503. However, the situation deteriorated following the accession of Henry VIII to the throne, after his father's death in 1509. The new king was eager to gain glory on the battlefields of Europe and to emulate the deeds of his ancestor Henry V. In 1511, he joined an international coalition against Louis XII of France known as the Holy League and made plans to invade France. Two years later, he landed at Calais at the head of a large army and soon afterwards joined forces with his ally Maximilian, the Holy Roman Emperor, with the intention of conquering France. However, despite spending huge sums of money, the only places conquered during the campaign were Thérouanne, which was destroyed, and Tournai. During Henry's absence overseas, James IV invaded the north of England in support of his French ally and laid siege to Norham Castle in August. The strong defences of the fortress meant that it was a difficult place to capture; the chronicler Thomas Hall claimed it was thought to be impregnable if well supplied. At first the Scots could make little headway against the defenders, despite inflicting significant damage to the walls with their artillery and making three attempts to storm the castle. However, Norham was eventually surrendered to them on the sixth day of the siege. Hall blamed the profligacy of the commander of the English garrison, John Ainslie, for the fall of the fortress. Supposedly, the defenders used up too much of their ammunition in repulsing the Scottish assaults and were therefore compelled to surrender under terms. Afterwards the Scots quickly took the nearby castles of Wark, Chillingham, Etal and Ford, all of which, except for Ford, were slighted. Yet in the meantime, the English commander, Thomas Howard, Earl of Surrey, had mobilised his forces and marched to confront the invaders. Despite their superior numbers, the Scots were defeated at the Battle of Flodden on 9 September, with James killed during the fighting. His death effectively removed the threat of a major Scottish invasion for some time, as he was succeeded by his one-year-old son, James V. During his long minority, Scotland was subjected to factional politics and internal conflicts. Nevertheless, the danger posed by the Scots due to cross-border raiding meant that significant sums of money were spent on improving and modernising key fortifications in the frontier region.[3]

Major works were carried out to overhaul the defences of the town and castle of Berwick. The walls were strengthened with an earthen bank to mitigate the effects of gunshot, with gunports inserted for the use of defensive guns. Artillery fortifications, known as bulwarks, were also added to the defences for the use of artillery. Bulwarks were made of earth, timber, masonry or brick and were intended to provide additional protection to vulnerable areas, often being situated in front of gatehouses. They had low thick walls with embrasures for guns and were a formidable obstacle for any attacker to overcome. The English first began to incorporate bulwarks into the defences of towns and castles on a regular basis in the second half of the fifteenth century, with the first bulwark added to Berwick's defences in the late 1480s. By 1522, the town and castle were protected by five bulwarks. Extensive building works were also carried out at the behest of the Bishop of Durham, Thomas Ruthall, to rebuild his castle of Norham. Extensive damage had been inflicted by the Scots, with Ruthall stating in a letter to Thomas Wolsey, Archbishop of York, dated September 1513, that only the keep and part of the wall remained standing. Yet little more than a month later, he could report to Wolsey that his workers had made good progress, with teams of carpenters, masons and smiths hard at work. By the early 1520s, the defences incorporated angular bastions and a bulwark known as Clapham's Tower, which were equipped with sixteen guns of various sizes.

Efforts were also made to restore other fortifications that had been damaged by the Scots with Thomas, Lord Dacre, tasked with overseeing the reconstruction of Wark Castle in 1517. Two years later, he submitted a detailed report on the state of the castle to Thomas Wolsey. The restored keep was said to be four storeys high, with each storey containing five embrasures for the use of large guns called bombards. He went so far as to claim that if Wark was provided with only a small garrison it would still be far more useful for the defence of the border than even Berwick. Four years later, these newly built defences were put to the test when the castle was besieged by a French army. The outbreak of war between England and France in 1522, led to Scotland joining the conflict on the side of their French ally in the following year. In response, the English carried out raids across the border, with Thomas Howard, Earl of Surrey, leading two forays in May and September. The governor of Scotland, John Stewart, Duke of Albany, retaliated by sending a mostly French force to attack Wark in October equipped with artillery. According to Hall, the besiegers numbered 3,000–4,000 men, while the garrison only consisted of 100 soldiers led by Sir William Lyle. The attackers succeeded in storming the outer ward of the castle, but were driven out of the inner ward by a fierce English counter-attack. This setback prompted the besiegers to lift the siege, as they had received news of the imminent arrival of the Earl of Surrey with a relief force. The latter reached the castle a short time later and stayed long enough to oversee the construction of new bulwarks of earth to strengthen the defences.[4]

Sizeable sums of money continued to be spent on maintaining and modernising the fortifications of the border regions in the later years of the reign of Henry VIII. Nevertheless, the level of expenditure was deemed to be inadequate by observers, with works often carried out in response to specific emergencies. Surveys carried out by Sir Robert Bowes and Sir Ralph Ellerker in 1541 reveal that many fortifications adjoining the Scottish border were deemed to be in an unsatisfactory condition. For example, Wark was said to be in a state of 'greatt & extreme decaye' due to the destruction caused by the Scots during the siege of 1523. Further to the west, Harbottle was characterised as being in 'extreme ruyne & decaye' due to a lack of repairs. However, despite the pessimistic nature of these reports, the castles of the region were generally in a better condition than those elsewhere in the kingdom. This can be seen from the writings of the poet and antiquarian John Leland. Leland travelled widely throughout England and Wales between 1538 and 1543 and described places he visited during his journeys. According to his testimony, many of the castles he saw were in a ruinous or semi-ruinous state. At Restormel Castle, the outer ward was said to be defaced but the large and fair keep was still standing. Whereas at Pickering, the walls and towers were said to be in good condition but the timber structures in the inner ward were in ruins. Other castles had failed less well due to neglect and deliberate destruction. Old Sarum was described as formerly having been 'a right fair and strong castelle', but only extensive ruins remained. Similarly, the buildings within Tintagel were stated to be 'sore wether beten and yn ruine', with sheep fed inside the remnants of the keep. As noted by Leland, some of these castles had been ruinous for hundreds of years. Yet others had been allowed to gradually deteriorate by their owners in more recent years. Some castles were retained as residences or as centres of local administration or justice, but many were deemed to be to surplus to requirements or too expensive to adequately maintain. This can be seen most clearly with castles in the possession of the Crown in the sixteenth century. Henry VII had acquired roughly forty castles after winning the throne in 1485, with further buildings subsequently obtained by forfeiture or inheritance. By the early sixteenth century, most of the principal castles of southern England and Wales were in royal hands. A minority of these structures were kept in good condition, such as Ludlow, which served as the headquarters of the Council in the Marches of Wales. However, little was spent on those castles that were considered to no longer have a residential, administrative or defensive function.[5]

The Break with Rome and the Defence of the Realm

Henry's determination to annul his marriage to his wife, Katherine of Aragon, and to marry Anne Boleyn, led to the break with Rome in 1533. His efforts to obtain an annulment from the papacy were systematically rebuffed, which eventually led to his decision to annul the marriage himself. This action led to him being

excommunicated by Pope Clement VII and the severing of all ties
with Rome. The passing of the Act of Supremacy by parliament in
the following year, which made the king the head of the church,
and efforts to dissolve the monasteries from 1534 onwards, led to
the outbreak of social unrest across the kingdom. The commons of
Lincolnshire rose in rebellion on 1 October 1536 in response to the
appointment of an episcopal commission to investigate the state of
the local clergy in the county, which was feared to be prelude to the
seizure of church property. This uprising was quickly suppressed
by royalist forces, but a far more serious insurrection broke out
soon afterwards in Yorkshire. This movement came to be called the
Pilgrimage of Grace, with leadership assumed by a lawyer, Robert
Aske. The rebels rapidly took control of most of the county, with
many of the common people and gentry joining their cause. On
16 October, Aske at the head of a large force entered York, which
had been surrendered without any resistance being offered. He
subsequently advanced towards nearby Pontefract Castle, where
many loyalist gentry from Yorkshire had taken refuge. Pontefract
was one of the principal royal castles in the north of England and
been kept in a good state of repair. However, the ability of the
garrison to resist a siege was hampered by a shortage of ordnance
and provisions, as its constable, Thomas, Lord Darcy, a prominent
northern magnate, conveyed to the king and other notables in a
series of increasingly desperate letters. On 13 October, he stated
that not one gun was ready to fire, there was no gunpowder or
gunners, and that only a small quantity of bows and arrows were
available, all of which were in a poor condition. Subsequent letters
stress the hostility of the local inhabitants, who refused to oppose
the rebels and prevented provisions from being sent to the fortress.
Despite these pleas for assistance, no help was forthcoming, and
the castle was yielded on 20 October. The surrender of Pontefract
was almost certainly motivated by the hopelessness of resisting
a siege. Nevertheless, Darcy was widely suspected of being in
league with the rebels, particularly as he, with other members
of the garrison, subsequently changed sides. The only place in
Yorkshire still in royalist hands was Scarborough Castle, which
was resolutely defended by its garrison, led by Sir Ralph Eure.
Scarborough was blockaded by the rebels, who were deterred

from making direct assaults due to its strong defences. However, the Crown succeeded in supplying the defenders by sea, with gunpowder and provisions sent to the castle. Nevertheless, the rebellion had spread into neighbouring counties, with castles, such as Barnard Castle in County Durham, falling into their hands. The royalist commanders were unable to counter the rebels militarily, as loyalist forces from the south of England were taking too long to assemble. Therefore, the king's principal military commander in the north, Thomas Howard, Duke of Norfolk, resorted to subterfuge to defeat his enemies. Norfolk persuaded the rebels to disperse their army in return for the promise of a royal pardon and for the summoning of a parliament to hear their grievances. However, the outbreak of further trouble early in the following year was used as the pretext for brutal reprisals being carried out against the rebels, with large numbers of people executed, including Aske and Darcy. Garrisons were also installed in major castles of the north to help pacify the region, with 100 men placed in Scarborough and fifty in Pontefract.[6]

Henry was soon to face another threat, this time from the Catholic monarchs of Europe, who threatened to invade England. On 18 June 1538, the Truce of Nice was agreed between the Holy Roman Emperor, Charles V, and Francis I of France, thereby ending hostilities between the forces of these two rulers. Pope Paul III sought to exploit the situation by persuading them to turn their energies against England, through the intercession of the exiled English cardinal Reginald Pole. On 17 December 1538, the pope published a bull that excommunicated Henry and called upon his subjects to overthrow him. In the event, neither monarch was willing to mount an invasion of England, but fears of such an eventuality prompted the carrying out of measures for the defence of the realm. Instructions were sent out for the mustering of soldiers, the manning of beacon stations, the hiring of mercenaries and the assembly of the royal fleet to protect the coastline. These actions were traditional responses to the threat of invasion, but the king went further by initiating an ambitious scheme of coastal defence, hitherto unparalleled in English history. Commissioners were sent to survey the coastline throughout the country to determine possible landing sites for enemy armies and where existing defences could be improved. The findings of these officials were sent to the king and his council who formulated a comprehensive scheme of coastal defence, known as the 'Device by the King', in February 1539. These plans were quickly acted upon, with work almost immediately beginning on the construction of castles, blockhouses, bulwarks and other fortifications in vulnerable areas. Previous measures for coastal defence in the Middle Ages had been localised and reactive to specific threats, such as the building of artillery fortifications in coastal settlements. By contrast, the works begun in 1539 were on a vast scale and were intended to be defended by small permanent garrisons. The Device programme was, therefore, the first national scheme of defence had that been carried out in English history. The significance of this project was recognised by contemporaries. In March 1539, a protégé of Thomas Cromwell stated that these fortifications would mean that England would be 'moch liker a castel, than a realme' in his newly published work, *An Exhortation to Styre all Englishe Men to the Defence of Theyr Countreye*. By the end of the year, sufficient progress had been made on twenty-four fortifications to necessitate the installation of garrisons within them, although many others were still under construction. Work finished on the Device forts in 1543, but fresh fears of an invasion in 1544 prompted a second phase of construction that lasted until 1547. These works were carried out at great speed, partly due to the threat of invasion but also due to Henry's enthusiasm for fortifications and ordnance. The king took a personal interest in the design and building of fortresses, with a report on the building work carried out at East Cowes on the Isle of Wight in April 1539 stating that it was carried out 'according to the platte devised by the King'. This process was aided by a revolution in cartography that took place in early sixteenth century England, with maps playing a key role in the planning and design of fortifications. Between 1539 and Henry's death in January 1547, the huge sum of some £376,500 had been expended on the Device project. Much of this money came from the colossal wealth acquired by the Crown during the dissolution of the monasteries, with ecclesiastical buildings stripped of their materials so that they could be reused in the construction of fortifications.[7]

The proximity of the coastline of Kent to the Continent meant that special attention was paid to the region. Fortifications were already present at the main settlements in the area, such as at Sandwich and Dover, but an area known as the Downs was identified as being particularly vulnerable to attack. This is an anchorage with a long, shingle beach, adjacent to deep water, which is sheltered from storms by the Goodwin Sands further out to sea. It was decided that three fortresses should be built there, near to each other, namely Deal, Walmer and Sandown, all fully equipped with ordnance.

The design of 'the castles in the Downs' was similar to that of other Henrician forts of the period, based on the principle of concentric defence. Unlike earlier castles, these fortifications had low, thick walls and towers and resembled Tudor roses in their appearance. A central tower or 'keep' was flanked by inner bastions, which were in turn encircled by outer bastions. The presence of numerous embrasures meant that guns of different sizes could be fired at multiple angles of fire. Work began on the castles in April 1539, with 1,400 men employed on their construction in May, with the structures finished by September of the following year. Further to the west, another castle was constructed at Camber in East Sussex to protect the nearby towns of Rye and Winchelsea. This was built on the site of an earlier artillery tower, which was extensively remodelled, with the addition of four bastions linked to stirrup towers. These works were carried out under the direction of an engineer from Moravia, Stephen von Haschenperg, who also oversaw the construction of the castles in the Downs at the same time. Building work initially finished in 1540, but problems with the initial design, caused by the high water table and the excessively low height of the structure, prompted a second phase of construction that lasted from 1542 to 1543. This saw the raising in height of the keep and the rebuilding of the bastions with much larger replacements. The south coast was another area of concern, which necessitated the construction of fortifications in the Solent. Castles and bulwarks were erected in Southampton Water at Netley and St Andrew's, at Southsea on Portsea Island and at Hurst facing the western approach to the Isle of Wight. Forts were also constructed on the Isle of Wight itself, at Sharpenode and Yarmouth in the west, at West Cowes and East Cowes in the north, and at St Helen's and Sandown in the east. These formidable defences meant that their garrisons effectively controlled the main shipping passages in the Solent. Other fortifications were built along the south-west coast, notably in Dorset and Cornwall. This included the construction of Portland Castle and Sandsfoot Castle to protect Weymouth, and Brownsea Castle to guard the approach to Poole. Further forts and bulwarks were erected in Cornwall with St Catherine's Castle situated to overlook the River Fowey, and St Mawes Castle to command the mouth of the River Fal. Fortifications were also constructed in other parts of the realm, notably at Hull, along the River Thames and at Milford Haven. An inventory of the late king's possessions compiled in 1547 reveals that the Device fortresses were heavily armed, with their stores filled with thousands of guns, handguns, bows, bills and other weapons. Yet they only saw limited action in this period, as the invasions that were feared in 1539 and 1544–5 failed to materialise. The French did land a small contingent on the Isle of Wight in 1545, but they were repulsed by local forces.[8]

Epilogue

To the Committees of Warwick and Northants. We conceive you cannot but observe the general disposition that is in the people to tumults and insurrections, and of what difficulty and length of time it is to take in places of strength when once possessed by the enemy. You know what a trouble it was to all the country about the castle of Banbury when it was last held by the enemy, yet we are informed its demolition is retarded for want of that money which is appointed for it in your county. We desire you forthwith to pay in the proportion of money assigned to your county by order of the Houses for the accomplishment of that work, so that the castle may be demolished and all future danger prevented from its being again surprised by any disaffected persons.
The Derby House Committee, 15 July 1648[1]

These instructions were issued by a parliamentary committee that met in Derby House in Westminster, which had been established by the parliamentarians during the First English Civil War in 1644. Their orders to destroy Banbury Castle were duly carried out by the local authorities in the area. Demolition of the site was thorough, with much of the masonry from the structure used to construct houses in the town. The destruction and ruination of many castles in England and Wales took place during the tumultuous years of the 1640s. A struggle for power between the supporters of Charles I and his parliamentary opponents led to the outbreak of the First English Civil War in 1642. Numerous castles were prepared for military action, some of which were damaged during the fighting. Following the parliamentary victory in 1646, the decision was taken to deliberately destroy many of these structures, both to render them indefensible and to punish the defeated royalists. This process of destruction was accelerated following the end of the Second Civil War three years later, to prevent future royalist rebellions. A small number of castles were maintained as fortresses, particularly in coastal areas in the late seventeenth century. Some of these buildings retained these functions in subsequent centuries, with places such as Portchester also being used for other military purposes, such as operating as Prisoner of War camps. Other castles remained in private hands, either as residences for wealthy landowners or as ruins. A change in the ownership of these buildings only began to take place in the nineteenth century, due to the growing popularity of the Gothic Revival movement. Public interest in visiting medieval ruins encouraged the development of the heritage industry, leading to the passing of legislation by parliament to provide protection for these structures, beginning with the Ancient Monuments Protection Act of 1882. Over the course of the nineteenth and twentieth centuries, many castles passed into the care of the State and other organisations, which were made available for the public to visit as attractions. Yet a minority of castles continued to be used by the armed forces into the twentieth century. Military requirements also saw the temporary reuse of some castles during the two World Wars, with even semi-ruined structures pressed into service, such as at Pevensey Castle.

The English Civil Wars

By the second half of the sixteenth century only a small number of castles in England and Wales were kept in a defensible condition. Many medieval castles fell gradually into ruin, with the aristocracy preferring to build new types of residences that emphasised domestic comfort, as opposed to defensive considerations. Other castles were converted to reflect sixteenth century architectural tastes. At Kenilworth, Robert Dudley, Earl of Warwick, transformed the site in the early 1570s by adding a new residential wing in the inner ward known as 'Leicester's Building', as well as a gatehouse and an elaborate Renaissance-style garden. Some royal castles in frontier regions were adapted for modern warfare in the late sixteenth century. Fears of an invasion from Spain prompted the carrying out of major works at Carisbrooke Castle at the end of the century. An Italian engineer, Federigo Gianibelli, converted Carisbrooke into an artillery fort by constructing massive outer defences, incorporating five bastions protected by flanker batteries. Large sums of money were also expended on improving the defences of Berwick-upon-Tweed and Carlisle during the reign of Elizabeth I. Yet these fortifications were neglected following the accession of James VI of Scotland to the English throne in 1603, as James I. The union of the two kingdoms meant that the Anglo-Scottish border defences were no longer considered desirable in the realm of 'Great Britain'. Nevertheless, garrisons were still maintained in the Henrician coastal fortresses and in the Channel Islands. The peace of the realm was shattered during the reign of Charles I in the early 1640s, with rebellions in Scotland and Ireland followed by the outbreak of the First English Civil War in 1642. The civil war rapidly took on the nature of a territorial conflict, with the royalists initially in control of most of Wales, as well as large parts of northern and western England. By contrast, the parliamentarians held the city of London, as well as much of southern and eastern England. The delipidated fortifications of towns and castles, as well as country houses and churches, were soon pressed into service by the warring parties. Outer earthwork defences were added to many castles, with their walls strengthened against gunshot by piling up mounds of earth behind them, a process known as 'countermuring'. The royalist Clifford family improved the fortifications of their castle at Skipton by employing masons to repair the stonework and labourers to stack turf against the walls. A gun platform was also constructed in the south-east corner of the castle, with artillery lifted onto the top of some of the towers. The garrison was well supplied with weaponry, although some of the ordnance kept in the castle stores was of considerable age, including guns captured from the Scots at Flodden in 1513.[2]

The military effectiveness of these medieval castles varied enormously during the conflict. Many royalist-held castles in the south-east of England were captured by the parliamentarians at the start of the war. Dover Castle was taken by a surprise night attack on 21 August 1642 by a daring group of men who scaled the cliffs, with the small garrison of Carisbrooke Castle surrendering to a much larger force from Newport in the next month. By contrast, the defenders of other castles offered more staunch resistance. At Corfe, a small group of men under the command of Mary, Lady Bankes, successfully resisted a parliamentary siege in 1643, with the castle only finally taken after the treachery of a member of the garrison in February 1646. The varying fortunes of war meant that castles frequently changed hands during the conflict. Old Wardour Castle was captured by the parliamentarians in May 1643, but seven months later was besieged by a royalist force led by the owner of the castle, Henry, Lord Arundell, who wished to recover his ancestral seat. However, during the the siege, gunpowder was accidentally ignited in one of the mines dug under the walls, resulting in the destruction of much of the structure. This allowed the attackers to take the castle a short time later, but at a considerable cost to the fabric of the building. Parliamentary victories meant that the royalists were increasingly on the defensive from 1644 onwards, with their castles systematically besieged and captured. The garrison of Scarborough Castle was isolated and placed under pressure following the royalist defeat at the Battle of Marston Moor on 2 July. By February 1645, the castle was under siege, with the attackers inflicting significant damage to Scarborough with their guns. Despite putting up a heroic resistance, the surviving members of the garrison were forced to yield in July, having run out of gunpowder and with their ranks depleted by disease. By contrast, other places were taken far more quickly. Sherborne Castle was surrendered after a eleven day siege, with its defenders having been forced to retreat to the keep after being subjected to a heavy artillery bombardment.[3]

The parliamentarians succeeded in striking a decisive blow against the royalists at the Battle of Naseby on 14 June 1645. This led to their victory in the conflict, with the last royalist-held fortress, Harlech Castle, surrendering to their forces on 15 March 1647. At first the victorious parliamentarians sought to negotiate a settlement with Charles, whereby he would remain as monarch in return for accepting major curbs to his power. However, the king duplicitously sought to exploit divisions between the two parliamentary factions, the Presbyterians and the Independents, as well as their Scottish allies. Following the suppression of rebellions against parliament during the Second Civil War, Charles's deceptions came to light and he was put on trial and executed on 30 January 1649. The outbreak of fresh fighting also encouraged parliament to accelerate its programme of slighting castles in the kingdom. Efforts had been made to destroy some defences from as early as 1645, particularly earthwork defences that had been added to existing fortifications. Yet this process was carried out with far more vigour from 1648 onwards. This stemmed from the practical need to render castles indefensible to prevent them being used in future rebellions and the desire to punish royalist supporters by destroying their properties. In some places the destruction carried out at this time was extensive, with further damage caused in subsequent years by the removal and reuse of materials by local people and landowners. Most castles were demolished by hand, using pickaxes and other tools, as opposed to using gunpowder, which was expensive to use in sufficient quantities to knock down well-built masonry structures. The sometimes substantial costs involved in carrying out this work explains why the scale of destruction varied from place to place, with orders sent out for some buildings to be rendered untenable as opposed to being fully dismantled. Henry Carey, Earl of Monmouth, succeeded in his petition that the apartment buildings at Kenilworth should be spared destruction, as he had a claim to its ownership. This measure failed to save most of the residential buildings within the castle, as they were stripped of their materials by the garrison. Yet Leicester's Gatehouse was converted into a comfortable residence by Colonel Joseph Hawkesworth, the parliamentary commander who oversaw the slighting of Kenilworth. The inhabitants of some places were resentful of the trouble caused by having a castle in their vicinity and petitioned parliament to slight them. Pontefract Castle was besieged on three occasions between 1644 and 1649, which necessitated long and expensive sieges. The townspeople were keen for this troublesome fortress to be thoroughly demolished, with work to dismantle the structure beginning in 1649. This work could be lucrative business, with in excess of £1,500 generated from the sale of lead stripped from Pontefract Castle.

However, these instructions were not universally popular, with the citizens of Winchester reluctant to destroy their magnificent castle. Eventually in response to frequent admonishments from parliament, the structure was almost comprehensively slighted, although the splendid thirteenth century Great Hall was retained for the holding of the county court quarter sessions for Hampshire. Elsewhere, local opposition proved to be more successful, with the people of Scarborough preventing any further destruction being inflicted on their castle. Nevertheless, large numbers of castles and stately homes were ruined and despoiled in the middle years of the seventeenth century.[4]

The Afterlife of Castles

A small number of castles were maintained and garrisoned for coastal defence in the late seventeenth century. This included Henrician forts, such as Deal Castle, whose defences were repaired following a siege of 1648, with a garrison of at least twenty men housed in the castle. Deal continued to be kept in a defensible state into the following century, with its arsenal in 1728 including eleven guns known as culverins. Wars with France in the eighteenth- and early nineteenth century meant that some efforts were made to adapt castle defences. For example, major repairs were carried out at Hurst Castle in the early 1800s, so that modern artillery could be mounted on the roof of its keep. Some fortresses were used as barracks in this period, with extensive tunnels carved beneath Dover Castle to provide extra space. The need to house the large numbers of enemy soldiers and sailors captured during these conflicts also resulted in the use of castles as Prisoner of War camps. At Portchester, men were kept in cramped conditions in the keep, with as many as 2,500 prisoners staying in the castle in 1747. Except for during times of military necessity, little effort was made by the authorities to spend much money on the maintenance of these structures, many of which gradually deteriorated over time. Yet they generally fared better than most other castles, which were quarried for building materials or left subject to the decay caused by the elements. However, in time they came to be regarded as the romantic ruins of a bygone age of chivalry. Public interest in castles and other ancient monuments developed over the course of the eighteenth and nineteenth centuries. This was sparked by the Gothic Revival architectural movement, as well as the writings of authors of historic fiction, such as Sir Walter Scott. His works were particularly influential, with large numbers of visitors flocking to visit Ashby de la Zouch Castle in Leicestershire, due to the popularity of his 1820 novel *Ivanhoe*, which featured the staging of a tournament in the grounds of the castle. Another important factor was the expansion of the rail network, which made it possible for tourists to easily travel across the country and to visit historic sites. In time these factors contributed to the development of the heritage industry, with the State recognising that it had a role to play in protecting the nation's history through the preservation of ancient monuments. This was carried out through the passing of legislation, starting with the Ancient Monuments Act of 1882, with the Ministry of Works gradually taking over the ownership of many medieval ruins. These were often acquired from private landowners, either through purchase or by bequest, with the managed sites then opened to the public as visitor attractions. Military requirements during the two World Wars meant that some castles were temporarily taken over for use by the armed forces in the first half of the twentieth century. Gun batteries were installed at forts, such as at Dartmouth and Hurst, to provide protection for merchant shipping. Scarborough Castle was even subjected to shelling from German warships in 1914, which caused damage to a barracks in the castle and part of its wall. Dover Castle was used as the headquarters for the evacuation of the British Expeditionary Force from Dunkirk in 1940, with its tunnels also extended for use as a secure underground hospital. Dover continued to have a military purpose into the 1980s, with some of its tunnels repurposed for use as a nuclear bunker in the event of a war with the Soviet Union. This role finished with the collapse of the Soviet Union in 1991. Castles in England and Wales are no longer used for the defence of the realm. Instead these structures are now principally heritage sites, with many of them in the possession of English Heritage, Cadw, the National Trust, local authorities and other organisations.[5]

Notes

Chapter One

1. Michael Swanton, ed., *The Anglo-Saxon Chronicles* (London: Phoenix, 2000), pp. 173–4.
2. Ibid, pp. 173, 175.
3. Patrick Wormald, 'Alfred (848/9–899)', *Oxford Dictionary of National Biography*, Oxford University Press, 2004; online edn, Oct 2006 [http://www.oxforddnb.com/view/article/183, accessed 9 Sept 2016]; EHD, vol 1, p. 498; Simon Keynes and Michael Lapidge, eds., *Alfred the Great: Asser's Life of King Alfred and Other Contemporary Sources* (Harmondsworth: Penguin Books, 1983), p. 102; Alexander R. Rumble, 'The Tribal Hidage: An Annotated Bibliography', in *The Defence of Wessex*, eds., David Hill and Alexander R. Rumble (Manchester: Manchester University Press, 1996), pp. 214–5, 221.
4. Sean Miller, 'Edward [Edward the Elder] (870s?–924)', *Oxford Dictionary of National Biography*, Oxford University Press, 2004; online edn, Sept 2011 [http://www.oxforddnb.com/view/article/8514, accessed 9 Sept 2016]; Sarah Foot, 'Æthelstan (893/4–939)', *Oxford Dictionary of National Biography*, Oxford University Press, 2004; online edn, Sept 2011 [http://www.oxforddnb.com/view/article/833, accessed 9 Sept 2016].
5. Simon Keynes, 'Æthelred II (c.966x8–1016)', *Oxford Dictionary of National Biography*, Oxford University Press, Oct 2009 [http://www.oxforddnb.com/view/article/8915, accessed 9 Sept 2016].

6. Frank Barlow, 'Edward [St Edward; known as Edward the Confessor] (1003x5–1066)', *Oxford Dictionary of National Biography, Oxford University Press*, 2004; online edn, May 2006 [http://www.oxforddnb.com/view/article/8516, accessed 12 Sept 2016]; Ann Williams, 'Godwine, earl of Wessex (d. 1053)', *Oxford Dictionary of National Biography*, Oxford University Press, 2004 [http://www.oxforddnb.com/view/article/10887, accessed 12 Sept 2016].

7. David Walker, 'Gruffudd ap Llywelyn (d. 1063)', Oxford Dictionary of National Biography, Oxford University Press, 2004 [http://www.oxforddnb.com/view/article/11695, accessed 21 Sept 2016]; Robin Fleming, 'Harold II (1022/3?–1066)', Oxford Dictionary of National Biography, Oxford University Press, 2004; online edn, Sept 2010 [http://www.oxforddnb.com/view/article/12360, accessed 21 Sept 2016]; Frank Barlow, 'Edward [St Edward; known as Edward the Confessor] (1003x5–1066)', Oxford Dictionary of National Biography, Oxford University Press, 2004; online edn, May 2006 [http://www.oxforddnb.com/view/article/8516, accessed 12 Sept 2016].

8. David Bates, *Normandy Before 1066* (London: Longman Group Limited, 1982), pp. 4, 8–9, 13–14.

9. Quotation taken from R. Allen Brown, *English Castles* (Woodbridge: The Boydell Press, 2004), p. 8; Charles Oman, *Castles* (London: Great Western Railways, 1926), pp. 4–5; Oliver H. Creighton, *Early European Castles* (London: Bristol Classical Press, 2012), pp. 29, 42.

10. Quotation taken from Brown, *English Castles*, p. 15; Creighton, *Early European Castles*, pp. 52–9, 89, 97–8; Edward Impey and Elisabeth Lorans, 'Langeais, Indre-Et-Loire. An Archaeological and Historical Study of the Early Donjon and its Environs', *Journal of the British Archaeological Association*, 151 (1998), pp. 69, 72–6, 94–5; Bernard S. Bachrach, 'The Angevin Strategy of Castle Building in the Reign of Fulk Nerera', *The American Historical Review*, 88 (1983), p. 558, n. 89.

11. Brown, *English Castles*, p. 9; David Charles Douglas, *William the Conqueror: The Norman Impact upon England* (London: Eyre & Spottiswoode, 1964), pp. 140–1; Bates, *Normandy Before 1066*, pp. 46–7, 68–70; Elisabeth M. C. Van Houts,

The Gesta Normannorum Ducum of William of Jumiéges, Orderic Vitalis, and Robert of Torigni, volume 2, (Oxford: Clarendon Press, 1995), pp. 57–9.

12. Douglas, *William the Conqueror*, pp. 37–52; Bates, *Normandy Before 1066*, pp. 114–5; Glyn S. Burgess, ed., *The History of the Norman People: Wace's Roman De Rou* (Woodbridge: The Boydell Press, 2004), pp. 130–4; David Bates, *William the Conqueror* (London: Yale University Press, 2016), pp. 49–85.

13. Douglas, *William the Conqueror*, pp. 53–71; David Bates, 'William I (1027/8–1087)', *Oxford Dictionary of National Biography*, Oxford University Press, 2004; online edn, May 2011 [http://www.oxforddnb.com/view/article/29448, accessed 16 Sept 2016]; Bates, *William the Conqueror*, pp. 86–133.

14. Douglas, *William the Conqueror*, pp. 72–80, 173–5; Marjorie Chibnall, ed., *The Ecclesiastical History of Orderic Vitalis, Vol. II, Books 3 and 4* (Oxford: Clarendon Press, 2002), pp. 117–9; R.H.C. Davis and Marjorie Chibnall, eds., *The Gesta Guillelmi of William of Poitiers* (London: Clarendon Press, 1998), pp. 60–7; Bates, *William the Conqueror*, pp. 162–87.

15. Douglas, *William the Conqueror*, pp. 178–195; Davis and Chibnall, *The Gesta Guillelmi of William of Poitiers*, pp. 75–6, 100–113; Bates, *William the Conqueror*, pp. 200–34.

Chapter Two

1. Marjorie Chibnall, ed., *The Ecclesiastical History of Orderic Vitalis, Vol. II, Books 3 and 4* (Oxford: Clarendon Press, 2002), p. 219.

2. Marjorie Chibnall, 'Orderic Vitalis on Castles', in *Anglo-Norman Castles*, ed. by Robert Liddiard (Woodbridge: Boydell Press, 2003), pp. 119–132; J. O. Prestwich, 'Orderic Vitalis (1075–c.1142)', *Oxford Dictionary of National Biography*, Oxford University Press, 2004; online edn, Oct 2006 [http://www.oxforddnb.com/view/article/20812, accessed 30 Sept 2016].

3. R.H.C. Davis and Marjorie Chibnall, eds., *The Gesta Guillelmi of William of Poitiers* (London: Clarendon Press, 1998), pp. 114–5; Elisabeth M. C. Van Houts, *The Gesta Normannorum Ducum of William of Jumiéges, Orderic*

Vitalis, and Robert of Torigni, volume 2, (Oxford: Clarendon Press, 1995), p. 167; David Charles Douglas, *William the Conqueror: The Norman Impact upon England* (London: Eyre & Spottiswoode, 1964), pp. 193–8; David Bates, *William the Conqueror* (London: Yale University Press, 2016), pp. 234–8.

4. Davis and Chibnall, *The Gesta Guillelmi of William of Poitiers*, pp. 128–149; R. A. B. Maynors, R. M. Thomson and M. Winterbottom, eds., *William of Malmesbury: Gesta Regum Anglorum*, volume 1, (Oxford: Clarendon Press, 1998), pp. 453–5; Douglas, *William the Conqueror*, pp. 198–207; Michael Swanton, ed., *The Anglo-Saxon Chronicles* (London: Phoenix, 2000), pp. 199–200; Bates, *William the Conqueror*, pp. 238–57.

5. Chibnall, *The Ecclesiastical History of Orderic Vitalis, Vol. II, Books 3 and 4*, pp. 194–7, 202–7; Thomas Forester, ed., *The Chronicle of Florence of Worcester* (London: Henry G. Bohn, 1854), pp. 171–2; Douglas, *William the Conqueror*, pp. 208–212; Swanton, *The Anglo-Saxon Chronicles*, p. 200; Houts, *The Gesta Normannorum Ducum of William of Jumiéges, Orderic Vitalis, and Robert of Torigni*, volume 2, pp. 176–9; Bates, *William the Conqueror*, pp. 268–9, 283.

6. Swanton, *The Anglo-Saxon Chronicles*, p. 201; Chibnall, *The Ecclesiastical History of Orderic Vitalis, Vol. II, Books 3 and 4*, pp. 212–5; Robert Liddiard, *Castles in Context: Power, Symbolism and Landscape, 1066 to 1500* (Macclesfield: Windgather Press Ltd, 2005), pp. 20–2; Douglas, *William the Conqueror*, p. 213; Bates, *William the Conqueror*, pp. 288–90.

7. Douglas, *William the Conqueror*, pp. 213–4; Chibnall, *The Ecclesiastical History of Orderic Vitalis, Vol. II, Books 3 and 4*, pp. 209, 214–21; Swanton, *The Anglo-Saxon Chronicles*, pp. 202–3; Forester, *The Chronicle of Florence of Worcester*, p. 172; Houts, *The Gesta Normannorum Ducum of William of Jumiéges, Orderic Vitalis, and Robert of Torigni*, volume 2, p. 183; Bates, *William the Conqueror*, pp. 290–300.

8. Bates, *William the Conqueror*, pp. 303–21; Douglas, *William the Conqueror*, pp. 214–5, 218–221; Chibnall, *The Ecclesiastical History of Orderic Vitalis, Vol. II, Books 3 and 4*, pp. 227–37; Swanton, *The Anglo-Saxon Chronicles*, pp. 202–6.

9. Bates, *William the Conqueror*, pp. 310–12; Douglas, *William the Conqueror*, pp. 218–20; Chibnall, *The Ecclesiastical History of Orderic Vitalis, Vol. II, Books 3 and 4*, pp. 227–30; Swanton, *The Anglo-Saxon Chronicles*, pp. 203–4; Forester, *The Chronicle of Florence of Worcester*, pp. 172–4.

10. Bates, *William the Conqueror*, pp. 331–4, 346–8, 360–1; Douglas, *William the Conqueror*, pp. 221–2, 226–7; Swanton, *The Anglo-Saxon Chronicles*, pp. 205, 208.

11. Bates, *William the Conqueror*, pp. 378–83; Douglas, *William the Conqueror*, pp. 331–3; Swanton, *The Anglo-Saxon Chronicles*, pp. 210–11; Chibnall, *The Ecclesiastical History of Orderic Vitalis, Vol. II, Books 3 and 4*, pp. 311–7.

12. R. R. Davies, *The Age of Conquest Wales 1063–1415* (Oxford: Oxford University Press, 1991), pp. 6–14, 24, 71.

13. Swanton, *The Anglo-Saxon Chronicles*, p. 200; Chibnall, *The Ecclesiastical History of Orderic Vitalis, Vol. II, Books 3 and 4*, pp. 260–1; Bates, *William the Conqueror*, pp. 342–3; Douglas, *William the Conqueror*, pp. 241–2; H. C. Darby, 'The Marches of Wales in 1086', *Transactions of the Institute of British Geographers*, 11 (1986), pp. 259–266; Davies, *The Age of Conquest Wales 1063–1415*, pp. 28–9.

14. Chibnall, *The Ecclesiastical History of Orderic Vitalis, Vol. II, Books 3 and 4*, pp. 260–3; Bates, *William the Conqueror*, pp. 342–3, 429–33; Douglas, *William the Conqueror*, pp. 241–2; Darby, 'The Marches of Wales in 1086', pp. 267–76; Swanton, *The Anglo-Saxon Chronicles*, p. 214; Davies, *The Age of Conquest Wales 1063–1415*, pp. 29–31; John Kenyon, 'Fluctuating Frontiers: Normanno-Welsh Castle Warfare c. 1075 to 1240' in *Anglo-Norman Castles*, ed. by Robert Liddiard (Woodbridge: The Boydell Press, 2003), pp. 247–9; Arthur Jones, ed., *The History of Gruffydd ap Cynan: The Welsh Text with Translation, Introduction, and Notes* (Manchester: Manchester University Press, 1910), p. 117.

15. Swanton, *The Anglo-Saxon Chronicles*, p. 216; Bates, *William the Conqueror*, pp. 298–9, 458–9, 462–3; C.G. Harfield, 'A Hand-list of Castles Recorded in the Domesday Book', *The English Historical Review*, 106 (1991), pp. 371–392.

16. Richard Eales, 'Royal Power and Castles in Norman England', in *Anglo-Norman Castles*, ed. by Robert Liddiard (Woodbridge: The Boydell Press, 2003), pp. 41–68; Oliver H. Creighton, *Castles and Landscapes: Power, Community and Fortification in Medieval England* (London: Equinox Published Ltd, 2002), pp. 36, 46; Bates, *William the Conqueror*, pp. 285–7, 298–300, 324; Sidney Painter, 'Castle-Guard', *The American Historical Review*, 40 (1935), pp. 450–9; Roland B. Harris, 'Recent Research on the White Tower: Reconstructing and Dating the Norman Building' in *Castles and the Anglo-Norman World*, ed. by John A. Davies, Angela Riley, Jean-Marie Levesque and Charlotte Lapiche (Oxford: Oxbow Books, 2016), p. 177–189.

17. Swanton, *The Anglo-Saxon Chronicles*, p. 220; Bates, *William the Conqueror*, pp. 396–404, 481–8.

18. Frank Barlow, *William Rufus* (London: Yale University Press, 2000), pp. 71–83; Swanton, *The Anglo-Saxon Chronicles*, p. 222–5; Marjorie Chibnall, ed., *The Ecclesiastical History of Orderic Vitalis, Vol. IV, Books 7 and 8* (Oxford: Clarendon Press, 1973), pp. 124–9; Maynors, Thomson and Winterbottom, *William of Malmesbury*, volume 1, pp. 544–9.

19. Frank Barlow, 'William II (c. 1060–1100)', *Oxford Dictionary of National Biography*, Oxford University Press, 2004 [http://www.oxforddnb.com/view/article/29449, accessed 29 March 2017); Maynors, Thomson and Winterbottom, *William of Malmesbury*, volume 1, pp. 548–53; Barlow, *William Rufus*, pp. 296–8.

20. Thomas Jones, ed., *Brut Y Tywysogyon, or, The Chronicle of the Princes. Red Book of Hergest Version* (Cardiff: University of Wales, 1955), pp. 32–3; Barlow, *William Rufus*, pp. 318–24; John Edward Lloyd, *A History of Wales: From the Earliest Times to the Edwardian Conquest*, volume 2 (London: Longmans, Green, and Co., 1912), pp. 385–403; Davies, *The Age of Conquest Wales 1063–1415*, p. 34; Jones, *The History of Gruffydd ap Cynan*, pp. 132–4; Chibnall, *The Ecclesiastical History of Orderic Vitalis, Vol. IV, Books 7 and 8*, pp. 136–43.

21. Jones, *The History of Gruffydd ap Cynan*, pp. 136–9; Davies, *The Age of Conquest Wales 1063–1415*, p. 35; Jones, *Brut Y*

Tywysogion, pp. 32–7; Barlow, *William Rufus*, pp. 337–55; Lloyd, *A History of Wales*, pp. 403–5; Swanton, *The Anglo-Saxon Chronicles*, p. 231.

22. Maynors, Thomson and Winterbottom, *William of Malmesbury*, volume 1, p. 553; Jones, *Brut Y Tywysogion*, pp. 36–7; Barlow, *William Rufus*, p. 354; Jones, *The History of Gruffydd ap Cynan*, pp. 140–1; Lloyd, *A History of Wales*, pp. 405–8; Swanton, *The Anglo-Saxon Chronicles*, p. 231; Forester, *The Chronicle of Florence of Worcester*, pp. 201–3.

23. Swanton, *The Anglo-Saxon Chronicles*, p. 234; Forester, *The Chronicle of Florence of Worcester*, p. 204; Jones, *The History of Gruffydd ap Cynan*, pp. 143–9; Lloyd, *A History of Wales*, pp. 408–11; Jones, *Brut Y Tywysogion*, pp. 36–9.

24. C. Warren Hollister, 'Henry I (1068/9–1135)', *Oxford Dictionary of National Oxford University Press*, 2004 [http://www.oxforddnb.com/view/article/12948, accessed 21 September 2016]; Frank Barlow, 'William II (c.1060–1100)', *Oxford Dictionary of National University Press*, 2004 [http://www.oxforddnb.com/view/article/29449, accessed 21 September 2016]; Maynors, Thomson and Winterbottom, *William of Malmesbury*, volume 1, pp. 716–19; Swanton, *The Anglo-Saxon Chronicles*, pp. 235–7; C. Warren Hollister, *Henry I* (London: Yale University Press, 2001), pp. 136–41.

25. Swanton, *The Anglo-Saxon Chronicles*, pp. 237–41; Maynors, Thomson and Winterbottom, *William of Malmesbury*, volume 1, pp. 718–25; Marjorie Chibnall, ed., *The Ecclesiastical History of Orderic Vitalis, Vol. VI, Books 11, 12 and 13* (Oxford: Clarendon Press, 1978), pp. 20–37; Forester, *The Chronicle of Florence of Worcester*, pp. 210–11; C. Warren Hollister, 'Henry I (1068/9–1135)', *Oxford Dictionary of National Oxford University Press*, 2004 [http://www.oxforddnb.com/view/article/12948, accessed 21 September 2016].

26. H. M. Colvin, *The History of the King's Works*, volume 1 (London: H. M. S. O, 1963), pp. 37–40; Paul Bennett, Sheppard Frere and Sally Stow, *The Archaeology of Canterbury Vol. 1, Excavations at Canterbury Castle* (Maidstone: Kent Archaeological Society for the Canterbury Archaeological Trust, 1982), pp. 70–7.

27. Swanton, *The Anglo-Saxon Chronicles*, pp. 442–3; Maynors, Thomson and Winterbottom, *William of Malmesbury*, volume 1, pp. 726–9; Lloyd, *A History of Wales*, pp. 423–32; Jones, *Brut Y Tywysogion*, pp. 48–105; Davies, *The Age of Conquest Wales 1063–1415*, pp. 36–44, 99–100.

28. Lloyd, *A History of Wales*, pp. 433–5; Jones, *Brut Y Tywysogion*, pp. 86–103; Davies, *The Age of Conquest Wales 1063–1415*, pp. 42–4.

Chapter Three

1. Michael Swanton, ed., *The Anglo-Saxon Chronicles* (London: Phoenix, 2000), pp. 263–4.

2. Edmund King, *King Stephen* (London: Yale University Press, 2012), pp. 210–15; K. R. Potter and R. H. C. Davis, eds., *Gesta Stephani* (Oxford: Claredon Press, 1976), pp. 150–5; Edmund King and K. R. Potter, eds., *William of Malmesbury, Historia Novella: The Contemporary History*, (Oxford: Clarendon Press, 1998), pp. 70–1.

3. King, *King Stephen*, pp. 11–49; J. A. Giles, ed., *William of Malmesbury's Chronicle of the Kings of England. From the Earliest Period to the Reign of King Stephen. With Notes and Illustrations* (London: Henry G. Bohn, 1847), pp. 454–7; C. Warren Hollister, 'William (1102–1128)', *Oxford Dictionary of National Biography*, Oxford University Press, 2004 [http://www.oxforddnb.com/view/article/58402, accessed 28 April 2017].

4. King, *King Stephen*, pp. 43–54; Davis, *Gesta Stephani*, pp. 3–7; King and Potter, *William of Malmesbury*, pp. 26–41; Marjorie Chibnall, ed., *The Ecclesiastical History of Orderic Vitalis, Vol. VI, Books 11, 12 and 13* (Oxford: Clarendon Press, 1978), pp. 444–7, 454–5.

5. King, *King Stephen*, pp. 64–7, 70, 73; Davis, *Gesta Stephani*, pp. 30–45; Thomas Forester, ed., *The Chronicle of Henry of Huntingdon. Comprising the History of England, from the Invasion of Julius Caesar to the Accession of Henry II. Also, the Acts of Stephen, King of England and Duke of Normandy* (London: Henry G. Bohn, 1853), p. 265; Oliver H. Creighton and Duncan W. Wright, eds., *The Anarchy: War and Status*

in 12th-Century Landscapes of Conflict (Liverpool: Liverpool University Press, 2016), pp. 56–8.

6. King, *King Stephen*, pp. 67–8, 70–73; Davis, *Gesta Stephani*, pp. 14–23; R. R. Davies, *The Age of Conquest Wales 1063–1415* (Oxford: Oxford University Press, 1991), pp. 45–6, 48, 67; Thomas Jones, ed., *Brut Y Tywysogyon, or, The Chronicle of the Princes. Red Book of Hergest Version* (Cardiff: University of Wales, 1955), pp. 112–7; John Edward Lloyd, *A History of Wales: From the Earliest Times to the Edwardian Conquest*, volume 2 (London: Longmans, Green, and Co., 1912), pp. 470–7; Thomas Forester, ed., *The Chronicle of Florence of Worcester* (London: Henry G. Bohn, 1854), pp. 251–2.

7. King, *King Stephen*, pp. 78–86; Forester, *The Chronicle of Henry of Huntingdon*, pp. 266–7; Davis, *Gesta Stephani*, pp. 46–55; Edmund King, 'Stephen (c.1092–1154)', *Oxford Dictionary of National Biography*, Oxford University Press, 2004; online edn, Sept 2010 [http://www.oxforddnb.com/view/article/26365, accessed 2 May 2017]; Forester, *The Chronicle of Florence of Worcester*, pp. 258–9.

8. King, *King Stephen*, pp. 87–90; Forester, *The Chronicle of Henry of Huntingdon*, p. 267; Davis, *Gesta Stephani*, pp. 56–71; King and Potter, *William of Malmesbury*, pp. 40–3; David Crouch, 'Robert, first earl of Gloucester (b. before 1100, d. 1147)', *Oxford Dictionary of National Biography*, Oxford University Press, 2004; online edn, May 2006 [http://www.oxforddnb.com/view/article/23716, accessed 2 May 2017].

9. King, *King Stephen*, pp. 90–4, 105–6; Forester, *The Chronicle of Florence of Worcester*, pp. 263–5; Forester, *The Chronicle of Henry of Huntingdon*, pp. 266–70; Richard Howlett, ed., *Chronicles of the Reigns of Stephen, Henry II., and Richard I, Vol III* (London: Longman & co, 1886), pp. 155–66.

10. King, *King Stephen*, pp. 106–110, 113–14, 134; Forester, *The Chronicle of Henry of Huntingdon*, pp. 270–1; Davis, *Gesta Stephani*, pp. 72–5; King and Potter, *William of Malmesbury*, pp. 44–59; Creighton and Wright, *The Anarchy*, pp. 208–10; Chibnall, ed., *The Ecclesiastical History of Orderic Vitalis, Vol. VI, Books 11, 12 and 13*, pp. 530–5.

11. King, *King Stephen*, p. 134; Davis, *Gesta Stephani*, pp. 80–5; Creighton and Wright, *The Anarchy*, pp. 59–60; Duncan Wright, Michael Fradley and Oliver H. Creighton, 'Corfe, 'The Rings', Dorset' in *Castles, Siegeworks and Settlements Surveying the Archaeology of the Twelfth Century*, ed. by Duncan Wright and Oliver H. Creighton (Oxford: Archaeopress Publishing Ltd, 2016), p. 40–48.

12. King, *King Stephen*, pp. 115–21; Forester, *The Chronicle of Florence of Worcester*, pp. 270–1; King and Potter, *William of Malmesbury*, pp. 60–5, 72–5; Davis, *Gesta Stephani*, pp. 87–97; Creighton and Wright, *The Anarchy*, pp. 64–8; Chibnall, ed., *The Ecclesiastical History of Orderic Vitalis, Vol. VI, Books 11, 12 and 13*, pp. 534–7; Forester, *The Chronicle of Henry of Huntingdon*, p. 272.

13. King, *King Stephen*, pp. 125–44; Creighton and Wright, *The Anarchy*, pp. 191–2, 252, 256–9; King and Potter, *William of Malmesbury*, pp. 74–7; Davis, *Gesta Stephani*, pp. 98–111; Forester, *The Chronicle of Florence of Worcester*, pp. 273–9; Janet Fairweather, ed., *Liber Eliensis: A History of the Isle of Ely from the Seventh Century to the Twelfth* (Woodbridge: The Boydell Press, 2005), pp. 389–90.

14. King, *King Stephen*, pp. 145–54; King and Potter, *William of Malmesbury*, pp. 80–7; Davis, *Gesta Stephani*, pp. 110–15; Chibnall, ed., *The Ecclesiastical History of Orderic Vitalis, Vol. VI, Books 11, 12 and 13*, pp. 538–51.

15. King, *King Stephen*, pp. 154–63, 167–73; King and Potter, *William of Malmesbury*, pp. 86–109, 114–5; Davis, *Gesta Stephani*, pp. 116–37; Forester, *The Chronicle of Florence of Worcester*, pp. 279–86; Creighton and Wright, *The Anarchy*, pp. 209–11.

16. King, *King Stephen*, pp. 181–8; King and Potter, *William of Malmesbury*, pp. 126–33; Davis, *Gesta Stephani*, pp. 138–45.

17. King, *King Stephen*, pp. 190–9; Davis, *Gesta Stephani*, pp. 144–71; Forester, *The Chronicle of Henry of Huntingdon*, p. 281; Creighton and Wright, *The Anarchy*, pp. 259–75; Duncan Wright, Michael Fradley and Oliver H. Creighton, 'Burwell Castle, Cambridgeshire' in *Castles, Siegeworks and Settlements Surveying the Archaeology of the Twelfth Century*,

ed. by Duncan Wright and Oliver H. Creighton (Oxford: Archaeopress Publishing Ltd, 2016), pp. 6–25.

18. King, *King Stephen*, pp. 222–9; Davis, *Gesta Stephani*, pp. 170–97, 237; Forester, *The Chronicle of Henry of Huntingdon*, pp. 281–4; Creighton and Wright, *The Anarchy*, pp. 58, 68–9.

19. King, *King Stephen*, pp. 237–43; Davis, *Gesta Stephani*, pp. 198–209; Marjorie Chibnall, 'Matilda (1102–1167)', *Oxford Dictionary of National Biography*, Oxford University Press, 2004 [http://www.oxforddnb.com/view/article/18338, accessed 8 May 2017].

20. King, *King Stephen*, pp. 250–8; Davis, *Gesta Stephani*, pp. 210–25; W. L. Warren, *Henry II* (London: Yale University Press, 2000), pp. 36–8

21. Davies, *The Age of Conquest Wales 1063–1415*, pp. 46–51; Lloyd, *A History of Wales*, pp. 489–94; Jones, *Brut Y Tywysogion*, pp. 120–33; Lawrence Butler, 'The Castles of the Princes of Gwynedd', in *The Impact of the Edwardian Castles in Wales*, ed. by Diane M. Williams and John R. Kenyon (Oxford: Oxbow Books, 2010), p. 27; Huw Pryce, 'Rhys ap Gruffudd (1131/2–1197)', *Oxford Dictionary of National Biography*, Oxford University Press, 2004 [http://www.oxforddnb.com/view/article/23464, accessed 10 May 2017].

22. King, *King Stephen*, pp. 257–68; Davis, *Gesta Stephani*, pp. 228–31; Creighton and Wright, *The Anarchy*, pp. 69–71; Forester, *The Chronicle of Henry of Huntingdon*, pp. 287–9; Warren, *Henry II*, pp. 38–48.

23. King, *King Stephen*, pp. 270–83, 290; Davis, *Gesta Stephani*, pp. 230–41; Forester, *The Chronicle of Henry of Huntingdon*, pp. 291–6; Creighton and Wright, *The Anarchy*, pp. 72–4; Warren, *Henry II*, pp. 49–53; Richard Howlett, ed., *Chronicles of the Reigns of Stephen, Henry II., and Richard I, Vol IV* (London: Eyre and Spottiswoode, 1889), pp. 173–4.

Chapter Four

1. Joseph Stevenson, ed., *The Church Historians of England. Vol. IV.–Part II. Containing The History of William of Newburgh: The Chronicles of Robert de Monte.* (London: Beeleys, 1856), p. 444.

2. Thomas Forester, ed., *The Chronicle of Henry of Huntingdon. Comprising the History of England, from the Invasion of Julius Caesar to the Accession of Henry II. Also, the Acts of Stephen, King of England and Duke of Normandy* (London: Henry G. Bohn, 1853), p. 295; Richard Howlett, ed., *Chronicles of the Reigns of Stephen, Henry II., and Richard I, Vol IV* (London: Eyre and Spottiswoode, 1889), p. 183; William Stubbs, ed., *The Historical Works of Gervase of Canterbury, Vol. I* (London: Longman & Co., 1879), p. 161; W. L. Warren, *Henry II* (London: Yale University Press, 2000), pp. 57–9; Oliver H. Creighton and Duncan W. Wright, eds., *The Anarchy: War and Status in 12th-Century Landscapes of Conflict* (Liverpool: Liverpool University Press, 2016), pp. 82–4, 111–5; H. M. Colvin, *The History of the King's Works,* volume 1 (London: H. M. S. O., 1963), pp. 51–6.

3. Stevenson, *The Church Historians of England. Vol. IV,* pp. 444–5; Stubbs, *The Historical Works of Gervase of Canterbury,* pp. 161–2; Warren, *Henry II,* pp. 53–69; Joseph Hunter, ed., *The Great Rolls of the Pipe for the Second, Third, and Fourth Years of the Reign of King Henry the Second, A. D. 1155, 1156, 1157, 1158* (London: George E. Eyre and Andrew Spottiswoode, 1844), pp. 126, 132; R. Allen Brown, 'Framlingham Castle and Bigod 1154–1216', *Proceedings of the Suffolk Institute of Archaeology and History,* 25.2 (1950), pp. 127–48.

4. Warren, *Henry II,* pp. 69–71, 160–1; R. R. Davies, *The Age of Conquest Wales 1063–1415* (Oxford: Oxford University Press, 1991), pp. 51–2; Thomas Jones, ed., *Brut Y Tywysogyon, or, The Chronicle of the Princes. Red Book of Hergest Version* (Cardiff: University of Wales, 1955), pp. 134–41; John Edward Lloyd, *A History of Wales: From the Earliest Times to the Edwardian Conquest,* volume 2 (London: Longmans, Green, and Co., 1912), pp. 494–510; Huw Pryce, 'Rhys ap Gruffudd (1131/2–1197)', *Oxford Dictionary of National Biography,* Oxford University Press, 2004 [http://www.oxforddnb.com/view/article/23464, accessed 5 April 2017]; Huw Pryce, 'Owain Gwynedd (d. 1170)', *Oxford Dictionary of National Biography,* Oxford University Press, 2004 [http://www.

oxforddnb.com/view/article/20979, accessed 5 April 2017]; F. Suppe, 'The Garrisoning of Oswestry: A Baronial Castle on the Welsh Marches', in *The Medieval Castle: Romance and Reality*, ed. by Kathryn Reyerson and Faye Powe (Kendall/ Hunt: Dubuque, 1984) pp. 63–78.

5. Suppe, 'The Garrisoning of Oswestry: A Baronial Castle on the Welsh Marches', pp. 63–78; Warren, *Henry II*, pp. 96–100; 162–4; Pryce, 'Rhys ap Gruffudd (1131/2–1197)'; Pryce, 'Owain Gwynedd (d. 1170)'; Lloyd, *A History of Wales*, pp. 511–22. 536–44; Jones, *Brut Y Tywysogion*, pp. 142–59; Davies, *The Age of Conquest Wales 1063–1415*, pp. 53–4, 67, 102, 218–39.

6. Warren, *Henry II*, pp. 97–130; Francisque Michel, ed., *Chronicle of the War Between the English and the Scots in 1173 and 1174* (London: J. B. Nichols and Son, 1840), pp. 22–59; William Stubbs, ed., *Ranulfi de Diceto Decani Lundoniensis Opera Historica. The Historical Works of Master Ralph de Diceto, Dean of London. Edited from the Original Manuscripts*, volume 1 (London: H. M. S. O. 1876), p. 376; Stevenson, *The Church Historians of England. Vol. IV*, pp. 488–9; William Stubbs, ed., *Chronica Magistri Rogeri de Houedene*, volume 2 (London: Longmans, Green, Reader and Dyer, 1868), p. 47; Stubbs, *The Historical Works of Gervase of Canterbury*, pp. 242–6; Valerie Potter, Margaret Poulter and Jane Allen, eds., *The Building of Orford Castle: A Translation from the Pipe Rolls 1163–78* (Woodbridge: Orford Museum, 2002), pp. 22–3; John S. Moore, 'Anglo-Norman Garrisons', *Anglo-Norman Studies*, 22 (1999), p. 234.

7. Warren, *Henry II*, pp. 129–42; Michel, *Chronicle of the War Between the English and the Scots in 1173 and 1174*, pp. 66–83; Stubbs, *Ranulfi de Diceto Decani Lundoniensis Opera Historica*, pp. 377–85; Stevenson, *The Church Historians of England. Vol. IV*, pp. 490–7; Stubbs, *Chronica Magistri Rogeri de Houedene*, volume 2, pp. 58–65; Stubbs, *The Historical Works of Gervase of Canterbury*, pp. 246–51.

8. H. M. Colvin, *The History of the King's Works*, volume 1 (London: H. M. S. O, 1963), pp. 51–73; R. Allen Brown, 'Royal Castle-Building in England, 1154–1216', *The English*

Historical Review, 70 (1955), pp. 353–98; Warren, *Henry II*, p. 234.

9. H. M. Colvin, *The History of the King's Works*, volume 2 (London: H. M. S. O, 1963), pp. 630–2, 746, 756, 769–70, 829–30, 855–7, 865; Joseph Stevenson, ed., *The Church Historians of England. Vol. V.–Part 1.* (London: Beeleys, 1858), pp. 221–2; Steven Brindle, *Dover Castle* (London: English Heritage, 2012), pp. 9, 13, 40–2; Potter, Poulter and Allen, *The Building of Orford Castle*; John Goodall, *The English Castle, 1066–1650* (New Haven: Yale University Press, 2011), pp. 140–4.

10. Quotation taken from W. L. Warren, *King John* (London: Yale University Press, 1997), p. 40; Ibid, pp. 38–42; William Stubbs, ed., *Chronica Magistri Rogeri de Houedene*, volume 3 (London: Longman & Co., 1870), pp. 25–190; Richard Howlett, ed., *Chronicles of the Reigns of Stephen, Henry II., and Richard I, Vol III* (London: Longman & co, 1886), pp. 383–422, 430–5.

11. Quotation taken from Warren, *King John*, p. 45; Ibid, pp. 42–6; Stubbs, ed., *Chronica Magistri Rogeri de Houedene*, volume 3, pp. 194–240; John Gillingham, *Richard I* (London: Yale University Press, 1999), pp. 269–70.

Chapter Five

1. J. A. Giles, ed., *Roger of Wendower's Flowers of History*, volume 2, (Oxford: Henry G. Bohn, 1849), p. 338.

2. The extract from the Barnwell chronicle is quoted by Charles Coulson, *Castles in Medieval Society: Fortresses in England, France, and Ireland in the Central Middle Ages* (Oxford: Oxford University Press, 2003), p. 160; H. M. Colvin, *The History of the King's Works,* volume 1 (London: H. M. S. O., 1963), p. 65.

3. W. L. Warren, *King John* (London: Yale University Press, 1997), pp. 51–99, 193–7.

4. R. R. Davies, *The Age of Conquest Wales 1063–1415* (Oxford: Oxford University Press, 1991), pp. 223–31; Thomas Jones, ed., *Brut Y Tywysogyon, or, The Chronicle of the Princes. Red Book of Hergest Version* (Cardiff: University of Wales, 1955), pp. 170–83; John Edward Lloyd, *A History of Wales: From the*

Earliest Times to the Edwardian Conquest, volume 2 (London: Longmans, Green, and Co., 1912), pp. 574–86.

5. Davies, *The Age of Conquest Wales 1063–1415*, pp. 239–41; Jones, *Brut Y Tywysogion*, pp. 184–91; Lloyd, *A History of Wales*, pp. 590, 612–39; Sidney Painter, *The Reign of King John* (Baltimore: The John Hopkins Press, 1949), p. 266; Warren, *King John*, pp. 197–200; William Stubbs, ed., *The Historical Collections of Walter of Coventry*, volume 2 (London: Longman & co., 1873), pp. 203–7.

6. Warren, *King John*, pp. 200–17; J. C. Holt, *The Northerners: A Study in the Reign of King John* (Oxford: Clarendon Press, 1992), p. 84; John S. Moore, 'Anglo-Norman Garrisons', *Anglo-Norman Studies*, 22 (1999), p. 243; Stubbs, *The Historical Collections of Walter of Coventry*, volume 2, pp. 207–16.

7. Warren, *King John*, pp. 217–44; Stubbs, *The Historical Collections of Walter of Coventry*, volume 2, pp. 216–22.

8. H. M. Colvin, *The History of the King's Works*, volume 1 (London: H. M. S. O., 1963), p. 65; H. M. Colvin, *The History of the King's Works*, volume 2 (London: H. M. S. O., 1963), pp. 617–9, 683, 688, 692, 766–7; Holt, *The Northerners*, pp. 104–7; Painter, *The Reign of King John*, pp. 352–60; Richard Eales, 'Castles and Politics in England, 1215–24', *Thirteenth Century England*, eds., P. Coss and S. Lloyd (Woodbridge: Boydell Press, 1988), pp. 27–30; John Goodall, *Scarborough Castle* (London: English Heritage, 2013), p. 27; T. Duffus Hardy, ed., *Rotuli Litterarum Clausarum in Turri Londinensi Asservati*, volume 1 (London: Eyre and Spottiswoode, 1833), pp. 176, 178, 185, 194–5.

9. Quotation from R. Allen Brown, *English Castles* (Woodbridge: The Boydell Press, 2004), p. 131; Warren, *King John*, pp. 245–8; Giles, *Roger of Wendower's Flowers of History*, pp. 335–9; Painter, *The Reign of King John*, pp. 360–5; Stubbs, *The Historical Collections of Walter of Coventry*, volume 2, pp. 226–7; John Goodall, *The English Castle, 1066–1650*, (New Haven: Yale University Press, 2011), p. 169; Hardy, *Rotuli Litterarum Clausarum, 1204–27*, volume 1, p. 231.

10. Giles, *Roger of Wendower's Flowers of History*, pp. 348–51; Warren, *King John*, pp. 248–9; Holt, *The Northerners*,

pp. 129–33; Painter, *The Reign of King John*, pp. 366–9; Stubbs, *The Historical Collections of Walter of Coventry*, volume 2, p. 229; Joseph. Stevenson, ed., *Radulphi de Coggeshall Chronicon Anglicanum* (London: Longman & Co., 1875), pp. 173–6; Joseph Stevenson, ed., *Chronica de Mailros* (Edinburgh: Typis Societatis Edinburgensis, 1835), pp. 121–2.

11. Giles, *Roger of Wendower's Flowers of History*, pp. 352–8; Warren, *King John*, pp. 249–51; Holt, *The Northerners*, pp. 133–5; Painter, *The Reign of King John*, pp. 369–72; Stubbs, *The Historical Collections of Walter of Coventry*, volume 2, p. 229; R. Allen Brown, 'Framlingham Castle and Bigod 1154–1216' *Proceedings of the Suffolk Institute of Archaeology and History*, 25.2 (1950), pp. 142–5.

12. Giles, *Roger of Wendower's Flowers of History*, pp. 364–74; Warren, *King John*, pp. 122–3, 251–2; Painter, *The Reign of King John*, pp. 374–5; Stubbs, *The Historical Collections of Walter of Coventry*, volume 2, p. 229–30; Stevenson, *Radulphi de Coggeshall Chronicon Anglicanum*, p. 181–2; Francisque Michel, ed., *Histoire des Ducs de Normandie et des Rois D'Angleterre* (Paris: Société de l'histoire de France, 1840), pp. 171–6.

13. Giles, *Roger of Wendower's Flowers of History*, pp. 374–5; Painter, *The Reign of King John*, p. 376; Stubbs, *The Historical Collections of Walter of Coventry*, volume 2, p. 230; John Goodall, 'Dover Castle and the Great Siege of 1216', *Château Gaillard*, 19 (2000), pp. 91–101; Stevenson, *Radulphi de Coggeshall Chronicon Anglicanum*, p. 182; Michel, *Histoire des Ducs de Normandie et des Rois D'Angleterre*, pp. 170, 177–82; Henry Richards Luard, ed., *Matthæi Parisiensis, Monachi Sancti Albani, Chronica Majora*, volume 3 (London: Longman & Co., 1876), p. 28.

14. Giles, *Roger of Wendower's Flowers of History*, pp. 366, 375–8; Painter, *The Reign of King John*, pp. 376–7; Warren, *King John*, pp. 253–5; Stubbs, *The Historical Collections of Walter of Coventry*, volume 2, pp. 230–5.

15. Quote from D. A. Carpenter, *The Minority of Henry III* (London: Methuen London, 1990), pp. 13–27; Giles, *Roger of Wendower's Flowers of History*, pp. 379–87; Warren, *King John*, pp. 255–6; Stubbs, *The Historical Collections of Walter*

of Coventry, volume 2, p. 232–5; Luard, *Matthæi Parisiensis*, volume 3, pp. 3–5.

16. Giles, *Roger of Wendower's Flowers of History*, pp. 389–97; Warren, *King John*, pp. 256–7; Stubbs, *The Historical Collections of Walter of Coventry*, volume 2, p. 236–7; Nicholas Vincent, *Peter des Roches: An Alien in English Politics, 1205–1238* (Cambridge: Cambridge University Press, 1996), pp. 135–6; Carpenter, *The Minority of Henry III*, pp. 27–49.

17. Davies, *The Age of Conquest Wales 1063–1415*, pp. 239–43; Jones, *Brut Y Tywysogion*, pp. 198–219; Lloyd, *A History of Wales*, pp. 640–54; A. D. Carr, 'Llywelyn ab Iorwerth (c.1173–1240)', *Oxford Dictionary of National Biography*, Oxford University Press, 2004 [http://www.oxforddnb.com/view/article/16874, accessed 29 May 2017]; Carpenter, *The Minority of Henry III*, pp. 42–3, 64–7.

Chapter Six

1. C. D. Yonge, ed., *The Flowers of History, especially such as relate to the Affairs of Britain. From the Beginning of the World to the Year 1307. Collected by Matthew of Westminster*, volume 2 (London: Henry G. Bohn, 1853), p. 444.

2. D. A. Carpenter, *The Minority of Henry III* (London: Methuen London, 1990), pp. 50–77; T. Duffus Hardy, ed., *Rotuli Litterarum Clausarum in Turri Londinensi Asservati*, volume 1 (London: Eyre and Spottiswoode, 1833), p. 379b.

3. Carpenter, *The Minority of Henry III*, pp. 84–198; William Stubbs, ed., *The Historical Collections of Walter of Coventry*, volume 2 (London: Longman & co., 1873), p. 245; Walter Waddington Shirley, ed., *Royal and Other Historical Letters Illustrative of the Reign of Henry III*, volume 1 (London: Longman, Green, Longman, and Roberts, 1862), pp. 56–100; J. A. Giles, ed., *Roger of Wendower's Flowers of History*, volume 2, (Oxford: Henry G. Bohn, 1849), pp. 404–5, 427–8.

4. Carpenter, *The Minority of Henry III*, pp. 217–39; Stubbs, *The Historical Collections of Walter of Coventry*, volume 2, pp. 247–9; R. R. Davies, *The Age of Conquest Wales 1063–1415* (Oxford: Oxford University Press, 1991),

p. 244; Shirley, *Royal and Other Historical Letters Illustrative of the Reign of Henry III*, volume 1, p. 150; Thomas Jones, ed., *Brut Y Tywysogyon, or, The Chronicle of the Princes. Red Book of Hergest Version* (Cardiff: University of Wales, 1955), pp. 220–1; John Edward Lloyd, *A History of Wales: From the Earliest Times to the Edwardian Conquest*, volume 2 (London: Longmans, Green, and Co., 1912), pp. 659–60; Giles, *Roger of Wendower's Flowers of History*, pp. 428–9; The National Archives, SC 1/1/143.

5. Carpenter, *The Minority of Henry III*, pp. 306–14; R. R. Davies, *The Age of Conquest Wales 1063–1415* (Oxford: Oxford University Press, 1991), p. 244; Jones, *Brut Y Tywysogion*, pp. 220–7; Lloyd, *A History of Wales*, pp. 660–3; Giles, *Roger of Wendower's Flowers of History*, pp. 432–3, 443–4; R. F. Walker, 'Hubert de Burgh and Wales, 1218–1232', *The English Historical Review*, 87 (1972), pp. 474–6. Carpenter, *The Minority of Henry III*, pp. 318–29, 346–61; G. Herbert Fowlers, 'Munitions in 1224', *Bedfordshire Historical Records Society*, 5 (1920), pp. 117–32; Stubbs, *The Historical Collections of Walter of Coventry*, volume 2, pp. 252–3; Joseph Stevenson, ed., *Radulphi de Coggeshall Chronicon Anglicanum* (London: Longman & Co., 1875), pp. 205–6; Henry Richards Luard, ed., *Annales Monastici*, volume 3 (London: Longmans, Green, Reader, and Dyer, 1866), p. 86; Giles, *Roger of Wendower's Flowers of History*, pp. 446–52.

7. Carpenter, *The Minority of Henry III*, pp. 361–78, 389; Stubbs, *The Historical Collections of Walter of Coventry*, volume 2, pp. 253–4, 265–8; Stevenson, *Radulphi de Coggeshall Chronicon Anglicanum*, pp. 206–8; Luard, ed., *Annales Monastici*, volume 3, pp. 86–9; Shirley, *Royal and Other Historical Letters Illustrative of the Reign of Henry III*, volume 1, pp. 224, 232–6, 543–4; Giles, *Roger of Wendower's Flowers of History*, pp. 452–4.

8. Carpenter, *The Minority of Henry III*, p. 389; Davies, *The Age of Conquest Wales 1063–1415*, p. 298; Jones, *Brut Y Tywysogion*, pp. 226–9; Lloyd, *A History of Wales*, pp. 667–76; Giles, *Roger of Wendower's Flowers of History*, pp. 509–41; H. M. Colvin, *The History of the King's Works*, volume 2 (London: H. M. S. O., 1963), p. 775; Walker, 'Hubert de

Burgh and Wales, 1218–1232', pp. 484–90; Luard, *Annales Monastici*, volume 3, p. 127.

9. Davies, *The Age of Conquest Wales 1063–1415*, pp. 298–302; Jones, *Brut Y Tywysogion*, pp. 230–3; Lloyd, *A History of Wales*, pp. 677–93; Giles, *Roger of Wendower's Flowers of History*, pp. 567–81; J. A. Giles, ed., *Matthew Paris's English History, From the Year 1235 to 1273*, volume 1 (London: Henry G. Bohn, 1852), pp. 47, 69–70, 237–9, 260.

10. *Calendar of the Liberate Rolls Preserved in the Public Record Office. Henry III. Vol. 3: A. D. 1240–1245* (London: H. M. S. O, 1930), pp. 69–70, 94, 102; Davies, *The Age of Conquest Wales 1063–1415*, pp. 300–2; Lloyd, *A History of Wales*, pp. 695–700; Jones, *Brut Y Tywysogyon*, pp. 236–41; Giles, *Matthew Paris's English History*, volume 1, pp. 260–409; Colvin, *The History of the King's Works*, volume 2, pp. 644–5; *The Royal Commission on the Ancient and Historical Monuments and Constructions in Wales and Monmouthshire: An Inventory of the Ancient Monuments in Wales and Monmouthshire. II, County of Flint* (London: H. M. S. O, 1912), pp. 20–1; Richard Copley Christie, ed., *Annales Cestrienses; or, Chronicle of the Abbey of S. Werburg, at Chester* (The Record Society, 1887), pp. 62–3.

11. Christie, *Annales Cestrienses*, pp. 62–5; Giles, *Matthew Paris's English History*, volume 1, pp. 487–510; J. A. Giles, ed., *Matthew Paris's English History, From the Year 1235 to 1273*, volume 2 (London: Henry G. Bohn, 1853), pp. 5–140; Jones, *Brut Y Tywysogyon*, pp. 238–41; Davies, *The Age of Conquest Wales 1063–1415*, p. 302; Lloyd, *A History of Wales*, pp. 700–5; M. A. Pollock, *Scotland, England and France After the Loss of Normandy, 1204–1296: 'Auld Amitie'* (Woodbridge: The Boydell Press, 2015), pp. 152–4; Colvin, *The History of the King's Works*, volume 2, pp. 624–6; J. Goronwy Edwards, ed., *Calendar of Ancient Correspondence Concerning Wales* (Cardiff: University Press Board, 1935), pp. 21–2.

12. Giles, *Matthew Paris's English History*, volume 2, pp. 114–245; Michael Prestwich, *Edward I* (London: Yale University Press, 1997), pp. 11–17; Jones, *Brut Y Tywysogion*, pp. 244–9; Lloyd, *A History of Wales*, pp. 705–18; Christie, *Annales Cestrienses*, pp. 72–3; Davies, *The Age of Conquest Wales*

1063–1415, pp. 303–10; J. A. Giles, ed., *Matthew Paris's English History, From the Year 1235 to 1273*, volume 3 (London: Henry G. Bohn, 1854), pp. 200–204.

13. Prestwich, *Edward I*, pp. 18–24; Jones, *Brut Y Tywysogion*, pp. 248–51; Lloyd, *A History of Wales*, pp. 719–25; Christie, *Annales Cestrienses*, pp. 74–5; Davies, *The Age of Conquest Wales 1063–1415*, pp. 310–11; Giles, *Matthew Paris's English History*, volume 3, pp. 217–269.

14. Giles, *Matthew Paris's English History*, volume 3, pp. 286–338; Adrian Jobson, *The First English Revolution: Simon de Montfort. Henry III and the Barons' War* (London: Bloomsbury Academic, 2012), pp. 15–71; H. W. Ridgeway, 'Henry III (1207–1272)', *Oxford Dictionary of National University Press, 2004*; online edn, Sept 2010 Biography, Oxford [http://www.oxforddnb.com/view/article/12950, accessed 21 Sept 2016]; F. W. Powicke, *King Henry III and the Lord Edward: The Community of the Realm in the Thirteenth Century*, volume 2 (Oxford: Clarendon Press, 1947), pp. 411–25.

15. Prestwich, *Edward I*, pp. 38–9; Christie, *Annales Cestrienses*, pp. 80–7; Jones, *Brut Y Tywysogion*, pp. 252–3; Lloyd, *A History of Wales*, pp. 730–1; Jobson, *The First English Revolution*, pp. 73–86; Powicke, *King Henry III and the Lord Edward*, pp. 426–38; Edwards, *Calendar of Ancient Correspondence Concerning Wales*, p. 27.

16. Prestwich, *Edward I*, pp. 39–41; Christie, *Annales Cestrienses*, pp. 84–7; Giles, *Matthew Paris's English History*, volume 3, pp. 338–43; Powicke, *King Henry III and the Lord Edward*, pp. 438–54; Jobson, *The First English Revolution*, pp. 86–105.

17. Prestwich, *Edward I*, pp. 42–4; Christie, *Annales Cestrienses*, pp. 86–9; Giles, *Matthew Paris's English History*, volume 3, p. 344; Powicke, *King Henry III and the Lord Edward*, pp. 456–62; Jobson, *The First English Revolution*, pp. 107–11; R. F. Treharne, 'The Battle of Northampton, 5th April 1264', *Northamptonshire Past and Present*, 2 (1955), pp. 73–90; Luard, *Annales Monastici*, volume 3, pp. 227–31; James Orchard Halliwell, ed., *The Chronicle of William de Rishanger, of The Barons' War. The Miracles of Simon de Montfort* (London: John Bowyer Nichols and Son, 1840),

pp. 20–6; Henry Richards Luard, ed., *Annales Monastici*, volume 4 (London: Longmans, Green, Reader, and Dyer, 1869), pp. 142–7; Yonge, *The Flowers of History*, pp. 412–4.

18. Prestwich, *Edward I*, pp. 44–7; Halliwell, *The Chronicle of William de Rishanger*, pp. 26–34; Luard, *Annales Monastici*, volume 4, pp. 147–62; Luard, *Annales Monastici*, volume 3, pp. 231–5; Yonge, *The Flowers of History*, pp. 419–25; Christie, *Annales Cestrienses*, pp. 90–5; Jobson, *The First English Revolution*, pp. 111–31; Powicke, *King Henry III and the Lord Edward*, pp. 462–97; *Calendar of the Liberate Rolls Preserved in the Public Record Office. Henry III. Vol. 5: A. D. 1260–1267* (London: H. M. S. O, 1961), p. 152; Fergus Oakes, 'King's Men without the King: Royalist Castle Garrison Resistance between the Battles of Lewes and Evesham', *Thirteenth Century England*, 15 (2015), pp. 51–68; William Aldis Wright, ed., *The Metrical Chronicle of Robert of Gloucester*, volume 2 (London: printed for H. M. S. O. by Eyre and Spottiswoode, 1887), pp. 571–2.

19. Prestwich, *Edward I*, pp. 48–53; Christie, *Annales Cestrienses*, pp. 94–5; Giles, *Matthew Paris's English History*, volume 3, pp. 353–5; Powicke, *King Henry III and the Lord Edward*, pp. 498–502; Jobson, *The First English Revolution*, pp. 131–47; Luard, *Annales Monastici*, volume 3, p. 239; Yonge, *The Flowers of History*, pp. 425–38; Luard, *Annales Monastici*, volume 4, pp. 163–74; Lloyd, *A History of Wales*, pp. 736–7.

20. Prestwich, *Edward I*, pp. 53–60; Christie, *Annales Cestrienses*, pp. 94–9; Giles, *Matthew Paris's English History*, volume 3, pp. 358–70; Benjamin L. Wild, 'The Siege of Kenilworth Castle, 1266', *English Heritage Historical Review*, 5 (2010), pp. 13–23; Powicke, *King Henry III and the Lord Edward*, pp. 503–47; Jobson, *The First English Revolution*, pp. 149–160; Luard, *Annales Monastici*, volume 3, pp. 239–46; Lloyd, *A History of Wales*, pp. 738–41; Richard K. Morris, *Kenilworth Castle* (London: English Heritage, 2012), pp. 39–41.

Chapter Seven

1. Thomas Wright, ed., *The Chronicle of Pierre de Langtoft, in French Verse, from the Earliest Period to the Death of King*

Edward. Volume 2 (London: Longmans, Green, Reader, and Dyer, 1868), pp. 216–9.

2. Lawrence Butler, 'The Castles of the Princes of Gwynedd', in *The Impact of the Edwardian Castles in Wales*, eds. by Diane M. Williams and John R. Kenyon (Oxford: Oxbow Books, 2010), pp. 27–36; John Goodall, *The English Castle, 1066–1650*, (New Haven: Yale University Press, 2011), pp. 192–4, 203–9; R. R. Davies, *The Age of Conquest Wales 1063–1415* (Oxford: Oxford University Press, 1991), pp. 251–81; Michael Prestwich, *Edward I* (London: Yale University Press, 1997), pp. 170–3.

3. Prestwich, *Edward I*, pp. 173–6; *Calendar of the Close Rolls Edward I 1272–1279* (London: H. M. S. O., 1900), p. 51; Davies, *The Age of Conquest Wales 1063–1415*, pp. 314–30; John Edward Lloyd, *A History of Wales: From the Earliest Times to the Edwardian Conquest*, volume 2 (London: Longmans, Green, and Co., 1912), pp. 739–58; Thomas Jones, ed., *Brut Y Tywysogyon, or, The Chronicle of the Princes. Red Book of Hergest Version* (Cardiff: University of Wales, 1955), pp. 260–5; Richard Copley Christie, ed., *Annales Cestrienses; or, Chronicle of the Abbey of S. Werburg, at Chester* (The Record Society, 1887), pp. 102–3.

4. Christie, *Annales Cestrienses, pp. 104–5;* C. D. Yonge, ed., *The Flowers of History, especially such as relate to the Affairs of Britain. From the Beginning of the World to the Year 1307. Collected by Matthew of Westminster*, volume 2 (London: Henry G. Bohn, 1853), p. 471; Prestwich, *Edward I*, pp. 176–9; Henry Richard Luard, ed., *Bartholomæi de Cotton, Monachi Norwicensis, Historia Anglicana (A.D. 449–1298)* (London: London: Longman, Green, Longman and Roberts, 1859), pp. 154–5; Jones, *Brut Y Tywysogion*, pp. 264–7; Hans Claude Hamilton, ed., *Chronicon Domini Walteri de Hemingburgh*, volume 2 (London: English Historical Society, 1849), p. 5; Henry Richards Luard, ed., *Annales Monastici*, volume 4 (London: Longmans, Green, Reader, and Dyer, 1869), p. 271; John E. Morris, *The Welsh Wars of Edward I* (Oxford: Clarendon Press, 1901), pp. 110–29; Lloyd, *A History of Wales*, pp. 757–8; Davies, *The Age of Conquest Wales 1063–1415,* p. 333; J. Goronwy

Edwards, ed., *Calendar of Ancient Correspondence Concerning Wales* (Cardiff: University Press Board, 1935), pp. 32–3.

5. *Christie, Annales Cestrienses, pp. 104–5;* Yonge, *The Flowers of History*, volume 2, p. 471; Prestwich, *Edward I*, pp. 179–82; Luard, *Bartholomæi de Cotton,* pp. 155–6; Jones, *Brut Y Tywysogion*, pp. 266–9; Hamilton, *Chronicon Domini Walteri de Hemingburgh*, volume 2, p. 5; Luard, *Annales Monastici*, volume 4, pp. 271–4; Morris, *The Welsh Wars of Edward I*, pp. 129–43; H. M. Colvin, *The History of the King's Works,* volume 1 (London: H. M. S. O., 1963), pp. 308–10; Lloyd, *A History of Wales*, pp. 758–9; Davies, *The Age of Conquest Wales 1063–1415*, pp. 334–7.

6. Colvin, *The History of the King's Works,* volume 1, pp. 293–308; Morris, *The Welsh Wars of Edward I*, pp. 143–5; David M. Brown, 'Builth Castle and Aberystwyth Castle 1277–1307', in *The Impact of the Edwardian Castles in Wales*, ed. by Diane M. Williams and John R. Kenyon (Oxford: Oxbow Books, 2010), pp. 59–71.

7. Colvin, *The History of the King's Works,* volume 1, pp. 308–27; Morris, *The Welsh Wars of Edward I*, pp. 146–8; Jones, *Brut Y Tywysogyon*, pp. 266–7; J. Goronwy Edwards, 'The Building of Flint', *Flintshire Historical Society Journal*, 12 (1951), pp. 5–20; Davies, *The Age of Conquest Wales 1063–1415*, p. 339; *Calendar of Various Chancery Rolls, 1277–1326* (London: H. M. S. O, 1912), p. 164; John Goodall, *The English Castle, 1066–1650*, (New Haven: Yale University Press, 2011), pp. 213–6.

8. Christie, *Annales Cestrienses*, pp. 108–9; Yonge, *The Flowers of History*, p. 476; Colvin, *The History of the King's Works*, volume 1, pp. 330–2, 354–7; Prestwich, *Edward I*, pp. 182–90; Luard, *Bartholomæi de Cotton*, pp. 161–2 Jones, *Brut Y Tywysogion*, pp. 268–71; Wright, *The Chronicle of Pierre de Langtoft, in French Verse*, pp. 176–7; Hamilton, *Chronicon Domini Walteri de Hemingburgh*, volume 2, p. 9; Luard, *Annales Monastici*, volume 4, pp. 287–8; Lloyd, *A History of Wales*, pp. 760–2; Davies, *The Age of Conquest Wales 1063–1415*, pp. 341–50; *Calendar of Various Chancery Rolls*, pp. 212–3.

9. Christie, *Annales Cestrienses*, pp. 108–13; Yonge, *The Flowers of History*, p. 477; Colvin, *The History of the King's Works,*

volume 1, pp. 354–7; Prestwich, *Edward I*, pp. 190–201; Luard, *Bartholomæi de Cotton*, pp. 162–4; Wright, *The Chronicle of Pierre de Langtoft, in French Verse*, pp. 178–83; Hamilton, *Chronicon Domini Walteri de Hemingburgh*, volume 2, pp. 10–14; Luard, *Annales Monastici*, volume 4, pp. 289–94; Lloyd, *A History of Wales*, pp. 762–3; Davies, *The Age of Conquest Wales 1063–1415*, pp. 351–4.

10. Yonge, *The Flowers of History*, p. 478; Colvin, *The History of the King's Works*, volume 1, pp. 330–94; Morris, *The Welsh Wars of Edward I*, pp. 149–96; Davies, *The Age of Conquest Wales 1063–1415*, pp. 355–60; *Calendar of Various Chancery Rolls*, p. 292; Goodall, *The English Castle*, pp. 217–21; Abigail Wheatley, 'Caernarfon Castle and its Mythology' in *The Impact of the Edwardian Castles in Wales*, ed. by Diane M. Williams and John R. Kenyon (Oxford: Oxbow Books, 2010), pp. 129–39.

11. Yonge, *The Flowers of History*, pp. 482–3; Prestwich, *Edward I*, pp. 218–9; Luard, *Bartholomæi de Cotton*, p. 168; Luard, *Annales Monastici*, volume 4, pp. 309–11; Morris, *The Welsh Wars of Edward I*, pp. 204–19; Davies, *The Age of Conquest Wales 1063–1415*, pp. 360–81; R. A. Griffiths, 'Rhys ap Maredudd (d. 1292)', *Oxford Dictionary of National Biography*, Oxford University Press, 2004; online edn, Jan 2008 [http://www.oxforddnb.com/view/article/48563, accessed 11 Sept 2017].

12. Yonge, *The Flowers of History*, p. 506; R. F. Walker, 'Madog ap Llywelyn (fl. 1277–1295)', *Oxford Dictionary of National Biography*, Oxford University Press, 2004 (http://www.oxforddnb.com/view/article/17765, accessed 6 Aug 2017); J. Griffiths, 'The Revolt of Madog ap Llywelyn, 1294–5', *Transactions of the Caernarfonshire Historical Society*, 16 (1955), pp. 12–15; Prestwich, *Edward I*, pp. 219–21; Luard, *Bartholomæi de Cotton*, p. 253; Wright, *The Chronicle of Pierre de Langtoft, in French Verse*, pp. 216–7; Hamilton, *Chronicon Domini Walteri de Hemingburgh*, volume 2, pp. 57–8; Luard, *Annales Monastici*, volume 4, p. 339; Morris, *The Welsh Wars of Edward I*, pp. 242–54; Davies, *The Age of Conquest Wales 1063–1415*, pp. 382–3; Colvin, *The History of the King's Works*, volume 1, pp. 377–8.

13. Walker, 'Madog ap Llywelyn'; Colvin, *The History of the King's Works,* volume 1, pp. 395–408; J. Goronwy Edwards, 'The Battle of Maes Madog and the Welsh Campaign of 1294–5', *The English Historical Review,* 39 (1924), pp. 1–12; R. F. Walker, 'The Hagnaby Chronicle and the Battle of Maes Moydog', *Welsh History Review,* 8 (1976–7), pp. 125–38; Yonge, *The Flowers of History,* pp. 506–7; Griffiths, 'The Revolt of Madog ap Llywelyn', pp. 16–23; Prestwich, *Edward I,* pp. 221–5; Luard, *Bartholomæi de Cotton,* p. 253; Wright, *The Chronicle of Pierre de Langtoft, in French Verse,* pp. 218–23; Hamilton, *Chronicon Domini Walteri de Hemingburgh,* volume 2, pp. 58–9; Luard, *Annales Monastici,* volume 4, p. 339; Morris, *The Welsh Wars of Edward I,* pp. 254–67; Davies, *The Age of Conquest Wales 1063–1415,* pp. 383–5.

Chapter Eight

1. Wendy R. Childs, ed., *Vita Edwardi Secundi* (Oxford: Oxford University Press, 2005), pp. 82–5.

2. Michael Prestwich, *Edward I* (London: Yale University Press, 1997), pp. 356–75; C. D. Yonge, ed., *The Flowers of History, especially such as relate to the Affairs of Britain. From the Beginning of the World to the Year 1307. Collected by Matthew of Westminster,* volume 2 (London: Henry G. Bohn, 1853), pp. 486–516; Fiona J. Watson, *Under the Hammer: Edward I and Scotland, 1286–1306* (Edinburgh: John Donald, 2005), pp. 6–27; Herbert Maxwell, ed., *The Chronicle of Lanercost, 1272–1346* (Glasgow: James Maclehose and Sons, 1913), pp. 39–42, 114; Herbert Maxwell, ed., *Scalacronica: The Reigns of Edward I, Edward II and Edward III* (Glasgow: James Maclehose & Sons, 1907), pp. 14–15.

3. Prestwich, *Edward I,* pp. 469–76; Yonge, *The Flowers of History,* volume 2, pp. 517–9; Maxwell, *Scalacronica,* p. 16; Maxwell, *The Chronicle of Lanercost,* pp. 115–44; Thomas Wright, ed., *The Chronicle of Pierre de Langtoft, in French Verse, from the Earliest Period to the Death of King Edward,* volume 2 (London: Longmans, Green, Reader, and Dyer, 1868), pp. 264–7; Joseph Bain, ed., *Calendar of Documents Relating to*

Scotland, Volume 2. A.D. 1272–1307 (Edinburgh: H. M. General Register House, 1884), pp. 176–8; Hans Claude Hamilton, ed., *Chronicon Domini Walteri de Hemingburgh*, volume 2 (London: English Historical Society, 1849), pp. 89–113; H. M. Colvin, *The History of the King's Works*, volume 2 (London: H. M. S. O., 1963), pp. 563–4; Geoffrey W. S. Barrow, *Robert Bruce & the Community of the Realm of Scotland* (Edinburgh: Edinburgh University Press, 1999), pp. 79–78.

4 Prestwich, *Edward I*, pp. 476–83; Yonge, *The Flowers of History*, volume 2, pp. 526–7; Maxwell, *The Chronicle of Lanercost*, p. 164–6; Maxwell, *Scalacronica*, pp. 20–1; Barrow, *Robert Bruce*, pp. 78–104; Joseph Stevenson, ed., *Documents Illustrative of the History of Scotland*, volume 2 (Edinburgh: H. M. General Register House, 1870), pp. 206–9; Hamilton, *Chronicon Domini Walteri de Hemingburgh*, volume 2, pp. 127–82.

5. Prestwich, *Edward I*, pp. 483–90; Yonge, *The Flowers of History*, volume 2, p. 533; Maxwell, *The Chronicle of Lanercost*, p. 170; Maxwell, *Scalacronica*, p. 23; Nicholas Harris Nicolas, ed., *The Siege of Carlaverock* (London: J. B. Nichols and Son, 1828), pp. 2–87; H. M. Colvin, *The History of the King's Works*, volume 1 (London: H. M. S. O., 1963), pp. 411–12.

6. Bain, *Calendar of Documents Relating to Scotland*, volume 2, p. 305; Maxwell, *The Chronicle of Lanercost*, pp. 171–2; Prestwich, *Edward I*, pp. 490–8; Colvin, *The History of the King's Works*, volume 1, pp. 412–16; Barrow, *Robert Bruce*, pp. 120–2; Hamilton, *Chronicon Domini Walteri de Hemingburgh*, volume 2, pp. 189–222.

7. Prestwich, *Edward I*, pp. 498–500; Bain, *Calendar of Documents Relating to Scotland*, volume 2, pp. 345, 355, 366, 455; Colvin, *The History of the King's Works*, volume 1, pp. 415–19; Barrow, *Robert Bruce*, pp. 124–9; Yonge, *The Flowers of History*, volume 2, pp. 564–6; Hamilton, *Chronicon Domini Walteri de Hemingburgh*, volume 2, pp. 222–3.

8. Prestwich, *Edward I*, pp. 499–504; Yonge, *The Flowers of History*, volume 2, pp. 570–5; Maxwell, *Scalacronica*, pp. 25–6; Barrow, *Robert Bruce*, pp. 128–44; Bain, *Calendar of Documents Relating to Scotland*, volume 2, pp. 389–90,

399, 405, 412–3, 419–20, 455; Joseph Bain, ed., *Calendar of Documents Relating to Scotland, Volume 4. A.D. 1357–1509. Addenda-1221–1435* (Edinburgh: H. M. General Register House, 1888), p. 466; Hamilton, *Chronicon Domini Walteri de Hemingburgh*, volume 2, pp. 231–2.

9. Maxwell, *The Chronicle of Lanercost*, pp. 176–84; Prestwich, *Edward I*, pp. 505–14, 557; Yonge, *The Flowers of History*, volume 2, pp. 583–96; Maxwell, *Scalacronica*, pp. 29–36; Barrow, *Robert Bruce*, pp. 145–73; Hamilton, *Chronicon Domini Walteri de Hemingburgh*, volume 2, pp. 245–66.

10. Maxwell, *Scalacronica*, p. 50; Seymour Phillips, *Edward II* (London: Yale University Press, 2011), pp. 89–157; Colvin, *The History of the King's Works*, volume 2, p. 724; Childs, *Vita Edwardi Secundi*, pp. 4–13, 26–31; J. S. Hamilton, 'Gaveston, Piers, earl of Cornwall (d. 1312)', *Oxford Dictionary of National Biography*, Oxford University Press, 2004; online edn, Jan 2008 [http://www.oxforddnb.com/view/article/10463, accessed 26 Sept 2017]; Maxwell, *The Chronicle of Lanercost*, pp. 184–9.

11. Phillips, *Edward II*, pp. 161–71; T. F. Tout, *The Place of the Reign of Edward II in English History* (Manchester: At the University Press, 1914), pp. 13–14; Maxwell, *The Chronicle of Lanercost*, pp. 190–4; David Cornell, 'A Kingdom Cleared of Castles: The Role of the Castle in the Campaigns of Robert Bruce', *The Scottish Historical Review*, 87 (2008), pp. 240–2; Barrow, *Robert Bruce*, pp. 173–92; Childs, *Vita Edwardi Secundi*, pp. 18–27.

12. Childs, *Vita Edwardi Secundi*, pp. 30–51; Maxwell, *The Chronicle of Lanercost*, pp. 197–8; Phillips, *Edward II*, pp. 171–91; Harry Rothwell, ed., *English Historical Documents, 1189–1327*, volume 3 (London: Eyre & Spottiswoode Ltd, 1975), pp. 531–42; *Calendar of the Patent Rolls Edward II 1307–1313* (London: H. M. S. O., 1884), pp. 469–70; *Calendar of the Close Rolls Edward II 1307–1313* (London: H. M. S. O., 1892), pp. 448–9; Hamilton, 'Gaveston, Piers, earl of Cornwall (d. 1312)'; Pierre Chaplais, *Piers Gaveston: Edward II's Adoptive Brother* (Oxford: Clarendon Press, 1994), pp. 86–8.

13. Childs, *Vita Edwardi Secundi*, pp. 52–77; Phillips, *Edward II*, pp. 192–217; *Calendar of the Patent Rolls Edward II 1307–1313*, pp. 486–7; Hamilton, 'Gaveston, Piers, earl of Cornwall (d. 1312)'; J. R. S. Phillips, *Aymer de Valence, Earl of Pembroke, 1307–1324: Baronial Politics in the Reign of Edward II* (Oxford: At the Clarendon Press, 1972), pp. 32–5; J. R. Maddicott, *Thomas of Lancaster, 1307–1322: A Study in the Reign of Edward II* (Oxford: Oxford University Press, 1970), pp. 124–9.

14. Childs, *Vita Edwardi Secundi*, pp. 82–9; Phillips, *Edward II*, pp. 219–27; Maxwell, *The Chronicle of Lanercost*, pp. 194–206; Maxwell, *Scalacronica*, pp. 51–2; Cornell, 'A Kingdom Cleared of Castles', pp. 242–52; Barrow, *Robert Bruce*, pp. 190–207; Colm McNamee, *The Wars of the Bruces: Scotland, England and Ireland 1306–1328* (Edinburgh: John Donald, 2006), pp. 72–7; George Eyre–Todd, ed., *The Bruce being the Metrical Historical of Robert the Bruce King of Scots Compiled A.D. 1375 by Master John Barbour* (London: Gowans & Gray Limited, 1907), pp. 148–81.

15. Childs, *Vita Edwardi Secundi*, pp. 89–99; Phillips, *Edward II*, pp. 227–61; Maxwell, *The Chronicle of Lanercost*, pp. 207–15; Maxwell, *Scalacronica*, pp. 52–8; Barrow, *Robert Bruce*, pp. 208–38; John. E. Morris, 'Cumberland and Westmorland Military Levies in the time of Edward I. and Edward II.', *Transactions of the Cumberland and Westmorland Antiquarian and Archaeological Society*, 3 (1903), pp. 316–9; Michael R. McCarthy, *Carlisle Castle: A Survey and Documentary History* (London: English Heritage, 1990), pp. 135–7; McNamee, *The Wars of the Bruces*, pp. 72–81.

16. Phillips, *Edward II*, pp. 264–79; Maxwell, *The Chronicle of Lanercost*, pp. 216–7; Childs, *Vita Edwardi Secundi*, pp. 114–7; Maxwell, *Scalacronica*, p. 58; Joseph Bain, ed., *Calendar of Documents Relating to Scotland, Volume 3. A.D. 1307–1357* (Edinburgh: H. M. General Register House, 1887), pp. 88–91; The National Archives, SC 8/218/10871.

17. Maxwell, *The Chronicle of Lanercost*, pp. 217–8; Maxwell, *Scalacronica*, pp. 58–60; Michael Prestwich, 'Middleton, Sir Gilbert (d. 1318)', *Oxford Dictionary of National Biography*, Oxford University Press, 2004 [http://www.

oxforddnb.com/view/article/53089, accessed 2 Oct 2017]; Henry Thomas Riley, ed., *Johannis de Trokelowe, et Henrici de Blaneforde, Chronica et Annales* (London: Longmans, Green, Reader, and Dyer, 1866), pp. 99–101; Arthur E. Middleton, *Sir Gilbert de Middleton* (Newcastle: Mawson Swan and Morgan Limited, 1918), pp. 28–64; Phillips, *Edward II*, pp. 297–327; Childs, *Vita Edwardi Secundi*, pp. 140–3; *Calendar of the Close Rolls Edward II 1313–1318* (London: H. M. S. O., 1893), p. 523, 529, 575; The National Archives, SC 8/80/3994; Phillips, *Aymer de Valence*, pp. 100–130; Maddicott, *Thomas of Lancaster*, pp. 204–8.

18. Bain, *Calendar of Documents Relating to Scotland*, volume 3, pp. 125–6; Maxwell, *Scalacronica*, pp. 58–66; Maxwell, *The Chronicle of Lanercost*, pp. 219–28; Phillips, *Edward II*, pp. 328–52; Childs, *Vita Edwardi Secundi*, pp. 150–79; R. C. Fowler, ed., *Calendar of Chancery Warrants 1244–1326*, volume 1 (London: Published by his Majesty's Stationery Office, 1927), pp. 501–2; Phillips, *Aymer de Valence*, pp. 184–8.

19. Phillips, *Edward II*, pp. 353–94; J. Conway Davies, 'The Despenser War in Glamorgan', *Transactions of the Royal Historical Society*, 9 (1915), pp. 21–64; Maxwell, *The Chronicle of Lanercost*, pp. 229–30; J. S. Hamilton, 'Despenser, Hugh, the Younger, first Lord Despenser (d. 1326)', *Oxford Dictionary of National Biography*, Oxford University Press, 2004; online edn, Sept 2012 [http://www.oxforddnb. com/view/article/7554, accessed 3 Oct 2017]; Childs, *Vita Edwardi Secundi*, pp. 186–93; *Calendar of the Patent Rolls Edward II 1317–1321* (London: H. M. S. O., 1903), pp. 569, 573–5, 584; J. Goronwy Edwards, ed., *Calendar of Ancient Correspondence Concerning Wales* (Cardiff: University Press Board, 1935), pp. 180–1, 219–21; Phillips, *Aymer de Valence*, pp. 199–211; Natalie Fryde, *The Tyranny and Fall of Edward II, 1321–1326* (Cambridge: Cambridge University Press, 1979), pp. 37–49; Maddicott, *Thomas of Lancaster*, pp. 259–92.

20. Phillips, *Edward II*, pp. 385, 394–401; Maxwell, *Scalacronica*, pp. 66–7; Maxwell, *The Chronicle of Lanercost*, p. 231; Childs, *Vita Edwardi Secundi*, pp. 196–9; *Calendar of the Close Rolls*

Edward II 1318–1323 (London: H. M. S. O., 1895), pp. 437, 502–4; *Calendar of the Fine Rolls Edward II 1319–1327* (London: H. M. S. O., 1912), pp. 71, 76; Charles Wykeham Martin, *The History and Description of Leeds Castle, Kent* (Westminster: Nichols and Sons, 1869), pp. 111–16; Reginald R. Sharpe, ed., *Calendar of Letter-Books of the City of London, Letter-Book E* (London: J. E. Francis, 1903), pp. 152–4; *Calendar of the Patent Rolls Edward II 1317–21* (London: H. M. S. O., 1904), pp. 38–45; Adam Chapman, *Welsh Soldiers in the Later Middle Ages, 1282–1422* (Woodbridge: The Boydell Press, 2015), p. 48; Phillips, *Aymer de Valence*, pp. 214–20; Fryde, *The Tyranny and Fall of Edward II*, pp. 49–51; Maddicott, *Thomas of Lancaster*, pp. 293–5.

21. Phillips, *Edward II*, pp. 402–15; Maxwell, *Scalacronica*, pp. 66–7; Chapman, *Welsh Soldiers in the Later Middle Ages*, p. 48; Maxwell, *The Chronicle of Lanercost*, pp. 231–4; Childs, *Vita Edwardi Secundi*, pp. 200–15; *Calendar of the Patent Rolls Edward II 1317–1321*, pp. 45–51, 67–79, 108, 157; Phillips, *Aymer de Valence*, pp. 220–5; Fryde, *The Tyranny and Fall of Edward II*, pp. 51–7; Maddicott, *Thomas of Lancaster*, pp. 295–312.

22. Phillips, *Edward II*, pp. 416–35; Maxwell, *Scalacronica*, pp. 67–9; Maxwell, *The Chronicle of Lanercost*, pp. 237–47; Bain, *Calendar of Documents Relating to Scotland*, volume 3, pp. 143–8; Michael Prestwich, *Armies and Warfare in the Middle Ages: The English Experience* (London: Yale University Press, 1996), pp. 117, 134; *Calendar of the Patent Rolls Edward II 1321–1324* (London: H. M. S. O., 1904), pp. 93–100, 123–33; Phillips, *Aymer de Valence*, pp. 228–30.

23. Phillips, *Edward II*, pp. 436–519; Maxwell, *Scalacronica*, pp. 69–74; Maxwell, *The Chronicle of Lanercost*, pp. 250–6; Hamilton, 'Despenser, Hugh, the Younger, first Lord Despenser (d. 1326)'; Nigel Saul, 'The Despensers and the Downfall of Edward II', *The English Historical Review*, 99 (1984), pp. 1–33; Childs, *Vita Edwardi Secundi*, pp. 218–47; *Calendar of the Patent Rolls Edward II 1324–1327* (London: H. M. S. O., 1904), pp. 302–3, 309–11; Chapman, *Welsh Soldiers in the Later Middle Ages*, pp. 52–3; The National Archives,

E 372/181, m. 34d; *Calendar of the Patent Rolls Edward III 1327–1330* (London: H. M. S. O., 1891), p. 13; Fryde, *The Tyranny and Fall of Edward II*, pp. 176–94.

24. W. Mark Ormrod, *Edward III* (London: Yale University Press, 2013), pp. 55–73; Ranald Nicholson, 'The Last Campaign of Robert Bruce', *The English Historical Review*, 77 (1962), pp. 233–46; Maxwell, *Scalacronica*, pp. 79–82; Maxwell, *The Chronicle of Lanercost*, pp. 256–8; Michael Prestwich, *The Three Edwards: War and State in England 1272–1377* (London: Methuen & Co. Ltd, 1981), pp. 57–8; Barrow, *Robert Bruce*, pp. 251–61.

25. Ormrod, *Edward III*, pp. 74–154; Maxwell, *Scalacronica*, pp. 85–97; Maxwell, *The Chronicle of Lanercost*, pp. 265–86; Bain, *Calendar of Documents Relating to Scotland*, volume 3, p. 201; Caroline Shenton, 'Edward III and the Coup of 1330', in *The Age of Edward III*, ed., James Bothwell (York: York Medieval Press, 2001), pp. 13–34; G. A. Holmes, 'The Rebellion of the Earl of Lancaster, 1328–9', *Bulletin of the Institute of Historical Research*, 28 (1955), pp. 84–9.

26. Ormrod, *Edward III*, pp. 154–77; Maxwell, *Scalacronica*, pp. 98–104; Maxwell, *The Chronicle of Lanercost*, pp. 291–300; Bain, *Calendar of Documents Relating to Scotland*, volume 3, pp. 199–201; *Calendar of the Close Rolls Edward III 1333–1337* (London: H. M. S. O., 1898), pp. 22–9, 37–38, 48–9; Ranald Nicholson, 'The Siege of Berwick, 1333', *The Scottish Historical Review*, 40 (1961), pp. 19–42.

Chapter Nine

1. David Preest and James G. Clark, eds., *The Chronica Maiora of Thomas Walsingham 1376–1422* (Woodbridge: Boydell, 2005), pp. 45–6.

2. W. Mark Ormrod, *Edward III* (London: Yale University Press, 2013), pp. 179–204; Eleanor Searle and Robert Burghart, 'The Defence of England and the Peasants' Revolt', *Viator*, 3 (1972), pp. 365–75; Jonathan Sumption, *The Hundred Years War: Volume I, Trial by Battle* (London: Faber, 1990), pp. 164–6; *Calendar of the Patent Rolls Edward III 1343–1345* (London: H. M. S. O., 1902), p. 427; *Calendar of the Close Rolls*

Edward III 1333–1337 (London: H. M. S. O., 1898), p. 715; *Calendar of the Close Rolls Edward III 1337–1339* (London: H. M. S. O., 1900), pp. 254–5, 542–3; Herbert J. Hewitt, *The Organization of War under Edward III, 1338–62* (Manchester: Manchester University Press, 1996), pp. 6–9; The National Archives, E 372/191, m. 52.

3. Ormrod, *Edward III*, pp. 204–12; *Calendar of the Close Rolls Edward III 1339–1341* (London: H. M. S. O., 1901), pp. 7, 22–3, 65, 74, 101, 208, 221, 354, 368, 444, 499; *Calendar of the Patent Rolls Edward III 1334–1338* (London: H. M. S. O., 1895), pp. 240–1; *Calendar of the Patent Rolls Edward III 1338–1340* (London: H. M. S. O., 1898), pp. 138–9, 180–1, 286–7; Herbert Maxwell, ed., *Scalacronica: The Reigns of Edward I, Edward II and Edward III* (Glasgow: James Maclehose & Sons, 1907), p. 106; H. M. Colvin, *The History of the King's Works*, volume 2 (London: H. M. S. O., 1963), pp. 592–3, 605; Sumption, *The Hundred Years War: Volume I*, pp. 226–7, 246–51, 260–5, 449–50, 492.

4. Ormrod, *Edward III*, pp. 174–7, 247–8, 283–5; Herbert Maxwell, *The Chronicle of Lanercost, 1272–1346* (Glasgow: James Maclehose and Sons, 1913), pp. 299–331; Maxwell, *Scalacronica*, pp. 98–119; H. M. Colvin, *The History of the King's Works*, volume 1 (London: H. M. S. O., 1963), pp. 421–2; Colvin, *The History of the King's Works*, volume 2, p. 819; *Calendar of the Close Rolls Edward III 1339–1341*, pp. 11, 208; Joseph Bain, ed., *Calendar of Documents Relating to Scotland, Volume 3. A.D. 1307–1357* (Edinburgh: H. M. General Register House, 1887), pp. 215–16, 226–7, 234–5, 241–2, 252–3, 255, 283, 347–68.

5. Ormrod, *Edward III*, pp. 212–497; *Calendar of the Close Rolls Edward III 1358–1360* (London: H. M. S. O., 1911), pp. 411–16; Colvin, *The History of the King's Works*, volume 2, pp. 662–6, 793–801; John Goodall, *The English Castle, 1066–1650* (New Haven: Yale University Press, 2011), pp. 291–2; T. F. Tout, 'Firearms in England in the Fourteenth Century', *The English Historical Review*, 26 (1911), p. 692; The National Archives, E 364/23, rot. F.

6. Ormrod, *Edward III*, pp. 498–576; Preest and Clark, *The Chronica Maiora of Thomas Walsingham 1376–1422*, pp. 36–7, 45–6, 109–110; 120–31; Jonathan Sumption, *The Hundred Years War: Volume III, Divided Houses* (London: Faber, 2009), pp. 135, 143, 173, 278, 283, 287–9; Nigel Saul, *Richard II* (New Haven: Yale University Press, 1997), pp. 24–82; The National Archives, E 101/36/23.

7. Colvin, *The History of the King's Works*, volume 2, pp. 623, 813–15, 842–4, Goodall, *The English Castle*, pp. 307, 317–20; Tout, 'Firearms in England in the Fourteenth Century', pp. 689–99; *Calendar of the Patent Rolls Richard II 1385–1389* (London: H. M. S. O., 1895), p. 196; Barry Cunliffe and Julian Munby, *Excavations at Portchester Castle, IV: Medieval, The Inner Bailey* (London: The Society of Antiquaries of London, 1985), pp. 150–1.

8. Sumption, *The Hundred Years War: Volume III*, pp. 541–57; Thomas Johnes, ed., *Sir John Froissart's Chronicles of England, France, Spain and the Adjoining Countries*, volume 7 (London: Longman, 1805), pp. 52–76; Kenneth H. Vickers, *A History of Northumberland, Volume XI. The Parishes of Carham, Branxton, Kirknewton, Wooler and Ford* (Newcastle Upon Tyne: Andrew Reid, 1922), pp. 51–3; 'Richard II: November 1384', in *Parliament Rolls of Medieval England*, ed. Chris Given–Wilson, Paul Brand, Seymour Phillips, Mark Ormrod, Geoffrey Martin, Anne Curry and Rosemary Horrox (Woodbridge, 2005), British History Online http://www.british-history.ac.uk/no-series/parliament-rolls-medieval/november-1384 [accessed 16 October 2017]; Saul, *Richard II*, pp. 135–47; L. C. Hector, ed., *The Westminster Chronicle 1381–1394* (Oxford: Clarendon Press, 1982), pp. 40–3, 56–9, 104–5, 132–5, 138–9; Preest and Clark, *The Chronica Maiora of Thomas Walsingham 1376–1422*, pp. 210–30.

9. Preest and Clark, *The Chronica Maiora of Thomas Walsingham 1376–1422*, pp. 231–47; Sumption, *The Hundred Years War: Volume III*, pp. 584–606; Goodall, *The English Castle*, pp. 314–17; Saul, *Richard II*, pp. 148–75; Dan Spencer, 'Edward Dallingridge: Builder of Bodiam Castle', *Ex Historia*, 6 (2014), pp. 81–98; Thomas Johnes, ed., *Sir John Froissart's*

Chronicles of England, France, Spain and the Adjoining Countries, volume 8 (London: Longman, 1808), pp. 95–156; The National Archives, E 403/515, m. 19.

10. Chris Given-Wilson, *Henry IV* (London: Yale University Press, 2016), pp. 41–118; Saul, *Richard II*, pp. 176–404; Anthony Goodman, *The Loyal Conspiracy: The Lords Appellant under Richard II* (London: Routledge and Kegan Paul Ltd, 1971), pp. 16–167.

11. S. K. Walker, 'Letters to the Dukes of Lancaster in 1381 and 1399', *The English Historical Review*, 106 (1991), pp. 75–9; Chris Given-Wilson, ed., *Chronicles of the Revolution, 1397–1400: The Reign of Richard II* (Manchester: Manchester University Press, 1993), pp. 115–61, 247–53; Robert Somerville, *History of the Duchy of Lancaster*, volume 1 (London: Chancellor and Council of the Duchy of Lancaster, 1953), pp. 136–7, Saul, *Richard II*, pp. 405–34; Given-Wilson, *Henry IV*, pp. 119–54; *Calendar of the Patent Rolls Richard II 1396–1399* (London: H. M. S. O., 1909), p. 596.

Chapter Ten

1. Alec Reginald Myers, ed., *English Historical Documents, 1327–1485*, volume 4 (London: Eyre & Spottiswoode Ltd, 1969), pp. 190–1.

2. Chris Given-Wilson, *Henry IV* (London: Yale University Press, 2016), pp. 160–70; Edward Maunde Thompson, ed., *Chronicon Adae De Usk* (London: Oxford University Press, 1904), pp. 197–8; David Preest and James G. Clark, eds., *The Chronica Maiora of Thomas Walsingham 1376–1422* (Woodbridge: Boydell, 2005), pp. 315–18; F. C. Hingeston, ed., *Royal and Historical Letters during the Reign of Henry the Fourth, King of England and of France, and Lord of Ireland. Vol I. A.D. 1399–1404* (London: Longman, Green, Longman, and Roberts, 1860), pp. 4–14; Anne Curry, 'New Regime, New army? Henry IV's Scottish Expedition of 1400', *The English Historical Review*, 125 (2010), pp. 1382–1413; *Calendar of the Patent Rolls Henry IV 1399–1401* (London: H. M. S. O., 1903), p. 287.

3. Given-Wilson, *Henry IV*, pp. 170–94; Davies, *The Revolt of Owain Glyn Dŵr*, pp. 103–6; Thompson, *Chronicon*

Adae De Usk, pp. 226–39; Hingeston, *Royal and Historical Letters during the Reign of Henry the Fourth, Vol I.*, pp. 69–72; Preest and Clark, *The Chronica Maiora of Thomas Walsingham 1376–1422*, pp. 318–19; *Calendar of the Patent Rolls Henry IV 1399–1401*, pp. 469–70; R. R. Davies, *The Revolt of Owain Glyn Dŵr* (Oxford: Oxford University Press, 1995), pp. 102–3; Gideon Brough, 'Owain's Revolt? Glyn Dŵr's Role in the Outbreak of the Rebellion', *Studies in History, Archaeology, Religion and Conservation*, 2 (2015), pp. 1–27; James Hamilton Wylie, *History of England Under Henry the Fourth, Vol. I. 1399–1404* (London: Longmans, Green and Co, 1884), pp. 146–8, 212–16, 244–9; Llinos Smith, 'Glyn Dŵr, Owain (c.1359–c.1416)', *Oxford Dictionary of National Biography*, Oxford University Press, 2004; online edn, Jan 2008 [http://www.oxforddnb.com/view/article/10816, accessed 23 Oct 2017].

4. Quotation from *The Life and Reign of Richard the Second* taken from Davies, *The Revolt of Owain Glyn Dŵr*, pp. 106–110 (p. 110); Given-Wilson, *Henry IV*, pp. 194–206; Thompson, *Chronicon Adae De Usk*, pp. 246–8; Preest and Clark, *The Chronica Maiora of Thomas Walsingham 1376–1422*, pp. 320–5. Given-Wilson, *Henry IV*, pp. 197–201, 218–30; Davies, *The Revolt of Owain Glyn Dŵr*, pp. 111–12; Thompson, *Chronicon Adae De Usk*, pp. 252–3; Preest and Clark, *The Chronica Maiora of Thomas Walsingham 1376–1422*, pp. 326–9; *Calendar of the Patent Rolls Henry IV 1401–1405* (London: H. M. S. O., 1905), pp. 137–40; Henry Ellis, ed., *Original Letters Illustrative of English History*, second series, volume 1 (London: Harding and Lepard, Pall-Mall East, 1827), pp. 15–16.

6. Given-Wilson, *Henry IV*, pp. 233–9; Davies, *The Revolt of Owain Glyn Dŵr*, pp. 112–15, 273–5; Thompson, *Chronicon Adae De Usk*, pp. 254–5; Henry Ellis, *Original Letters Illustrative of English History*, second series, volume 1, pp. 14–34; Hingeston, *Royal and Historical Letters during the Reign of Henry the Fourth, Vol I*, pp. 136–62; *Calendar of the Patent Rolls Henry IV 1401–1405*, p. 439; Wylie, *History of England Under Henry the Fourth, Vol. I.*, pp. 345–7; H. M. Colvin, *The History of*

the King's Works, volume 2 (London: H. M. S. O., 1963), pp. 685–6.

7. Given-Wilson, *Henry IV,* pp. 240–3; Davies, *The Revolt of Owain Glyn Dŵr,* pp. 115–17, 162–5, 213–14; Thompson, *Chronicon Adae De Usk,* p. 257; Ellis, *Original Letters Illustrative of English History,* pp. 33–8; Preest and Clark, *The Chronica Maiora of Thomas Walsingham 1376–1422,* pp. 331–2; *Calendar of the Patent Rolls Henry IV 1401–1405,* p. 440; *Calendar of the Close Rolls Henry IV 1402–1405* (London: H. M. S. O., 1929), pp. 478–9; Myers, *English Historical Documents, 1327–1485,* volume 4, pp. 190–1; Wylie, *History of England Under Henry the Fourth, Vol. I.,* pp. 431–2; The National Archives, E 364/40, rot. C; E 364/39, rot. E; E 364/45, rot. 3d; F. C. Hingeston, ed., *Royal and Historical Letters during the Reign of Henry the Fourth, King of England and of France, and Lord of Ireland. Vol II. A.D. 1405–1413* (London: H. M. S. O., 1965), pp. 15–24.

8. Davies, *The Revolt of Owain Glyn Dŵr,* pp. 117–18, 166–72, 193–4, 248–52; Thompson, *Chronicon Adae De Usk,* p. 282; Hingeston, *Royal and Historical Letters during the Reign of Henry the Fourth, Vol II. A.D. 1405–1413,* pp. 76–9; Ellis, *Original Letters Illustrative of English History,* pp. 38–41; *Calendar of the Patent Rolls Henry IV 1405–1408* (London: H. M. S. O., 1907), pp. 5–6; Preest and Clark, *The Chronica Maiora of Thomas Walsingham 1376–1422,* pp. 339–40.

9. Given-Wilson, *Henry IV,* pp. 266–71; Davies, *The Revolt of Owain Glyn Dŵr,* p. 119; Dan Spencer, '"The Scourge of the Stones": English Gunpowder Artillery at the Siege of Harfleur', *Journal of Medieval History,* 43 (2017), p. 61; Preest and Clark, *The Chronica Maiora of Thomas Walsingham 1376–1422,* pp. 336–9; James Hamilton Wylie, *History of England Under Henry the Fourth, Vol. II. 1405–1406* (London: Longmans, Green and Co, 1894), pp. 254–73; Hingeston, *Royal and Historical Letters during the Reign of Henry the Fourth, Vol I.,* pp. 206–7; J. L. Kirby, ed., *Calendar of Signet Letters of Henry IV and Henry V (1399–1422)* (London: H.M. Stationery Off., 1978), p. 95; Edward Barrington de Fonblanque, *Annals of the House of Percy, from the Conquest to the Opening of*

the Nineteenth Century, volume 2 (London: Richard Clay & Sons, 1887), pp. 532–4.

10. Given-Wilson, *Henry IV*, pp. 303–19; Davies, *The Revolt of Owain Glyn Dŵr*, pp. 121–5, 253; Spencer, '"The Scourge of the Stones"', pp. 61–2; Preest and Clark, *The Chronica Maiora of Thomas Walsingham 1376–1422*, pp. 341, 356–60; *Calendar of the Patent Rolls Henry IV 1405–1408*, pp. 361–2; James Hamilton Wylie, *History of England Under Henry the Fourth, Vol. III. 1407–1410* (London: Longmans, Green and Co, 1896), pp. 265–6; Christopher Allmand, *Henry V* (London: Yale University Press, 1997), pp. 32–3.

11. Davies, *The Revolt of Owain Glyn Dŵr*, p. 126; Allmand, *Henry V*, p. 341; Nicholas Harris Nicolas, ed., *Proceedings and Ordinances of the Privy Council of England*, volume 2 (London: Record Commission, 1834), pp. 136–8, 146–7; James Hamilton Wylie, *The Reign of Henry the Fifth, Vol. I. 1413–1415* (Cambridge: Cambridge University Press, 1914), pp. 52–7, 328, 456, 516, 520; Preest and Clark, *The Chronica Maiora of Thomas Walsingham 1376–1422*, p. 437; Dan Spencer, 'Adapting to New Technology: Roxburgh Castle and the Scottish Marches', *Emergence*, 6 (2014), pp. 1–4; Michael R. McCarthy, *Carlisle Castle: A Survey and Documentary History* (London: English Heritage, 1990), pp. 157–8; R. A. Griffiths, *The Reign of Henry VI* (Stroud: Sutton Publishing Limited, 2004), pp. 154–5; Joseph Bain, ed., *Calendar of Documents Relating to Scotland, Volume 4. A.D. 1357–1509. Addenda-1221–1435* (Edinburgh: H. M. General Register House, 1888), pp. 176–84.

12. Griffiths, *The Reign of Henry VI*, pp. 155–62, 402–11; Spencer, 'Adapting to New Technology', pp. 4–7; H. M. Colvin, *The History of the King's Works*, volume 2 (London: H. M. S. O., 1963), pp. 569–71, 599–60, 820–1; McCarthy, *Carlisle Castle*, pp. 158–60; Bain, *Calendar of Documents Relating to Scotland, Volume 4. A.D. 1357–1509*, pp. 222–3.

Chapter Eleven

1. Note that the Middle English text has been modernised. James Orchard Halliwell, ed., *A Chronicle of the First Thirteenth*

Years of the Reign of King Edward the Fourth by John Warkworth, D. D. Master of the St Peter's College, Cambridge (London: Camden Society, 1839), pp. 36–8.

2. Michael Hicks, *The Wars of the Roses* (London: Yale University Press, 2012), pp. 22–92; R. A. Griffiths, *The Reign of Henry VI* (Stroud: Sutton Publishing Limited, 2004), pp. 443–686; Henry Thomas Riley, ed., *Ingulph's Chronicle of the Abbey of Croyland with the Continuations by Peter of Blois and Anonymous Writers* (London: Henry G. Bohn, 1854), pp. 413–14; Nicholas Harris Nicolas, ed., *Proceedings and Ordinances of the Privy Council of England*, volume 2 (London: Record Commission, 1834), p. 95; *Fifth Report of the Royal Commission on Historical Manuscripts: Part 1. Report and Appendix* (London: George Edward Eyre and William Spottiswoode, 1876), p. 520; Frederick Devon ed., *Issues of the Exchequer: Being a Collection of Payments Made out of His Majesty's Revenue, From King Henry III to King Henry VI Inclusive: with an Appendix/ Extracted and Translated From the Original Rolls of the Ancient Pell Office* (London: J. Murray, 1837), pp. 471–2; *Calendar of the Patent Rolls Henry VI 1446–1452* (London: H. M. S. O., 1909), p. 388; James Gairdner, ed., *The Historical Collections of a Citizen of London in the Fifteenth Century* (London: Camden Society, 1876), pp. 190–4.

3. Anthony Goodman, *The Wars of the Roses: Military Activity and English Society, 1452–97* (London: Routledge, 1981), pp. 19–49; Hicks, *The Wars of the Roses*, pp. 93–161; Griffiths, *The Reign of Henry VI*, pp. 686–875; Riley, *Ingulph's Chronicle of the Abbey of Croyland with the Continuations by Peter of Blois and Anonymous Writers*, pp. 421, 453–6; Friedrich W. D. Brie, ed., *The Brut or The Chronicles of England* (London: Kegan Paul, Trench, Trübner & Co., 1906), pp. 520–31; Dan Spencer, 'The Lancastrian Armament Programme of the 1450s and the Development of Field Guns', *The Ricardian*, 25 (2015), pp. 61–70.

4. Hicks, *The Wars of the Roses*, pp. 162–76; Goodman, *The Wars of the Roses*, pp. 50–8; Riley, *Ingulph's Chronicle of the Abbey of Croyland with the Continuations by Peter of*

Blois and Anonymous Writers, pp. 425–6; Brie, *The Brut or The Chronicles of England*, pp. 532–3; Charles Ross, *Edward IV* (London: Eyre Methuen, 1974), pp. 45–6; James Gairdner, ed., *The Paston Letters, 1422–1509 A.D.*, volume 2 (Edinburgh: John Grant, 1910), p. 13.

5. Hicks, *The Wars of the Roses*, pp. 176–80; Goodman, *The Wars of the Roses*, pp. 58–61; Ross, *Edward IV*, pp. 50–1; Cora L. Scofield, *The Life and Reign of Edward the Fourth: King of England and of France and Lord of Ireland*, volume 1 (London: Longmans, Green, 1923), pp. 243–9; James Gairdner, ed., *Three Fifteenth-Century Chronicles with Historical Memoranda by John Stowe, the Antiquary, and Contemporary Notes of Occurrences Written by Him in the Reign of Queen Elizabeth* (Westminster: J. B. Nichols and Sons, 1843), pp. 157–9.

6. Gairdner, *The Historical Collections of a Citizen of London in the Fifteenth Century*, p. 219–27; Halliwell, *A Chronicle of the First Thirteen Years of the Reign of King Edward The Fourth*, pp. 37–8; Goodman, *The Wars of the Roses*, pp. 61–5; Hicks, *The Wars of the Roses*, pp. 176–80.

7. Hicks, *The Wars of the Roses*, pp. 178–80; Goodman, *The Wars of the Roses*, p. 186; Gairdner, *The Historical Collections of a Citizen of London in the Fifteenth Century*, p. 237; The National Archives, SC 6/74/1, no. 67; SC 6/1224/8; James Gairdner, ed., *The Paston Letters, 1422–1509 A.D.*, volume 4 (London: Chatto & Windus, 1905), pp. 96–7; Anne Crawford, *Yorkist Lord: John Howard, Duke of Norfolk, c.1425–1485* (London: Continuum, 2010), pp. 39–40; Howell T. Evans, *Wales and the Wars of the Roses* (Cambridge: Cambridge University Press, 1915), pp. 143–70.

8. Hicks, *The Wars of the Roses*, pp. 186–206; Goodman, *The Wars of the Roses*, pp. 66–85; Riley, *Ingulph's Chronicle of the Abbey of Croyland with the Continuations by Peter of Blois and Anonymous Writers*, pp. 446–81; Ross, *Edward IV*, pp. 104–295; C. F. Richmond, 'Fauconberg's Kentish Rising of May 1471', *The English Historical Review*, 85 (1970), pp. 673–92.

9. Hicks, *The Wars of the Roses*, pp. 215–32; Goodman, *The Wars of the Roses*, pp. 86–95; Riley, *Ingulph's Chronicle of*

the Abbey of Croyland with the Continuations by Peter of Blois and Anonymous Writers, pp. 491–505; Charles Ross, *Richard III* (London: Yale University Press, 1999), pp. 63–226; S. B. Chrimes, *Henry VII* (London: Yale University Press, 1999), pp. 3–67.

Chapter Twelve

1. Note that the Middle English text has been modernised. Henry Ellis, ed., *Hall's Chronicle* (London: Johnson; F. C. and J. Rivington; T. Payne; Wilkie and Robinson; Longman, Hurst, Rees and Orme; Cadell and Davies; and J. Mawman, 1809), p. 828.

2. Ian Arthurson, *The Perkin Warbeck Conspiracy 1491–1499* (Stroud: Sutton Publishing Limited, 1997), pp. 121–75; S. B. Chrimes, *Henry VII* (London: Yale University Press, 1999), pp. 69–94; Ellis, *Hall's Chronicle*, pp. 555–64; Anthony Goodman, *The Wars of the Roses: Military Activity and English Society, 1452–97* (London: Routledge, 1981), pp. 95–116; Michael Hicks, *The Wars of the Roses* (London: Yale University Press, 2012), pp. 233–51.

3. Chrimes, *Henry VII*, pp. 90–1; J. J. Scarisbrick, *Henry VIII* (London: Eyre & Spottiswoode, 1968), pp. 21–4; Gervase Phillips, *The Anglo-Scots Wars 1513–1550. A Military History* (Woodbridge: The Boydell Press, 1999), pp. 109–47.

4. Phillips, *The Anglo-Scots Wars 1513–1550*, pp. 89–90; J. R. Kenyon, 'Wark Castle and its Artillery Defences in the Reign of Henry VIII', *Post-Medieval Archaeology*, 11 (1977), pp. 50–60; H. M. Colvin, *The History of the King's Works*, volume 4 (London: H. M. S. O., 1982), pp. 607–93; J. S. Brewer, ed., *Letters and Papers, Foreign and Domestic of the Reign of Henry VIII, Volume 1, 1509–1514* (London: H. M. S. O., 1920), nos. 2283, 2381–2, 2394; Trevor Pearson, 'Norham Castle, Northumberland', *English Heritage Report*, AI/25/2002 (2002), pp. 12–13; Henry Ellis, 'A Memoir on the State of Norham Castle in the Time of Henry the Eight', *Archaeologia*, 17 (1814), pp. 201–6; C. J. Bates, 'The Border Holds of Northumberland', *Archaeologia Aeliana*, 14 (1891), pp. 342–4; Henry Ellis, ed., *Original Letters Illustrative of*

English History, first series, volume 1 (London: Printed for Harding, Triphook and Lepard, 1824), pp. 232–5; Ellis, *Hall's Chronicle*, pp. 649–66.

5. Colvin, *The History of the King's Works*, volume 4, pp. 607–93; M. W. Thompson, *The Decline of the Castle* (Cambridge: Cambridge University Press, 1987), pp. 104–7; Bates, 'The Border Holds of Northumberland', pp. 28–49; James P. Carley, 'Leland, John (c.1503–1552)', *Oxford Dictionary of National Biography*, Oxford University Press, 2004; online edn, May 2006 [http://www.oxforddnb.com/view/article/16416, accessed 16 Nov 2017]; Lucy Toulmin Smith, ed., *The Itinerary of John Leland In Or About the Years 1535–1543. Parts I to III* (London: George Bell and Sons, 1907), pp. 63, 177, 205, 261; H. M. Colvin, 'Castles and Government in Tudor England', *The English Historical Review*, 83 (1968), pp. 225–34.

6. E. W. Ives, 'Henry VIII (1491–1547)', *Oxford Dictionary of National Biography*, Oxford University Press, 2004; online edn, May 2009 Biography, Oxford [http://www.oxforddnb. com/view/article/12955, accessed 21 Sept 2016]; R. W. Hoyle, 'Aske, Robert (c.1500–1537)', *Oxford Dictionary of National Biography*, Oxford University Press, 2004; online edn, Oct 2008 [http://www.oxforddnb.com/view/article/797, accessed 17 Nov 2017]; R. W. Hoyle, 'Darcy, Thomas, Baron Darcy of Darcy (b. in or before 1467, d. 1537)', *Oxford Dictionary of National Biography*, Oxford University Press, 2004; online edn, Jan 2008 [http://www.oxforddnb.com/view/article/7148, accessed 17 Nov 2017]; Katy Kenyon, *Barnard Castle, Egglestone Abbey and Bowes Castle* (London: English Heritage, 2016); John Goodall, *Scarborough Castle* (London: English Heritage, 2013); James Gairdner, ed., *Letters and Papers, Foreign and Domestic of the Reign of Henry VIII, Volume 11, July–December 1536* (London: H. M. S. O., 1888), nos. 692, 729, 739, 760, 883, 1045, 1086, 1136, 1155, 1410; H. M. Colvin, *The History of the King's Works*, volume 3 (London: H. M. S. O., 1982), pp. 287–8; Scarisbrick, *Henry VIII*, pp. 338–48.

7. Colvin, *The History of the King's Works*, volume 4, pp. 367–95; P. D. A. Harvey, *Maps in Tudor England* (London: The Public Record Office and The British Library, 1993), pp. 6–41; Ives,

'Henry VIII (1491–1547)'; Richard Morison, *An Exhortation to Styrre all Englyshe Men to the Defence of Theyr Countreye, 1539*, Early English Books Online, [http://gateway.proquest.com/openurl?ctx_ver=Z39.88-2003&res_id=xri:eebo&rft_id=xri:eebo:image:4495:28, accessed 23 Nov 2017]; David Loades, *The Tudor Navy. An Administrative, Political and Military History* (Aldershot: Scolar Press, 1992), pp. 119–22; James Gairdner and R. H. Brodie, eds., *Letters and Papers, Foreign and Domestic of the Reign of Henry VIII, Volume 14, part 1, January–July 1539* (London: H. M. S. O., 1894), nos. 143–4, 899.

8. Colvin, *The History of the King's Works,* volume 4, pp. 415–606; Jonathan Coad, *Deal Castle* (London: English Heritage, 2014); Jonathan Coad, *Hurst Castle* (London: English Heritage, 2013); Stanley C. Jenkins, 'St Mawes Castle, Cornwall', *Fort*, 35 (2007), pp. 153–5; Martin Biddle, Jonathan Hiller, Ian Scott and Anthony Streeten, *Henry VIII's Coastal Artillery Fort at Camber Castle, Rye, East Sussex: An Archaeological, Structural and Historical Investigation* (Oxford: Oxford Archaeological Unit for English Heritage, 2001), pp. 21–33; Gairdner and Brodie, eds., *Letters and Papers, Foreign and Domestic of the Reign of Henry VIII, Volume 14, part 1, January–July 1539*, nos. 529, 573, 685, 899.

Chapter Thirteen

1. William Douglas Hamilton, ed., *Calendar of State Papers, Domestic Series, of the Reign of Charles I. 1648–1649* (London: H. M. S. O., 1893), p. 192.

2. Richard K. Morris, *Kenilworth Castle* (London: English Heritage, 2010), pp. 46–8; Christopher Young, *Carisbrooke Castle* (London: English Heritage, 2013), pp. 31–3; Mark A. Kishlansky, John Morrill, 'Charles I (1600–1649)', *Oxford Dictionary of National Biography*, Oxford University Press, 2004; online edn, Oct 2008 [http://www.oxforddnb.com/view/article/5143, accessed 27 Nov 2017]; Stephen Bull, *The Furie of the Ordnance: Artillery in the English Civil Wars* (Woodbridge: The Boydell Press, 2008), pp. 86–7, 95.

3. Young, *Carisbrooke Castle*, p. 35; Ronald Hutton and Wylie Reeves, 'Sieges and Fortifications', in *The Civil Wars: A Military History of England, Scotland, and Ireland 1638–1660*, eds., by John Kenyon and Jane Ohlmeyer (Oxford: Oxford University Press, 1998), pp. 225–31; Bull, *The Furie of the Ordnance*, pp. 103, 118–20; Peter White, *Sherborne Old Castle* (London: English Heritage, 2016), p. 36; Steven Brindle, *Dover Castle* (London: English Heritage, 2012), p. 48; Brian K. Davison, *Old Wardour Castle* (London: English Heritage, 1999), pp. 29–33; John Goodall, *Scarborough Castle* (London: English Heritage, 2013), pp. 34–5; National Trust, *Corfe Castle* (London: The National Trust, 2003), pp. 43–58.

4. M. W. Thompson, *The Decline of the Castle* (Cambridge: Cambridge University Press, 1987), pp. 142–56, 179–93; Morris, *Kenilworth Castle*, pp. 50–1; John R. Kenyon, *Helmsley Castle* (London: English Heritage, 2017), pp. 43–4; Goodall, *Scarborough Castle*, p. 35; Hamilton, *Calendar of State Papers, Domestic Series, of the Reign of Charles I. 1648–1649*, pp. 158, 192, 323,

5. Thompson, *The Decline of the Castle*, pp. 158–64; Jonathan Coad, *Deal Castle* (London: English Heritage, 2014), pp. 30–2; John Goodall, *Pevensey Castle* (London: English Heritage, 2016), p. 28; Paul Pattison, *Dartmouth Castle* (London: English Heritage, 2013), pp. 34–7; White, *Sherborne Old Castle*, pp. 38–9; Jonathan Coad, *Hurst Castle* (London: English Heritage, 2013), pp. 30–9; Brindle, *Dover Castle*, pp. 48–52; John Goodall, *Portchester Castle* (London: English Heritage, 2013), pp. 36–40; Morris, *Kenilworth Castle*, pp. 50–1; Davison, *Old Wardour Castle*, pp. 34–5; Goodall, *Scarborough Castle*, pp. 39–40; Simon Thurley, *Men from the Ministry: How Britain Saved its Heritage* (London: Yale University Press, 2014), pp. 6–23, 40–1, 54–8, 68–74, 111–22, 148–61.

Bibliography

Unprinted manuscripts consulted at The National Archives, Kew

E 101 – King's Remembrancer, Accounts Various.

E 364 – Exchequer, Pipe Office, Foreign Account Rolls.

E 372 – Exchequer, Pipe Office, Pipe Rolls.

E 403 – Exchequer of Receipt, Issue Rolls.

SC 1 – Special Collections: Ancient Correspondence of the Chancery and the Exchequer.

SC 6 – Special Collections, Ministers Accounts.

SC 8 – Special Collections, Ancient Petitions.

Printed primary sources

Bain, Joseph, ed., *Calendar of Documents Relating to Scotland, Volume 2. A.D. 1272–1307* (Edinburgh: H. M. General Register House, 1884).

Bain, Joseph, ed., *Calendar of Documents Relating to Scotland, Volume 3. A.D. 1307–1357* (Edinburgh: H. M. General Register House, 1887).

Bain, Joseph, ed., *Calendar of Documents Relating to Scotland, Volume 4. A.D. 1357–1509. Addenda-1221–1435* (Edinburgh: H. M. General Register House, 1888).

Brewer, J. S., ed., *Letters and Papers, Foreign and Domestic of the Reign of Henry VIII, Volume 1, 1509–1514* (London: H. M. S. O., 1920).

Brie, Friedrich W. D., ed., *The Brut or The Chronicles of England* (London: Kegan Paul, Trench, Trübner & Co., 1906).

Burgess, Glyn S., ed., *The History of the Norman People: Wace's Roman De Rou* (Woodbridge: The Boydell Press, 2004).

Calendar of the Close Rolls Edward I 1272–1279 (London: H. M. S. O., 1900).

Calendar of the Close Rolls Edward II 1307–1313 (London: H. M. S. O., 1892).

Calendar of the Close Rolls Edward II 1313–1318 (London: H. M. S. O., 1893).

Calendar of the Close Rolls Edward II 1318–1323 (London: H. M. S. O., 1895).

Calendar of the Fine Rolls Edward II 1319–1327 (London: H. M. S. O., 1912).

Calendar of the Close Rolls Edward III 1333–1337 (London: H. M. S. O., 1898).

Calendar of the Close Rolls Edward III 1337–1339 (London: H. M. S. O., 1900).

Calendar of the Close Rolls Edward III 1339–1341 (London: H. M. S. O., 1901).

Calendar of the Close Rolls Edward III 1358–1360 (London: H. M. S. O., 1911).

Calendar of the Close Rolls Henry IV 1402–1405 (London: H. M. S. O., 1929).

Calendar of the Liberate Rolls Preserved in the Public Record Office. Henry III. Vol. 3: A. D. 1240–1245 (London: H. M. S O, 1930).

Calendar of the Liberate Rolls Preserved in the Public Record Office. Henry III. Vol. 5: A. D. 1260–1267 (London: H. M. S O, 1961).

Calendar of the Patent Rolls Edward II 1307–1313 (London: H. M. S. O., 1884).

Calendar of the Patent Rolls Edward II 1317–21 (London: H. M. S. O., 1904).

Calendar of the Patent Rolls Edward II 1321–1324 (London: H. M. S. O., 1904).

Calendar of the Patent Rolls Edward III 1327–1330 (London: H. M. S. O., 1891).

Calendar of the Patent Rolls Edward III 1334–1338 (London: H. M. S. O., 1895).

Calendar of the Patent Rolls Edward III 1338–1340 (London: H. M. S. O., 1898).

Calendar of the Patent Rolls Edward III 1343–1345 (London: H. M. S. O., 1902).

Calendar of the Patent Rolls Henry IV 1399–1401 (London: H. M. S. O., 1903).

Calendar of the Patent Rolls Henry IV 1401–1405 (London: H. M. S. O., 1905).

Calendar of the Patent Rolls Henry IV 1405–1408 (London: H. M. S. O., 1907).

Calendar of the Patent Rolls Henry VI 1446–1452 (London: H. M. S. O., 1909).

Calendar of the Patent Rolls Richard II 1385–1389 (London: H. M. S. O., 1895).

Calendar of the Patent Rolls Richard II 1396–1399 (London: H. M. S. O., 1909).

Calendar of Various Chancery Rolls, 1277–1326 (London: H. M. S. O, 1912).

Chibnall, Marjorie, ed., *The Ecclesiastical History of Orderic Vitalis, Vol. II, Books 3 and 4* (Oxford: Clarendon Press, 2002).

Chibnall, Marjorie, ed., *The Ecclesiastical History of Orderic Vitalis, Vol. IV, Books 7 and 8* (Oxford: Clarendon Press, 1973).

Chibnall, Marjorie, ed., *The Ecclesiastical History of Orderic Vitalis, Vol. VI, Books 11, 12 and 13* (Oxford: Clarendon Press, 1978).

Christie, Richard Copley, ed., *Annales Cestrienses; or, Chronicle of the Abbey of S. Werburg, at Chester* (The Record Society, 1887).

Davis, R. H. C., and Marjorie Chibnall, eds., *The Gesta Guillelmi of William of Poitiers* (London: Clarendon Press, 1998).

Devon, Frederick, ed., *Issues of the Exchequer: Being a Collection of Payments Made out of His Majesty's Revenue, From King Henry III to King Henry VI Inclusive: with an Appendix/ Extracted and Translated From the Original Rolls of the Ancient Pell Office* (London: J. Murray, 1837).

Edwards, J. Goronwy, ed., *Calendar of Ancient Correspondence Concerning Wales* (Cardiff: University Press Board, 1935).

Ellis, Henry, ed., *Hall's Chronicle* (London: Johnson; F. C. and J. Rivington; T. Payne; Wilkie and Robinson; Longman, Hurst, Rees and Orme; Cadell and Davies; and J. Mawman, 1809).

Ellis, Henry, ed., *Original Letters Illustrative of English History*, first series, volume 1 (London: Printed for Harding, Triphook and Lepard, 1824).

Ellis, Henry, ed., *Original Letters Illustrative of English History*, second series, volume 1 (London: Harding and Lepard, Pall-Mall East, 1827).

Eyre-Todd, George, ed., *The Bruce being the Metrical Historical of Robert the Bruce King of Scots Compiled A.D. 1375 by Master John Barbour* (London: Gowans & Gray Limited, 1907).

Fairweather, Janet, ed., *Liber Eliensis: A History of the Isle of Ely from the Seventh Century to the Twelfth* (Woodbridge: The Boydell Press, 2005).

Fifth Report of the Royal Commission on Historical Manuscripts: Part 1. Report and Appendix (London: George Edward Eyre and William Spottiswoode, 1876).

Forester, Thomas, ed., *The Chronicle of Florence of Worcester* (London: Henry G. Bohn, 1854).

Forester, Thomas, ed., *The Chronicle of Henry of Huntingdon. Comprising the History of England, from the Invasion of Julius Caesar to the Accession of Henry II. Also, the Acts of Stephen, King of England and Duke of Normandy* (London: Henry G. Bohn, 1853).

Fowler, R. C., ed., *Calendar of Chancery Warrants 1244–1326*, volume 1 (London: Published by his Majesty's Stationery Office, 1927).

Gairdner, James, ed., *Letters and Papers, Foreign and Domestic of the Reign of Henry VIII, Volume 11, July–December 1536* (London: H. M. S. O., 1888).

Gairdner, James, ed., *The Historical Collections of a Citizen of London in the Fifteenth Century* (London: Camden Society, 1876).

Gairdner, James, ed., *The Paston Letters, 1422–1509 A.D.*, volume 2 (Edinburgh: John Grant, 1910).

Gairdner, James, ed., *The Paston Letters, 1422–1509 A.D.*, volume 4 (London: Chatto & Windus, 1905).

Gairdner, James, ed., *Three Fifteenth-Century Chronicles with Historical Memoranda by John Stowe, the Antiquary, and Contemporary Notes of Occurrences Written by Him in the Reign of Queen Elizabeth* (Westminster: J. B. Nichols and Sons, 1843).

Gairdner, James, and R. H. Brodie, eds., *Letters and Papers, Foreign and Domestic of the Reign of Henry VIII, Volume 14, part 1, January–July 1539* (London: H. M. S. O., 1894).

Giles, J. A., ed., *Matthew Paris's English History, From the Year 1235 to 1273*, volume 1 (London: Henry G. Bohn, 1852).

Giles, J. A., ed., *Matthew Paris's English History, From the Year 1235 to 1273*, volume 2 (London: Henry G. Bohn, 1853).

Giles, J. A., ed., *Matthew Paris's English History, From the Year 1235 to 1273*, volume 3 (London: Henry G. Bohn, 1854).

Giles, J. A., ed., *Roger of Wendower's Flowers of History*, volume 2, (Oxford: Henry G. Bohn, 1849).

Giles, J. A., ed., *William of Malmesbury's Chronicle of the Kings of England. From the Earliest Period to the Reign of King Stephen. With Notes and Illustrations* (London: Henry G. Bohn, 1847).

Halliwell, James Orchard, ed., *A Chronicle of the First Thirteenth Years of the Reign of King Edward the Fourth by John Warkworth, D. D. Master of the St Peter's College, Cambridge* (London: Camden Society, 1839).

Halliwell, James Orchard, ed., *The Chronicle of William de Rishanger, of The Barons' War. The Miracles of Simon de Montfort* (London: John Bowyer Nichols and Son, 1840).

Hamilton, Hans Claude, ed., *Chronicon Domini Walteri de Hemingburgh*, volume 2 (London: English Historical Society, 1849).

Hamilton, William Douglas, ed., *Calendar of State Papers, Domestic Series, of the Reign of Charles I. 1648–1649* (London: H. M. S. O., 1893).

Hardy, T, Duffy, ed., *Rotuli Litterarum Clausarum in Turri Londinensi Asservati*, volume 1 (London: Eyre and Spottiswoode, 1833).

Hector, L. C., ed., *The Westminster Chronicle 1381–1394* (Oxford: Clarendon Press, 1982).

Hingeston, F. C., ed., *Royal and Historical Letters during the Reign of Henry the Fourth, King of England and of France, and Lord of Ireland. Vol I. A.D. 1399–1404* (London: Longman, Green, Longman, and Roberts, 1860).

Hingeston, F. C., ed., *Royal and Historical Letters during the Reign of Henry the Fourth, King of England and of France, and Lord of Ireland. Vol II. A.D. 1405–1413* (London: H. M. S. O., 1965).

Houts, Elisabeth M. C. Van, ed., *The Gesta Normannorum Ducum of William of Jumiéges, Orderic Vitalis, and Robert of Torigni*, volume 2, (Oxford: Clarendon Press, 1995).

Howlett, Richard, ed., *Chronicles of the Reigns of Stephen, Henry II., and Richard I, Vol III* (London: Longman & co, 1886).

Howlett, Richard, ed., *Chronicles of the Reigns of Stephen, Henry II., and Richard I, Vol IV* (London: Eyre and Spottiswoode, 1889).

Hunter, Joseph, ed., *The Great Rolls of the Pipe for the Second, Third, and Fourth Years of the Reign of King Henry the Second, A. D. 1155, 1156, 1157, 1158* (London: George E. Eyre and Andrew Spottiswoode, 1844).

Johnes, Thomas, ed., *Sir John Froissart's Chronicles of England, France, Spain and the Adjoining Countries*, volume 7 (London: Longman, 1805).

Johnes, Thomas, ed., *Sir John Froissart's Chronicles of England, France, Spain and the Adjoining Countries*, volume 8 (London: Longman, 1808).

Jones, Arthur, ed., *The History of Gruffydd ap Cynan: The Welsh Text with Translation, Introduction, and Notes* (Manchester: Manchester University Press, 1910).

Jones, Thomas, ed., *Brut Y Tywysogyon, or, The Chronicle of the Princes. Red Book of Hergest Version* (Cardiff: University of Wales, 1955).

Keynes, Simon, and Michael Lapidge, eds., *Alfred the Great: Asser's Life of King Alfred and Other Contemporary Sources* (Harmondsworth: Penguin Books, 1983).

King, Edmund, and K. R. Potter, eds., *William of Malmesbury, Historia Novella: The Contemporary History*, (Oxford: Clarendon Press, 1998).

Kirby, J. L., ed., *Calendar of Signet Letters of Henry IV and Henry V (1399–1422)* (London: H.M. Stationery Off., 1978).

Luard, Henry Richards, ed., *Annales Monastici,* volume 3 (London: Longmans, Green, Reader, and Dyer, 1866).

Luard, Henry Richards, ed., *Annales Monastici,* volume 4 (London: Longmans, Green, Reader, and Dyer, 1869).

Henry Richard Luard, ed., *Bartholomæi de Cotton, Monachi Norwicensis, Historia Anglicana (A.D. 449–1298)* (London: London: Longman, Green, Longman and Roberts, 1859).

Luard, Henry Richards, ed., *Matthæi Parisiensis, Monachi Sancti Albani, Chronica Majora,* volume 3 (London: Longman & Co., 1876).

Maynors, R, A, B., R. M. Thomson and M. Winterbottom, eds., *William of Malmesbury: Gesta Regum Anglorum,* volume 1, (Oxford: Clarendon Press, 1998).

Maxwell, Herbert, ed., *Scalacronica: The Reigns of Edward I, Edward II and Edward III* (Glasgow: James Maclehose & Sons, 1907).

Maxwell, Herbert, ed., *The Chronicle of Lanercost, 1272–1346* (Glasgow: James Maclehose and Sons, 1913).

Michel, Francisque, ed., *Chronicle of the War Between the English and the Scots in 1173 and 1174* (London: J. B. Nichols and Son, 1840).

Michel, Francisque, ed., *Histoire des Ducs de Normandie et des Rois D'Angleterre* (Paris: Société de l'histoire de France, 1840).

Morison, Richard, *An Exhortation to Styrre all Englyshe Men to the Defence of Theyr Countreye, 1539,* Early English Books Online, [http://gateway.proquest.com/openurl?ctx_ver=Z39.88-2003&res_id=xri:eebo&rft_id=xri:eebo:image:4495:28, accessed 23 Nov 2017].

Myers, Alec Reginald, ed., *English Historical Documents, 1327–1485,* volume 4 (London: Eyre & Spottiswoode Ltd, 1969).

Nicolas, Nicholas Harris, ed., *Proceedings and Ordinances of the Privy Council of England,* volume 2 (London: Record Commission, 1834).

Nicolas, Nicholas Harris, ed., *The Siege of Carlaverock* (London: J. B. Nichols and Son, 1828).

Potter, K. R., and R. H. C. Davis, eds., *Gesta Stephani* (Oxford: Claredon Press, 1976).

Preest, David, and James G. Clark, eds., *The Chronica Maiora of Thomas Walsingham 1376–1422* (Woodbridge: Boydell, 2005).

Riley, Henry Thomas, ed., *Ingulph's Chronicle of the Abbey of Croyland with the Continuations by Peter of Blois and Anonymous Writers* (London: Henry G. Bohn, 1854).

Riley, Henry Thomas, ed., *Johannis de Trokelowe, et Henrici de Blaneforde, Chronica et Annales* (London: Longmans, Green, Reader, and Dyer, 1866).

Rothwell, Harry, ed., *English Historical Documents, 1189–1327*, volume 3 (London: Eyre & Spottiswoode Ltd, 1975).

Sharpe, Reginald R., ed., *Calendar of Letter-Books of the City of London, Letter-Book E* (London: J. E. Francis, 1903).

Shirley, Walter Waddington, ed., *Royal and Other Historical Letters Illustrative of the Reign of Henry III*, volume 1 (London: Longman, Green, Longman, and Roberts, 1862).

Smith, Lucy Toulmin, ed., *The Itinerary of John Leland In Or About the Years 1535–1543. Parts I to III* (London: George Bell and Sons, 1907).

Stevenson, Joseph, ed., *Documents Illustrative of the History of Scotland*, volume 2 (Edinburgh: H. M. General Register House, 1870).

Stevenson, Joseph, ed., *Chronica de Mailros* (Edinburgh: Typis Societatis Edinburgensis, 1835).

Stevenson, Joseph, ed., *Radulphi de Coggeshall Chronicon Anglicanum* (London: Longman & Co., 1875).

Stevenson, Joseph, ed., *The Church Historians of England. Vol. IV.–Part II. Containing The History of William of Newburgh: The Chronicles of Robert de Monte.* (London: Beeleys, 1856).

Stevenson, Joseph, ed., *The Church Historians of England. Vol. V.–Part 1.* (London: Beeleys, 1858).

Stubbs, William, ed., *Chronica Magistri Rogeri de Houedene*, volume 3 (London: Longman & Co., 1870).

Stubbs, William, ed., *Ranulfi de Diceto Decani Lundoniensis Opera Historica. The Historical Works of Master Ralph de Diceto, Dean of London. Edited from the Original Manuscripts*, volume 1 (London: H. M. S. O. 1876).

Stubbs, William, ed., *The Historical Collections of Walter of Coventry*, volume 2 (London: Longman & co., 1873).

Stubbs, William, ed., *The Historical Works of Gervase of Canterbury, Vol. I* (London: Longman & Co., 1879).

Swanton, Michael, ed., *The Anglo-Saxon Chronicles* (London: Phoenix, 2000).

Thompson, Edward Maunde, ed., *Chronicon Adae De Usk* (London: Oxford University Press, 1904).

Wright, Thomas., ed., *The Chronicle of Pierre de Langtoft, in French Verse, from the Earliest Period to the Death of King Edward*. Volume 2 (London: Longmans, Green, Reader, and Dyer, 1868).

Wright, William Aldis, ed., *The Metrical Chronicle of Robert of Gloucester*, volume 2 (London: printed for H. M. S. O. by Eyre and Spottiswoode, 1887).

Yonge, C. D., ed., *The Flowers of History, especially such as relate to the Affairs of Britain. From the Beginning of the World to the Year 1307. Collected by Matthew of Westminster*, volume 2 (London: Henry G. Bohn, 1853).

Printed secondary sources

Allmand, Christopher, *Henry V* (London: Yale University Press, 1997).

Arthurson, Ian, *The Perkin Warbeck Conspiracy 1491–1499* (Stroud: Sutton Publishing Limited, 1997).

Bachrach, Bernard S., 'The Angevin Strategy of Castle Building in the Reign of Fulk Nerera', *The American Historical Review*, 88 (1983), pp. 553–60.

Barlow, Frank, *William Rufus* (London: Yale University Press, 2000).

Barrow, Geoffrey W. S., *Robert Bruce & the Community of the Realm of Scotland* (Edinburgh: Edinburgh University Press, 1999).

Bates, C. J., 'The Border Holds of Northumberland', *Archaeologia Aeliana*, 14 (1891).

Bates, David, *Normandy Before 1066* (London: Longman Group Limited, 1982).

Bates, David, *William the Conqueror* (London: Yale University Press, 2016).

Bennett, Paul, Sheppard Frere and Sally Stow., *The Archaeology of Canterbury Vol. 1, Excavations at Canterbury Castle* (Maidstone: Kent Archaeological Society for the Canterbury Archaeological Trust, 1982).

Biddle, Martin, Jonathan Hiller, Ian Scott and Anthony Streeten, *Henry VIII's Coastal Artillery Fort at Camber Castle, Rye, East Sussex: An Archaeological, Structural and Historical Investigation* (Oxford: Oxford Archaeological Unit for English Heritage, 2001).

Brindle, Steven, *Dover Castle* (London: English Heritage, 2012).

Brough, Gideon, 'Owain's Revolt? Glyn Dŵr's Role in the Outbreak of the Rebellion', *Studies in History, Archaeology, Religion and Conservation*, 2 (2015), pp. 1–30.

Brown, David M., 'Builth Castle and Aberystwyth Castle 1277–1307', in *The Impact of the Edwardian Castles in Wales*, ed. by Diane M. Williams and John R. Kenyon (Oxford: Oxbow Books, 2010), pp. 59–71.

Brown, R. Allen, *English Castles* (Woodbridge: The Boydell Press, 2004).

Brown, R. Allen, 'Framlingham Castle and Bigod 1154–1216', *Proceedings of the Suffolk Institute of Archaeology and History*, 25.2 (1950), pp. 127–48.

Brown, R. Allen, 'Royal Castle-Building in England, 1154–1216', *The English Historical Review*, 70 (1955), pp. 353–98.

Bull, Stephen, *The Furie of the Ordnance: Artillery in the English Civil Wars* (Woodbridge: The Boydell Press, 2008).

Butler, Lawrence, 'The Castles of the Princes of Gwynedd', in *The Impact of the Edwardian Castles in Wales*, ed. by Diane M. Williams and John R. Kenyon (Oxford: Oxbow Books, 2010), pp. 27–36.

Carpenter, D. A., *The Minority of Henry III* (London: Methuen London, 1990).

Chaplais, Pierre, *Piers Gaveston: Edward II's Adoptive Brother* (Oxford: Clarendon Press, 1994).

Chapman, Adam, *Welsh Soldiers in the Later Middle Ages, 1282–1422* (Woodbridge: The Boydell Press, 2015).

Chibnall, Marjorie, 'Orderic Vitalis on Castles', in *Anglo-Norman Castles*, ed. by Robert Liddiard (Woodbridge: Boydell Press, 2003), pp. 119–32.

Childs, Wendy R., ed., *Vita Edwardi Secundi* (Oxford: Oxford University Press, 2005).

Chrimes, S. B., *Henry VII* (London: Yale University Press, 1999).

Coad, Jonathan, *Deal Castle* (London: English Heritage, 2014).

Coad, Jonathan, *Hurst Castle* (London: English Heritage, 2013).

Colvin, H. M., 'Castles and Government in Tudor England', *The English Historical Review*, 83 (1968), pp. 225–34.

Colvin, H. M., *The History of the King's Works*, volume 1 (London: H. M. S. O, 1963).

Colvin, H. M., *The History of the King's Works*, volume 2 (London: H. M. S. O, 1963).

Colvin, H. M., *The History of the King's Works*, volume 3 (London: H. M. S. O., 1982).

Colvin, H. M., *The History of the King's Works*, volume 4 (London: H. M. S. O., 1982).

Cornell, David, 'A Kingdom Cleared of Castles: The Role of the Castle in the Campaigns of Robert Bruce', *The Scottish Historical Review*, 87 (2008), pp. 233–57.

Coulson, Charles, *Castles in Medieval Society: Fortresses in England, France, and Ireland in the Central Middle Ages* (Oxford: Oxford University Press, 2003).

Crawford, Anne, *Yorkist Lord: John Howard, Duke of Norfolk, c.1425–1485* (London: Continuum, 2010).

Creighton, Oliver H., *Castles and Landscapes: Power, Community and Fortification in Medieval England* (London: Equinox Published Ltd, 2002).

Creighton, Oliver H., *Early European Castles* (London: Bristol Classical Press, 2012).

Creighton, Oliver H., and Duncan W. Wright, eds., *The Anarchy: War and Status in 12th-Century Landscapes of Conflict* (Liverpool: Liverpool University Press, 2016).

Cunliffe, Barry, and Julian Munby, *Excavations at Portchester Castle, IV: Medieval, The Inner Bailey* (London: The Society of Antiquaries of London, 1985).

Curry, Anne, 'New Regime, New army? Henry IV's Scottish Expedition of 1400', *The English Historical Review*, 125 (2010), pp. 1382–1413.

Darby, H. C., 'The Marches of Wales in 1086', *Transactions of the Institute of British Geographers*, 11 (1986), pp. 259–78.

Davies, J. Conway, 'The Despenser War in Glamorgan', *Transactions of the Royal Historical Society*, 9 (1915), pp. 21–64.

Davies, R. R., *The Age of Conquest Wales 1063–1415* (Oxford: Oxford University Press, 1991).

Davies, R. R., *The Revolt of Owain Glyn Dŵr* (Oxford: Oxford University Press, 1995).

Davison, Brian K., *Old Wardour Castle* (London: English Heritage, 1999).

Douglas, David Charles, *William the Conqueror: The Norman Impact upon England* (London: Eyre & Spottiswoode, 1964).

Eales, Richard, 'Royal Power and Castles in Norman England', in *Anglo-Norman Castles*, ed. by Robert Liddiard (Woodbridge: The Boydell Press, 2003), pp. 41–68.

Edwards, J. Goronwy, 'The Building of Flint', *Flintshire Historical Society Journal*, 12 (1951), pp. 1–20.

Edwards, J. Goronwy, 'The Battle of Maes Madog and the Welsh Campaign of 1294–5', *The English Historical Review*, 39 (1924), pp. 1–12.

Ellis, Henry, 'A Memoir on the State of Norham Castle in the Time of Henry the Eight', *Archaeologia*, 17 (1814), pp. 201–6.

Evans, Howell T., *Wales and the Wars of the Roses* (Cambridge: Cambridge University Press, 1915).

Fonblanque, Edward Barrington de, *Annals of the House of Percy, from the Conquest to the Opening of the Nineteenth Century*, volume 2 (London: Richard Clay & Sons, 1887).

Fowlers, G. Herbert, 'Munitions in 1224', *Bedfordshire Historical Records Society*, 5 (1920), pp. 117–32.

Fryde, Natalie, *The Tyranny and Fall of Edward II, 1321–1326* (Cambridge: Cambridge University Press, 1979).

Gillingham, John, *Richard I* (London: Yale University Press, 1999).

Given-Wilson, Chris, *Henry IV* (London: Yale University Press, 2016).

Goodall, John, 'Dover Castle and the Great Siege of 1216', *Château Gaillard*, 19 (2000), pp. 91–102.

Goodall, John, *Scarborough Castle* (London: English Heritage, 2013).

Goodall, John, *The English Castle, 1066–1650* (New Haven: Yale University Press, 2011).

Goodman, Anthony, *The Loyal Conspiracy: The Lords Appellant under Richard II* (London: Routledge and Kegan Paul Ltd, 1971).

Goodman, Anthony, *The Wars of the Roses: Military Activity and English Society, 1452–97* (London: Routledge, 1981).

Griffiths, J., 'The Revolt of Madog ap Llywelyn, 1294–5', *Transactions of the Caernarfonshire Historical Society*, 16 (1955), pp. 12–24.

Griffiths, R. A., *The Reign of Henry VI* (Stroud: Sutton Publishing Limited, 2004).

Harfield, C. G., 'A Hand-list of Castles Recorded in the Domesday Book', *The English Historical Review*, 106 (1991), pp. 371–92.

Harris, Roland B., 'Recent Research on the White Tower: Reconstructing and Dating the Norman Building' in *Castles and the Anglo-Norman World*, ed. by John A. Davies, Angela Riley, Jean-Marie Levesque and Charlotte Lapiche (Oxford: Oxbow Books, 2016), pp. 177–90.

Harvey, P. D. A., *Maps in Tudor England* (London: The Public Record Office and The British Library, 1993).

Hewitt, Herbert J., *The Organization of War under Edward III, 1338–62* (Manchester: Manchester University Press, 1996).

Hicks, Michael, *The Wars of the Roses* (London: Yale University Press, 2012).

Holmes, G. A., 'The Rebellion of the Earl of Lancaster, 1328–9', *Bulletin of the Institute of Historical Research*, 28 (1955), pp. 84–9.

Holt, J. C., *The Northerners: A Study in the Reign of King John* (Oxford: Clarendon Press, 1992).

Hutton, Ronald, and Wylie Reeves, 'Sieges and Fortifications', in *The Civil Wars: A Military History of England, Scotland, and Ireland 1638–1660*, eds., by John Kenyon and Jane Ohlmeyer (Oxford: Oxford University Press, 1998), pp. 195–233.

Impey, Edward, and Elisabeth Lorans, 'Langeais, Indre-Et-Loire. An Archaeological and Historical Study of the Early Donjon and its Environs', *Journal of the British Archaeological Association*, 151 (1998), pp. 43–106.

Jenkins, Stanley C., 'St Mawes Castle, Cornwall', *Fort*, 35 (2007), pp. 153–72.

Jobson, Adrian, *The First English Revolution: Simon de Montfort. Henry III and the Barons' War* (London: Bloomsbury Academic, 2012).

Kenyon, John, R. 'Fluctuating Frontiers: Normanno-Welsh Castle Warfare c. 1075 to 1240' in *Anglo-Norman Castles*, ed. by Robert Liddiard (Woodbridge: The Boydell Press, 2003), pp. 247–58.

Kenyon, John R., *Helmsley Castle* (London: English Heritage, 2017).

Kenyon, John, R. 'Wark Castle and its Artillery Defences in the Reign of Henry VIII', *Post-Medieval Archaeology*, 11 (1977), pp. 50–60.

Kenyon, Katy, *Barnard Castle, Egglestone Abbey and Bowes Castle* (London: English Heritage, 2016).

King, Edmund, *King Stephen* (London: Yale University Press, 2012).

Liddiard, Robert, *Castles in Context: Power, Symbolism and Landscape, 1066 to 1500* (Macclesfield: Windgather Press Ltd, 2005).

Lloyd, John Edward, *A History of Wales: From the Earliest Times to the Edwardian Conquest*, volume 2 (London: Longmans, Green, and Co., 1912).

Loades, David, *The Tudor Navy. An Administrative, Political and Military History* (Aldershot: Scolar Press, 1992).

Maddicott, J. R., *Thomas of Lancaster, 1307–1322: A Study in the Reign of Edward II* (Oxford: Oxford University Press, 1970).

Martin, Charles Wykeham, *The History and Description of Leeds Castle, Kent* (Westminster: Nichols and Sons, 1869).

McCarthy, Michael R., *Carlisle Castle: A Survey and Documentary History* (London: English Heritage, 1990).

McNamee, Colm, *The Wars of the Bruces: Scotland, England and Ireland 1306–1328* (Edinburgh: John Donald, 2006).

Middleton, Arthur E., *Sir Gilbert de Middleton* (Newcastle: Mawson Swan and Morgan Limited, 1918).

Moore, John S., 'Anglo-Norman Garrisons', *Anglo-Norman Studies*, 22 (1999), pp. 205–60.

Morris, John. E., 'Cumberland and Westmorland Military Levies in the time of Edward I. and Edward II.', *Transactions of the*

Cumberland and Westmorland Antiquarian and Archaeological Society, 3 (1903), pp. 307–27.

Morris, John E., *The Welsh Wars of Edward I* (Oxford: Clarendon Press, 1901).

Morris, Richard K., *Kenilworth Castle* (London: English Heritage, 2012).

National Trust, *Corfe Castle* (London: The National Trust, 2003).

Nicholson, Ranald, 'The Last Campaign of Robert Bruce', *The English Historical Review*, 77 (1962), pp. 233–46.

Nicholson, Ranald, 'The Siege of Berwick, 1333', *The Scottish Historical Review*, 40 (1961), pp. 19–42.

Oakes, Fergus, 'King's Men without the King: Royalist Castle Garrison Resistance between the Battles of Lewes and Evesham', *Thirteenth Century England*, 15 (2015), pp. 51–68.

Oman, Charles, *Castles* (London: Great Western Railways, 1926).

Ormrod, W. Mark, *Edward III* (London: Yale University Press, 2013).

Painter, Sidney, 'Castle-Guard', *The American Historical Review*, 40 (1935), pp. 450–9.

Painter, Sidney, *The Reign of King John* (Baltimore: The John Hopkins Press, 1949).

Pattison, Paul, *Dartmouth Castle* (London: English Heritage, 2013).

Pearson, Trevor, 'Norham Castle, Northumberland', *English Heritage Report*, AI/25/2002 (2002).

Phillips, Gervase, *The Anglo-Scots Wars 1513–1550. A Military History* (Woodbridge: The Boydell Press, 1999).

Phillips, J. R. S., *Aymer de Valence, Earl of Pembroke, 1307–1324: Baronial Politics in the Reign of Edward II* (Oxford: At the Clarendon Press, 1972).

Phillips, Seymour, *Edward II* (London: Yale University Press, 2011).

Pollock, M. A., *Scotland, England and France After the Loss of Normandy, 1204–1296: 'Auld Amitie'* (Woodbridge: The Boydell Press, 2015).

Potter, Valerie, Margaret Poulter and Jane Allen, eds., *The Building of Orford Castle: A Translation from the Pipe Rolls 1163–78* (Woodbridge: Orford Museum, 2002).

Powicke, F. W., *King Henry III and the Lord Edward: The Community of the Realm in the Thirteenth Century*, volume 2 (Oxford: Clarendon Press, 1947).

Prestwich, Michael, *Armies and Warfare in the Middle Ages: The English Experience* (London: Yale University Press, 1996).

Prestwich, Michael, *Edward I* (London: Yale University Press, 1997).

Prestwich, Michael, *The Three Edwards: War and State in England 1272–1377* (London: Methuen & Co. Ltd, 1981).

Richmond, C. F., 'Fauconberg's Kentish Rising of May 1471', *The English Historical Review*, 85 (1970), pp. 673–92.

Ross, Charles, *Edward IV* (London: Eyre Methuen, 1974).

Rumble, Alexander R., 'The Tribal Hidage: An Annotated Bibliography', in *The Defence of Wessex*, eds., David Hill and Alexander R. Rumble (Manchester: Manchester University Press, 1996), pp. 182–8.

Saul, Nigel, *Richard II* (New Haven: Yale University Press, 1997).

Saul, Nigel, 'The Despensers and the Downfall of Edward II', *The English Historical Review*, 99 (1984), pp. 1–33.

Scarisbrick, J. J., *Henry VIII* (London: Eyre & Spottiswoode, 1968).

Scofield, Cora L., *The Life and Reign of Edward the Fourth: King of England and of France and Lord of Ireland*, volume 1 (London: Longmans, Green, 1923).

Searle, Eleanor, and Robert Burghart, 'The Defence of England and the Peasants' Revolt', *Viator*, 3 (1972), pp. 365–88.

Shenton, Caroline, 'Edward III and the Coup of 1330', in *The Age of Edward III*, ed., James Bothwell (York: York Medieval Press, 2001), pp. 13–34.

Spencer, Dan, 'Adapting to New Technology: Roxburgh Castle and the Scottish Marches', *Emergence*, 6 (2014), pp. 1–7.

Spencer, Dan, 'Edward Dallingridge: Builder of Bodiam Castle', *Ex Historia*, 6 (2014), pp. 81–98.

Spencer, Dan, 'The Lancastrian Armament Programme of the 1450s and the Development of Field Guns', *The Ricardian*, 25 (2015), pp. 61–70.

Spencer, Dan, '"The Scourge of the Stones": English Gunpowder Artillery at the Siege of Harfleur', *Journal of Medieval History*, 43 (2017), pp. 59–73.

Sumption, Jonathan, *The Hundred Years War: Volume I, Trial by Battle* (London: Faber, 1990).

Sumption, Jonathan, *The Hundred Years War: Volume III, Divided Houses* (London: Faber, 2009).

Suppe, F., 'The Garrisoning of Oswestry: A Baronial Castle on the Welsh Marches', in *The Medieval Castle: Romance and Reality*, ed. by Kathryn Reyerson and Faye Powe (Kendall/Hunt: Dubuque, 1984), pp. 63–78.

The Royal Commission on the Ancient and Historical Monuments and Constructions in Wales and Monmouthshire: An Inventory of the Ancient Monuments in Wales and Monmouthshire. II, County of Flint (London: H. M. S. O, 1912).

Thompson, M. W., *The Decline of the Castle* (Cambridge: Cambridge University Press, 1987).

Thurley, Simon, *Men from the Ministry: How Britain Saved its Heritage* (London: Yale University Press, 2014).

Tout, T. F., 'Firearms in England in the Fourteenth Century', *The English Historical Review*, 26 (1911), pp. 666–702.

Tout, T. F., *The Place of the Reign of Edward II in English History* (Manchester: At the University Press, 1914).

Treharne, R, F,, 'The Battle of Northampton, 5th April 1264', *Northamptonshire Past and Present*, 2 (1955), pp. 13–30.

Vickers, Kenneth H., *A History of Northumberland, Volume XI. The Parishes of Carham, Branxton, Kirknewton, Wooler and Ford* (Newcastle Upon Tyne: Andrew Reid, 1922).

Vincent, Nicholas, *Peter des Roches: An Alien in English Politics, 1205–1238* (Cambridge: Cambridge University Press, 1996).

Walker, R. F., 'Hubert de Burgh and Wales, 1218–1232', *The English Historical Review*, 87 (1972), pp. 465–94.

Walker, R. F., 'The Hagnaby Chronicle and the Battle of Maes Moydog', *Welsh History Review*, 8 (1976–7), pp. 125–38.

Walker, S. K., 'Letters to the Dukes of Lancaster in 1381 and 1399', *The English Historical Review*, 106 (1991), pp. 68–79.

Warren, W. L., *Henry II* (London: Yale University Press, 2000).

Warren, W. L., *King John* (London: Yale University Press, 1997).

Watson, Fiona J., *Under the Hammer: Edward I and Scotland, 1286–1306* (Edinburgh: John Donald, 2005).

Wheatley, Abigail, 'Caernarfon Castle and its Mythology' in *The Impact of the Edwardian Castles in Wales*, ed. by Diane M. Williams and John R. Kenyon (Oxford: Oxbow Books, 2010), pp. 129–39.

White, Peter, *Sherborne Old Castle* (London: English Heritage, 2016).

Wild, Benjamin L., 'The Siege of Kenilworth Castle, 1266', *English Heritage Historical Review*, 5 (2010), pp. 12–23.

Wright, Duncan, Michael Fradley and Oliver H. Creighton, 'Burwell Castle, Cambridgeshire' in *Castles, Siegeworks and Settlements Surveying the Archaeology of the Twelfth Century*, ed. by Duncan Wright and Oliver H. Creighton (Oxford: Archaeopress Publishing Ltd, 2016), pp. 6–25.

Wright, Duncan, Michael Fradley and Oliver H. Creighton, 'Corfe, 'The Rings', Dorset' in *Castles, Siegeworks and Settlements Surveying the Archaeology of the Twelfth Century*, ed. by Duncan Wright and Oliver H. Creighton (Oxford: Archaeopress Publishing Ltd, 2016), pp. 40–8.

Wylie, James Hamilton, *History of England Under Henry the Fourth, Vol. I. 1399–1404* (London: Longmans, Green and Co, 1884).

Wylie, James Hamilton, *History of England Under Henry the Fourth, Vol. II. 1405–1406* (London: Longmans, Green and Co, 1894).

Wylie, James Hamilton, *History of England Under Henry the Fourth, Vol. III. 1407–1410* (London: Longmans, Green and Co, 1896).

Young, Christopher, *Carisbrooke Castle* (London: English Heritage, 2013).

Online secondary sources

Barlow, Frank, 'Edward [St Edward; known as Edward the Confessor] (1003x5–1066)', *Oxford Dictionary of National Biography, Oxford University Press*, 2004; online edn, May 2006 [http://www.oxforddnb.com/view/article/8516, accessed 12 Sept 2016].

Barlow, Frank, 'William II (c. 1060–1100)', *Oxford Dictionary of National Biography*, Oxford University Press, 2004 [http://www.oxforddnb.com/view/article/29449, accessed 29 March 2017).

Bates, David, 'William I (1027/8–1087)', *Oxford Dictionary of National Biography*, Oxford University Press, 2004; online edn, May 2011 [http://www.oxforddnb.com/view/article/29448, accessed 16 Sept 2016].

Carley, James P., 'Leland, John (c.1503–1552)', *Oxford Dictionary of National Biography*, Oxford University Press, 2004; online edn, May 2006 [http://www.oxforddnb.com/view/article/16416, accessed 16 Nov 2017].

Carr, A. D., 'Llywelyn ab Iorwerth (c.1173–1240)', *Oxford Dictionary of National Biography*, Oxford University Press, 2004 [http://www.oxforddnb.com/view/article/16874, accessed 29 May 2017].

Chibnall, Marjorie, 'Matilda (1102–1167)', *Oxford Dictionary of National Biography*, Oxford University Press, 2004 [http://www. oxforddnb.com/view/article/18338, accessed 8 May 2017].

Crouch, David, 'Robert, first earl of Gloucester (b. before 1100, d. 1147)', *Oxford Dictionary of National Biography*, Oxford University Press, 2004; online edn, May 2006 [http://www. oxforddnb.com/view/article/23716, accessed 2 May 2017].

Fleming, Robin, 'Harold II (1022/3?–1066)', *Oxford Dictionary of National Biography*, Oxford University Press, 2004; online edn, Sept 2010 [http://www.oxforddnb.com/view/article/12360, accessed 21 Sept 2016].

Foot, Sarah, 'Æthelstan (893/4–939)', *Oxford Dictionary of National Biography*, Oxford University Press, 2004; online edn, Sept 2011 [http://www.oxforddnb.com/view/article/833, accessed 9 Sept 2016].

Griffiths, R. A., 'Rhys ap Maredudd (d. 1292)', *Oxford Dictionary of National Biography*, Oxford University Press, 2004; online edn, Jan 2008 [http://www.oxforddnb.com/view/article/48563, accessed 11 Sept 2017].

Hamilton, J. S., 'Despenser, Hugh, the Younger, first Lord Despenser (d. 1326)', *Oxford Dictionary of National Biography*, Oxford University Press, 2004; online edn, Sept 2012 [http://www. oxforddnb.com/view/article/7554, accessed 3 Oct 2017].

Hamilton, J. S., 'Gaveston, Piers, earl of Cornwall (d. 1312)', *Oxford Dictionary of National Biography*, Oxford University

Press, 2004; online edn, Jan 2008 [http://www.oxforddnb.com/view/article/10463, accessed 26 Sept 2017].

Hollister, C. Warren, 'Henry I (1068/9–1135)', *Oxford Dictionary of National Oxford University Press*, 2004 [http://www.oxforddnb.com/view/article/12948, accessed 21 September 2016].

Hollister, C. Warren, 'William (1102–1128)', *Oxford Dictionary of National Biography*, Oxford University Press, 2004 [http://www.oxforddnb.com/view/article/58402, accessed 28 April 2017].

Hoyle, R. W., 'Aske, Robert (c.1500–1537)', *Oxford Dictionary of National Biography*, Oxford University Press, 2004; online edn, Oct 2008 [http://www.oxforddnb.com/view/article/797, accessed 17 Nov 2017].

Ives, E. W., 'Henry VIII (1491–1547)', *Oxford Dictionary of National Biography*, Oxford University Press, 2004; online edn, May 2009 Biography, Oxford [http://www.oxforddnb.com/view/article/12955, accessed 21 Sept 2016].

Keynes, Simon, 'Æthelred II (c.966x8–1016)', Oxford Dictionary of National Biography, Oxford University Press, Oct 2009 [http://www.oxforddnb.com/view/article/8915, accessed 9 Sept 2016].

King, Edmund, 'Stephen (c.1092–1154)', *Oxford Dictionary of National Biography*, Oxford University Press, 2004; online edn, Sept 2010 [http://www.oxforddnb.com/view/article/26365, accessed 2 May 2017].

Kishlansky, Mark A., John Morrill, 'Charles I (1600–1649)', *Oxford Dictionary of National Biography*, Oxford University Press, 2004; online edn, Oct 2008 [http://www.oxforddnb.com/view/article/5143, accessed 27 Nov 2017].

Miller, Sean, 'Edward [Edward the Elder] (870s?–924)', *Oxford Dictionary of National Biography*, Oxford University Press, 2004; online edn, Sept 2011 [http://www.oxforddnb.com/view/article/8514, accessed 9 Sept 2016].

Prestwich, J. O., 'Orderic Vitalis (1075–c.1142)', *Oxford Dictionary of National Biography*, Oxford University Press, 2004; online edn, Oct 2006 [http://www.oxforddnb.com/view/article/20812, accessed 30 Sept 2016].

Prestwich, Michael, 'Middleton, Sir Gilbert (d. 1318)', *Oxford Dictionary of National Biography*, Oxford University Press,

2004 [http://www.oxforddnb.com/view/article/53089, accessed 2 Oct 2017].

Pryce, Huw, 'Owain Gwynedd (d. 1170)', *Oxford Dictionary of National Biography*, Oxford University Press, 2004 [http://www.oxforddnb.com/view/article/20979, accessed 5 April 2017].

Pryce, Huw, 'Rhys ap Gruffudd (1131/2–1197)', *Oxford Dictionary of National Biography*, Oxford University Press, 2004 [http://www.oxforddnb.com/view/article/23464, accessed 10 May 2017].

Ridgeway, H. W., 'Henry III (1207–1272)', *Oxford Dictionary of National University Press, 2004*; online edn, Sept 2010 Biography, Oxford [http://www.oxforddnb.com/view/article/12950, accessed 21 Sept 2016].

Smith, Llinos, 'Glyn Dŵr , Owain (c.1359–c.1416)', *Oxford Dictionary of National Biography*, Oxford University Press, 2004; online edn, Jan 2008 [http://www.oxforddnb.com/view/article/10816, accessed 23 Oct 2017].

Walker, David, 'Gruffudd ap Llywelyn (d. 1063)', Oxford Dictionary of National Biography, Oxford University Press, 2004 [http://www.oxforddnb.com/view/article/11695, accessed 21 Sept 2016]

Walker, R. F., 'Madog ap Llywelyn (fl. 1277–1295)', *Oxford Dictionary of National Biography*, Oxford University Press, 2004 (http://www.oxforddnb.com/view/article/17765, accessed 6 Aug 2017).

Wormald, Patrick, 'Alfred (848/9–899)', *Oxford Dictionary of National Biography*, Oxford University Press, 2004; online edn, Oct 2006 [http://www.oxforddnb.com/view/article/183, accessed 9 Sept 2016].

'Richard II: November 1384', in *Parliament Rolls of Medieval England*, ed. Chris Given-Wilson, Paul Brand, Seymour Phillips, Mark Ormrod, Geoffrey Martin, Anne Curry and Rosemary Horrox (Woodbridge, 2005), British History Online http://www.british-history.ac.uk/no-series/parliament-rolls-medieval/november-1384 [accessed 16 October 2017].

Index

Also available from Amberley Publishing

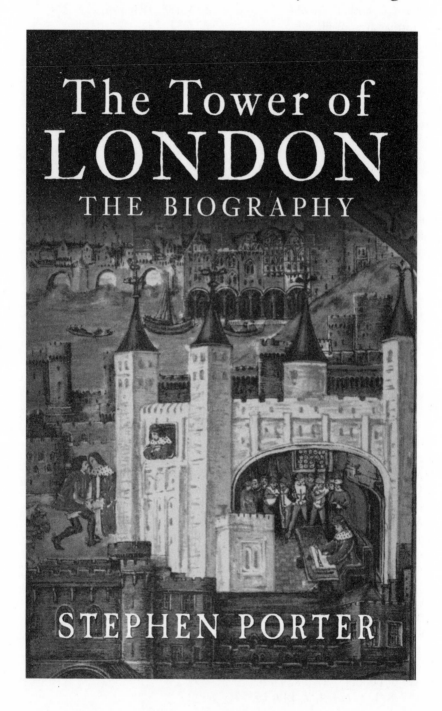

The Tower of
LONDON
THE BIOGRAPHY

STEPHEN PORTER

Available from all good bookshops or to order direct
Please call **01453-847-800**
www.amberley-books.com